KU-392-939

PROGRAMMING LANGUAGES
Paradigm and Practice

Doris Appleby
Marymount College

McGraw-Hill, Inc.
New York St. Louis San Francisco Auckland Bogotá Caracas Hamburg
Lisbon London Madrid Mexico Milan Montreal New Delhi Paris
San Juan São Paulo Singapore Sydney Tokyo Toronto

PROGRAMMING LANGUAGES: Paradigm and Practice
International Edition 1991

Exclusive rights by McGraw-Hill Book Co. — Singapore for manufacture and export. This book cannot be re-exported from the country to which it is consigned by McGraw-Hill.

Copyright © 1991 by McGraw-Hill, Inc. All rights reserved. Except as permitted under the United States Copyright Act of 1976, no part of this publication may be reproduced or distributed in any form or by any means, or stored in a data base or retrieval system, without the prior written permission of the publisher.

1 2 3 4 5 6 7 8 9 0 FSP AGA 9 0 9 8 7 6 5 4 3 2 1

This book was designed and electronically typeset in Palatino and Univers by Ocean View Technical Publications.
The editor was Eric M. Munson.
The production supervisor was Annette Mayeski.
Cover design was by Terry Earlywine.
Copyediting was by P. J. Schemenauer.
Text programming was by Bruce Boston and Brooke Nicholson.
The index was prepared by Linda Fetters.
Project supervision was by Business Media Resources.

Library of Congress Cataloging-in-Publication Data

Trademarked products cited:
Arity is a trademark of Arity Corporation
dBASE III PLUS is a registered trademark of Ashton Tate
Eiffel is a trademark of Interactive Software Engineering
Escort GT is a trademark of the Ford Motor Company
GALILEO is a trademark of the Krell Software Corporation
GEM is a trademark of Digital Research
IBM is a registered trademark of International Business Machines
Macintosh is a registered trademark of Apple Computer Incorporated
MS-DOS and Microsoft are trademarks of the Microsoft Corporation
Objective-C is a trademark of the Stepstone Corporation
R:BASE for DOS is a trademark of Microrim, Inc.
Smalltalk-80 is a trademark of the Xerox Corporation
Sun-3, Sun-4, and SunOS are trademarks of Sun Microsystems, Inc.
Turbo Pascal, Turbo C, Turbo C++, and Turbo Pascal 5.5 are registered trademarks of Borland International
UNIVAC is a registered trademark of the Information Systems Group of the Sperry Corporation
UNIX is a registered trademark of AT&T Bell Laboratories
VAX, VMS, DEC System-10 and PDP are trademarks of the Digital Equipment Corporation

When ordering this title use ISBN 0-07-100971-X

Printed in Singapore

CONTENTS

PART II IMPERATIVE LANGUAGES

PART III FORM AND STRUCTURE

PART IV DECLARATIVE LANGUAGES

BRIEF THEORETICAL EXCURSIONS

HISTORICAL VIGNETTES

LABS

PREFACE

A great deal has happened since the standard programming language texts were written in the 1970s and revised for the 1980s. The books of the 1970s concentrated almost entirely on imperative languages, those that facilitate changes to a computer's physical state. Revisions included some modest reference to declarative languages, which allow the specification of relations or functions.

This book gives equal weight to imperative and declarative language paradigms, while emphasizing theoretical foundations for different language types. This text is divided into five parts:

    I. Preliminary Concepts
    II. Imperative Languages
    III. Form and Structure
    IV. Declarative Languages
    V. Languages for Special Purposes

It includes 10 tutorials on underlying mathematical theory, 15 historical vignettes on prominent language innovators, and 23 laboratory assignments employing nine different languages: Ada, BASIC, C, C++, LISP, Object Pascal, Pascal, PROLOG, SETL, and SQL. Accompanying the text are low-cost language "MiniManuals," sufficient for completing the labs or for individual language workshops.

These materials are intended for a one-semester or one-quarter course in programming languages including two or more hours of lecture and a 1½ hour lab each week. The intended audience is students who can program well in at least one high-level language. Knowledge of assembly language is not assumed, although it would be helpful in understanding some topics.

Computer science students are sometimes lacking in the mathematical background necessary to understand and use a language effectively. The reader will find brief theoretical excursions, or tutorials, on mathematical logic, the lambda calculus, the relational calculus, and set theory. These may be covered quickly or omitted entirely by knowledgable students. The six other excursions include abstract data types, modularization, objects, classes of objects, synchronization of parallel processes, and formal languages and machines.

BACKGROUND

The year 1988 saw completion of the report of the ACM Task Force on Computing as a Discipline [Denning, 1989]. It presents a "new intellectual framework for the discipline of computing and a new basis for computing curricula." The report sees curriculum design as a blueprint for lifelong learning, rather than a method for developing particular skills. It stresses conceptual depth and rigor coupled with practice with particular implementations exemplifying the principle being studied. Each of the nine subject areas of computing is described in terms of its theory, abstractions, and issues of design and experimentation.

The report lists the elements of theory necessary for the subject matter of programming languages as:

1. Formal languages and automata, including theories of parsing and language translation.

2. Turing machines (base for procedural languages), Post systems (base for string-processing languages), lambda calculus (base for functional languages).

3. Formal semantics: methods for defining mathematical models of computers and the relationships among the models, language syntax, and implementation. Primary methods include denotational, algebraic, operational, and axiomatic semantics.

4. As supporting areas: predicate logic, temporal logic, modern algebra and mathematical induction.

The elements of abstraction for programming languages are:

1. Classification of languages based on their syntactic and dynamic semantic models; e.g., static typing, dynamic typing, functional, procedural, object-oriented, logic specification, message passing, and dataflow.

2. Classification of languages according to intended application area; e.g., business data processing, simulation, list processing, and graphics.

3. Classification of major syntactic and semantic models for program structure; e.g., procedure hierarchies, functional composition, abstract data types, and communicating parallel processes.

4. Abstract implementation models for each major type of language.

5. Methods for parsing, compiling, interpretation, and code optimization.

6. Methods for automatic generation of parsers, scanners, compiler components and compilers.

Design and experimentation issues include:

1. Specific languages that bring together a particular abstract machine (semantics) and syntax to form a coherent, implementable whole. Examples: procedural (COBOL, FORTRAN, ALGOL, Pascal, Ada, C), functional (LISP), dataflow (SISAL, VAL), object-oriented (Smalltalk, CLU), logic (PROLOG), strings (SNOBOL), and concurrency (CSP, Occam, Concurrent Pascal, Modula 2).

2. Specific implementation methods for particular classes of languages: run-time models, static and dynamic execution methods, typing checking, storage and register allocation, compilers, cross compilers, and interpreters, systems for finding parallelism in programs.

3. Programming environments.

4. Parser and scanner generators (e.g., YACC, LEX), compiler generators.

5. Programs for syntactic and semantic error checking, profiling, debugging, and tracing.

6. Applications of programming language methods to document-processing functions such as creating tables, graphs, chemical formulas, spreadsheets equations, input and output, and data handling. Other applications such as statistical processing.

In this text, I have included the report's elements of theory except for parsing and language translation, which will be left for a course on compilers, as will items (5) and (6)—the elements of abstraction, and item (4)—the design and experimentation issues.

THEORETICAL ORGANIZATION

The presentation of languages is organized around the paradigm schema of Peter Wegner, which I first encountered in his IEEE tutorial [Wegner, 1988] while searching for a way to organize the disparate topics of programming languages into a manageable whole. Recent papers on these views are "Introduction to Programming Language Paradigms" [Wegner, 1989] and "Concepts and Paradigms of Object-Oriented Programming" [Wegner, 1990].

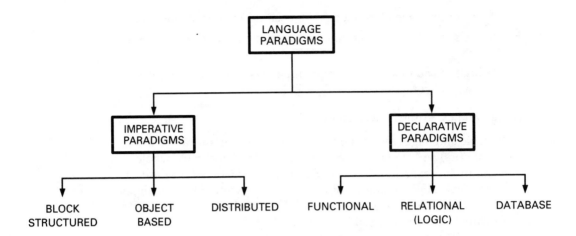

Figure P.1

A paradigm is a simple collection of abstract features that categorize a group of languages. The two top-level classes of paradigms are *imperative* and *declarative*. Each has three subcategories, as shown in Figure P.1. We will look at one or more example languages of each subtype.

The final section on languages for special purposes, includes rapid prototyping, the needs of novice programmers and business and "little languages" for special tasks. Programming environments, including editors, debuggers, browsers, profilers, etc., are addressed through the laboratory assignments.

Although "a blueprint for lifetime learning" may be the main goal of education, students also need training in language skills. It is both for this skill-building needed for the world of work and for the reinforcement that dealing with concrete languages provides for conceptual learning, that I have included laboratory assignments. A student who successfully completes a weekly lab will have gained some modest skill in the several languages used.

There are 23 assignments for formal labs of about 1½ hours each, which is far too many for a one-quarter or semester course. An instructor may choose which labs to use depending on the focus of the course. The labs can be found in the *Instructor's Manual*, although the objectives are listed in the body of the text. Labs address 23 topics exemplifying a particular language feature, and some can be executed in a choice of language. The instructor may choose languages in which to provide programming experiences.

MiniManuals are available for:

Imperative languages

1. Ada by George Benjamin	Block structured, object-based and distributed paradigms
2. C and C++ by Maryam and Bill Hastings	Block structured and object-oriented paradigms
3. Pascal and Object Pascal by Steve Andrianoff	Block structure and object-oriented paradigms

Declarative languages

4. SCHEME by Dick Hull	Functional paradigm
5. PROLOG by Tom Hankins	Relational (logic) paradigm

Labs are also available using BASIC, Modula-2, SETL (rapid prototyping) and SQL (database), although no MiniManuals have been provided.

I believe that students learn languages best by examining exemplary programs and making modifications as well as by writing their own programs. A student completing a course using this text will not be able to claim competency, only familiarity, in the three or four languages in which programs are written. However, by viewing languages organized by their features, students should understand the different programming styles in use today.

COURSE ORGANIZATION

In my experience, the programming languages course benefits students most if they actively program in several of the languages studied. But when they have lab in addition to classroom assignments, it is usually the latter that gets slighted. There are numerous exercises in the text, but none that require computer solution. Thus I would expect students to come to class prepared with answers to only some of the exercises, while successfully completing all the labs assigned.

A typical undergraduate semester is composed of 15 weeks, or 14, if we exclude class periods used for testing and review. A class meeting three hours a week for lecture, plus once a week for a 1 to 2 hour lab, should be able to finish all 10 chapters of the text and complete 14 of the 23 labs. Some of these are closed labs, where students are expected to finish the assignment within the allotted time, and others are open, where extra work outside the scheduled lab period can be expected. If a college cannot provide a closed lab situation, all assignments can be completed as open labs, with students working at computers whenever they can.

In a system of 10-week quarters, one might omit Chapter 5, "Formal Languages," and Part V, "Languages for Special Purposes." These students could be expected to complete nine labs.

TEACHING MATERIALS

In addition to the MiniManuals, the following are available from McGraw-Hill to adopters of the text:

1. An *Instructor's Manual* containing solutions to paper-and-pencil exercises contained in the text, as well as laboratory assignments.
2. A lab files diskette containing the source files necessary to do the labs.

ACKNOWLEDGMENTS

The text includes 15 historical vignettes, written by my former student, Laurie Sexton, who also served as research assistant, reader, and critic.

The MiniManual authors, Steve Andrianoff, of St. Bonaventure University; George Banjamin, Muhlenberg College; Maryam Hastings, Marymount College; Dick Hull, Lenoir-Rhyne; Tom Hankins, West Virginia College of Graduate Studies; and also Jay VandeKopple, Marymount, read materials related to the languages they were working with and offered many suggestions and corrections. They also wrote, tested, and debugged lab assignments using the languages addressed in their manuals.

The text also benefitted from careful readings by several reviewers who were anonymous to me at the time. Chapter 2, in particular was extensively rewritten in conformance with their suggestions. I appreciate all their careful thought and comments. They are:

Jane Hill, Dickinson College
Jim Beug, California Polytechnic, San Luis Obispo
Jon Manney, North Carolina State University
Richard Salter, Oberlin College
Rob Lyndon, Ohio University
Walter Pharr, College of Charleston
Stan Seltzer, Ithaca College
Tom Meyers, Colgate University
Dale Hanchey, Oklahoma Baptist University
David Jackel, LeMoyne College

Special thanks must go to Marymount College, which provided me with a year of course reductions plus a year-long sabbatical to complete this work.

And finally, I must acknowledge my three editors, David Shapiro and Eric Munson from McGraw-Hill, and Raleigh Wilson, from Business Media Resources. I needed their generous "TLC" to persevere through to the end from conception (which, I must admit, was Raleigh's) to final proofing. Without Ingrid Reselmaier and Carolyn Patsos, David and Eric's able assistants, the book would never have seen the light of day. Jennifer Ballentine and her staff at Ocean View Technical Publications did far more than their assigned tasks of editing and typesetting. They caught many stylistic as well as substantive errors in the materials submitted to them.

P A R T

I

PRELIMINARY
CONCEPTS

0

INTRODUCTION

0.0 PROBLEM SOLVING

When we use a computer we are attempting to solve a problem. It may be a business problem involving profit and loss, a scientific problem employing models of physical behavior, a statistical investigation, assessing the chance of some event occurring, a linguistic exercise, interpreting natural language, or just plain word processing. People solved problems long before computers became common place resulting in a wealth of experience to benefit from today.

Charles Hoare claims that "the primary purpose of a programming language is to help the programmer in the practice of his art" [Hoare, 1973]. This practice consists of program design, coding, documentation, and debugging. Classic problem-solving aids can benefit programmers in many ways, including the design of programs.

Devices from Mathematics

Any problem that can be expressed numerically is included in the realm of mathematics. Thus it is in this discipline that most computer languages are based. Mathematicians have attempted different ways to represent facts in economical and unambiguous ways. We can represent the addition of one and two by 1 + 2, PLUS(1,2) or ADD 0001 0010. These representations are three different *syntaxes* for the same idea.

Each mathematical or program statement has *syntax*, or form, and *semantics*, or meaning. The semantics for each of the representations of "one plus two" should adhere to the standard notions of the addition of two natural numbers. In any programming language, each statement must be both syntactically and semantically unambiguous. Furthermore, a compiler or interpreter must be able to decide whether a program is syntactically correct. If so, the run-time system must then execute the program in accordance with its semantics. Our understanding of these notions owes much to mathematicians and logicians.

Logic

Logic is the science of reasoning. If we follow its syntax and rules, we can deduce new facts from old ones. We will also know that the new facts are just as correct as the old ones were. For example, if "All birds can fly" and "Tweety is a bird" are true, we can deduce, "Tweety can fly," applying the rules of the predicate calculus.

To reason logically, we must first decide what constitutes a sentence and what does not. If the statements above are deducible, they must also be valid. What constitutes a valid statement (well-formed formula or WFF) is specified by the *syntax* of the language being used in a particular system of logic. Similarly, a programming language has only certain statements that are valid. In BASIC, X = 5 is valid, but X + 1 = 4 + 1 is not.

A programming language is much closer to a formal language in the mathematical sense than to the natural languages we use in everyday parlance. In Spanish there are two words for language, *idioma* and *lenguaje*. *Idioma* also means tongue and is never used for a computer language, which is *un lenguaje de máquina*. It is important to keep in mind the distinction between natural languages, with their semantic ambiguities, and precise formal languages. The study of programming languages themselves is much more straightforward when approached from a formal perspective than from the method of trial and error.

Around the turn of the century, mathematicians thought that all of mathematics could be expressed in formal logic. Although this turned out to be untrue, just as it is untrue that all problems can be solved by the computer, the methods developed have proved valuable in mathematics, linguistics and computer science. We will look closer at this concept in Chapter 6.

Set theory

The theory of sets formalizes much of mathematics. Practitioners in many fields work comfortably with sets and find them advantageous for solving problems. Thus many programming languages incorporate sets directly into the available structures. One very high-level language, developed primarily for the early testing of a new system called rapid prototyping, is based entirely on set theory. We will explore SETL in Chapter 9.

Lambda calculus

After the failures of both formal logic and set theory to incorporate all of mathematics, Alonzo Church attempted the task through functions. A function, as the word implies, specifies some sort of action or transformation of information. Addition is a function, which transforms two numbers into a third according to particular rules. A computer program can be thought of as a function as well, transforming its input into its output. Languages based on functions have been especially useful in the field of artificial intelligence (AI). Although Church's original program to express all of mathematics through functions failed, the most popular AI language, LISP, owes both its syntax and part of its semantics to his lambda calculus.

Recursive function theory

Investigation into the properties of functions did not stop with Church. Among the problems considered in computing theory are what sorts of functions are computable, what sorts will compute but never end, and what the relationships are among languages, computers and problems. A class of functions that map the natural numbers into the natural numbers is particularly useful in this regard. These are called recursive functions since they may be defined in terms of each other. For example:

$$ODD(1) = 1; ODD(n) = ODD(n-1) + 2;$$

is a recursive function, with range all the odd natural numbers. If we want to find the fourth odd number, ODD(4), we proceed:

$$
\begin{aligned}
ODD(4) = ODD(3) + 2 \\
ODD(3) = ODD(2) + 2 \\
ODD(2) = ODD(1) + 2 \\
3 = \quad 1 + 2 \\
5 = \quad 3 + 2 \\
7 = 5 + 2
\end{aligned}
$$

The most general of all programming languages can be described using recursive functions and can be used as input to the most general of all computers, the Turing machine. We will discuss these theoretical matters briefly in Chapter 5.

Conceptual and Implementation Levels

Any programming language can be considered equivalent to any other, in that each changes values of the store.[1] They can, however, be quite different at both the conceptual and the implementation level. A language is organized around a particular conceptual model. A LISP programmer does not bother with the store, but thinks in terms of functions, atoms and lists. One programming in logic considers relations and clauses. When working in Pascal, we think "top-

---

1 The store of a computer is usually thought of as an array of cells in which values are kept. Each cell has a unique name that can be recognized through a legal identifier of a programming language. The store may be implemented variously in the hardware of different physical computers.

down" in terms of procedures accomplishing particular tasks. Assignments to variables change the store directly, but we are operating at the conceptual level. Our thought processes are devoted to certain concepts, and we remain free from consideration of bits and bytes.

Once a language has been developed conceptually, it must be implemented so that its basic structures can be represented at the bit level. This is the job of the compiler designer, who also works at various conceptual levels. In this text, we will mention implementations, but will work largely at the conceptual level.

0.1 LANGUAGE PARADIGMS

The notion of scientific paradigms can be found in Thomas Kuhn's *The Structure of Scientific Revolutions* [Kuhn, 1962]. He defines them as "universally recognized scientific achievements that for a time provide model problems and solutions to a community of practitioners" [p. x]. Peter Wegner [Wegner, 1988, p. 5, Wegner, 1990] extends the notion to programming language paradigms, which "may be defined intensionally by their properties or extensionally by one or more instances." These terms, *intension* and *extension*, are borrowed from set theory. A set may be defined intensionally by describing the members of the set. For example, "S is the set of all black and white dogs," defines the set S intensionally. Any black and white dog is intended to be in S. D = {Spot, Snoopy, Tyge}, is defined extensionally. D is built from the empty set $\emptyset$, by extending it three times, D = $\emptyset \cup$ {Spot} $\cup$ {Snoopy} $\cup$ {Tyge}. The block-structured language paradigm can be described intensionally as the set of all programming languages that support nested block structures, including procedures, or it can be described extensionally by listing particular languages with this feature, e.g., BlockStructuredLanguages = {ALGOL, Pascal, Ada, Modula, C}. In defining a paradigm, no attempt is made to ensure that the list of language exemplars is exhaustive. Kuhn uses the term *exemplar* for an example that helps to define a paradigm. A single language incorporating all the features of a paradigm is called an *exemplar*, an exemplary realization of the paradigm. We may investigate a particular paradigm by exploring the features of one or more representative languages. You will not be far wrong if you relate a language paradigm to a very good example language for a collection of related ideas.

A paradigm, and also its exemplars, is most useful when it is simple and clearly differentiates one language from another. Exemplars may be manufactured to serve as a model, as are some experimental languages, or may already exist as languages. We may say that Ada is "block structured" and also "object based." It is not, however, "object oriented." Thus Ada belongs to both the block-structured and object-based paradigms, but not to the object-oriented paradigm. Whether or not Ada can serve as an exemplar depends on your view of Ada.

In this text we will explore the paradigms selected by Wegner and his colleagues as representing the languages predominantly in use today by significant groups of programmers and researchers.

Kuhn's essay has been widely praised and is considered to have raised the level of discussion about the nature of science. He claims that notable scientific achievements often precede the recognition of an abstract paradigm. Such achievements serve to define the legitimate problems and research methods in an area of scientific inquiry for succeeding generations of practitioners. When a significant new paradigm is made known, it draws a group of adherents *away from* competing methodologies. It also must be open ended enough to leave all sorts of problems to be solved. Examples of classic competing paradigms are Aristotelian vs. Newtonian dynamics or Ptolemaic vs. Copernican astronomy. A more recent example is the wave vs. quantum theory of electrical current. Each paradigm serves a useful purpose in particular applications. Kuhn [Kuhn, 1962, p. 43] holds that "despite occasional ambiguities, the paradigms of a mature science can be determined with relative ease."

Wegner believes that computer science is becoming mature, and that the paradigms for programming languages fall into two classifications, imperative and declarative. *Imperative languages* specify how a computation is performed by sequences of changes to the computer's store, while *declarative languages* specify what is to be computed.

Kuhn holds that paradigms help specify appropriate puzzles to be solved, and that a scientist is motivated "to succeed in solving a puzzle that no one before has solved or solved so well." Wegner refers to problems in need of solution, rather than puzzles, and the paradigms as descriptions of "patterns of thought for problem solving" [Wegner, 1988, p. 7]. These patterns are so elusive that in practice, paradigms are abstracted from models of computation, example languages and language features. The abstractions, and not the individual languages, are of major importance when considering programming languages as a group. We will deal with notions of abstraction in Chapter 1.

Kuhn traces new paradigms from the breakdown of an older one in an application. He comments [Kuhn, 1962, p. 76] that "retooling is an extravagance to be reserved for the occasion that demands it." A recent breakdown was recognized by the Department of Defense (DOD), which was floundering in a sea of software written in hundreds of sometimes unmaintainable and often fragile languages. The development of the Ada language involved the simultaneous development of both paradigm and example.

Perhaps the most startling part of Kuhn's work describes scientific revolutions within their social context. When contrasting paradigms exist, the choice of which will hold sway is not always based on merit or proximity to "truth."

One community or another decides which problems are more important to solve, and then supports the most promising paradigm for attacking them. This decision is sometimes made acrimoniously, with hostile camps supporting different models. Many criticisms were leveled at *The Structure of Scientific Revolutions* when it first appeared. There was confusion over the paradigm notion itself. In a postscript to the second edition [Kuhn, 1970], Kuhn attempts to separate the notion into two parts: the constellation of beliefs, values, and techniques shared by a community of practitioners, and the concrete models or examples themselves. He identifies four components of a discipline organized around a particular paradigm. The first he calls symbolic generalizations, the written rules or laws of the paradigm. Second are the beliefs of the community of practitioners, the particular ways of proceeding that appear to be most fruitful. Third are the values of a group about what is most important. Simplicity, such as is found in Pascal or pure LISP, might be valued more than widespread applicability, one of the goals of PL/I. The fourth and final component is the exemplars themselves, including the problems to be solved and with their solutions.

Programming language paradigms and languages themselves are not immune from champions and detractors. And eventually, certain languages become *linguae francae* for commercial, scientific or other reasons. We will recognize all of Kuhn's four components as we look closer at the paradigms and their particular language exemplars.

EXERCISES

1. Consider a language you know well and discuss it in terms of the four paradigm components mentioned by Kuhn.
   a. Symbolic generalization: What are the written rules of the language?
   b. Beliefs of the practitioners: What particular features of the language are believed to be "better" than in other languages?
   c. Values: What thinking or programming style did the originators believe best?
   d. Exemplars: What sort of problems can be solved most easily in the language?

2. If you know more than one language, repeat exercise 1, comparing this second language with the first.

3. FORTRAN, an acronym for FORmula TRANslation, was the first language to let programmers express their problems in familiar mathematical notation. Name some examples that are perfectly good algebraic formulas, but do not work well as programming expressions (one was mentioned in the section, "Logic," p. 4). What is the problem? You might consider both the limitations of computers as finite computational devices and the limi-

tations of particular equipment, such as keyboards and visual displays. How about the symbols themselves?

4. ALGOL was the first ALGOrithmic Language. What devices must be implemented to deal successfully with algorithms?

5. If shortness of source code is valued, we might rank languages in terms of how many lines are needed to write code for a particular problem. APL, C, BASIC, Pascal, and COBOL are listed here in order from shortest to longest average program length. Discuss the features that promote brief code in five languages with which you are familiar. ■

Imperative Paradigms

Imperative paradigms are those that facilitate computation by means of state changes. By a state, we mean the condition of a computer's random access memory (RAM). It is sometimes helpful to think of computer memory as a sequence of "snapshots," each one capturing the values in all the memory cells at a particular time.

When a program is entered, associated data exists in a certain condition, e.g., an unsorted list offline. It is the programmer's job to specify a sequence of changes to the store that will produce the desired final state, perhaps a sorted list. The store involves much more than data and a stored program, of course. It includes symbol tables, a run-time stack(s), an operating system and its associated queues and stacks, etc. The complete program, data, and even the CPU itself can be viewed as part of the initial state. The first task might be to input the unsorted list and the final one to output the sorted list. We will discuss the formal connections between languages and state transitions in Chapter 5.

The block structured paradigm

FORTRAN, the first language with program blocks, partitions the state into blocks representing subroutines and common data. FORTRAN blocks can be thought of as a flat file, where each block follows its predecessors. Because of this flat structure, FORTRAN is no longer considered to be a block-structured language, but is an example of a procedure-oriented language, where programs are executed through successive calls to separate procedures. FORTRAN's libraries of tested procedures are one of its useful features.

The term *block structure* now refers to nested blocks. That is, procedures may be nested within procedures. The state represents a stack with a reference to the procedure block currently active on top. No restriction applies to duplicate items on this stack, so recursion is supported, which is not possible using FORTRAN's flat structure. In block-structured languages, the procedure is the principal building block of programs. Language examples are ALGOL 60, Pascal, ALGOL 68, and C.

The object-based paradigm

The object-based paradigm describes languages that support interacting objects. An object is a group of procedures that share a state [Wegner, 1988, p. 9]. Since data is also part of a state, data and all the procedures or functions that apply to it can be captured in a single object. Examples are Ada, where objects are called packages; Modula, where they are called modules; and Smalltalk, where objects are called (rightfully) objects.

Objects have been differentiated from packages or modules by certain properties that place them in the object-oriented paradigm. We will discuss these distinctions in Chapter 3.

The distributed programming paradigm

Concurrent programming has been divided into two broad categories, loosely or tightly coupled systems. The term *distributed* usually refers to languages for loosely coupled systems that support a group of programmers working on a particular program simultaneously and communicating through message passing over a communications channel, such as a point-to-point link or a local area network (LAN) [Bal, 1988, p. 82]. In a loosely coupled distributed system, a language need not support simultaneous memory sharing, thus skirting some problems.

A tightly coupled system allows more than one running process to access the same memory location. Associated languages must synchronize the memory sharing so that only one process writes to a shared variable at a time, and so that a process can wait until certain conditions are fulfilled before continuing to execute. Shared memory has the advantage of speed.

Concurrent programming is associated with more than one CPU operating simultaneously in parallel, with or without data sharing. Multiple CPU's are not essential for this paradigm, however. What is essential is that work on a particular problem can be shared. Ada is perhaps the best-known language supporting concurrency. In Ada, two or more procedures execute independently. The sharing of results occurs through a process called a *rendezvous*.

Recently, work has been done on languages that blur the distinction between the loosely and tightly coupled paradigms. Languages such as Concurrent PROLOG, Linda, and Emerald have some features of both paradigms. In Chapter 4, we will consider both the distributed and shared-variable paradigms.

Declarative Paradigms

A declarative language is one in which a program specifies a relation or function [Wegner, 1988]. When programming in the declarative style, we make no assignments to program variables. The interpreter or compiler for the particular language manages memory for us. These languages are "higher level" than imperative languages, in that the programmer operates more remotely from the CPU itself.

The three declarative paradigms are taken from mathematics: logic, the theory of functions, and the relational calculus.

Logic programming

Logic programming is based on a subset of the predicate calculus, including statements written as Horn clauses. The predicate calculus provides axioms and rules so that one can deduce new facts from other known facts. Horn clauses allow only one new fact to be deduced in any single statement. Statements expressed as Horn clauses allow a particularly mechanical method of proof called resolution.

A logic-based program consists of a series of axioms or facts, rules of inference, and a theorem or query to be proved. The output is true if the facts support the query, and false otherwise. PROLOG is the exemplar for logic programming languages.

Functional programming

Purely functional languages operate only through functions, which return a single value, given a list of parameters. No side effects are permitted, so a program is a function call with parameters possibly calling other functions to produce actual parameter values. Functions themselves are first-class values that can be passed to other functions. Thus functional programming provides the ability for a program to modify itself, i.e., learn.

In practice, there are few purely functional languages, since basic side effects such as input and output are desirable. LISP, an acronym for List Processing, is the best-known functional language. Pure LISP exists and has a devoted following, but production versions of LISP include many nonfunctional features.

Database languages

The properties that distinguish languages designed to deal with databases are persistence and the management of change. Database entities do not disappear after a program terminates, but live on indefinitely, as originally structured. Since the database itself is permanent, these languages must also support change. The data itself may change and so may the relationships between data entities or objects.

A database management system usually includes a *data definition language (DDL)* for describing a new collection of facts, or data, and a *data manipulation language (DML)* for interacting with existing data bases.

Database languages can often be embedded in other programming languages for greater flexibility. An effort is also afoot to make them easy to use, so that nonprogrammers can manage the normal data of the world of business and affairs.

EXERCISES

1. The most familiar recursive procedure is the factorial function,

```
FACT(0) = 1
FACT(n) = n * FACT(n-1), (n > 0).
```

Suppose the reference to the block of code for FACT is F. Draw the stack for FACT(3). What information other than F must be on that stack to make the recursion work?

2. LISP expressions are implemented as binary nodes, the right half called the car and the left half the cdr (more on this in Chapter 7). (+ 2 5) becomes:[2]

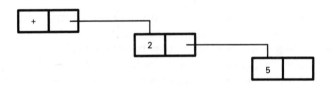

a. How would (+ 2 5 7) be implemented?
b. (* 2 (+5 7))?
c. (cats dogs)?
d. ((cats)(dogs))?

3. Horn clauses allow only one new fact to be derivable (after the "→") in each clause. A & B → C is a Horn clause, but A & B → C & D is not. Rewrite the following as Horn clauses (you may need more than one):

a. (The date is December 25) → (It's cold) & (Nights are long).
b. (The date is December 25) → (It's cold) OR (You're in the South). ■

---

2 There are and have been many dialects of LISP. Originally, they were grouped as "evalquote" or "eval" languages. One of the differences is that the former uses the functional syntax, fn(args), while the latter uses (fn args), where "fn" is a function name and "args" are the arguments to fn. McCarthy's original paper [McCarthy, 1960] defined LISP as an evalquote interpreter using evalquote syntax. Most modern LISPs, such as SCHEME and Common LISP use eval notation. Evalquote notation is more mathematical while eval notation follows the lambda calculus closer.

0.2 PRACTICAL CONSIDERATIONS

Computer programs are written to exploit the limits of computers and their problem-solving abilities. Sometimes their purpose is to solve efficiently some particularly tedious problem in the real word of science, industry and business. Thus languages are designed to incorporate particular features desired by the potential users. Particular languages designed with particular users in mind are COBOL for the business community and Ada for the DOD.

Programming in the Large

One of the things a computer does well is to remember large amounts of facts. It can also process these facts much faster than any human. Just think of the possibilities when a group of human beings work with a group of computers on a particularly difficult problem, such as predicting the weather. This is perfectly reasonable to tackle, since meteorologists know what sorts of data are needed, and good equipment exists to measure this data. Managing a world economy, where daily local fluctuations in currency and bond rates affect markets world-wide is another problem of large proportions. The Japanese have embarked on a "fifth-generation" computing project, largely directed toward managing the staggering amounts of potentially available information. Efforts at coordinating both human and machine efforts will be discussed in Chapters 4 and 6.

Special Problems

As computers have become more available, due to both increased capabilities and lowered prices, they are being used to accomplish more tasks. When a particular use becomes pervasive in an industry, it sometimes pays to develop both machines and languages specialized to the task at hand.

Data processing

One of the first areas where computers were obviously useful was in handling massive amounts of data. Herman Hollerith's tabulating machine was first used in compiling the 1890 U.S. census. For the past 50 years, every sizable corporation has had a data processing (DP) department. Dickens's Bob Cratchit was the classic data processor with his account books and quill pen. As these tasks became mechanized, fourth-generation languages (4GLs) were developed to meet these special needs.

Why fourth generation? Although different authors categorize languages differently, a reasonable grouping is to call machine languages first generation, assembly languages second generation, and procedural languages third generation.[3] These last include FORTRAN, COBOL, ALGOL, Pascal, and C. Gary Hansen [Hansen, 1988] describes 4GLs as languages with the following five properties:

1. Database structures and programming
2. A centralized data dictionary containing information about system components
3. Visual programming, such as using a mouse with icons
4. A graded-skill user interface allowing novices as well as database experts to use the programs
5. An interactive, integrated, multifunction programming environment

We will discuss these languages in Chapter 8.

Statistics

Statistics is the science of data analysis, which could be thought of as a subfield of data processing. We would not consider getting out the payroll to be a statistical process, but projecting a corporation's profits might be (given those salaries).

Statistics came to the attention of mathematicians in the nineteenth century, when Poincaré's wide-ranging interests included gambling. Much detailed work was conducted during the Great Depression of the 1930s, when statistical tables were compiled by hand by mathematicians working for the Works Progress Administration (WPA). Much of this work was agricultural in nature, as improving farming methods appeared to be a way out of rural poverty. Any undergraduate who has taken an introductory applied statistics course can appreciate the amounts of tedious calculation needed to compute even the simplest summary statistics, such as a mean and standard deviation.

Statistical work is done in all the natural and social sciences, often by researchers inexperienced in both computing and mathematics. Thus packages of programs and interactive languages for using them have been developed especially for this field.

Graphics

Graphics is, of course, concerned with graphs, charts, and other visual representations of data. Here we need languages that can manipulate individual dots (pixels) on a monitor or printing device. More difficult is incorporating

---

3 In this categorization of languages by generation, it is interesting that LISP fits nowhere. PROLOG is generally considered the language of the fifth generation, and Ada could be thought of as an extension of third-generation languages. Functional languages seem to be off in an unnamed category by themselves.

a graphics language within an existing programming language. We will look at this in Chapter 10, along with other "little languages" for special purposes.

Real-time embeddings

Computers complete tasks other than producing printed output from given numerical input. They may also signal apparatuses to do one thing or another, given certain conditions. In such a case, a computer and its languages may be embedded in another larger machine. Examples are medical monitors, which automatically regulate intravenous dosages depending on data taken from the patient, airplane automatic pilots, and the entire strategic defense initiative (SDI). One of the primary purposes of the DOD-sponsored language, Ada, is to facilitate these real time embeddings. We will see examples of language features supporting such activity throughout the text.

0.3 LANGUAGE CRITERIA

There are, or have been, literally hundreds of programming languages. Many are no longer used, while the notions of others have been incorporated in other languages. Throughout this text we will discuss the following criteria for considering a language meritorious. There are many other lists. These were first suggested by Barbara Liskov in a course at MIT and are reported in [Horowitz, 1984]. The criteria are interrelated, e.g., a language with a well-defined description may well be reliable and efficient, in part because of its description. We will merely define the terms here.

Well-Defined Descriptions

FORTRAN or PL/I programmers often worked as a group. If one didn't know or had forgotten how to write code to perform a particular function, the easiest solution was to walk down the hall and ask a friend. The manuals were huge, poorly organized volumes that instructed by example more often than by any other means. The designers of ALGOL 60 rectified this deficiency by providing a tidy, 18-page language description. Language syntax for ALGOL 60 is described in the formal Backus-Naur Form (BNF), followed by programming examples. For example, identifiers are described in BNF as:

```
<identifier> ::=
<letter>|<identifier><letter>|<identifier><digit>
```

Examples are: q, Soup, V17a, a34kTMNs and MARILYN.

The BNF definition can be read as, "An identifier is defined to be a letter, or an identifier followed by a letter, or an identifier followed by a digit." Letters and digits have been previously defined as:

```
<letter> ::= a|b|c|d|e|f|g|h|i|j|k|l|m|n|o|p|q|r|s|t|u|v|w|x|y|z|
A|B|C|D|E|F|G|H|I|J|K|L|M|N|O|P|Q|R|S|T|U|V|W|X|Y|Z
```

```
<digit> ::= 0|1|2|3|4|5|6|7|8|9.
```

By *syntax*, we mean a set of rules that differentiate valid from invalid programs. The BNF statements above are employed in making syntax definitions. Several formalisms describe syntax, including BNF and syntax diagrams.

A language must also be defined *semantically* by describing just what a particular statement means, e.g., the statement type `X : integer;` means in Pascal that storage sufficient for an integer will be set aside and identified as `X`. Then, `X := 12`, would store the integer 12 in that previously reserved location.

Natural language is notoriously ambiguous, so efforts are being made to describe language semantics formally as well as syntax. Two formal mathematical methods are being used to describe the semantics of languages. The first is axiomatic and the second denotational. Axiomatic semantics is based on the predicate calculus, which we will discuss in Chapter 6 when we study the declarative, logic-based language PROLOG. Axiomatic semantics makes statements about programs that are either true or false at various stages in a program's execution. These statements are usually in the form of pre- and postconditions, which are made before and after a statement such as a loop or procedure executes. If each condition can be proven true, regardless of the data input, the program will be guaranteed to be correct. Denotational semantics is based on the theory of functions. We will study these in Chapter 7. Each program and each procedure is associated with a function. If program P is associated with function f_P, and if $X_1, X_2, ..., X_n$ are inputs to P, then $f_P(X_1, ..., X_n)$ should produce a value corresponding to the desired output of P.

A third semantic method is to describe a theoretical machine for a language and how it operates. A compiler writer's job would then be to implement this machine for a particular piece of hardware. The designer will have already guaranteed that the language operates correctly on the theoretical machine. We will see an example of such a machine in Chapter 6.

Formal semantic methods are important for several reasons. They provide, first, an unambiguous language definition; second, standards so that a language will not vary from implementation to implementation; and third, a basis for correctness proofs of both compilers and programs. We will discuss formal semantics briefly in Chapter 5.

Provability

Proving with mathematical certainty that a program is correct is a slow-going process. C. A. R. Hoare believes, however, that "the practical advantages of program proving will eventually outweigh the difficulties, in view of the increasing costs of programming error" [Hoare, 1969]. Proving a program correct involves three steps: first, proving that the program accomplishes the intention of the programmer; second, proving that the compiler correctly translates the syntax and semantics of the language used into machine code; and third, proving that the machine itself operates correctly.

When considering a programming language, the goal is to prove that a compiler accurately interprets the language. This is often hard to do if the language definition includes natural language descriptions of what is meant by a particular bit of syntax. If syntax can be described in a formal language, and semantics described axiomatically, a compiler can be proved formally to fulfill both the syntactical and semantic definition of a language.

Pascal was defined axiomatically by its designers, Niklaus Wirth and C. A. R. Hoare; and PL/I was designed using the Vienna Definition Language. ALGOL 68 was defined in a two-level grammar, which formed a basis for proving compilers, but was too arcane for most users.

Reliability

Software is considered reliable if it behaves as advertised and produces results the user expects. When an error occurs, it should be easily detected and corrected. A programming language fosters the writing of reliable programs in often subtle ways. The goto statement is perhaps the most notorious language feature thought to result in unreliable programs [Dijkstra, 1968]. The underlying problem here is that programs with many back-and-forth goto's are hard for anyone but the originator to read, and thus hard to modify or debug.

Unusual syntax features may also foster errors. The C language uses "=" as an assignment operator. x = 5 assigns the value 5 to the storage location designated for x. For comparisons, "==" is used. x == 5 compares the value of x to five and is either true or false. Since C allows assignments almost anywhere in a statement, the inadvertent substitution of "=" for the unfamiliar "==" may produce no error, only unintelligible results. Modula-2 identifiers are case sensitive. Thus Count and count represent distinct variables, which are easily confused by both a programmer and subsequent reader.

A reliable language should be able to handle run-time errors. Arithmetic overflow occurs when an integer is computed that is larger than can be supported by the particular hardware involved. A variety of errors can occur during data input, from reading past the end of a file, to an unallowed value entered interactively. These kinds of errors are called *exceptions*, and language provisions for dealing with them are called *exception handlers*. Aborting a program is not always acceptable, particularly for real-time programs.

For programming languages, reliability will usually refer to mechanisms that promote the writing, maintaining, and debugging of correct programs, and the subsequent handling of exceptions when a program runs.

Fast Translation

The programming languages we will consider in this text are usually machine independent. That is, a program written in the language can be translated and then run on a variety of different machines. The program we write is in *source code*. This must be translated into a language the particular machine can recognize, and eventually into *machine code* that can actually run. The machine on which a program will run is called the *host* and its language(s), host language(s). We put the alternate (s) after language here, since a machine may have more than one host language. Any machine must have an associated low-level machine language written in binary code. It may also have a higher-level machine-specific assembly language. Often it is practical first to translate the source code into *target code* that is intermediate between the source code and machine code. Target code may or may not be one of the host languages.

Translation of source code involves three steps: lexical analysis, syntactic analysis, and semantic analysis. Lexical analysis, or *scanning*, identifies which tokens[4] represent numbers, identifiers, operators, etc. Syntactic analysis is called *parsing* and recognizes the valid statements while rejecting invalid statements of the source language. Semantic analysis determines the "meaning" of a statement. Some translators can perform two or more of these three processes in a single pass over the source code.

Translators are either *interpreters* or *generative translators*, which generate target code. If a language is interpreted, each statement is executed immediately after it is translated. Interpreters are usually easier to write than generative translators but execute more slowly.

The most common parts of a generative translator are the *compiler, linker,* and *loader.* The compiler translates source code into machine-oriented target code, called *object code*. The linker links together independently compiled target code into a single *load module*, resolving differences among tokens. Its output may be in the same target code as its input but is free of references from module to module. Resulting code is thus *relocatable*. The loader makes the final translation into machine code and loads the program into various memory locations. The output from the loader is an *executable module* in machine code. Names for programs often indicate what sort of code is involved, with source code having some extension indicative of the language, e.g., .PAS, .BAS., .C. Object modules may have a name with the extension .OBJ, relocatable code, .COM, and executable modules, .EXE.

It is important in some instances that source code translate quickly, e.g., an interactive application. If programs will be compiled only once, and run often, compilation speed may not be a primary concern. Successful attempts have

---

4 A token is any legal string of symbols denoting a single object. "COUNT", "4.532", "(", "*", and "13" are all tokens.

been made at one-pass compilers that scan the source code only once, while some translators make as many as 10 passes.

Efficient Object Code

After source code is compiled into object code, no further reference is made to the source language. Thus it is at compile time that matters of efficiency in both memory use and execution time must be considered. There is usually a trade-off between work that the programmer must do and work that the compiler can do. For example a language that has all type and variable declarations preceding other code can make efficient use of memory. The programmer will have to make all these declarations, of course, before a program can be compiled.

Some compilers, called *optimizing compilers*, execute one or two more steps after semantic analysis to increase the efficiency of the compiled code. The first optimizations, such as eliminating common subexpressions, are machine independent, while final improvements depend on the particular machine on which the program will run. Very high-level languages, where programs manipulate complex structures such as records, lists, relations, or sets, depend on optimizing compilers for efficiency. Programming languages run the gamut from ones like C where the programmer can work very close to the CPU itself to database manipulation languages (DMLs) where the underlying physical structures are largely hidden. In the lower-level languages, efficient object code often reflects the programmer's skill, while in very high-level languages it depends on the skill of compiler writers.

Orthogonality

The word orthogonal comes from the Greek and refers to straight lines meeting at right angles. Random variables are considered to be orthogonal if they are independent. It is in this sense of independence that language features can be considered orthogonal. Here we mean that components are independent of each other and that they behave in the same way in any circumstance.

One example is in the concepts of types and functions. A type describes the structure of data items. A function is a procedure that is passed a finite number of parameter values, and that returns a single value to the calling procedure. In an orthogonal language, types are independent from functions, and no restrictions apply to the types of parameters that can be passed or to the type of value that can be returned. Thus we would be able to pass a function to a function and receive a function back. LISP incorporates this particular feature, but certain inherent difficulties must be understood and dealt with.

ALGOL 68 was intended as an entirely orthogonal language. It has very few built-in constructs and the programmer is able to build what is wanted by combining features. It never became popular in the United States, in part

005, 13

58025087

because it was too orthogonal. Programmers wanted special built-in structures that behaved in predictable ways.

Nonorthogonality can be annoying and lead to errors. To the novice Pascal programmer, there seems to be no good reason why a function cannot return a record or that a file must be passed as a **var** parameter.

Generality

Generality is related to orthogonality. It refers to the existence of only the necessary language features, with others composed in a free and uniform manner without limitation and with predictable effects. If notions are independent of each other or orthogonal, such composition is possible.

Consistency and Common Notations

As we have mentioned before, problems for computer solution are often conceived in the languages of mathematics. Thus the notation of programming languages should be consistent with the commonly used notations of this field. We use "–" to indicate subtraction and negative numbers as well as the negation of a statement. Thus, $5 - 3$, -5, and $-$(Fido is Black) should all be allowed in languages supporting these notions.

$1 \in \{1, 2, 3\}$ is the common notation for set membership, and is thus preferable to 1 in [1, 2, 3]. However, not all character sets support "$\in$," "{," and "}," so substitutions are often made.

Uniformity

Related to consistency is uniformity. By this we mean that similar notions should look and behave in the same way. One uniformity issue has to do with the necessity for begins and ends. Should *every* "end" be preceded by a matching "begin"? Similarly, should every statement end with a ";"? In a completely uniform language, the answer would be yes to both questions.

Subsets

A subset of a language is an implementation of only part of it, without special features. The specifications for the DOD language, Ada, allow no subsets. Motivating this was the desire of the DOD to have its contractors produce software exploiting a full-featured Ada. After all, unnecessary features were not included. One of the disadvantages of this approach was that students could not begin learning the language until fully validated compilers were available, thus a corps of programmers did not exist until several years after the language had been completed.

Many languages are large, with many special components. These can run only on large machines, and so are unavailable to smaller companies and schools unless subsetted. A third advantage of subsets is incremental development of a language. By this we mean early release of a small core language, with other features being released as they are developed.

Extensibility

The converse of subsets is extensibility. A language may have a standard core, which is unvarying on every implementation, but various extensions. The advantages of subsets are enhanced when a language can be extended in useful ways.

Portability

A language is portable if its programs can be compiled and run on different machines without the source code having to be rewritten. To achieve portability, national and international standards organizations have been organized to produce language descriptions to which implementations must adhere. The most active of these are the American National Standards Institute (ANSI), British Standards Institute (BSI), International Organization for Standardization (ISO), and the Institute for Electrical and Electronic Engineering (IEEE). These groups have various official committees that prepare and revise standards for different languages. SC22/WG5 is the ISO working group for FORTRAN, and WG10 is charged with general recommendations on guidelines for standard preparation.

Standards can be developed after some experience has been gained with a particular language, as in the case of Pascal, or before a language is designed, as with Ada. Early standardization may perpetuate unrecognized poor design features, while delay fosters incompatible "dialects." LISP is perhaps the language with the greatest unstandardized longevity. LISP was designed and implemented in the early 1960s, but is only now being standardized to Common LISP. The standardized part will be only a small core, however, with different implementers free to make any extensions they wish.

EXERCISES

1. Well-defined descriptions must be written for both the syntax and semantics of a language. Find the definition of a "for" statement in two different formalisms. Two possibilities are syntax diagrams in Pascal and BNF for ALGOL 60 or Ada. Which do you find easier to read?

2. Using the descriptions you found for exercise 1, look at the semantic definitions. Are they formal or natural language definitions? To find these

semantic definitions, you may have to locate the official standard or report. Syntax charts often appear in textbooks, but the semantic definitions may be missing, with meaning explained in the body of the text.

3. When producing object code, optimization involves rearranging and changing operations to make the program run faster. One of these techniques is called *folding*, the process of computing at compile time arithmetic operations that are known [Gries, 1971]. Suppose our source code includes the following sequence of statements:

```
I := 1 + 1;   I := 3;   B := 6.2 + I.
```

These can be optimized to

```
I := 2;   I := 3; B := 9.2.
```

Optimize the following sequences of statements:

a. `X := 10; Y := X / 2; Z := SQR(X) - (X + Y);`

b. `X := 10; Y := X + Z; Z := SQR(X) - (X + Y);`

c.
```
case I of
        1:  Print (I * 2);
        2:  Print (I * 3);
        3:  Print (I * 4);
        otherwise Print (I)
   end case;
```

4. If you are familiar with some assembly language, convert the code sequences of exercise 3 into both optimized and unoptimized assembly code.

5. Find as many nonorthogonal or nongeneral features as you can of a language you are familiar with. For each, why do you think the restriction was made? ∎

0.4 NOTES ON REFERENCES

A well-written and fairly easy-to-read text on axiomatic semantics is [Gries, 1981]. The book has many easy examples, which allows for understanding, but that is also its drawback. Nowhere is a program of even average length or complexity analyzed using the pre- and post-condition methodology. [Tennent, 1976] and [Gordon, 1979] provide good introductions to denotational semantics. Both axiomatic and denotational semantics are considered in [Mandrioli, 1986].

The student interested in translators is referred to [Calingaert, 1988]. The coverage is on a "first-book" level, with material restricted to the translation of procedural languages.

Brief overviews on programming languages, language design, control structures, data types, Pascal and Ada, database management and exception handling, and experiences in designing new languages and axiomatic language definitions are contained in the *IEEE Tutorial* volume [Wasserman, 1980]. The collection also includes original articles by leading language implementers.

1

ABSTRACTION

"Euclid alone has looked on beauty bare." To Edna St. Vincent Millay, Euclid's abstraction of the geometry of the plane comprised "beauty bare," while others' more muddled views did not. Euclid perceived the bare bones of the plane and expressed them in nine general axioms and seven postulates. He showed that these are sufficient to describe the plane and its figures, and also that each axiom or postulate is necessary. Essential properties are lost if any are omitted. To abstract is to condense a larger object to its essential parts, ignoring details; to bare the underlying structure. When you write a paper, you might include a brief summary or abstract to let the potential readers know if they are interested in reading further. To abstract also means to find those essential parts of an example that must be shared by any other example considered similar. An abstract painting may have had all representations of visual reality removed except certain lines or colors to emphasize something particular. A series of paintings by Richard Albers includes nothing but single gray squares, investigating the essential nature of the color gray. Each painting is an example of grayness.

Many computer scientists, including Edsgar Dijkstra, have noted that the amount of complexity the human mind can cope with at any one time is considerably less than that needed for writing even fairly simple software. Peter Denning [Denning, 1989] describes abstraction in computer science as "modeling potential implementations. These models suppress details while retaining essential features; they are amenable to analysis and provide means for calculating predictions of the model's behavior." For example, two implementations for a linear list are an array or a linked list. The abstraction is the same for both, a list including the usual operations for manipulating it.

Much of mathematics is concerned with abstract systems that help us organize our world and our thinking. The seven postulates of Euclidean geometry may have been the first such system you encountered. They define the essential features of a flat world without perspective, in terms of the two undefined notions, point and line. This system does not work very well when describing the geometry of the eye, where parallel train tracks appear to meet in the distance. For this we use a different set of axioms to define projective geometry. An even different system, spherical geometry, is needed to model the globe.

Among programming languages, some systems work better for certain types of problems than do others. For programmers to be productive, the abstractions that have proved useful for applications need to be available in the languages they use. Abstractions in languages for programming computers are different from those in mathematical systems. We must consider the abstraction both in its relationship to problem solving and in its relationship to a physical machine. There is a certain "how to" about computing that may be missing in mathematics. We need to think about abstract machines as well as language paradigms. For our implemented list, an abstract machine might include consecutive storage locations with random access operations, or binary cells containing data in the first and the address of the succeeding cell in the second. Ideally, in an all-purpose programming language, all abstractions for all potential applications would be built in for the programmer to use.

Barbara Liskov of MIT and her colleagues [Liskov, 1977; Zilles, 1986] have identified three sorts of abstraction supported by programming languages: data abstraction, control abstraction, and procedural abstraction. A data abstraction consists of a set of objects and a set of operations characterizing their behavior. Control abstraction defines a method for sequencing arbitrary actions, and procedural abstraction specifies the action of a computation on a set of input objects and the output object(s) produced. We will discuss abstractions for data in section 1.1, control in 1.2, and modules and procedures in 1.3.

1.0 FROM LOW THROUGH HIGH TO VERY HIGH LEVEL

A language is considered low level if one can directly manipulate a machine's random access memory (RAM)[1] using statements in the language. Those at the lowest level are machine dependent and assign values of 0 or 1 to individual bits. A simplistic assembly language program for the PDP-11™ to initialize a five-element array to 0 is:

```
MOV #0.,R2                                    (1.1)
MOV R2.,428
MOV R2.,430
MOV R2.,432
MOV R2.,434
MOV R2.,436
```

---

1 The user can read or write to RAM in contrast to ROM, which is read-only memory.

After execution of the fragment, words 428 through 436 of RAM will contain the value 0. Equivalent code in Pascal is:

```
var                                              (1.2)
   IntArray : Array[1..5] of integer;
   I : 1..5;
begin For I := 1 to 5 do
   IntArray[I] := 0;
...
```

The Pascal code is easier to understand, but we have lost control over just which memory locations will house the array. The Pascal compiler does this, presumably, in an efficient manner.

In APL we can do the job with

```
V <- 5  0                                        (1.3)
```

Here the instruction is certainly quick and easy, but we have lost yet another element of control over the machine itself. When an APL program is executing, space must be found for the five-element vector V "on the fly."

```
V <- V,V
```

is also a perfectly good APL statement, which produces two copies of V catenated together, i.e., V is 0 0 0 0 0 0 0 0 0 0.

Languages such as APL, LISP, PROLOG, SETL, and SNOBOL are called "very high-level languages" because they allow the direct manipulation of complex data structures. In APL, the basic structures are arrays and matrices; in PROLOG, relations; in SETL, sets and maps; and in SNOBOL, it is patterns, or sets of strings. The goal of these languages is to make programming easier. Program specification and "coding up" are to be done in one straightforward step.

The price paid for efficient program writing may be execution efficiency. Very high-level programs often have large memory requirements and execute slowly. They are, however, very useful for prototyping, the testing of preliminary versions of new systems. The languages are often easy to learn, so suitable for beginning students and designers of programming languages and other computer applications. Compiler writers and machine builders are working to translate programs written in these languages directly into more efficient intermediate languages so that the expensive part of application development, the man years of programmer time, can be minimized.

EXERCISES

1. When modeling traffic crossing a bridge, an abstraction for a queue is needed. List as many abstractions as you can for the applications below.

   a. A grocery check-out counter

   b. A LIFO (last-in-first-out) accounting system; a FIFO (first-in-first-out) system

    c. Constructing a dictionary

    d. A word-processing package

    e. An automatic theorem prover

    f. An airline reservations system

    g. A computerized fuel-injection system in an automobile

2. Suppose we wish to print out the arrays defined in listings (1.1) to (1.3). Which would you expect to be printed the fastest? slowest? Why?

3. The BASIC language permits undeclared arrays of up to 10 elements. Why do you think the designers forced users to declare large arrays but not small ones? ■

1.1 DATA ABSTRACTION

The crossword puzzle clue for *data* is something like "raw material for a computer." Older dictionaries define it as "collected facts used as a basis for inference" while newer ones include the notion of computation to be performed on these facts. The *Random House Dictionary* defines data as "the plural of datum." In all these definitions, the emphasis is on individual items, which may be collected together in some way.

High-level programming languages look at data according to what can be done to and with it. For each sort of data, certain operations apply either to select out parts or to put parts together. For example, if our data is composed of names, i.e., character strings, one selector might print out the last name of a string. A constructor could, when combined with a selector, append an appropriate address to a name, or could produce a list of all names where the last name begins with A. What is important to remember is that only certain selectors and constructors apply to certain types of data. It makes no sense to multiply two names together to construct a single object from two others, or to select out the first name of an integer.

Data and the Store

The store, which is the collection of data values at a particular moment in the execution of a program, is composed of bits and can be thought of as a series of 0's and 1's. It may have no other defining characteristics.[2] High-level programming languages were developed to help programmers solve problems correctly. Structured programming methods are intended to enhance both the reliability

---

2 The store, of course, does have structure since it is organized into bytes, words, blocks, pages, etc. It also is addressed and differentiates between registers, RAM, ROM, and user-addressable and non-addressable sectors. Such organization need not concern one programming in a high-level language.

and understandability of programs. Very few programmers can assure themselves of the correctness of their programs if their only access to them is through pages and pages of bit strings. Grace Hopper, one of the developers of COBOL, reports that a supervisor would not let programmers use even assembly language, as it was felt that direct contact with the machine produced better programs. Current thinking has it that users will be able to employ computers more effectively if languages are available with built-in abstractions that are useful in their particular application areas. These abstractions include operations, data structures, and control structures.

Structuring Data

All data is structured in some way. Most programming languages have at least one built-in type, although there are typeless languages such as APL and MUMPS, where data objects can be coerced automatically from one type to another. Even here, the programmer is thinking and the program operating on some sort of structured type.

Integers are often built into a language. If the statement, $N = 5 + 3$, occurs in a program where "=" is the assignment operator, the contents of the storage location assigned to N will be thought of as the integer 8. On the other hand, if $N = 'O' + 'K'$, N will contain the string 'OK'. Each data type is recognized not only by its data items but by the operations associated with it. A set of data items is called a *data domain* (abbreviated D).[3] One or more data domains with associated operations is called an *abstract data type*.

As an example, the type, integer, in Pascal is described by:

$D = \{0, \pm1, \pm2, ..., \text{maxint}\}$ (1.4)
Constant identifier: maxint (machine dependent)
Operations:
    Unary operators = {+, –}
    Binary operators = {+, –, *, div, mod}

In LISP, the list is the basic built-in data type, and integers are described (in the SCHEME dialect) by:

$D_1 = \{0, \pm1, \pm2, ...\}$, $D_2 = \{\#t, \#f\}$ (1.5)
Constants: #t, #f (representing true and false)
Procedures:
    (* num1, num2) → num
    (+ num1, num2) → num
    (– num1, num2) → num
    (abs num) → num

---

3 What we have called a data domain is sometimes called a data object. We will reserve the term *object* to refer to a "container for data," following [Liskov, 1986]. Among object-oriented languages, the term is used to refer to hierarchical modules containing abstract data types.

(integer? obj) returns #t if obj is an integer, #f otherwise.
(zero? num) returns #t if num = 0, #f otherwise.

Underlying these descriptions is a common abstraction that defines integers and their properties, and underlying that is the abstraction for a ring,[4] which describes all structures with the same operations and behavior as the integers. The integers with their associated operations are expected to behave properly on any machine on which a program is run. Thus a further abstraction representing the integral properties of a CPU is needed to complete our abstract data type for integers. Actual compilers for particular computers represent implementations of these abstractions, as does the particular syntax used. A language standard, which specifies the necessary characteristics of any implementation of the language being considered, specifies some implementation details as well as syntax for data types.

EXERCISES

1. Give two reasons why an all-purpose language with all useful abstractions built in is impractical.

2. Using manuals for two or more languages available to you, respond to the following:

   a. What data types are built in?

   b. Write a description of one of these data types, including the data domain(s), associated constants, and operations, as in listings (1.4) and (1.5). ■

Data Types

Languages have varying numbers of data types, from pure LISP, with one essential type, the symbolic expression, or *S*-expression to a rich language like Ada, with six basic types: enumeration, integer, real, array, record, access, and types derived from these. Among the enumeration types are included character and Boolean types. Reals can be either fixed or floating point and included in arrays is a built-in string type. The user can define new types, including recursive types and subtypes as well. Ada also provides type variations such as generic types, which describe an entire class of similar types; private types, which hide an implementation from the user; limited private types, which hide the operations as well; and task types, which facilitate the naming of processes that can run concurrently.

---

4 A ring is a structure, R = <S, +, *, 0, 1>, where S is a set, and + and * are binary operations on S that have the same properties as integer addition and multiplication, e.g., a + b = b + a, a + −a = 0, a*a^{-1} = 1, and a * (c + d) = a*c + a*d, among others. For a complete definition see any modern algebra text, e.g., [MacLane, 1968].

LISP's *S*-expression is simplicity itself, defined as:

1. Atomic symbols are *S*-expressions.
2. If s_1 and s_2 are *S*-expressions, then $(s_1 . s_2)$ is an *S*-expression.

Whether a language should have few or many types is a matter of taste as well as controversy. If a language is simple like LISP, the programmer must be imaginative and creative to implement the necessary abstractions. Another issue is whether the type of each data domain should be explicitly declared or not. APL was designed with no type declarations at all. Variable types are determined implicitly by context. APL's developer, Kenneth Iverson, believes that implicit type definitions correspond more closely to a programmer's thought processes than do type declarations. In order to dispense with types, APL provides a greater number of operators than most other languages. For example, ρ is the array size operator, where $\rho V[0,1,2]$ generates 3, and $\rho 12$ generates a null value. The operator works on any type, here a vector or an integer.

Data independence

The approach to problem solving called *stepwise refinement* involves two activities: definition of the program modules needed to carry out the various activities involved in the solution, and defining data types, including their interaction with the solution activities. Consider the problem of laying out airplane routes. Some will be nonstop flights between cities while others will involve one or more connecting flights. When we start on the program, the form of the data is rather vague, perhaps a list of cities and the number of daily flights desired between them. Fairly early in the problem-solving process, it will be obvious that we will be working with a graph, since connections between two cities go both ways, and any single city might be connected to more than one other city. However, we need not worry about how to represent the graph with the types available in the language we have chosen at this level. All we need to do is think of the graph in relation to the operations we desire. Some of these operations might be:

connect(City1, City2, Day, Time),
disconnect(City1, City2, Day, Time),
Distance?(City1, City2),
list-all-cities, and
where-can-I-go-from?(City).

Each program module will know about the cities and the routes only through these known, but as yet unspecified, operations associated with the cities and the routes.

If, after the data and its associated operations have been specified, it becomes necessary to change the representation of the data, including the graph of routes, nothing else in the program need be changed but these operations. This property is known as *data independence*.

Programs written independently from the final data representations have many advantages. Among these is *information hiding*, which makes a program easier for the user to understand, makes programs portable between different languages and machines, and makes certain security measures practical. The principle of information hiding is to make visible all that is essential for the user to know, and to hide everything else. We will discuss this further below in "Brief Theoretical Excursion 2: Modularization."

User-defined data types

FORTRAN II had five simple data types: integer, real, double-precision real, complex and logical. The single-structured type was the array. Character strings were facilitated through a crippled Hollerith[5] type, which was really relegated to the integers. There were no other types, so users kept the "real meaning" of their data in their heads or described it through numerous comment lines.

ALGOL 68 was the first language to enable users to define their own types, called *modes*. The language was intended to be completely orthogonal, so there were no restrictions. For example,

```
mode functionset = [1:n] proc (real) real;
```

defines a dynamic array of real valued procedures. The declaration can be made at any place in a program with the size of the functionset depending on the value of n. The following block of code declares two functionsets, x with 15 elements and y with 75.

```
begin
  int n;
  n := 3;
  mode functionset = [1:n] proc (real) proc;
  n := 5 * n;
  functionset x;
  n := 75;
  functionset y;
  skip;    ; comment dummy statement. Each ALGOL block must have
           at least 1 executable statement.;
end
```

That n was assigned the value 3, when its mode was declared, has no effect on the size of x or y. What matters is the value of n at the time the mode of x and y are declared. See [Tanenbaum, 1976] for further discussion. Dynamic arrays cause problems for compiler writers, as storage must be found during execution to store them.

---

5 This was named for Herman Hollerith, who developed the punch card in the nineteenth century.

The chief design goal of Pascal was simplicity, rather than orthogonality; simplicity for compiler writers as well as programmers. Users can define their own Pascal types, but there are limitations. The most important of these is that all types (with one exception) must be declared before they are used, in a declaration block at the beginning of each program, function or procedure. The bounds of an array type must be declared along with the array. Pascal functions can have only pointers or simple, not structured, types as results. What Pascal loses in orthogonality and generality, it gains in simplicity of both implementation and the language itself.

Strong typing

A language is said to be strongly typed if it is not only required that all variables be declared as to type, but that these types be strictly enforced at both compile and run time. It is weakly typed if a programmer can declare types, but they may be either implicit or not enforced. Although Pascal is considered to be strongly typed, there are certain exceptions. One of these is in the variant record. Consider the following bit of code:

```
type Horrible = record                              (1.6)
   case b  : boolean of
     true  : (int : integer);
     false : (c2 : array [1..2] of char)
   end;
var
   H : Horrible;
begin
   H.int := 1;
   if (H.c2[1] = chr(0)) then
   ....
```

Just why is this fragment so Horrible? Before we answer this question, a little discussion of Pascal's variant record type is in order. A variant record is considered necessary in many applications, primarily to save space. For example, in a file of employee records, where most fixed field designations are the same for all, but certain ones vary for salaried and unsalaried workers, it is practical to allow these status-dependent fields to differ within the same record structure. Otherwise we would have to keep separate files for each category or maintain space-wasting void fields for those items not pertaining to a particular employee. A type that allows its variables to take on values of different types is called a *union*, since the data domain for the type is a union of two or more domains. Pascal allows a record to contain one variant part at the end of a record declaration.

Two assumptions are made (although not always honored):

1. The data will be overlaid in storage by the compiler writer,

2. Only one variant will be active at any one time.

That is, in the example of listing (1.6), H is a record containing either an integer or an array of characters, not both. The record, Horrible, has two fields: b, called the tag, or discriminant, which is either **true** or **false**, and the other, depending on the tag, either int or C2. Pascal 74 [Jensen, 1974], allowed switching back and forth between variants at will. Such a type is called a *free union* in which it is not necessary to specify the value of the tag before assigning values to the fields of the union part. The compiler or run-time system will pick it up in context. A union where tag specification is required is called a *discriminated union*. The Pascal 83 Standard [ANSI/IEEE, 1983] states that the fragment of listing (1.6) should cause an error. The H.int variant would be activated at the statement, H.int := 1; and the H.C2 variant would be completely undefined. An error should occur on encountering the inactive variant H.C2 in the Boolean expression, (H.C2[1] = chr(0)). Just what is meant by "completely undefined" and "cause an error," however, is left up to the compiler writer. Given either the Pascal 74 Standard or some lack of high-quality error detection on the part of a compiler, our example could still result in ambiguity.

Some machines store integers with the most significant 8 bits first and others last. Thus H.int (in octal form) could be represented by either 10 or 01. Then, *if* the variant fields are overlaid, and *if* a character occupies 8 bits, the value of (H.c2[1] = **chr**(0)) will be **true** in the first integer storage case and **false** in the second. If either of the *if*s is not true, our result could be either **true** or **false**.

The Ada language, which is based on Pascal, resolved the variant problem by requiring discriminated, static unions only so that consistency can be checked at compile time. Our variant record of listing (1.6) would be declared in Ada as:

```
type b : boolean;                                        (1.7)
type Not_so_Horrible(tag : b) is
  record
    case tag is
      when true => int : integer;
      when false => c2 : array [1..2] of char
    end case;
  end record;
var
  H1 : Not_so_Horrible(true);
  T  : b;
  H2 : Not_so_Horrible (T);
```

H1 would always have an int field and never a C2 field. H2 could have either, but the entire record must be specified, as in:

```
H2 := (false, ('O','K')); or
H2 := (true, 35);
```

Weak typing in C

A language developed with different design goals for data typing than those of Pascal and Ada is the C language. A short example from *The C Puzzle Book* [Feuer, 1982, p. 17] will suffice here. We will look further at C in Chapter 2.

```
#include <stdio.h>  /* standard I/O package */
#define PRINT(format,x) printf("x = %format\n",x)
    /* macro definition for more readable code to follow */
    /* variable declarations & initializations */
int  integer = 5
char character = '5'
char *string = "5"; /* pointer to the variable, string */
main()
{
  PRINT(d,string); PRINT(d,character); PRINT(d,integer);
  PRINT(s,string); PRINT(c,character);
  PRINT(c,integer=53); PRINT(d,( '5'>5 ));
}
```

PRINT(f,v) is a function to print the contents of variable v with format f. Formats used above are

```
d:  decimal          s:  string          c:  char.
```

The output will be, in order:

1. The address of the two-character array, [5,/0].

2. 53, the ASCII value of the character '5' (or other decimal value, if running on a non-ASCII machine).

3. The integer 5.

4. %s, or string format, instructs **printf** that the variable, string, contains a pointer to a string, or character array. **printf** prints out the contents of that array, 5.

5. %c, instructs **printf** to print the character its ASCII value represents, thus 5 is printed.

6. Since the ASCII value of '5' is 53, 5 is printed.

7. In order to test ('5' > 5), '5' is given its ASCII value, 53, which is larger than 5. Thus some nonzero decimal number meaning "true" will be printed.

Notice that machine addresses, or pointers, can be treated as decimal numbers (1), as can characters (2,7) or integers (3), without explicit conversion. A pointer value can be dereferenced[6] on the spot (5), and an integer converted automatically to its representing character (6). Each of these variables has a

---

6 A pointer (memory address) is said to be "dereferenced" to the value contained in the cell addressed. A reference is an address, while a dereference is the value pointed to.

declared type, but it can be converted to another type almost without the programmer being aware of it. C provides overt machine access, but can lead to hard-to-find bugs.

EXERCISES

1. What is the exception in Pascal to the rule that all types must be declared before they are used?

2. To avoid specific type declarations, in addition to providing a rich set of operators, APL also expands operators to other types. B mod A is written A | B in APL, with 2 | 5 generating the residue 1, as expected. 5 | –13.4 generates 1.6. What is APL's definition of the "mod" function for negative operands?

3. Consider the following four assumptions:

    1. Variant fields are overlaid.
    2. A single character occupies 8 bits.
    3. 16-bit integers are stored with the most significant digits first.
    4. 16-bit integers are stored with the least significant digits first.

    Trace the fragment of listing (1.6) under assumptions

    a. 1, 2, and 3
    b. 1, 2, and 4
    c. 1 and 3 with characters occupying 6 bits
    d. 1 and 4 with characters occupying 6 bits
    e. a through d without 1

4. Explain how Ada's rules governing variant records would resolve a through e above.

5. Define an abstract data type for pointers. Would you allow unlimited arithmetic operations, as in C? If not, which would you include?

6. In C, a Boolean variable, b, is considered "false" if b = 0, and "true" in all other cases. Consider the merits of this vs. "true" = 1 and "false" = 0, or "true" = some special reserved value, and "false" = some other special reserved value. ■

BRIEF THEORETICAL EXCURSION 1: Abstract Data Types

You may have wondered why the last section ending with a discussion of bits and machine storage of characters is included in a chapter titled "Abstraction." This gets us back to the difference between mathematical and computer-related abstractions, where the actual machine is always lurking in the background. We need assurance that abstractions developed for an application can be implemented both in the high-level language we are using and in its implementation through a compiler, in conformance with the common notions we had in mind. Just what sort of abstract machine represents our abstract data types, including their data domains and associated procedures? Before we can answer this question, we must be absolutely sure what is meant by abstract data types, which enable a programmer to postpone selection of actual data structures until all uses of the data are fully understood. They also facilitate program modification and maintenance to improve performance or accommodate new requirements.

Theoretical computer science employs the methods of mathematics to specify and prove semantic notions, the "meaning" of language constructs. Data abstraction can be defined briefly as the pair, [objects, operations]. Some discussions of abstract data types (ADTs) don't bother with objects at all. Any object that is subject to the various operations is OK. In this way of thinking, an ADT is described *entirely* by its operations. An ADT implemented on a (theoretical) computer includes the data abstraction and specifies the sorts of values a particular object or container for data can have. The container for data of course must be specified eventually in terms of bits, bytes, and computer words.

The burden of this theoretical excursion is to investigate how we can make these notions precise and prove that an implementation of a data type faithfully represents the abstract type. Two such approaches have been explored, the method of abstract models pioneered by C. A. R. Hoare [Hoare, 1972] and algebraic specification introduced by John Guttag [Guttag, 1977].

ABSTRACT MODELS

The method of abstract models embodies procedures plus conditions on the data on which they operate. These conditions can be of three kinds; preconditions, postconditions, and invariants. A precondition must be true before a procedure executes, a postcondition true when a procedure terminates, and an invariant true both on entry and exit from a procedure. It is the job of either the programmer or the compiler writer to specify and prove these conditions when implementing a procedure. As you explored in an exercise a few pages back, it is not possible or even desirable for a high-level language to include all the abstract data types a user might want. Thus verification of data types must be approached by both the language implementer and user.

The method was introduced by C. A. R. Hoare [Hoare, 1972], using the syntax of SIMULA 67 [Dahl, 1966]. SIMULA was the first class-based language. A class contains a data type, or types, plus a description of the associated operations. As an example, consider:

```
class SmallIntSet.                                    (1.8)
Data Types:  integer, boolean, SmallIntSet
Constants:   MaxSize : integer
```

Procedures:
```
p0:  initialize  -> s:SmallIntSet
p1:  size(s:SmallIntSet) -> integer
p2:  insert(s₁:SmallIntSet, i:integer) -> s₂:SmallIntSet
p3:  remove(s₁:SmallIntSet, i:integer) -> s₂:SmallIntSet
p4:  is_in(i:integer, s:SmallIntSet) -> boolean
```

An invariant for all five procedures is:

I: $0 \leq size(s{:}SmallIntSet) \leq MaxSize$.

Thus for any parameter, s, which represents a SmallIntSet, size(s) must be between 0 and whatever value has been set for MaxSize. For p0: initialize, there are no preconditions, since initialize has no parameters. The postcondition that must be proved in addition to the invariant I is:

P_{00}: s = {}.

For p1: size, the invariant must hold and also the postcondition, P_{10}: size(s) = |s|, where |s| is the cardinality of the set s.

For P2: insert, the invariant I must hold for both s_1 and s_2, and, in addition, the two postconditions:

```
P₂₀: if (i ∈ s₁) then |s₂| = |s₁|
        else |s₂| = |s₁| + 1;
P₂₁: s₂ =  s₁ ∪ {i}
```

Notice how these conditions are expressed using the language of set theory. Notice also that two previously defined types, **integer** and **boolean**, are included in SmallIntSet. The properties of the integers and Boolean values are inherited by SmallIntSet, which enables us to compare size(s) to MaxSize without specifically defining "<".

The method of abstract models is actually more detailed than we have presented here. There are three levels of abstraction involved. The highest, or most abstract, level is the set T, of all classes defined as data types. Second is the particular class or abstract type t, such as SmallIntSet. Included in the class t = SmallIntSet is a constant, MaxSize; data types, **integer** with parameter i, SmallIntSet, with parameters s, s_1, and s_2, and **boolean** with values true and false; and five procedures. At the lowest level are the implementations of the procedures and the data structure, SmallIntSet, and the specification of the data domains for **integer** and **boolean**. Hoare's method of abstract models provides mappings between each of these levels, which are formally proven to interpret the abstract data type (ADT) according to the invariants, pre- and postconditions.

ALGEBRAIC SPECIFICATION

The second method for formally proving that abstract data types actually do what we thought they would is due to John Guttag [Guttag, 1977]. An algebraic specification has two parts: a syntactic specification and a set of relations. An example of a specification for a queue follows.

Syntax

new :	→ Queue	
add : Queue X Item	→ Queue	
Front : Queue	→ Item	
Remove : Queue	→ Queue	
IsEmpty? : Queue	→ **boolean**	

(1.9)

Relations

(1) IsEmpty?(New) = true

(2) IsEmpty(Add(q,i)) = false

(3) Front(New) = error

(4) Front(Add(q,i)) = if IsEmpty?(q) then i
$\qquad\qquad\qquad$ else Front(q)

(5) Remove(New) = error

(6) Remove(Add(q,i)) = if IsEmpty?(q) then New
$\qquad\qquad\qquad$ else Add(Remove(q),i)

The advantage to this system is that we do not need to use any metalanguage,[7] such as the language of set theory above, to talk about the procedures we are defining. The disadvantage is that we must convince ourselves or prove that the relations are consistent and sufficiently complete.

When we say that P1 through P6 above are consistent, we mean that they do not contradict each other. That is, we cannot show that any of the P_i is false, given that the other five relations are true. To consider the specification complete, we must be sure that we have not missed any feature necessary to a queue. Boundary conditions, such as those causing errors above, are particularly easy to overlook.

In any implementation of an object of type Queue, we would need to demonstrate that the relations above hold. In addition, each of the five procedures can be furnished with invariants and pre- and postconditions. These are of two types, those inherent to the abstract data type itself, and those depending on the particular implementation. For example, if we implement a queue as an array, a dependent precondition on Add(q,i) would be that q was not already full. An inherent precondition on Remove(q) would be that q not be empty.

EXERCISES

1. Using a language familiar to you, suggest two different implementations of SmallIntSet.

2. What are the pre- and postconditions for P3: remove, and P4: is_in?

---

7 A theoretical system, S, is written in a particular language, L_S. When discussing S, we use L_S and the language of logic, the predicate calculus. This includes relations such as "=", "or", and "&". If we use any other language L to discuss S, L is called a *metalanguage*, i.e., L discusses S.

3. Choose one of your implementations from exercise 1, and write procedures for P1 through P4.

4. Convince yourself that relations 1 through 6 describe a queue completely. You might find using an example queue helpful. Are there any other procedures you might want? If so, what additional relations are needed?

5. Specify SmallIntSet of listing (1.8) algebraically, as in listing (1.9).

6. Specify Queue as an abstract model.

Language Examples

Zilles and her colleagues [Zilles, 1977] identify two requirements that must be satisfied by a language supporting data abstractions:

1. A linguistic construct is needed that permits a data abstraction to be implemented as a unit. The implementation involves selecting a representation for the data objects and defining an algorithm for each operation in terms of that representation.

2. The language must limit access to the representation to just the operations. This limitation is necessary to ensure that the operations completely characterize the behavior of the objects.

The first requirement means that the language itself must support some method for bundling data types and their associated operations into one class. The second facilitates verification of programs and data independence.

Data abstraction in Pascal

Pascal, which was modeled on ALGOL 60, provides the means for the abstraction of data objects, although abstract data types, which include procedures as well as objects, are not implemented directly. Liskov and Guttag [Liskov, 1986] suggest that the way to implement data abstractions in Pascal is through a comment describing the type, with procedures and functions discriminated by a single letter. They also suggest that each data type be implemented through a pointer into the heap, where dynamic variables are stored and released when a Pascal program executes. This pointer implementation serves two purposes. First, Pascal permits only simple types, including pointers, as values of functions. If an abstract type were represented as a record or other structured type, its values could not be returned by functions. Second, **var** parameters can be dangerous in procedures that are hidden. Side effects of which the user has no knowledge may occur causing program errors. Listing (1.10) shows part of the implementation of the queue of listing (1.9) as an abstract data type in Pascal.

```
{queue = data type is q_new, q_add, q_front, q_remove, q_is_empty.
item = data type is ...
```

Queues are used to store items in a FIFO manner. An auxiliary type for the sort of item stored is needed for each different sort of queue.

Operations

function q_New: queue   (1.10)
    effects: Returns a new queue with no elements in it.

procedure q_Destroy(q: queue);
    effects: Deallocates storage for all nodes in the q.

procedure q_Add(q: queue; i: item)
  modifies: q
  effects: adds i to the end of q

function q_Front(q : queue): item
  effects: returns the item at the front of the q.

procedure q_Remove(q: queue)
  modifies: q
  effects: removes the first item from q, unless q is
            empty, in which case an error occurs.

function q_Is_Empty(q: queue): **boolean**
  effects: returns true if q is empty, false otherwise.
end queue.
}

{Representation of abstract data type, Queue}

type
  Queue = ^Queue_rep;[8]
  Queue_rep = ^Queue_Node
  Queue_Node = **record**
    Element : item;
    Next: Queue_rep
  end {Queue_rep}

function q_New: Queue;
  var q : Queue;
begin
  q_New := **New**(q); q^ := **nil**; q_New := q;
end; {q_New}
. . .

---

8 "rep" stands here for representation. In this particular representation, we are using a record with one item field. In another representation, we might use an array. However, following [Liskov, 1986], we would still use the pointer into the representation, ^queue_rep.

Modula-2

Modula and its successor, Modula-2, were designed by Pascal's designer, Niklaus Wirth, for the programming of real-time systems. Wirth gives two criteria for any such language [Smedema, 1983]:

1. Facilities to program concurrent execution of several activities (e.g., several physical quantities have to be monitored at different frequencies).

2. Facilities to program input/output operations to any device (i.e., not only to standard devices like visual display unit, printer, and disk, but also to, e.g., analog-to-digital converter, external timer).

Wirth introduced the concept of a *module*, from which the name Modula derives. One of the capabilities of a module is to group data objects and their operations together, hiding their implementation from the user. In other words, the module supports abstract data types. Let's look at our ADT queue as implemented in Modula-2.

```
DEFINITION MODULE ItemQueues;

FROM Items IMPORT Item;
EXPORT QUALIFIED
    ItemQueue, Status, New, Destroy, Add, Front, Remove, Isempty;
TYPE
    ItemQueue;
VAR
    Status: CARDINAL;   (* Result of last procedure call.
                           0 = all OK;
                           1 = Can't find Front, Queue empty.
                           2 = Can't Remove, Queue empty. *)9
PROCEDURE New (VAR Q: ItemQueue);
PROCEDURE Destroy (VAR Q: ItemQueue);
PROCEDURE Add(VAR Q: ItemQueue; I: Item);
PROCEDURE Front(Q: ItemQueue; VAR I: Item);
PROCEDURE Remove(VAR Q: ItemQueue);

END Queue;
```

There are a few things to notice from this module definition. First, a **QUAL-IFIED** module allows for a procedure or type used in another module to be qualified by the module name. If module **USE**s ItemQueues and another module, say M, both contain procedures called New, we can qualify these procedures to ItemQueues.New or M.New to avoid confusion. Second, it assumes that a previous module has been defined and implemented that defines a type for an Item. Thus we **IMPORT** this information into the module Queue. The Items module also might provide access to objects of type Item, such as Read.

---

9 Status is based on a Queue module defined in [Beidler, 1986]. We include it here in order to demonstrate Modula-2's initialization capability.

The **EXPORT** clause lists all the procedures and data types that may be known outside ItemQueues. The only operations permitted on items of type ItemQueue are those defined in module ItemQueues, i.e., New, Destroy, Add, Front, and Remove. In a program **USE**ing ItemQueues, in which

    VAR Q : ItemQueue;

had been declared, the statement, Q:= NIL, would be illegal. The only assignments to Q must be made through New, Destroy, Add, or Remove.

Modula uses procedures with **VAR** parameters as functions, thus skirting Pascal's inability to return structured types from function calls. This can be done in Pascal, of course, but many programmers are used to working with functions and like to have them implemented directly.

Next, we proceed to the **IMPLEMENTATION MODULE**, which actually implements our procedures and may be both compiled separately and hidden from the user. A user, of course, needs access to the **DEFINITION MODULE** to be able to use the operations.

```
IMPLEMENTATION MODULE ItemQueues;

FROM Items    IMPORT Item;
FROM Storage IMPORT ALLOCATE, DEALLOCATE;
   (* ALLOCATE, AND DEALLOCATE are built-in functions to
      manage dynamic variables. *)
TYPE ItemQueue = POINTER to QueueNode;
     QueueNode  = RECORD;
        Element : Item;
        Next    : ItemQueue
     END QueueNode;
(* Procedure implementations will follow here. *)

BEGIN
    Status := 0;

END ItemQueues;
```

Notice here that the implemented (in contrast to the abstract) data type of ItemQueue is unknown to the user, who only sees the definition part. Also notice the initialization of Status to 0. Status will be global to all procedures within the ItemQueues module and will change if an error occurs. This initialization is also invisible to the user.

Ada

Ada builds on both Pascal and Modula in defining its modules, called packages. It also has facilities for defining types while hiding their implementation and even the operations associated with them. As one wag commented, "It's a great language for a police state." We will defer a discussion of packages *per se* until later, and restrict ourselves here to Ada's facilities for defining and implementing abstract data types.

Ada offers degrees of information hiding, whereas in Modula, the strictest rules apply to all operations. Let's look at an Ada package definition for Item-Queues.

```
package ItemQueues is                                          (1.11)

    with Items; --the type Item is defined in a separate
                --package
    Use Items;  --the type Item is available for use

    type ItemQueue is private; --type definition is hidden
    type StatusValues is limited private;
      --even comparisons for "=" are unavailable
      --outside the package

    function "=" (S1, S2: in StatusValues) return boolean;
      --the body of "=" must be given in the package body
      --equality may be used outside the package, but only
      --as defined in the hidden function definition.
    function NewQueue returns ItemQueue; --defined in package
                                          --body
    procedure Destroy(Q: in out ItemQueue);
    procedure Add(Q: in ItemQueue; I: in Item);
    function Front(Q: in ItemQueue) returns Item;
    procedure Remove(Q: in out ItemQueue);
    function Isempty(Q: in ItemQueue) returns boolean;

end ItemQueues;

package body ItemQueues is                                     (1.12)
    ...
end ItemQueues;
```

We will not complete the body of `ItemQueues` here. We do have, however, different levels of information hiding. Since type `ItemQueue` is private, but not limited private, we can compare two `ItemQueues`, Q1 and Q2, for equality and can assign Q1 to Q2. However, we are completely unaware of the implementation of an `ItemQueue` unless we have access to the package body itself.

Generics   One of the shortcomings of a language like Pascal is the necessity of writing new procedures and functions for every data type. We got a start on making an ItemQueue general to whatever type Item was wanted above. Suppose we change the definition of ItemQueues in listing (1.11) to:

```
generic                                                        (1.13)
    type Item is private;
package ItemQueues is
    type ItemQueue is private; --type definition is hidden
    ...
end ItemQueues;
```

All we have done is move the definition of Item outside the package definition and labeled it **generic**. We can now create and use an ItemQueue containing **real** items by:

```
declare                                                    (1.14)
    package Real_Queue is new ItemQueues(real);
    use Real_Queue;
    Q: ItemQueue;
begin
    NewQueue := Q;
    ...
end;
```

We could also declare other queues:

```
declare                                                    (1.15)
    package Char_Queue is new ItemQueues(char);
    use Char_Queue;
    Q: ItemQueue;
begin
    NewQueue := Q;
    ...
end;
```

```
declare                                                    (1.16)
    package Real_Queue2 is new ItemQueues(real);
    use Real_Queue2;
    Q: ItemQueue;
begin
    Real_Queue2.NewQueue := Q;
    ...
end;
```

The **new** instances above are generic packages. The generic facility need not be tied to packages, but it is also useful for declaring **new** instances of individual functions or procedures. With a generic package, we of course get versions of each procedure and function specialized to the particular data type(s) we want to use. Think how nice it would be to program a Swap procedure just once, and then declare new instances of it for pairs of values we wanted swapped!

LAB I: Abstract Data Types in Ada/Pascal

OBJECTIVES

1. To construct and use an abstract data type in a language with facilities for constructing modules

2. To compile the package or module separately, if possible, and incorporate it in another program

3. To investigate the security provisions in the language you are using by trying illegal operations on such things as private types ∎

Data abstraction in Smalltalk

In Smalltalk, abstract data types are called objects, and messages are passed between them. Objects are organized into classes, superclasses and subclasses, and objects of one class may respond differently to the same message. For example, suppose Tom, Dick, and Harry are three objects, and the message passed to them is, "Go home." Furthermore, suppose Tom is an object of the Smith class, Dick a Jones, and Harry a Black. Even though Smith, Jones, and Black may be subclasses of the same superclass, Person, Tom, Dick, and Harry may each respond to the message differently and go home using a different *method*. Tom will use the Smiths', Dick the Jones's, and Harry the Blacks' method.

The class **Object** of Figure 1.1 is a superclass of every other class. Figure 1.2 represents the predefined class structure of **Magnitude**.

Messages in Smalltalk correspond to the operations associated with an abstract data type. A message has three parts, a *receiver*, a message *selector*, and one or more *arguments*. The message 5 == 4 means, "send the argument 4 to the receiver 5, selecting method ==." Since 5 and 4 are **Integer** objects, == selects integer equality.

Objects are elements of classes and have associated with them a list of operation names and *methods* of responding to these operations. This list is called a *protocol* for *objects* of the *class*. == is an element of the protocol for the class **Integer**.

So far, there is not much difference from the abstract data types we have discussed: a collection of types, with associated operations—all or some of which may be hidden from the user. However, we did not encounter any class hierarchy among data types in languages such as Modula-2 or Ada. Objects can *inherit* methods from their superclasses.

An example may help here. Suppose the message 4 **abs** is sent. 4 is an object of class **Integer**. Thus the message will be received in the context of the **Integer** protocol. However, **abs** is not listed in this protocol, but is on the protocol of the superclass **Number**. The object will inherit the method **abs** and return the integer 4. Now suppose the message 4 / 2 is sent. **Number** contains a method for / for mixed-mode division, which is redefined in class Integer. The **Integer** method for / will be used, since both the receiver 4 and the argument

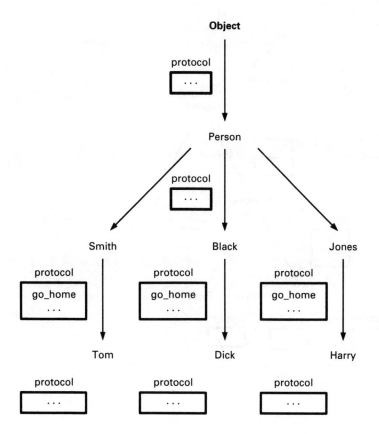

Figure 1.1

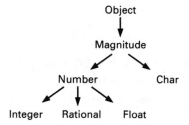

Figure 1.2

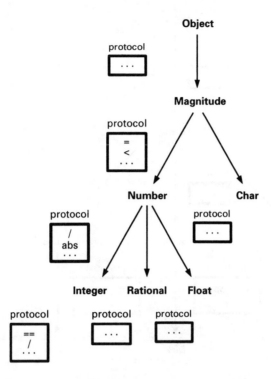

Figure 1.3

2 are integers. However, if the message 4.0 / 2 is sent, 4.0 and 2 both belong to the class **Number**, but not both to any subclass. Thus Number's method for / will be used, returning 2.0.[10]

EXERCISES

1. Check that the description of the abstract data type for queue of listing (1.10) satisfies the algebraic specification of listing (1.9).

2. a. Why are there two pointers, ^Queue_rep and ^Queue_Node, into our Pascal data type Queue?

   b. Why couldn't q_New have been implemented:

   ```
   function q_New : Queue;
     begin  q_New := nil; end;  ?
   ```

10 Digitalk's Smalltalk V [Digitalk, 1986] defines mixed-mode arithmetic in the class Number. In the Little Smalltalk System [Budd, 1987], mixed-mode division is implemented differently. When Number receives the message 4.0 / 2, it sends the message "4.0 / **coerce** 2" to the Float class, which uses the Float method /, returning 2.0.

3. Implement the other four operations on type Queue in Pascal.

4. Why did we have to discriminate the function NewQueue in the declaration of listing (1.16) and not that in listing (1.15)?

5. From the examples you saw in listings (1.11) and (1.12), explain how Modula's use of **VAR** parameters in procedures allows functions to have values with structured data types, while Pascal's functions are limited to values with simple or pointer types.

6. Write a generic Swap procedure in Ada and declare new versions of it for reals, integers, and characters.

7. Consider the Smalltalk message, 2 + 4.0.

   a. What would be the result if **Integer** were a subclass of **Float**, with the method for + in the object **Float**?

   b. What if **Float** were a subclass of **Integer**?

   c. What are the possible responses if **Integer** and **Float** are organized in Smalltalk as in Figure 1.2?

8. The Smalltalk object, **Magnitude**, is intended to capture linearly ordered subclasses. Thus it provides methods for =, <, <=, >, >=. What other subclasses might fit here in addition to those of Figure 1.2?

9. Smalltalk allows no variables of type **Magnitude**. How should this affect the message $A = 65? (Character variables in Smalltalk are preceded by "$", and 65 is the ASCII code for A.) ∎

1.2 CONTROL ABSTRACTION

Most programs are constructed to transform or respond to data. We have looked briefly at data abstractions above and will now consider mechanisms that allow us to move through a data structure, changing or maintaining values as we wish.

Branching

Ordinarily a program executes sequentially, beginning at the first statement and terminating at the last. Branching involves relocating program execution to a portion of our source code possibly different from the succeeding statement. Those who are familiar with an assembly language will recognize that branching can be implemented using (conditional) branch statements or a jump statement. On most machines, a relocation from a branch statement is restricted to a small range of addresses and/or labels, while a jump permits relocation to any word.

Jumps are necessary to implement procedures, but have also been implemented directly through the GOTO statement. Controversy still rages over the advisability of permitting GOTOs, beginning with Dijkstra's famous article, "Go To Statement Considered Harmful" [Dijkstra, 1968b].

It may be helpful to remember that the first high-level programming languages were written for particular machines and started with an assembly language that was then rewritten into something more like a conventional scientific language. Thus assembly constructs were improved to look like English. Such stylistic niceties are often called "syntactic sugar," since they may not be necessary, but make the language more appealing to a programmer. Modern language designers often start with the (scientific) language and worry about compilers and assemblers later.

The most common high-level branch statements are the *if...then...[else]* and *case* statements. The first provides a two-way and the second a multiway branch.

Consider the following fragment of C code.

```
y=1;                                            (1.17)
if (y==0) x=3;
else x=1;
PRINT1(d,x);    /* 1 will be printed */
    /* the "d" specifies decimal format */
if (z=y<0) if (y>0) x=3;
else x=5;
PRINT1(d,z,x);   /* 0,1 will be printed */
```

To see why the value of x remains 1 after the second **if** is executed, we should be aware that C's rule is that an **else** belongs with the nearest **if** that can accept it. Rewriting the statement as

```
if (z=y<0) {if (y>0) x=3; else x=5;},
```

illustrates its evaluation in C. z is assigned the Boolean value, false (0 in C), since the expression (y<0) is false. So the statement is **if** false {...}. The problem of more ifs than elses is called the "dangling-else" problem.

To avoid confusion, Ada has two if statements, one with and one without an else. In either case, the **if** is paired with an **end if**. The C statement above would be written in Ada:

```
if y > 0 then                                   (1.18)
   if y < 0 then x := 3;
            else x := 5;
   end if;
end if;
```

Notice in the Ada fragment, we have not used the expression, $(z = y > 0)$, as in the corresponding C statement. Languages where assignments can be made in the context of an expression are called *expression languages*. ALGOL and C are examples.

The case statement depends on a *discriminant*, to select the appropriate case. An example in Ada with discriminant TODAY is:

```
case TODAY is                                    (1.19)
   when MON..THU => WORK;
   when FRI      => WORK;
                    PARTY;
   when others   => null;
end case;
```

LISP uses the **cond** (for conditional) for both case and if statements. A **cond** function may have any number of arguments, each of which is a pair (condition, result). Evaluation of the **cond** proceeds through the pairs until it finds a true condition, whence the corresponding result is returned.

```
(define sales-tax                               (1.20)
   (lambda (state, cost)
     (cond
       [(= state 'AZ)(* .05 cost)]
       [(= state 'CA)(* .06 cost)]
       [(= state 'CT)(* .075 cost)]
       [(= state 'NJ)(* .06 cost)]
       [else  0]
)))
```

Then (sales-tax 'CT 100) => 7.5, (sales-tax 'AZ 100) => 6.0, and (sales-tax 'VT 100) => 0. In some LISP dialects, the last **cond** pair would be [**true** 0] or (**true** 0). The final statement will be executed if all the preceding **cond** expressions are false. SCHEME has substituted **else** as being more commonly understood. [11]

Iteration

By iteration, we mean moving through all the elements of an aggregate in an orderly fashion, visiting each just once. For example, if SilverWare is a set of flatware, we might like to go through it all, counting the number of forks, knives, spoons, etc. We may not care just how this is accomplished, just what result is achieved.

The simplest iterator is a *for* statement.

```
for i := 1 to 20 do Sum := Sum + i;            (1.21)
```

iterates over the integers between 1 and 20, computing their sum as we go. (We assume here that Sum was initialized to 0 elsewhere.) This can also be accomplished by a statement that repeats until some terminating condition is encountered.

---

11 SCHEME also includes an **if** statement for use with only two alternatives, and a **case** statement for use with a discriminant. The **cond** would be replaced by **case** (state), and an expression like (= state 'AZ) by 'AZ.

```
Sum := 0; i := 1; delta := 1; max := 20;                    (1.22)
repeat Sum := Sum + i;  i := i + delta; until i > max;
```

or through a statement that tests at the top of the loop rather than the bottom:

```
Sum := 0; i := 0; delta := 1; max := 20;                    (1.23)
while i < max do
begin i := i + delta; Sum := Sum + i; end;
```

Such systematic processing works well for data that is in some sort of linear order. But what about data collections with no order?

CLU provides iterators in the form of procedures. An iterator is specified by:

```
IteratorName = iter (...) yields (...) signals (...).
```

As we will investigate in "Brief Theoretical Excursion 2: Modularization," CLU formally abstracts a data type from its representation. When working with a variable of set type, the user may be unaware of its underlying implementation. This could be as an array, linked list, record or other type. An example of a sum operator over a set of integers in CLU is:

```
setsum = proc (s:intset) returns (int) signals (NumOverFlow) (1.24)
   sum: int := 0
   for e: int in intset$elements(s)¹²do
      sum := sum + e
      end
   return (sum)
   end setsum
```

SETL, which was designed with sets as its basic data structure, has set iterators built in. Summing the elements of a set, S, can be accomplished in any of the following three ways:

```
(for x in S) Sum + := x; end for;
(while S /= {}) x from S; Sum + := x; end while;
(until S = {}) do Sum + := x; end;
```

Declarative programming deals with the "what are" of data rather than the "how to." A typical declarative query might be,

```
which(x : x lives-in Michigan).
```

The system would iterate through the database in question and respond with all individuals living in Michigan. How this iteration is accomplished will be explored in Part IV.

---

12 In CLU, functions operate on objects. As we will see later, object-oriented programming includes polymorphic procedures and functions. Thus, the procedure named "elements" may work differently on objects of different types. The CLU syntax for this is <T>$<procedure name>, where T is a data type. A call of intset$elements(s) transfers control to the "elements" procedure operating on an object, s, of type intset.

Iterative and Recursive Procedures

Iteration may also describe the behavior of a procedure. In an iterative procedure statements are executed sequentially, even though control may be transferred temporarily to another procedure or function. For such procedures, one enters its *environment* at the "top" and exits in exactly one place. An environment is a collection of variable, function, and procedure names and their storage locations. As we have mentioned, the values stored at these locations are part of the *store*.

A recursive procedure differs in that one can create many different environments for the same procedure. For example, consider a recursive LISP function in the SCHEME dialect to sum the elements of a list.

```
(define (SumList s l)                                    (1.25)
  (lambda (s l)
    (cond ((= (length l)  0) s)
          (else (SumList (+ s  (car l)) (cdr l))))))
```

An environment for SumList will include three variable names: SumList, s, and l.

Let's trace the call for `(SumList 0 (1 2 3 4))`. We will not trace the transfer of control to the `length` function, but merely report its result. (Try to figure out as we go what values are returned by the two functions, **(car** l) and **(cdr** l), where l is a list.[13])

```
0) (SumList 0  (1 2 3 4))              => ?                (1.26)
         (= 4  0)  => nil
1)       (SumList (+ 0  1) (2 3 4))    => ?
         (= 3  0)  => nil
2)         (SumList (+ 1  2) (3 4))    => ?
           (= 2  0)   => nil
3)         (SumList (+ 3  3) (4))      => ?
             (= 1  0) => nil
4)            (SumList (+ 6  4) ())    =>  ?
              (= 0  0) => T
            (SumList 10  ())           => 10
3)        (SumList 6  (4))             => 10
2)      (SumList 3  (3 4))             => 10
1)    (SumList 1  (2 3 4))             => 10
0) (SumList 0  (1 2 3 4))              => 10
```

Five environments are in the execution, labeled 0 through 4. Each contains the same three names, SumList, s and l, but their locations are different. For example, in environment 2, s is (+ 1 2) = 3, and l is (3 4). On the first entry, SumList is and remains undefined. When we return to environment 2, s is still 3, l is still (3 4), and SumList becomes 10.

---

13 The functions **car** and **cdr** relate to the organization of the early IBM 704® machines on which LISP was run. **car** stands for "contents of the address register," and **cdr** signifies the "contents of the decrement register." They are pronounced "kar" and "kudder." **nil** represents either the empty list or "false."

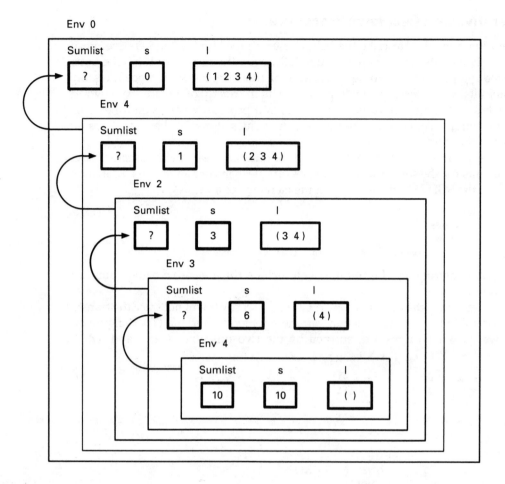

Figure 1.4

Figure 1.4 shows environments and their stores after the fourth recursive call has completed, and before the value of SumList is passed to Environments 3 through 0.

The alert reader may wonder why that value of 10 had to be passed all the way up the recursive stack. The answer of course is that it didn't. The value was known at step 5, so we could have quit there. A function whose value becomes defined at the bottom of the recursive stack is called *tail recursive*. Compilers or interpreters for newer versions of LISP, including SCHEME and Common LISP, have been optimized to terminate tail recursive functions at the bottom rather than the top of the stack. A nontail recursive version of SumList is:

```
(define (SumList2                                                    (1.27)
  (lambda (l)
    (cond ((= l nil) 0)
          (else (+ (SumList2 (cdr l)) (car l)))))))))
```

Exceptions

An *exception* occurs when program execution is interrupted because some unusual event occurs. If a program is running in real time, it is particularly important that such events be handled appropriately. Our astronauts might not be very happy to see "ERROR 12, ARRAY SUBSCRIPT OUT OF RANGE, PROGRAM ABORTING" flash on to their monitor when they were halfway to Mars. Similarly, a banking program might include a special routine if a customer tried to deposit an unusually large amount, outside the declared range of the input variable.

An exception is *raised* when the unusual event occurs, and control is transferred to an *exception handler*. An exception is *propagated* if it is not *handled* in the block in which it was raised, and control is transferred to a surrounding block.

Horowitz [Horowitz, 1984, p. 268] summarizes the design issues involved as:

1. Is there a way to access the interrupt capabilities of the underlying computer?
2. Can the system action be overriden?
3. Are user-defined exceptions possible? How are they raised?
4. What are the scope rules for an enabled exception? Can they be attached to statements, blocks, procedures, and/or expressions?
5. What are the scope and extent rules for an exception handler?
6. Is a resumption or termination model followed?
7. Can multiple exceptions be propagated?
8. Can signaled exceptions have parameters?
9. Is a mechanism provided for automatically catching all unexpectedly raised exceptions?
10. Can exceptions be raised in an exception handler, and what are the consequences?

PL/I pioneered the orderly management of unexpected program interrupts with *ON conditions*. The programmer can override whatever customary action would be taken by an operating system by writing

```
ON <condition> ON-unit
```

For example, `ON ZERODIVIDE X := -999`; this would assign to X the value –999 whenever an attempt was made to divide by 0. One can also raise an exception one's self, e.g.:

```
IF DELTA < 0.001 THEN SIGNAL ZERODIVIDE;
```

Here, the `ZERODIVIDE` routine would be invoked whenever the variable `DELTA` became less than 0.001, and X would be assigned the value, –999.

Just what happens after an exception occurs is treated somewhat inconsistently in PL/I. In particular, just which X becomes –999, after an attempt to divide by zero? Programmers are also able to disable exceptions so that program execution will continue. Depending on the exception, only nonsense might be generated subsequently.

EXERCISES

1. Uninitialized variables are those that have not been assigned any value. Left unrecognized, this can cause hard-to-find program errors. Discuss the merits of the following solutions:

    a. Forcing the programmer to assign initial values when a variable is created (APL)

    b. Initializing variables at compile time if the appropriate statement is encountered (FORTRAN)

    c. Automatically initializing numeric variables to 0 (BASIC)

    d. Initializing variables to some special indicator (SETL)

    e. Making initialization at the time of declaration easy, but not mandatory (Ada)

2. Some authors advocate eliminating statements like the "repeat" in listing (1.22) that iterate at least once, in favor of the "while" that tests before entering the loop. What is your opinion? In particular, what if there is a test condition such as reaching the end of an input file or data elements being in a certain range?

3. Trace the function (ListSum2 (1,2,3,4)) in listing (1.27), and discuss the difference between its execution and that of ListSum, in listing (1.25). ∎

1.3 MODULAR ABSTRACTION

Abstract data types can be considered as modules, in that they contain both a data structure and its associated operations. Here we will consider modules somewhat differently. In Parnas's terms [Parnas, 1972], a module is a "responsibility assignment." A program will have at least the following sections:

1. Input data
2. Process data
3. Output results

The program could be decomposed into three modules, one responsible for each of the three activities. We do not care how each part gets done, just how they interface with each other. These three parts could be procedures, but they could also be more. A module could include abstract data types as well as other functions and procedures. We can think of a module as a "black-box" function. Known inputs enter the box, and verifiable results come out. The details of what goes on in the box, however, are hidden.

We will consider modular abstraction by looking at collections of procedures and data types first. This will be followed by a discussion of procedures themselves.

BRIEF THEORETICAL EXCURSION 2: Modularization

Parnas states the benefits of modular programming as

1. Managerial—Development time should be shortened because separate groups would work on each module with little need for communication.
2. Product flexibility—It should be possible to make drastic changes to one module without a need to change others.
3. Comprehensibility—It should be possible to study the system one module at a time. The whole system can therefore be better designed because it is better understood.

A modular abstraction simplifying a program is achieved by specifying a function. For example, a publisher may use a large program to transform text supplied by an author into a book. One module might receive text at a certain stage in the process and produce an index. Here the function could be IndexModule(TextFiles) => Index. We must, of course, carefully specify requirements on the TextFiles, and also describe what the output will be. Although users need not be concerned with what happens inside IndexModule, the form of TextFiles must be specified completely and well so that a possibly naive user can prepare TextFiles for IndexModule to work properly.

Index may not be the final product. There may be other modules, such as:

```
ModuleAssemble(TextFiles, Index) => Galleys.
```

The TextFiles here might be subject to different requirements than when used as input to the IndexModule. So why not use a different name, such as IndexedTextFiles, to make the distinction clear? This might be a good idea, but certainly isn't necessary. The key point is that the description of TextFiles is in the *interface* between whichever modules it is coming from and going into. In a different interface, the description may be entirely different. We are quite comfortable with this notion when considering procedures. Find-ThirdLetter(x) certainly expects a different input x than would SquareRoot(x).

If we modify the TextFiles while constructing the index, our function Index-Module will produce a pair, rather than a single output, i.e.,

```
IndexModule2(TextFiles) => (NewTextFiles,Index).
```

In an ideal system, modularization would be completely orthogonal, with no restrictions on either input or output.

Definitions abound for the term module. Watson [Watson, 1987] lists some of these as:

1. A contiguous set of instructions that may be addressed by name
2. Ada packages, subprograms, and tasks
3. A single subroutine that is part of an activity
4. A contiguous sequence of program statements, bounded by boundary elements, having an aggregate identifier
5. A set of executable program statements that meets three criteria:
   a. It is a closed subroutine.
   b. It has the potential of being called from any other module in the program.
   c. It has the potential of being separately compiled.

Watson considers definition 4 above to be the most widely accepted, but suggests adding, "and being capable of being explicitly invoked from other parts of the program to which it is visible." The "aggregate identifier" refers to the notion that if a module is an aggregate of various program elements, such as declarations, procedures, and statements, the module itself has a name that can be referenced by another program statement. Boundary elements may be as simple as a begin...end sequence or may include declarations as well.

Some authors refer to objects as modules and modules as objects. When we use the term object in describing a module, we will assume it demonstrates persistence and inheritance, i.e., a module in which the state, or values of all its identifiers, is preserved between invocations and in which submodules inherit the attributes of the parent module.

INFORMATION HIDING

One principle of modularization is information hiding. By this we mean making visible only as much information as is needed for one to use a program correctly. Other information is hidden from the user. A module need only be understood through its interfaces to other modules and to the main program. If the interface does not change, a module can be completely implemented again without changing any program parts using it. Consider IndexModule, which receives text in the form of files, each containing chapters, paragraphs, sentences, etc., and produces an alphabetized index as a file. An author-user may be given some formal specifications pertaining to the text, but need know nothing of the internal workings of the indexing module. If the indexing can later be speeded up through separate submodules running in parallel, clients need not change their mode of operation. All they know is that they now get their indexes back in two days, rather than two months.

SEPARATE COMPILATION

One advantage of modularization is that self-contained program parts can be tested independently. Separate programming teams can write modules, and compile and debug them without communicating with the rest of the project team. This, of course, requires very specific design criteria so that everything will fit together when the time comes for assembling the entire program.

Languages supporting modularization provide for two sorts of modules, definition modules that formally describe the interfaces to the module, and implementation modules, which can be hidden from the user, and which implement the definition faithfully. We saw an example of both in Language Examples above and will discuss objects in detail in Chapter 3.

CONCURRENT EXECUTION

If modules are independent of each other, they can run concurrently, provided that multiple processors are available. Concurrency demands time synchronization as well as the specification of a data interface. One module may have to wait for another to complete before proceeding further.

A further complication arises when modules are not completely independent, but share data. If you work on a network, you may have experienced delays when using the same software as other users. Networks can provide for copying a particular compiler or editor into a user's individual workspace, in which case no sharing occurs. Other systems maintain only one copy of such software on the file server and users access it by some sort of time-sharing method. Here, the user, rather than changing the shared data (which may be a compiler, editor, or other utility) is only using it, so many synchronization problems do not apply. We will discuss concurrent execution in Chapter 4.

MODULE VARIETIES

The term, modularization, is used to describe several different notions. As we noted above, a module can be thought of as a "responsibility assignment" that performs a particular function. Another notion is that of independent program sections, each module being independent of all others. Such independence aids in proving programs to be correct. If each module does what it is supposed to do, and the module interfaces are correct, a program should produce the desired result, given appropriate input. As programs and systems have become more complex, modularization has become a necessity for understanding a system design, getting a large program completed in a reasonable amount of time, and demonstrating that it works properly.

Another important modular notion is the extent of information hiding realized. Just which variables, constants, types, procedures, and functions are accessible inside and outside a particular module? Those that are listed to be visible outside the module in which they are defined are said to be *exported* from a module, and those to be used, but defined and implemented in other modules, are *imported* into a module.

Different languages have given different names to their modules, and the notion of a module differs among them.

Modules in Modula-2

A Modula-2 module was exemplified above in our discussion of abstract data types. In both Modula and its successor Modula-2, a module is a collection of type declarations, constants, variables, and procedures. These module elements are hidden (inaccessible) from the rest of the program unless expressly listed in the **EXPORT** list. Similarly, external elements are inaccessible within a module unless expressly listed in an **IMPORT** list. The schema for a Modula module is:

```
module <module name>;                              (1.28)
IMPORT m₀, m₁, ...
EXPORT e₀, e₁, ...
const c₀ = expression₀, ...
type t₀ = type₀, ...
var v₀, v₁, ...
procedure p₀(...) ...end p₀;
procedure p₁(...) ...end p₁;
procedure p₂(...) ...end p₂;
. . .
begin
   <statements>
end <name>;
```

Here **IMPORT** precedes the list of module names, $m_0, m_1, ...$, from which procedures, variables, and constants are to be imported. Identifiers for these elements must be specifically listed on the export list of one of the m_i. **EXPORT** precedes the list of objects available for export from the module being defined, and possibly imported to other modules.[14] Adherence to these stated visibilities is checked at compile time, so no run-time checking is needed. The statements initialize module variables. Module A cannot use visible elements of module B without first declaring these elements for import in its (A's) IMPORT list. In this case these same elements must be listed on B's EXPORT list, or an error will occur.

---

14 Modula has alternate forms of **IMPORT** and **EXPORT** statements, e.g., **IMPORT from** <module name> $e_0, e_1, ...$, where the e_i are identifiers of objects such as procedures to be imported. In this case the objects may be used in the importing module without qualification. If the **from** form is not used, the e_i must be qualified with the exporting module's name in the importing module, e.g., A.proc(x, y, z).

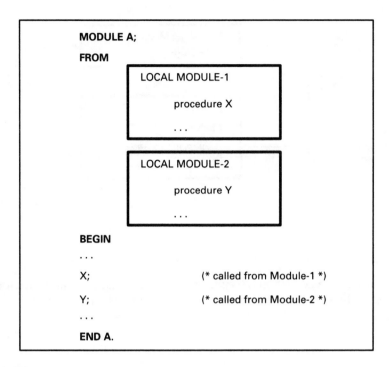

MODULE A;

FROM

LOCAL MODULE-1

    procedure X

    . . .

LOCAL MODULE-2

    procedure Y

    . . .

BEGIN

. . .

X;   (* called from Module-1 *)

Y;   (* called from Module-2 *)

. . .

END A.

Figure 1.5

Variables declared within a Modula-2 module are static. By this we mean that they retain their values from invocation to invocation, in contrast to a procedure where local variables cease to exist when the procedure terminates. Such variables that come and go as procedures are entered and exited are called *dynamic*. Static variables are sometimes called *own* variables (ALGOL's term), since the module owns these variables. When it is reentered, all its *own* variables still contain the last values assigned.

If a module is nested in another module, A, as in Figure 1.5, the elements need not be listed on its **IMPORT** list or A's **EXPORT** list. A module nested in module A, is local to A. Modula's local modules own variables only within the context of the surrounding module.

At first glance, it might seem that a local module adds nothing that procedures don't already provide. However, they differ in two ways [Cooling, 1988, p. 127]: first, variables can be brought into a local module only through the IMPORT process, avoiding the necessity of variables global to a group of procedures; and second, variables local to a module can be made visible outside through the EXPORT/IMPORT mechanism. Thus local modules provide more refined visibility control than do procedures.

Modula-2's modules offer options for separate compilation. A DEFINITION module must be compiled first, but an IMPLEMENTATION module, or any client (importing) modules can be compiled in any order.

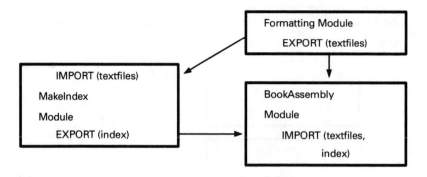

Figure 1.6

Clusters in CLU

A CLU program consists of a collection of separate modules. A module can be a procedure, an iterator or a CLUster. Modules cannot be nested in CLU, and communication between them occurs through explicitly passed arguments and results. Modules consist of a specification part, or header, and an implementation part. Only the header need be visible to a user. A cluster, which implements an abstract data type, also has a representation, or **rep**, part that describes the particular representation of the data object. The example below defines an abstract set of integers and is taken from [Liskov, 1986].

```
intset = cluster is create, insert, delete, member, size,          (1.29)
             choose
    rep = array[int]
          create = proc() returns (cvt)
                     return (rep$new())
                     end create

          %definition of delete comes here

          member = proc (s : cvt, x : int)
                     return (getind(s,x) <= rep$high(s))
                     end member

          %definitions of size & choose are here

          getind = proc (s : rep, x : int) returns (int)

          %definition follows here.
          %The index of the first occurrence
          %of x is returned or an integer greater than the
          %highest index of the representing array if
          %x is not found.

    end intset
```

The function, `getind`, is not listed in the header of `intset`, and thus may not be called by the user, although functions within the cluster, such as `member`, can access it. Only the header, intset = **cluster is** ..., needs to be visible to a user.

There are two CLU functions, **up** and **down**, which switch back and forth between an abstract intset and its **rep** as an array. The built-in keyword, **cvt** (convert) also ups a **rep** to an abstract object or `downs` an abstract object to a **rep** automatically. In the cluster of listing (1.29), the procedure `create` returns to its caller, an abstract intset, i.e., a data item accessible only through its listed operators. The actual procedure creates a **rep** for intset (in this case an array), which is automatically **upped** to an intset as part of the return. The function could have been written:

```
create = proc() returns (intset)
        return (up(rep$new()))
        end create
```

Cvt is just used for convenience. In the function, member, **cvt** is used to **down** the actual intset parameter for s to its array representation so that the function can do its work of checking for membership of x in s. The user deals only with abstract intsets, whereas the implemented functions and procedures operate on their representations.

CLU's procedures and iterators also have visible headers and hidden implementations. We shall not discuss these here, but direct the interested reader to [Liskov, 1986].

Packages and Tasks in Ada

One of the design specifications for the Ada language was that information hiding be supported. Packages were devised for this purpose as well as for encapsulating data types, grouping a collection of related subprograms, and naming a collection of declarations. "The package is probably the language's principal contribution to the programming art" [Brender, 1981].

As in Modula-2's module, a package has a specification part and an implementation part. Each can reside in a separate file and be compiled separately. The format for a package is:

```
(File A)                                                    (1.30)
package MY_PACKAGE is     --specification part
   . . .                  --public part
   private
   . . .                  --private part
end MY_PACKAGE;

(file B)
package body MY_PACKAGE is --implementation part
   . . .
end MY_PACKAGE;
```

Brender provides the following example of a specification part, which is all the user will ordinarily see:

```
package TEXT is                                                    (1.31)
   type FILE is private;
   NO_FILE : constant FILE;
   type MODE is (Read WRITE);
   IO_ERROR : exception;
   procedure OPEN(F: out FILE; M: in MODE; NAME: in STRING);
   procedure GET(F: in FILE; S: out STRING);
   procedure CLOSE(F: in FILE);
private
   type FILE is new INTEGER;
   NO_FILE : constant FILE := 0;
end TEXT;
```

The specification of the package, TEXT, may be compiled and incorporated in other packages or a main program without the package body. Thus this specification forms the interface to other program units. It has a logical part, the visible portion, and a physical part, the private section. This private part is visible to the user, in the sense that it can be read, and contains information needed by the particular compiler being used. The designation, **private**, for FILE and NO_FILE confine the user to accessing either using only the procedures, OPEN, GET, PUT and CLOSE. Thus FILE is an abstract data type.

If no changes are made to the specification, changes to the package body are guaranteed not to require changes to source programs referencing the package. Changes to the private part may require recompilation of source code, but will not require any changes to the source code itself. However, changes to the visible part may require source code changes, as well as recompilation. For example, if the procedure OPEN were changed to OPEN(F: out FILE; NAME: in STRING), all references to the procedure, with the former three parameters, would have to be rewritten.

Shumate and Nielsen [Shumate, 1988] classify Ada packages by intended use into the structure shown in Figure 1.7. An application package contains subprograms that accomplish the tasks set out by a software requirements statement. Communications packages provide data transfers between applications packages, and helper packages provide services to help an applications package do its job. Previously developed and library packages are often found in the helper category.

Brender does not consider the Ada package to be a module, since it cannot be invoked by name anyplace in a program. To make a package exist, one must introduce it with a "with" statement, e.g., **with** TEXT. This statement can only occur at the beginning of a unit to be compiled, and causes the package to be "elaborated." That is, space is laid out for its variables along with that for the including unit. Ada does have, however, Tasks that can be called anywhere.

Like a package, a Task is divided into a specification and a body. A task is a separate program thread and can run in parallel with other tasks. Tasks can be synchronized, with one waiting until another provides needed information. Such communication between tasks is called a *rendezvous*. Procedures in a task specification may be declared as entries to programs. A program accepts an *entry*. A certain amount of randomness is

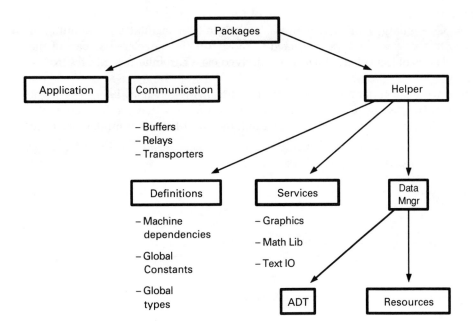

Figure 1.7

built into accept statements, or a program can **accept** different procedures at an entry point, depending on some condition or other. We will delay further discussion of tasks until Chapter 4, when we consider distributed programming.

Objects in C++

Object-oriented languages have been defined as those that support abstraction, encapsulation, inheritance and polymorphism. Data *encapsulation* by an object includes data private to an object, data shared with other objects, global data shared by all objects, and a set of messages, or protocol, to which an object responds. *Polymorphism*, meaning "many forms," refers to the ability of different objects to respond to the same message differently, e.g., Successor('A') and Successor(3)   will elicit different responses. (The "message" is "Successor", and the objects are 'A' and 3.) Neither Modula-2's modules, CLU's clusters, nor Ada's packages support inheritance, so these languages can be considered object based, but not object oriented. *Inheritance* implies subobjects that inherit the attributes of a parent object.

We saw a bit of the object-oriented language Smalltalk when we discussed abstract data types. Here we will look at the classes of C++, as another example of object-oriented modularization. C++ is an extension of the C language. "++" is the increment operator,[15] so C++ enlarges, or increments C. A class in C++ facilitates the defining of new types, with access to the type restricted to those functions declared as part of the class. A C++ class is object oriented because a derived class can inherit attributes from a base class.

Suppose we want to simulate the activities of trains [Goldstein, 1989]. We might first define an abstract class, Container, which captures objects that can hold contents. The class, Vehicle, can then be derived from Container, and finally, Train derived from Vehicle.

```
/* Represent the abstract world of all Containers */          (1.32)

class Container
{       int capacity;
        void *contents[MAX];

/* Here, void represents the unknown base type of contents.
   *contents returns the object pointed to by contents. */

public:
/* add or remove an object, checking to make sure there is
   room */

        addObject(void *anObject);
        removeObject(void *anObject);
};      /* end of Container interface */

/* Represent abstract notion of Vehicles */
        class Vehicle : public Container
{       protected : int position, velocity;
}   /* end of Vehicle interface */

class Train : Public Vehicle
{       train();  /* constructor for object of type Train */
        private :
                int maxObtainableSpeed;
                int maxNumberOfPassengers;
        public :
                /* set train's speed */
                setSpeed(int speed);
                addPassenger(void *passenger);

}
```

In an actual simulation, we can declare an object, WabashCannonBall, to be of type Train by the declaration: `Train WabashCannonBall;`

The member variables, MaxObtainableSpeed and MaxNumberOfPassengers, are private, so user attempts to access these variable will cause an error. These Maxes are set

---

15 In C (and in C++), ++x means x = x + 1, that is, x is increased by 1. x++ is the old value of x before it was incremented. If x has the value 3, then; y = x++; z = ++x; will result in values for x, y, and z, of 5, 3, 5, respectively.

in C++ hidden implementation code. The **protected** designation for position and velocity prevent a user from creating instances of them directly, although these identifiers can be inherited in subclasses such as Train.

C++ supports the notions of derivation, as above, and of composition. Derivation describes the *is-a* relation, such as, "a train is-a vehicle," while composition describes *has-a*. "A train has-a maximum obtainable speed." The Container and Vehicle classes are abstract, and are never implemented as such, but they do guarantee that any class derived from Vehicle will have addObject and removeObject operators, as well as position and velocity. C++ also allows the building of abstract superclasses from classes with operators in common.

EXERCISES

1. A Modula-2 module may not be imported into another module, but procedures, types, variables and constants may. How might the importing of entire modules violate visibility rules?

2. Rewrite the CLU function, member, using **up** and/or **down** in place of **cvt**.

3. Discuss the purposes of keeping a CLU cluster's **rep**resentation and function implementations hidden.

4. Suppose that in the package specification of listing (1.31), the private part is changed to read, **type** FILE **is new** FLOAT;

   a. Why will a source file using TEXT need no rewriting?

   b. Why might it need recompilation?

5. Suppose we declared a C++ class of Vehicles (see listing (1.32)) called Bicycle. How might we define position and velocity for Bicycle differently from Train?

Procedural Abstraction

Although we considered modules above as aggregates or collections of declarations and/or procedures and functions, a single procedure can be thought of as a program module itself. Certainly Parnas's definition of a module as a responsibility assignment will include procedures. Watson's definition, "a contiguous sequence of program statements, bounded by boundary elements, having an aggregate identifier, and being capable of being explicitly invoked from other parts of the program to which it is visible," will also include single procedures if we allow aggregates of one. Thus we include procedural abstraction here as the simplest module.

Abelson and the Sussmans [Abelson, 1985, p. 29] define a procedure as "a pattern for the local evolution of a computational process." By local, they mean that a procedure carries out its responsibility assignment in an environment separate from the rest of the program. That a procedure is a pattern allows its work to be performed on various actual objects in similar ways, depending on the objects present.

A procedure is an abstraction in two senses. First, by parameterization, where we abstract from the identity of various data instances. Here actual data values are unimportant; our concern is with the number and types of the data items. The second sense is abstraction by specification. We specify the behavior of a procedure only by what results the user can expect. Just how these are accomplished is irrelevant. This is sometimes thought of as a black-box, where the "how" details are hidden from the user. These two abstractions working together allow procedures to be separated from the rest of a program (enhancing understandability and correctness), and modified individually, without changing parts of a system that call them.

Functions are procedures of a special type that return a single value. We could avoid functions altogether by using procedures that modify only one value, as in Modula-2. This, however, makes the usual mathematical notion of function composition hard to express. Functional languages, such as pure LISP, avoid procedures entirely, working only with functions. For our purposes, we will use the word *procedure* to include both procedures and functions.

Parameterization

Parameters are associated with procedures, specifying the form or pattern of data objects with which they will work. `SquareRoot(X : `**`in`**` real; Y: `**`out`**` real)`,[16] has two real-numbered formal parameters, X and Y. When the calling module calls `SquareRoot(2, Result)`, 2 and Result will take the place of X and Y and are called *actual* parameters. The procedure, SquareRoot, actually works with 2 and places its result in the data container named Result.

By an environment, we mean the assignment or binding of names to storage locations. These may name subprocedures, variables, etc. When a procedure is called, control is transferred to the environment of the procedure, which may or may not have portions in common with the calling environment. If communication is desired between the caller and the callee, arrangements must be made for passing values back and forth through the procedure's parameters.

Reference Parameters   A reference parameter behaves somewhat like a global variable, in that any changes to a formal parameter result in changes to the corresponding actual parameter as well. This is accomplished by passing to the procedure the address of the actual parameter, rather than its value. Such an address is called a reference to a variable, hence the term, reference parameter.

---

16 The modifiers **in** and **out** are Ada syntax. An **in** parameter must be supplied a value at the time of a procedure call, whereas the procedure itself will provide a value for an **out** parameter.

In ALGOL-like languages the programmer has no direct access to the reference. In C, however, arithmetic on pointers is not only permitted but encouraged as a programming technique. For example, a string in C may be declared:
```
char *s
```
The "*" indicates that s is a pointer, and that it points to a location holding a character. s can be incremented, using ordinary integer arithmetic. Thus the statement,

```
for  (i = 0; i < 100; s++) *s = "a";
```

will produce a string consisting of 100 "a's." Such access to addresses also makes variable length arrays simple to implement.

Value Parameters A value parameter is one into which the value of the actual parameter is copied into the location identified with the name of the corresponding formal parameter. Value parameters are associated closely with functions, in which only one value is to be computed and returned by a procedure, all other parameters remaining unchanged in the calling environment. Value parameters are sometimes called IN parameters, since they come in to a procedure, but provide no new outgoing information.

In the 1950s, FORTRAN was the only high-level language that was widely available. Its only parameter-passing mode was by reference. Thus any parameter could be IN, OUT or IN OUT. A procedure, ADDONETO (X) could result in the value of X being increased by one. Contrary to most programmers' intentions, however, ADDONETO (2) might result in the constant 2 being increased to 3. A reference to the location of a constant need be no different than a reference to the location assigned to a variable. This could not happen if the 2 were passed by value, since 2 would be copied into ADDONETO's formal parameter.

Result Parameters A result parameter is one that has no value on entry to its procedure and is assigned a value during the procedure's execution, which is subsequently available to the calling module. In Ada these are called OUT parameters.

Value-Result Parameters A value-result parameter behaves like a value parameter, up until control returns to the calling environment. As part of this transfer of control, the new value, or result, computed for that parameter in the environment of the procedure, is copied back into the actual parameter.

If no exception occurs, so that a procedure is interrupted abnormally, a user would notice no difference in performance between reference and value-result parameters, except possibly excessive memory use. Thus some language designers have left the choice up to the compiler builder.

Name Parameters The designers of ALGOL 60 included reference, value and name parameters. All parameters that were not declared explicitly in the body of a procedure to be passed by value or reference were considered to be passed by name. Passing by name means that the name of an actual parameter is substituted for the formal parameter in the body (between the **begin** and the **end**) of a procedure to which it is passed.

```
real procedure increment(x, d);
value d;
real x, d;
begin
x := x + d;
end;
```

A call of increment(a, .01); would result in:

```
real procedure increment(x, d);
value d;
real x, d;
begin
a := a + .01;
end;
```

Pass by name is powerful, since functions and procedures can be passed as well as simple and structured variables. The usual example demonstrating this power is:

```
real procedure SIGMA(i,l,u,x); value l,u; integer i,l,u; real x;     (1.33)
begin real s; s:= 0;
for i := 1 step 1 until u do s := s + x;
SIGMA := s end;
```

A call to SIGMA(i,1,m,SIGMA(j,1,n,A[i,j]), computes

$$\sum_{i=1}^{m}\sum_{j=1}^{n} A[i,j],$$

a facility afforded by few other languages. You will be asked to explore some of the dangers of pass by name in exercise 7, (d) and (e), below (p. 78).

Binding and scope

A *binding* of a variable occurs when it is declared. The set of expressions for which a binding defines a name is called the *scope* of the binding. In the Pascal procedure below the expressions between the **begin** and **end** are in the scope of L, I and Size. They constitute the entire scope of L, I but not of Size. L and I are bound to the particular values assigned to them in the procedure and are called *bound variables*. Size is free in AddList, i.e., its scope is larger than that of I and L.

```
procedure AddList(L: ArrayType);                              (1.34)
   var I : integer;
begin
   Sum := 0;
   for I := 1 to Size do Sum := Sum + L[I];
   write('The sum is: ',Sum)
end;
```

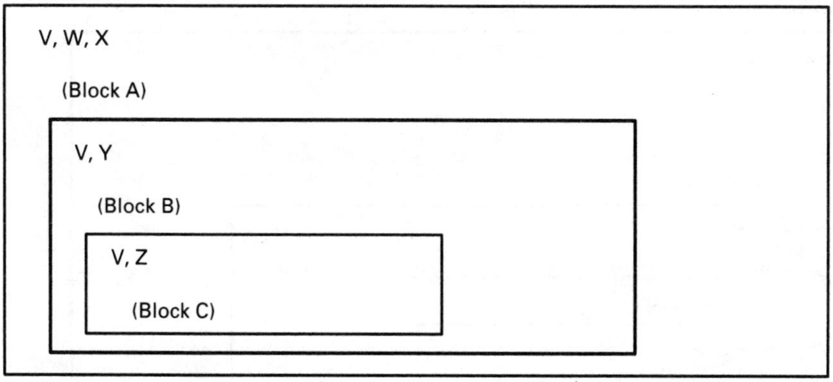

Figure 1.8

Procedures, of course, may have local variables, such as I above, as well as parameters. They may also have subprocedures, which are bound to the parent procedure, with free variables. By a free variable, we mean one that is not bound to the particular procedure in which it is used. The variable, Size, above is free in AddList. In many languages, bound variables include value parameters and variables declared to be local to a procedure. Global variables are free in all but the main procedure. What happens to these free variables depends on the type of binding that occurs.

In Figure 1.8, V is bound to each of Blocks A, B, and C, separately. Thus it names a different variable in each of the three blocks. It is sometimes helpful to think of them as A.V, B.V, and C.V. W is bound in Block A, but is free in both Blocks B and C, and is thus a global variable. Y is bound in Block B, but free in C, while Z is bound only in C.

Static Binding If binding is static, a variable that is free in a procedure gets its value from the environment in which the procedure is defined, rather than from where the procedure is called. This means that the binding of a variable is determined by the structure of a program, not by what happens at run time. In Figure 1.8, if Y occurs in Block C, it would be bound to its value in Block B, since this is the nearest environment in which Y is bound. Since we can determine the binding of a variable by looking at the source code to find the innermost environment or block in which the variable name is bound, static binding is also called lexical scoping.

Dynamic Binding Dynamic binding should not be confused with dynamic variables, which are either reference variables that can be created or destroyed at run time, or variables local to a procedure that are created when the scope of the procedure is entered and cease to exist when it is exited. By

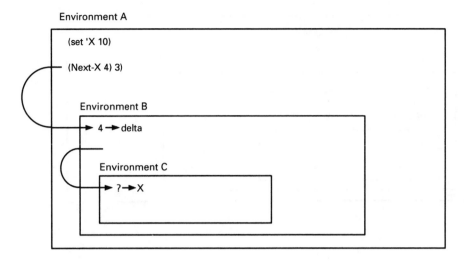

Environment A
(set 'X 10)
(Next-X 4) 3)
Environment B
4 → delta
Environment C
? → X

Figure 1.9

dynamic binding, we mean that a free variable gets its value from the environment from which it is called, rather than from the environment in which it is defined. Consider the following LISP fragment:

```
(define Next-X                                          (1.35)
  (lambda (delta)
    (lambda (X)
      (+ X delta))))
```

The semantics of this code is that a function named NEXT-X is being defined with a single bound variable, *delta*. This definition includes a second, unnamed function with bound variable X. A call of (Next-X 4 (3)) would, in a statically scoped LISP return the value 7. To see what happens in a dynamically scoped LISP, consider Figure 1.9.

X would take its value from environment A, the calling environment, and not from B. If this were 10, as in the figure, the value of Next-X would be 13. Here we say that the X of Next-X was captured by the X of environment A. With such nonintuitive variable bindings, one might ask why any language designer would consider dynamic binding. As a functional language, LISP was designed to treat functions as first-class objects that could be passed between other functions. Abelson [Abelson, 1985, p. 322] provides the following simple example of the sort of mechanisms that were desired:

```
(define sum-powers                                      (1.36)
  (lambda (a b n)
    (sum nth-power a 1+ b)))

(define product-powers
  (lambda (a b n)
    (product nth-power a 1+ b)))
```

```
(define nth-power
  (lambda(x)
    (expt x n)))
```

The first two functions return the sum and product of the powers of integers between a and b, respectively. (sum-powers 1 3 2) would yield $1^2 + 2^2 + 3^2$ = 14, and (product-powers 1 3 2) yields $1^2 * 2^2 * 3^2$ = 36. nth-power is shared by both functions, and has a single free variable, n. In a statically scoped LISP, nth-power would have to be defined in the environment of n, i.e., in each of sum-powers and product-powers.

```
(define sum-powers            (define product-powers
  (lambda (a b n)               (lambda (a b n)
    (define nth-power             (define nth-power
      (lambda (x)                  (lambda (x)
        (expt x n)))                 (expt x n)))
    (sum nth-power a 1+ b)))      (product nth-power a 1+ b))).
```

John McCarthy [McCarthy, 1960 and 1965] designed LISP as a dynamically scoped language in order to make possible sharing of code with free variables, such as that in listing (1.36). More recent versions, such as SCHEME [Steele, 1978] and Common LISP [Steele, 1984], have used lexical scoping to avoid the capturing of variables.

Coroutines and concurrent processes

The procedures we have been considering above are sequential processes. They execute statements one at a time and deliver the same result each time the process runs. A procedure may be in a *slave* relationship to some other *master* procedure. Sometimes the master is no more than a *driver* for various slaves, i.e., it consists of only declarations and procedure calls.

We might envision our procedures somewhat differently, however. Two or more procedures might fulfill coequal responsibilities, where none are master and none slave, but control is passed from one to the other as their functions dictate. Procedures might also run at the same time. Two procedures are called *concurrent* if execution of one begins before the other has terminated. Concurrent procedures may be coequal or not, but synchronization is vital, if data is passed between them or shared memory locations are accessed.

In addition to communication and synchronization, concurrency involves the notion of managing partial failure. If one process fails, others should be allowed to continue. Programming techniques for managing concurrent processes are called *multiprogramming*, whether or not multiple CPUs are used. Here we will look at two multiprogramming examples, coroutines as implemented in Modula-2 and Ada's tasks. Underlying concepts and other language examples will be considered in Chapter 4.

Coroutines In the usual master-slave procedure call, when the master calls the slave, the current state of the calling program is saved, control branches to the top of the slave, and it executes through to the end. After the slave completes, control returns to the word of code in the master immediately following the procedure call.

```
Master Program                                              (1.37)

A:      Call to Slave
            Execute Slave

            Return to Master
A+1:    Resume Master

B:      Call Slave again
            Execute Slave

            Return to Master
B+1:    Resume Master
```

In contrast to the procedure of listing (1.37),[17] among coroutines there is no master-slave relationship. However, only one process may use the CPU at one time. Transfer of control may occur at any point in either coroutine, but it must be implemented by the currently running process. Listing (1.38) should help explain the relationship between the two coroutines, C1 and C2. We have left the first coroutine, C1, running at the bottom of the diagram. We could just as well have left C2 running, as the processes are coequal. Program termination could occur from either as well.

```
Process C1                                                  (1.38)

A:      Stop C1
        Activate coroutine, C2
                                    Execute C2

                            X:      Stop C2
                                    Return to C1
A+1: Resume C1

B:      Stop C1
        Activate coroutine, C2
                            X+1: Resume C2 at X+1

                            Y: Stop C2
                               Return to C1
B+1: Resume C1
```

Coroutines are implemented in SIMULA 67 and Modula-2. They can be used to simulate concurrency, but assume that only one CPU is available, and that only a single coroutine will be active at any one time. One abstraction implementable through coroutines is a game simulation with two or more

---

17 Listings (1.37) and (1.38) are adapted from [Cooling, 1988, p. 233].

opponents. Control would be passed to the next player after each play. The notion of coroutines is sometimes used at the machine-code level in processing lists where items may be formatted differently, and in complex search and/or matching applications.

Tasks   A *task* is Ada's procedure type for a concurrent process. Like a package, a task has a public *specification* and a possibly private *body*. A *task type* may also be declared, so that numerous actual tasks can be declared [Wegner, 1983]:

```
procedure Airplanes is                                        (1.39)
   task type Airplane is
      entry TakeOff (Home, Destination : in Location);
      entry Mission (Plan : MissionType);
      entry Return (LandingPlace : out Location)
   end;
   type AirplanePtr is access Airplane;
   Squadron : array (1..100) of AirplanePtr;
   task body Airplane is separate;        --private task body
begin
   for I in 1..100 loop
      Squadron(I) := new Airplane;        --activate tasks
   end loop;
   --exit when all tasks are terminated
end Airplanes;
```

To send the entire squadron off on a mission, we could execute the following statement:

```
for I in 1..100 do
   Squadron(I).TakeOff("AndrewsAFB", SecretTarget);
end for;
```

Notice, these Airplanes are not communicating with each other, just operating concurrently.

A disk buffer is an area of storage on a disk used to temporarily store input and output data. Usually, buffers are fast-access devices that store a fixed amount of data before transferring it to a CPU (input) or an output device, such as a printer. Let's see how a DiskBuffer would look as an Ada task (listing (1.40)).

```
task DiskBuffer is                  --task specification     (1.40)
   entry Send (Block : in Page);    --procedures through
   entry Receive (Block : in Page); --which other tasks can
                                     --access a DiskBuffer
end;
task body DiskBuffer is             --may be hidden
   --variable declarations go here
begin loop
   select
      when Length < Limit =>         --guarded accept
         accept Send (Block : in Page) do
```

```
            DiskWrite (Base + Tail, Block);
        Tail := (Tail + 1) mod Limit;
        Length := Length + 1;
    end;
or
    when Length > 0 =>
        accept Receive (Block : out Page) do
            ...
        end;
    end select;
end loop;
end DiskBuffer;
```

The **entry** Send is executed in some other task, which controls an input device, or Console. Similarly, the **entry** Receive transfers data from a Virtual-Disk. Synchronization of possibly concurrently running **tasks** calling Send and Receive is accomplished through the Ada *rendezvous*.

Notice several things in this example. First, only the specification part need be visible to a user. The task may be used to either Send or Receive a Block of code. If a cooperating task executes a DiskBuffer.Send call, and the buffer is full (Length >= Limit), the calling task can be suspended until one or more calls to DiskBuffer.Receive have been executed, and (Length < Limit). **Accept** statements are said to be *guarded* by the Boolean conditions or *guards*, (Length >= Limit and Length < Limit). An Ada **select** statement is not required to have a single true guard among its alternatives. If multiple guards evaluate to true, some random process of the compiler selects among them. Thus Ada tasks may be nondeterminate, giving different results from different invocations.

Two concurrently executing tasks are synchronized in a rendezvous when the calling task has executed its entry call, and the called task is ready to **accept** the call. After the two processes communicate, control is returned to each to continue execution.

Comparisons We have not discussed implementation details here, but suffice it to say, another piece of software is needed. One solution, called a *semaphore*, delays requests until other traffic has cleared, and gives a go-ahead signal for waiting traffic to restart. Semaphores were first implemented in ALGOL 68. Another solution is a *monitor*, which is an interface between concurrent user processes and provides a set of procedures callable by the users, a mechanism for scheduling calls to these procedures if another concurrently executing process requests usage before the procedure has terminated, and a mechanism for suspending a calling procedure until a resource is available and then reawakening the process. A monitor has no access to nonlocal variables and can communicate with other monitors only by calling procedures in them. Thus a monitor, which was first used in Concurrent Pascal, serves as a third-party policeman between two or more cooperating processes. We will consider semaphores and monitors further when we discuss distributed programming in Chapter 4.

Coroutines function as procedures with equal standing and **transfer** control back and fourth. On a single-processor machine, only a single coroutine can be running at one time. A suspended coroutine resumes where execution stopped in its previous invocation. Coroutines can also form the basis for concurrently executing processes if multiple processors are available, and each coroutine runs independently on its own processor. A module will be necessary to synchronize communication between processes using Modula-2's **transfer** procedure. True concurrent programming is impossible using coroutines, since they are all equal in status, i.e., if one fails they all fail.

Ada **tasks** need no third party. Each task serves as a resource manager, and a request to use a resource is represented by an **entry** call to a **task** that "owns" the resource. The resource is allocated by its manager **task** when it executes an **accept** statement. A coroutine explicitly mentions which process is to be resumed when executing its **continue** statement. In Ada, when a task **selects** which option to execute, preference may be given to one calling task or another. There is also the possibility for asynchronous interrupts from remote computers. Thus just which task resumes after being suspended is not entirely specified in Ada. The semantics of cooperating tasks are quite complex, due in part to the special requirements imposed by the DOD on its designers.

EXERCISES

1. Suppose a language provided only procedures and no functions. How would you implement a procedure to compute the length of the hypotenuse of a triangle, if procedures Square(X, Y) and SquareRoot(X, Y) were provided? What methods of parameter-passing should be used for X and for Y?

2. Why does the Pascal language provide procedures in addition to functions?

3. a. Why would an array passed by value-result require more memory than the same array passed by reference?

    b. In real-time programming, which are more desirable, value-result or reference parameters? Can you think of situations where your answer would differ?

4. In C, $*$s indicates the data object pointed to by s and &x gives the address of variable x, what are &*s and *&x?

5. If a reference parameter behaves somewhat like a global variable, what advantages are there in passing by reference instead of using global variables?

6. Redraw the environment diagram of Figure 1.8, assigning the correct value to X if:

   a. The LISP is statically scoped.

   b. The LISP is dynamically scoped.

7. Consider the following procedure to exchange the values of two variables, *X* and *Y*.

   ```
   swap(X, Y);
   temp;
         begin temp = X;  X := Y; Y := temp; end;
   ```

   Suppose `I` = 1, and `A[1]` = 2, and `A[2]` = 3, when we call `swap(A[I], I)`. What are the values of `I`, `A[1]`, and `A[2]`, on completion of the swap procedure if:

   a. X and Y are passed by value?

   b. X is passed by value, and Y by reference?

   c. X and Y are passed by reference?

   d. X and Y are passed by name?

   e. Repeat a through d if the call is `swap (I, A[I])`.

8. How would you compute the triple sum of all the elements of a three-dimensional matrix, A[i,j,k], using the ALGOL procedure, SIGMA, of listing (1.33), and call by name?

9. Complete the **entry procedure** Receive, of listing (1.40), completely parallel to the **entry procedure** Send. ∎

LAB II: Cooperating Processes in Ada

OBJECTIVE

1. To construct and use tasks in Ada. ∎

1.4 A COMPREHENSIVE ABSTRACTION

Some very high-level languages combine abstractions for data, control, and procedures into one comprehensive structure. One such language is BETA [Kristensen, 1987], developed through the Joint Language Project (JLP) at various Norwegian universities. The single abstraction method is called a *pattern*. Instances of patterns, called *objects*, may be used as variables, data structures, procedures, functions, coroutines or concurrent systems. A pattern P has the form:

```
P: (#                      {begin object description}              (1.41)
    D₁; D₂; ...Dₙ          {list of declarations}
    enter In               {input parameters}
    do    Imp              {imperatives to be executed}
    exit  Out              {output parameters}
    #)
```

For example, the pattern:

```
Point: (# x, y: @Integer;         {2 object attributes}          (1.42)
          Move:                   {a pattern attribute}
                (# dx, dy: @Integer
                   enter (dx, dy)
                   do x + dx -> x;
                      y + dy -> y
                   exit  (dx, dy)
                   #)
          #)
```

We can declare `P1,P2:@Point` and assign `(1,2) -> P1` and `(-1,-1)->P2`. Then, the assignment `(2,3)->P1.Move` results in a moving of P1 to (3,5). Furthermore, since `P1.Move,` has `(dx,dy)` listed in its **exit** part, dx=2 and dx=3 act like own variables. `(1,1)->P1.Move->P2.Move->P1.Move` will result in a move of P1 to (5,7) and P2 to (1,2).

BETA has three kinds of objects (instances of patterns), *system*, *component*, and *item*. A system object can run concurrently with other system objects. A component object (coroutine) can run alternately with other components, and an item object may be static, as is Point above, inserted during evaluation, or created dynamically.

The designers claim that "The main advantage of having only one abstraction mechanism is uniform treatment of abstraction mechanisms and their instances" [Kristensen, 1987, p. 42]. A hierarchical classification is also possible, as are virtual patterns.

1.5 SUMMARY

We have looked in this chapter at abstractions that raise a programming language above the level of the machine. These abstractions are grouped into three categories: data, control, and procedural or modular abstraction.

The principle methods of abstracting data from the underlying bits and bytes are through simple data types such as integers, reals, and characters; structured data types such as records, arrays, lists, and sets; and through abstract data types, where data is packaged with and defined by its associated operations. Differences among languages reflect the level of abstraction and whether typing is enforced or not. We also looked at two methods for proving theoretically that an implementation of a data type faithfully represents an abstract type, abstract models and algebraic specification.

Control abstraction involves run-time moving around in a program. Methods for two-way or multiway branching, iteration, and recursion were examined in several languages.

Procedural abstraction involves the assigning of individual tasks to procedures and their interfaces. Here we considered both iterative and recursive procedures as well as modules including data and associated procedures. One of the important advantages of modularization is information hiding so that users know everything they need, but nothing more. Such hiding promotes understanding by removing unnecessary details, and facilitates program revision and security. Modularization also fosters top-down program development, which may be done by independent members of a team, and concurrency, where more than one module may execute at the same time.

This ends our consideration of preliminary concepts. In succeeding chapters, we will see how these abstractions have been implemented in various languages. In Part II, we will look at imperative languages, and consider block structure, objects and concurrency. Part IV deals with declarative languages designed on the basis of functions, mathematical logic, or the foundations for designing and maintaining databases.

1.6 NOTES ON REFERENCES

Hoare's introductory article on abstract models [Hoare, 1972] is rather tough going for those unfamiliar with the notation of mathematical logic and formal proof theory. A more accessible treatment is contained in [Zilles, 1986], Chapter 4. An earlier article by Liskov and Zilles [Liskov, 1975] discusses the purposes of formal specification techniques, criteria for evaluating such techniques, and a discussion of the methods of both abstract models and algebraic specification. The article is well written and accessible to undergraduates. It could provide the basis for a good seminar report. John Guttag has developed a system to aid in the automatic generation of algebraic specifications. References to this work can be found in [Guttag, 1977].

A good, concise discussion of Modula-2, as implemented for PCs, can be found in [Cooling, 1988].

C++ is so new that there are few manuals or texts. [Stroustrup, 1986] is the definitive description and language reference manual. There is also a newsletter, *The C++ Report*, in which tutorials, literature summaries, and implementation details are reported.

Some of the vagaries of pass-by-name are documented in [Knuth, 1967]. Insecurities and ambiguities in the construct were so extensive that pass-by-name has not been implemented in most modern languages.

Elementary examples of coroutines are hard to come by. Marcotty and Ledgard [Marcotty, 1976, p. 316] present an adaptation of a contrived example contained in [Grune, 1977], which solves a list-processing problem involving looking ahead to the next two elements to be input from the list.

A good article discussing the differences between processes, coroutines, tasks, and monitors is [Wegner, 1983]. They consider differences between Ada, monitors, and the experimental language CSP.

II

IMPERATIVE LANGUAGES

2

BLOCK STRUCTURE

2.0 BLOCKS, PROCEDURES, AND RECURSION

The block-structured paradigm is characterized by nested blocks, procedures, and recursion. A block is a contiguous section of code in which variables can be localized. Thus any information that is to be used exclusively within a block, and need not be known by surrounding blocks, can be hidden.

This characteristic is advantageous for several reasons. First, it localizes changes that might be made in the future. Local variables can affect performance only in the block(s) in which they are visible. Second, when proving correctness, assumptions can be made at the beginning and end of a block. If the structure of the block can be used to show that the end assumptions necessarily follow from those at the beginning and the operations performed within the block, complex proofs are made easier. Third, an individual or a group of programmers need not concern themselves with conflicting names for any variables local to a block. Finally, block structure facilitates program organization if a block embodies a single concept. The structure of ALGOL 60 was a step in this direction.

Once blocks have been implemented, procedures follow naturally, as named blocks that can be called from other parts of a program and that facilitate explicit information exchange between the calling and the called blocks through parameters. The implementation model for blocks is the stack. Only one block can be active at any one time, and its allocated storage occupies the top of the run-time stack. When a block terminates, its memory allocation will be released, and memory for the calling block reactivated. The stack implementation supports recursion, as successive invocations of a recursive procedure can be pushed onto the run-time stack and popped in reverse order, passing values back up the stack.

ALGOL's blocks were a good start, but not enough to ensure local modification and correctness for large complex systems. The first paper outlining the needs for more explicit information hiding and connections between modules was [Parnas, 1971]. He proposed that systems designers should control the distribution of design information, since "a good programmer makes use of the usable information given him," and somebody has to be in charge. In the descendants of blocks, modules and objects, explicit control of information has been implemented. Data, procedures or entire modules can be visible or invisible to a user or programmer using, but unable to modify, hidden features.

2.1 ALGOL 60

HISTORICAL VIGNETTE 1: Design by Committee

It is commonly accepted that nothing good can come from a committee. Since many are involved, compromise is inevitable, so better results are more likely from an individual's efforts. If one were to take a superficial look at ALGOL's (ALGOrithmic Language) history, one might conclude that this opinion was valid. ALGOL failed to come even close to its goal of becoming a universal programming language. Looked at differently, it is a success story in which the main character, ALGOL, became one of the most important conceptual milestones in the history of computer science.

The story began in 1957. FORTRAN had just entered the computer scene, and a programming revolution was underway. New languages surfaced everywhere. Many users' groups in the United States began to see that the situation was getting out of hand. If a programmer moved, it was almost inevitable that he or she would have to learn a new programming language. Time and resources were being wasted. The groups asked the Association for Computing Machinery (ACM) to come up with a solution. A German organization, the Society for Applied Mathematics and Mechanics (GAMM), was struggling with the same problem, so in May 1958, ACM and GAMM joined forces. A joint committee met in Zurich to develop a universal programming language.

FORTRAN's close ties to IBM and its products would have made its choice seem like "the U.S. Department of Transportation endorsing United Airlines or Ford Escorts™" [Baron, 1986, p. 108]. Thus this initial committee of eight embarked on the design of an entirely new programming language.

After eight days of work, the group completed a rough draft of the ALGOL language, originally known as International Algebraic Language (IAL). Although the draft was put together in a short time, all did not run smoothly at committee meetings. At one point, a meeting came to a complete deadlock over decimals. Americans use a period while Europeans use a comma. One committee member pounded the table, vowing "never (to) use a period for a decimal point." This conflict was resolved by the decision that ALGOL would be represented at three levels: as a reference language, a hardware language, and a publication language. This gave everyone the freedom to represent decimals however they liked in the publication language.

The product of the committee's work, the ALGOL 58 report, set forth the objectives of the new language:

> The new language should be as close as possible to standard mathematical notation and be readable with little further explanation.

> It should be possible to use it for the description of computing processes and publications.

> It should be mechanically translatable into machine programs.

This report generated considerable interest, and IBM considered abandoning FORTRAN in favor of ALGOL.

It is interesting that "many of the European framers of the language...recognized 'ALGOL'[1] as the name of the second-brightest star in the constellation Perseus. The amount of light emanating from ALGOL changes, for roughly every 69 hours the star is eclipsed by a large dark body, its partner star, which is about six million miles away. Yet ALGOL always manages to regain its brilliance. The double meaning was not lost on the Europeans: The ALGOL language was not to be eclipsed by FORTRAN" [Baron, 1986, p. 110]. But ALGOL *was* eclipsed when IBM made the decision to stick with FORTRAN. ALGOL was still in rough draft form, so that programmers could make suggestions about its final form, while FORTRAN was complete and debugged.

In January 1969, 13 members of ACM and GAMM met in Paris for six days to transform ALGOL 58 into a complete language, ALGOL 60. The resulting report was unique in that the language's syntax was described in the new Backus-Naur form (BNF), developed by committee members John Backus and Peter Naur. Semantics were described in clear, unambiguous English, which resulted in a very readable report [Naur, 1963]. "The brevity and elegance of this report contributed significantly to ALGOL's reputation as a simple, elegant language" [MacLennan, 1987, p. 102].

ALGOL 60 proved to be a major breakthrough in computer science. The European passion for orderliness influenced its metamorphosis into the first structured, second-generation programming language. Important language constructs were introduced, such as [Wegner, 1976, p. 7]:

- Block structure
- Explicit type declarations for variables
- Scope rules for local variables
- Dynamic, as opposed to static lifetimes for variables
- Nested if-then-else expressions and statements
- Call by value and call by name for procedure parameters

---

1 In most circles, the rule on capitalization for the names of programming languages is that all letters are capitalized if the name is an acronym, e.g., ALGOL, standing for "ALGOrithmic Language," and only the first letter capitalized for proper names, e.g., Pascal. I have followed this custom except for nonconforming quotations. I have not used hyphens in ALGOL 60 and ALGOL 68, as they are not used in the original reports. They are often used in the literature, however. Modula-2 was hyphenated in Wirth's writings, and the hyphen is only occasionally omitted.

- Recursive subroutines
- Arrays with dynamic bounds

These new constructs led directly to the development of Pascal, Modula-2, and Ada. The BNF notation, first used in the ALGOL 60 report, made the development of a formal theory of programming languages possible, which facilitates successful compiler design. Thus ALGOL, a commercial failure, is considered a scientific triumph.

IBM wasn't solely responsible for ALGOL's downfall in the marketplace. For one thing, ALGOL 60 had no input/output statements. This seemingly major flaw was intended by its designers to make ALGOL machine independent, as is fitting for a truly universal language. Instead, a library of I/O routines was to be provided, specific to each implementation. This notion of separating I/O from the language specification is continued in Ada, but a standard library is included. Eventually, this I/O situation was corrected in ALGOL 68, but it was too late. That the ALGOL 68 report was generally considered to be unreadable didn't help matters. The designers of ALGOL 68 strove to provide language constructs of maximal generality and flexibility. These constructs proved, however, to be too complex to be readily learned by an applications programmer.

ALGOL 68's future is bleak. Its users are almost extinct in the United States, and they are an endangered species in Europe as well. But its successors, Pascal, Modula-2, and Ada are successful, both commercially and scientifically. And the C programming language, descended from ALGOL 68, is thriving.

Concepts from ALGOL 60

ALGOL has had such a large influence on programming languages that the term "ALGOL-like" is used widely to describe languages with the following six features [Horowitz, 1984, pp. 11–12]:

1. It is an algorithmic language, i.e., it facilitates the step-by-step solution of problems, including loops.
2. The algorithm is conveyed to the computer as a sequence of changes to the store (memory).
3. The basic units of computation are the block and the procedure.
4. Variables are typed, and types are checked at compile and/or run time.
5. It uses the lexical (static) scoping rule, i.e., the environment of a procedure is that in which it is defined.
6. It is designed to be compiled, rather than interpreted.

Although many of these ideas were mentioned in Chapter 1, we will examine them further in the sections that follow.

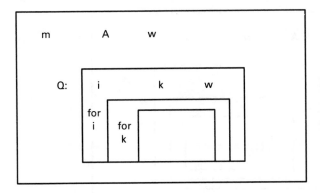

Figure 2.1   ALGOL's **for** statements

Block structure

ALGOL 60 defines a block as either labeled or unlabeled. The report provides the following example:

```
Q:          begin integer i, k ; real w ;
                for i := 1 step 1 until m do
                for k := i+1 step 1 until m do
                begin w := A[i,k] ;
                      A[i,k] := A[k,i];
                      A[k,i] := w
                end for i and k
            end block Q;
```

An unlabeled block could be the same if the two references to the label Q were deleted.

The important things to note are that a block is enclosed by **begin...end**, and that variables may be declared which are local to the block. Following the declarations and preceding the **end**, a block includes one or more statements. The second **begin...end** for i and k sequence is a block with no declaration part, called a *compound statement*. The local variables i, k, and w come into existence when block Q is entered and cease to exist after **end** block Q; is executed. Any variable outside block Q named i, k, or w is completely inaccessible inside block Q.

In the Figure 2.1, there are four blocks. In the outer block, the variables m, A, and w are known, while in the inner ones, only m and A are still accessible. The local variables i, k and w exist, but the outer w is completely hidden from the three inner blocks. One of the four blocks is labeled Q, and thus may be accessed from outside via a statement such as **goto** Q.

In Pascal, a subtle change was made. Since the control variables of a **for** loop (here i, k and m) are intended to control the number of iterations and do

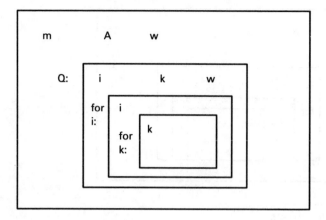

Figure 2.2   Pascal's **for** statements

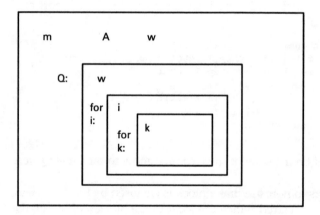

Figure 2.3   Ada's **for** loop

nothing else, two rules were made: first, the body of the loop can contain no statement changing these variables, and second, they are completely undefined on exit from the loop. (See Figure 2.2.)

The designers of Ada took this notion one step further. In the Ada statement:

```
for I in 1..MAX loop ... end loop;
```

I does not appear in the declaration section of the block containing the **for** statement, but is implicitly declared to be of integer subtype 1..MAX on entrance to the for loop, may not be altered in the body of the loop, and ceases to exist on execution of **end loop**. (See Figure 2.3.)

In PL/I and Ada, both labeled and unlabeled blocks have been implemented, while in Pascal local variables may be declared only in procedures or functions.

In ALGOL, a procedure is declared and defined in the head, or declaration, section of a block. Variables in the surrounding block are known to an included procedure as in any other block. When a procedure is called, its environment is entered, its statements executed, and its environment exited. Control then returns to the environment of the caller. This situation is called *static binding* because the environment of the procedure is that of the block where it was declared and not that of the caller.

```
B1:                                                      (2.1)
    integer a;
    procedure P
    begin
        print(a);
    end;
    begin
      a := 7;

    B2:    integer a;
           begin
              a := 0;
              P;
           end block B2;
    end block B1;
```

In the program fragment shown in listing (2.1), 7 will be printed, rather than the 0 of the caller's environment B2, since procedure P was defined in the environment B1, where a = 7.

In Pascal, all procedures are declared and defined before the main block is defined or any variables assigned values. Pascal uses static binding, however, so any global variable (such as the "a" of procedure P) must be declared before a procedure referencing it.

Explicit type declarations for variables and procedures

FORTRAN provides for declaring variables, but allows the implicit declaration of integers and reals. Unless otherwise declared, any variable beginning with I, J, K, L, M, or N is an integer, and all others are real. ALGOL 60 has three simple variable types: **integer**, **real**, and **boolean**, and all variables must be explicitly declared. A **boolean** variable may have the value **true** or **false**. Characters and strings are not typed, but can be passed by name as an actual parameter. The only structured types are **array**s, which are ordered sets of the same type. For example, **integer array** A[1:20], describes a one-dimensional array of 20 integers. **integer array** B[**if** c<0 **then** 2 **else** 1:20] declares an array, B, similar to A, unless the variable c has a value less than 0, in which case B has only 19 storage locations, indexed from 2 to 20. We will discuss arrays

with dynamic bounds further below. ALGOL 68 added the **record** and character types, among others, where a record is a template for an aggregate containing items of possibly different types.

Any ALGOL 60 type declaration can be preceded by the designation **own**,
e.g., **own integer array** A[5..100]. In this case, on exit from the block in
which A is declared, its value will be retained and may be accessed on reentry
to the block. Local variables and their values in Pascal, Modula, and Ada are
destroyed on exit from the block in which they are declared. In PL/I, however,
the notion of "own" variables has been implemented. A PL/I variable declared
to be **STATIC** will retain its values for the life of the program, whereas **AUTO-
MATIC** variables (the default storage class) are destroyed on exit from their
defining block.

Scope rules for local variables

Storage for variables declared local to a block is not allocated until entry to
the block and is deallocated on exit from the block. There are, however, certain
exceptions to this rule. The first is for **own** variables, as noted previously. Second
is in execution of the **switch** statement, which is ALGOL's case statement. It is
really a disguised "go to" statement. An example of a **switch** statement is:

    switch S := S1, S2, Q[m], **if** v > -5 **then** S3 **else** S4.

Each of the four expressions on the right-hand side of the statement evaluates to
a label. If S = 3, then control will be switched to the statement labeled by the
value of the third expression, Q[m]. ALGOL allows this label to refer to a line of
code outside the block in which the **switch** statement occurs. The report states
that in such a case, "conflicts between the identifiers for the quantities in this
expression and the identifiers whose declarations are valid at the place of the
switch designator will be avoided through suitable systematic changes of
the latter identifiers." This means that if m = 5 in the block B2, where the switch
statement is encountered, and the value of Q[5] is a label in block B, outside B2,
the name of the variable m may be changed in B if its value differs from the
value of m in B2. (See exercise 5 for a further exploration of this situation.)

The rather baroque **switch** statement of ALGOL 60 is similar to
FORTRAN's computed **GOTO**, where **GOTO**(L₁, ..., Lₙ) S switches execution
to the statement labeled L_i if the value of S = i. Since FORTRAN has no nested
blocks, a goto is quite straightforward, and execution continues at the statement
labeled appropriately. In block-structured languages, however, variables must
be deallocated on exit from a block, so the rules become quite strict. In Pascal, a
goto can reference a statement only in the block in which the label is declared.
One may not transfer into a compound statement, such as a **for**, **if** or **case**
statement, as the control variable(s) would not be active. In Ada, the rules are
somewhat more complex, to accommodate packages and tasks. As a general
rule, Ada **goto**'s may transfer into the same lexical level.

Because of resulting program disorganization and subsequent errors, goto's are generally discouraged, but allowed for special uses, such as block or program termination on error. Transfer is not permitted into a contained block, and if execution is transferred to a surrounding block, the block where the goto occurs and all intermediate blocks must be deactivated during the transfer. In the figure below, if control is transferred from block S to the statement labeled 1 in block P, blocks S, R, and Q must be deactivated during the transfer.

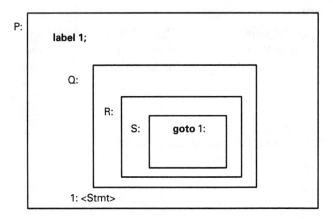

Nested if-then-else expressions and statements

ALGOL was the first language that permitted nested statements as well as blocks. A statement

```
if A then S1 else S2
```

has no restrictions on statements S1 and S2. Either can be an if..then..else to any level of nesting. The ALGOL 60 report gives the following as an example of a valid ALGOL statement:

```
if if if a then b else c then d else f then g else h<k
```

Can you sort this out? Which variables necessarily represent Boolean expressions?

Call by value and call by name

A procedure, as we know, may have formal parameters. It is called from another environment with actual parameters. Thus a function may be:

```
procedure Increment(u, inc) ;
begin    value u,inc  ; real u, inc  ;
         u := u + inc;
end;
```

and the call may be Increment(x + y, z). Here the actual parameters, x + y and z, are passed by value to the formal parameters, u and inc. On entry to the procedure block for Increment, storage is allocated for two real numbers, and the values of x + y and z are stored at locations for u and inc, respectively. Neither x nor y is changed by the Increment procedure. No link exists between the actual and formal parameters after the initial copying of the actuals into the formals.

In contrast, consider

```
procedure Increment2(u, inc) ; real u, inc  ;
begin u := u + inc; end;
```

Here the parameters are passed by name, the ALGOL 60 default. The effect is that the call, Increment2(x, z), is replaced *in the environment of the caller* by the body of Increment2 with the name x substituted for the formal parameter u and z for inc, i.e.,

```
begin x := x + z end;
```

Here the value of x is changed.

If the call were Increment2(x,y+z), the substitution would be

```
begin x := x + thunk; end;
```

The *thunk* provides an address of code for the expression y + z. Whenever the thunk is encountered, control switches to that address, x + y is calculated, and its value returned in place of the thunk.

Call by name is very powerful, as we have seen. As another example, consider the ALGOL procedure, Integral:

```
real procedure Integral (func,low,high,interval);
real procedure func; real low, high, interval;
begin  integer i, n; real LastInterval;
   n := entier (high - low);          ;comment entier ≡ truncate;
   Integral := 0;
   for i:= 1 step 1 until n do
      Integral := func (low + i*interval/2) * interval;
   LastInterval := high - (low+n*interval);
   Integral := func (LastInterval/2) * LastInterval;
end;
```

Suppose the call was Integral(sqrt, 0, 10, 0.001). Each time "func" is encountered, control will transfer to code for the "sqrt" function (via a thunk), where the appropriate value will be computed and returned to Integral.

All is not well, however, with call by name. We considered a simple swap procedure in exercise 7, following the section "Procedural Abstraction: in Chaper 1, where you found (I hope) that using name parameters made a call to swap(I, A[I]) impossible.

Because of irregularities such as this, call by name has essentially disappeared from modern programming languages. Smalltalk-76 is one of the few to have implemented it.

Recursive subroutines

The ALGOL 60 report makes no explicit mention of recursion. It is allowed by what it doesn't say. A procedure is defined in the BNF of the report as:

```
<procedure declaration> ::=
  procedure <procedure heading><procedure body> |
   <type> procedure <procedure heading><procedure body>.
<procedure body> ::= <statement> | <code>
```

Code refers to non-ALGOL procedures. The designers envisioned FORTRAN or assembly language procedures being imported into an ALGOL program. Just how this was to be done was left to the hardware and/or publication languages, and not specified in the report, which considered only the reference language.

The definition of the procedure body specified that it be a statement or code, but did not put any restrictions on the statement. One sort of statement is a procedure call, so a call to P within the procedure P is quite all right. PL/I, which was being developed about the same time, also allowed recursive procedures, but only if they were declared to be so, e.g., a recursive version of the factorial function would be declared as

```
Factorial: procedure (n) recursive;
```

in PL/I, but as

```
integer procedure Factorial (n);
```

in ALGOL. It was left to the ALGOL compiler writer to recognize that Factorial was indeed recursive and to implement it properly.

Arrays with dynamic bounds

In a language such as Pascal, the size or dimension of an array must be declared before a program is compiled. Thus its storage can be allocated before the program is run. A second advantage is that the index type need only be checked once. If its maximum value is within the array bounds, no further checks need be done. Checking a simple index type for its maximum may be faster than other more complex tests. In a situation where the size of an array depends on some value computed by the program, it is sometimes declared to be of maximum estimated size, and then only partially filled. An array is considered abstractly as a random access structure. That is, we can access the ith element just as quickly as the first or last. Thus there needs to be some method for computing element locations. This poses no problem if we know both the size of each element and that the entire array is stored contiguously in storage. The ith element will then be found at

```
location_i = starting-address + (i-1) * element-length
```

ALGOL 60, PL/I, and Ada prescribe arrays with *dynamic bounds*. These bounds can be computed at run time, but must be known before the array is used. Storage is then found for the entire array, just as it is for dynamic variables. ALGOL 68 calls for arrays with *flexible bounds*, which may change after the array has been created and storage allocated for it. APL is even less demanding, and any variable can have an array of any size as its value, simply by assigning an array to it.

EXERCISES

1. Discuss the advantages and disadvantages of the **own** designation in ALGOL 60. What would a programmer have to consider about an **own** variable on the first entry into the block where it is declared? subsequent entries?

2. Consider the following Pascal program:

```
program StaticScope;
var a: integer;
procedure P;
begin
  write(a);
end;

procedure Q;
a : integer;
begin
  a := 0;
  P;
end;

begin
  a := 7;
  Q;
end.
```

What value of a will be printed? Why?

3. The control variable in an Ada for-loop is implicitly declared on entry to the loop. Suppose an Ada loop is

```
for COUNT in 1.. MAX loop ... end loop;
```

and that

```
type COUNT is (MON..SUN);
```

appeared in the declaration section of the surrounding block. What will happen? Why?

4. ALGOL allows arrays with dynamic bounds. If **own array** A[1..100] is declared in a procedure P, what happens to the retained values if P initializes all 100 elements of A, and then changes the bounds of A to, say, 1..50? What is available on the second invocation? (Don't panic! This is a compiler writer's problem and various solutions are acceptable.)

5. Trace the value of the variables B.m and B2.m in the following ALGOL 60 code observing the semantics of the report. (Here B.m refers to m in Block B, and B2.m, the m in Block B2.)

```
B:begin integer array Q[1..20];   real m, r;
   Q[2] := 1;
   m := 3.1416;   r := 2.0;
   1:  begin print (m*2*r); end;

   B2:  begin integer m;
           m := 2; S := 3;
           switch S := S1, S2, Q[m], if v>-5 then S3 else S4
           end;
   end;
```

6. Can you see why a call of Increment2(x+y,z) is not allowed in ALGOL 60?

7. In numerical computations, it is quite common to sum the elements of an array, Σ A[i], (i = j to n). Pass by name accomplishes this quite neatly using a technique called Jensen's Device.

```
real procedure Sigma(A, i, low, high);
value low, high; real A; integer i, low, high;
begin  integer i; real sum;
  for i := low step 1 until high do
    sum := sum + A
  Sigma := sum
end;
```

a. Why are low and high value parameters?

b. Trace the call total := Sigma(A[k], k, 1, 20). Be careful to substitute correctly for the name parameters A and i.

c. Why did we need to pass explicitly to the index variable i?

8. Why can't arrays expand and contract? For example, what is wrong with connecting two portions of an array of size n with a pointer from the first i-elements to the last (n − i)?

9. APL is usually interpreted, rather than compiled. Why would this make it easier to assign arrays to any variable? ∎

Trouble Spots in ALGOL 60

In 1967 the *Communications of the ACM* published an article by Donald Knuth [Knuth, 1967] collecting all the ambiguities and errors noticed in the ALGOL 60 report. By an ambiguity, Knuth means that a number of knowledgeable people find different meaning in a part of the report. An error constitutes an ambiguity on which nearly everyone is agreed on the correction needed. We mention them here, as various remedies will be seen in the successors to ALGOL 60.

There are nine ambiguities.

1. If side effects are allowable, then the order of computation must be specified. (A function has a side effect if in addition to computing a value, changes are made to other nonlocal variables.) Knuth gives the following example, which we leave for exercise 1, to find the 11 possible answers.

```
begin
   integer procedure f(x,y); value y,x; integer y,x;
      a := f := x + 1;

   integer procedure g(x);   integer x;
      x := g := a + 2;

   a := 0;
   outreal² (1, a + f(a, g(a))/g(a))
end;
```

Notice that each of the procedures f and g has a side effect. f increases the value of the global variable a by 1, and g increases it by 2. Notice also that x and y are value parameters in procedure f, but name parameters in g. One of the outputs is 4 1/2, which occurs if the order of computation is:

1. g(a) is computed first as the denominator of a fraction.
2. f(a, g(a)), the numerator is computed second.
3. The **value** parameters in f are computed with a first, and g(a) second
4. a + f(a,g(a))/g(a) is computed and output last.

2. Allowability of a **goto** statement within a procedure. Goto's violate the principle of one-entry/one-exit in a procedure, which makes debugging difficult. The idea of a procedure embodies the transfer of control from a calling routine to a callee. The callee is entered at the top, and when exited, returns to the statement immediately following that from which it was called. Goto's allow return to (almost) anywhere.[3]

3. Confusion on whether variable V, expressions A, B, and C, and procedure S use call by value or call by name in the statement:

```
for V := A step B until C do S
```

---

2 "Outreal (1,---)" indicates that an output procedure should be supplied by the compiler writer for output onto device number 1. It is an expression of the reference language and may be different in any particular publication language for ALGOL 60.

3 R. L. Clark [Clark, 1973] suggested that the "go-to" problem was really a "come-from" problem. If a program contains several statements of the form "goto L," and if an error occurs at or subsequent to the statement labeled L, we may not know where to search for the error, since we won't know where we "came from."

Again, different values may be computed by programs employing the statement.

4. To what extent do variable types have to be specified, and what automatic type changes may occur? For example, if x and y are integers, is x := x/y, always allowed? If so, is x rounded? truncated?

5. What happens to repeated parameters, e.g., G(x,x)?

6. May the value of a label be undefined?

7. Own variables are a disaster.

8. Can labels be numbers? Is the following a valid ALGOL procedure?

```
procedure P(q); if q < 5 then go to q;
```

9. No precision is specified for real numbers. In particular, when can two reals be considered equal?

Among the corrections, only three will be mentioned here.

1. Division by 0 should result in an error.
2. The report suggests that "certain identifiers should be reserved for the standard functions of analysis." It goes on to suggest, but not specify, that these might include abs, sign, sqrt, sin, cos, and arctan. Knuth suggests that this would cause confusion, unless the list is strictly adhered to, and not added to, in all implementations.
3. Call by name should be restricted. (See exercise 6).

Language Specification

ALGOL 60 was the first language to have a complete defining description, as detailed in the *Report on the Algorithmic Language ALGOL 60* [Naur, 1963]. Any compiler written for ALGOL had to implement faithfully each language element as defined. The report consists of five chapters totaling 17 pages:

1. Structure of the Language
2. Basic Symbols, Identifiers, Numbers, and Strings
3. Expressions
4. Statements
5. Declarations

The report is written in the *reference language. Publication languages* are also to be permitted, which might differ from country to country, but, "correspondence with the reference representation must be secured." The intention for different publication languages is to ease communication between computer professionals so a more natural language style is allowed.

Closely related to publication languages are hardware representations, which relate to individual machines. For example, the reference language defines:

<relational operator> : := < | ≤ | = | ≥ | > | ≠

where "|" represents "or". Most keyboards are not equipped to handle ≤ , ≥ , or ≠. The particular substitutions can be listed for a hardware representation, but their meaning must conform with the usual mathematical notions represented in the reference.

One of the greatest contributions of the report is the use of Backus-Naur (Backus-Normal) Form, or BNF, to define the reference language. In the fifties, the linguist, Noam Chomsky [Chomsky, 1965] was attempting to develop a mathematical theory of natural languages, i.e., those in everyday use for communication between people. Although his four types do not include all spoken or written languages, the hierarchy has been very useful for formal and programming languages. Although Backus's work proceeded independently from that of Chomsky, it was quickly recognized that BNF notation was equivalent to Chomsky's type 2, or *context-free* grammars. Both use recursive definitions to identify valid units of a language. The report uses the following example to explain BNF.

<ab> ::= (| [| <ab>(| <ab><d> ...

It indicates that <ab> may have the value (, or [, or that given some legitimate value of <ab>, another may be formed by following it with the character (or by following it with some value of the variable <d>. If the values of <d> are the decimal digits, some values of <ab> are:

[((((1(37(
(12343(
(((
[86

We will look at formal languages and their relationship to theoretical machines further in Chapter 5.

EXERCISES

1. Since the ALGOL 60 report does not specify in which order computations must proceed, or in which order parameters labeled **value** are to be evaluated, there are 11 possible values printed on output device 1 at execution of the statement outreal(1, a + f(a,g(a))/g(a)) discussed previously. Find as many as you can.

2. It is hard to imagine a real-world example of a function, such as f(a,g(a))/g(a)). Why do you think Donald Knuth paid any attention to it?

3. If you were a compiler writer confronted with handling a procedure call such as G(x,x), what possible interpretations might you consider?

4. In ambiguity number 8, if the procedure is valid, what would be wrong with a call of P(2)?

5. Different programming languages use different strategies on identifiers with special meanings. For example, in FORTRAN, it is perfectly valid to say if = 2. Supposedly, a compiler should be able to figure out whether "if" is part of an if..then statement, or a variable name. ALGOL did not specify any reserved words, but suggested that certain familiar functions should be provided. Discuss the pros and cons of

   1. No reserved words
   2. As few reserved words as possible
   3. A rich list of special functions named by reserved words (ALGOL 68 had more than one hundred)
   4. A rich list of defined functions, which could be redefined by the user (PL/I's solution)
   5. A small list of reserved words plus a list of defined functions and procedures that can be redefined by the user (Pascal's solution)

6. a. Suggest some values for the variable <d> if it is defined in BNF as:
   ```
   <d> ::= <digit> | <d><digit>
   <digit> ::= 0 | 1 | 2 | 3 |4 | 5 | 6 | 7 | 8 | 9
   ```

   b. Can you supply a different BNF definition for <d> to allow only decimal natural numbers without leading 0's? ■

2.2 ALGOL 68

ALGOL 68 was the first language to be described completely in a formal grammar, a W-grammar, sometimes called a vW-grammar.[4] In BNF, which was used for the ALGOL 60 report, the authors were able to describe syntax, but not the semantics of the language. Even though a language is completely expressible in the W-grammar, readers found it extremely hard to understand. This obscurity[5] is often cited as one of the reasons for ALGOL 68's demise.

   The defining feature of ALGOL 68 is its orthogonality. "An orthogonal language has a small number of basic constructs and rules for combining them in regular and systematic ways. A very deliberate attempt is made to elim-

---

4 The vW-grammar is named after its inventor, A. van Wijngaarden. It is *context sensitive* while BNF is *context free*. For example, the FORTRAN statement IF (IF = 1) X = 2 is sensitive to the context in which the IF is used, the first IF being a conditional and the second a variable name. We will discuss these differences in Part III.

5 Programmers were not expected to learn ALGOL 68 using the definition, and several tutorials were written for them, e.g., [Tanenbaum, 1976].

inate arbitrary restrictions" [Tanenbaum, 1976]. For example, a function maps parameters onto a single result. In orthogonal ALGOL, each parameter and the functional result can be of any type, whereas only scalar or pointer values can be returned by a Pascal or PL/I function. Arbitrary rules and restrictions are eliminated in ALGOL 68, reducing program errors and programmer frustration.

Procedures in ALGOL 68 are of mode[6] **proc**. Since any mode can be either passed to a procedure or returned as a functional value, procedures can also. It would seem impractical to transfer a procedure as a segment of code into or out of another procedure, thus the facility is usually implemented as a pointer. A pointer, or reference, to the code segment becomes the actual parameter or functional value. Tanenbaum [Tanenbaum, 1976] provides the elementary example shown in listing (2.2) to produce a sum of functional values, f(1) + f(2) +...+ f(n), for an arbitrary function, f.

```
proc sum = (int n, proc (real) real f) real:              (2.2)
begin real sum := 0;
for i to n do sum := sum+f(i) od
sum
end
```

A call to sum might be sum(100, **sin**), which would yield $sin(1) + sin(2)$ +...+ $sin(100)$. Notice in the definition of the procedure, the formal parameter i of sum is used as a counter (integer) and the real valued parameter for sin. The integral i of the **for** loop is automatically transformed into a real, for use with f(i).

In the mid-sixties the notion of procedures as first-class objects was present in LISP and being experimented with in SIMULA, the first of the object-oriented languages. Procedure passing survived in Pascal only in limited form.

Another of the genuine achievements of ALGOL 68 was its use of operators. An *operator* is a symbol representing a procedure or function, such as the arithmetic binary operators, '+' and '*', or the unary, '–'. 2 + 3, 5 * 6, and –2 are familiar to us all. One operator may have *precedence* over another so that 2 + 3 * 5, evaluates to 17, rather than 25. Not only can one define new operators in ALGOL 68, but define and redefine precedence as well. Thus if one wants 2 + 3 * 5 = 25, as on some simple hand-held calculators where * does not have precedence over +, one can have it in ALGOL 68. The orthogonal principle dictates that we can redefine built-in precedents in ALGOL, since we can define them for user-defined operators. The designers of Ada included user-defined operators, as have those defining declarative languages, such as PROLOG.

Although ALGOL 68 gained little popularity in the United States, many of its pioneering features have been used in other languages.

---

6 Types in ALGOL 68 are called modes. Many common notions were renamed to warn the user that the ideas were somewhat different than in other languages.

2.3 PASCAL

In contrast to the much more complicated ALGOL 68, ALGOL 60 influenced a simpler language, designed for teaching good programming principles and style. This is the Pascal language.

HISTORICAL VIGNETTE 2: Pascal and Modula-2: Niklaus Wirth

> Complexity has and will maintain a strong fascination for many people. It is true that we live in a complex world and strive to solve inherently complex problems, which often do require complex mechanisms. However, this should not diminish our desire for *elegant* solutions, which convince by their clarity and effectiveness. Simple, elegant solutions are more effective, but they are *harder* to find than complex ones, and they require more time, which we often believe to be unaffordable. [Niklaus Wirth, Turing Award Lecture, 1984.]

During the mid- to late sixties, ALGOL was the focus of much attention in the world of computer programming. Niklaus Wirth was in the midst of it all, working on improved versions of ALGOL 60 at the ETH laboratory in Zurich. The need for a successor to ALGOL had become apparent after the release of the revised report. Although it contained many brilliant conceptual ideas, the language lacked such practical capabilities as character variables and I/O. Wirth and Tony Hoare, of Oxford University, but both at Stanford University at the time, suggested to the ALGOL Committee several modest but important improvements to ALGOL 60. The ideas were rejected and the successor became the overly complex ALGOL 68.

Wirth, refusing to be daunted by a closed-minded committee, developed his own successor to ALGOL 60, called ALGOL-W. During the next four years, with the help of three assistants, he developed a successor to that language. This language came to be known as Pascal, after Blaise Pascal, the French mathematician, scientist, and religious writer.

Pascal is in many ways an elegant[7] version of ALGOL 60. "Like ALGOL 60, the standard Pascal language contains all the code necessary for implementation on computers" [Baron, 1986, p. 286]. It is both beautiful and practical. Wirth had designed Pascal with the following two goals in mind [Cooper, 1982, p. xvii]:

1. To provide a teaching language that would bring out concepts common to all languages while avoiding inconsistencies and unnecessary detail.

2. To define a truly standard language that would be cheap and easy to implement on any computer.

---

7 In mathematics, *elegant* is often used to describe a theory or construct that is parsimonious. That is, it contains everything that is necessary but excludes any unneeded adornments. Fred Astaire is elegant, whereas Liberace is not.

These goals have been realized. Many universities and colleges teach Pascal as a first programming language, and it is the language used for the AP Computer Science Exam for high school students. That Pascal is a structured language has a lot to do with its popularity in the world of education. According to Wirth, programs are designed "according to the same principles as electronic circuits, that is, clearly subdivided into parts with only a few wires going across the boundaries." He believes that students should program this way, *especially* in the beginning of their education since "the language in which the student is taught to express his[/her] ideas profoundly influences his[/her] habits of thought and invention" [Jensen, 1974].

An important milestone in the history of Pascal occurred when Kenneth Bowles developed a Pascal compiler and operating system for use on mini- and microcomputers, including a text editor, assembler, and linker. This system is University of California at San Diego (UCSD) Pascal and was distributed to educational institutions as well as industry. Since 1984, interpreted versions and the fast Turbo Pascal® have added to its popularity. Wirth, however, has moved on to newer interests, in particular, concurrent programming.

Languages such as FORTRAN, ALGOL, BASIC, and Pascal are sequential languages. Each action of a sequential program is initiated only after the action of its predecessor is completed. Procedures are executed one at a time. In concurrent programming (also known as multiprogramming) more than one process can be executing at the same time.

Concurrent programming interested Wirth, since it could make efficient use of computers, but also because concurrent programming more accurately models many real-world situations, where many things happen at once, than does sequential processing. A program that controls many different subway cars, for example, has to be concurrent. Processes that control events as they occur are incorporated in "real-time" programs. "Real-time programming is at once the darling and the nightmare of computer scientists" [Baron, 1986]. On the one hand, it enables computers to control extremely complex situations; on the other, real-time programming languages tend to be just as complex and tricky as the situations they are designed to control. And they must be very reliable. In some cases, such as that of an antiballistic missile system, they must be 100 percent error free. "Ada [which is based on Pascal] is just the last in a long series of languages that have grown to resemble wild thickets as opposed to the neat English gardens so easily possible with sequential languages" [Baron, 1986, p. 271].

In the mid-seventies, Wirth set out to design a real-time programming language that would be efficient and conceptually well structured at the same time. He named his new special-purpose language Modula. It is a subset of Pascal with some important features added. One of these, which is responsible for the name Modula, is the module concept. Modules are like programs within a larger program, which can hide information from each other and can be compiled or executed independently. Modula also provides for low-level machine access.

In 1976, Wirth took a sabbatical from Switzerland to Xerox PARC, in Palo Alto, California. There, he decided to build a complete computer system for real-time programming. For this, he created another new language, Modula-2, a child of both Pascal and Modula. The computer itself was called Lilith, who was, according to Jewish folklore, Adam's first wife, before Eve. She flew away from Adam and became a night monster, with demonic powers over children. I leave it to you, dear reader, to decide why the name is appropriate for a concurrent computer system.

As with Pascal, it took a while for the public to become interested in Modula-2. Some believe that it will eventually replace Pascal as the first language students learn. But the real competition is not between Pascal and Modula-2, but between Modula-2 and Ada. Even though Ada is overly complex and has several costly features, it has the support of the Department of Defense, which shows no signs of shifting its allegiance.

Niklaus Wirth's tenacious adherence to an elegant and strict programming discipline has made him one of the major architects of computer science. In his 1984 Turing Award Lecture, he stated, "The subject [computer languages] seemed to consist of 1 percent science and 99 percent sorcery, and this tilt had to be changed." Wirth's commitment to this change has molded the conceptual framework of computer science and will continue to influence it for years to come.

Philosophy and Structure

Wirth's purposes in designing Pascal [Wirth, 1971] were to:

1. Allow the systematic and precise expression of programming concepts and structure

2. Allow systematic program development

3. Demonstrate that a language with a rich set of flexible data and program structuring facilites can be implemented efficiently

4. Demonstrate that the use of a machine-independent language with flexible data and program structures for compiler writing leads to an increase in the compiler's readability, verifiability, and consequently its reliability, without loss of efficiency

5. Help gain more insight into methods of organizing large programs and managing software projects

6. Have extensive error-checking facilities and thus be a good-vehicle for teaching programming

Thus Pascal was not envisioned as a production language, but as an experimental and teaching language. The DOD's selection of Pascal as the basis for Ada gives evidence to Wirth's attaining his goals.

A Pascal program is block structured, with nesting allowed to any depth, but in a special way. Its form is as shown in listing (2.3).

```
program name(list of file identifiers);                    (2.3)
    label declarations
    constant declarations
```

> **type** declarations
> **var**iable definitions
> **procedure** and **function** definitions
> program body enclosed by **begin**...**end.**

The list of procedure and function definitions may be long indeed, separating the main program's variable list from its body. One might need to look back at several pages of source code to find just what the range of IndexType is, or whether X is **real** or **integer** valued. Local blocks encapsulating a section of related code are not a part of Pascal. Each block must be either a procedure, function, the main program block, or a statement block, such as a **for** or **while** construction. This structure is simple, but encourages global variables or variables with unnecessarily large scope.

Strong data typing

Pascal insists (up to a point) on strongly typed data. Every variable, every constant, and every procedure or function must be declared before it is used. Strong typing helps avoid programming errors and also eases the compiler writer's job.

A useful definition of strong typing is due to Gehani [Feuer, 1982]:

1. Every object in the language belongs to exactly one type.
2. Type conversion occurs by converting a *value* from one type to another. Conversion does not occur by viewing the representation of a value as a different type.

Pascal's types adhere to this definition with two exceptions. Variant records may include free unions in the variant part, and procedures passed as parameters are not typed objects. We will look at variant records in the next section. An example of Pascal's procedure-passing facilities is shown in listing (2.4).

```
function RealFunctionSum (a, b : integer;                    (2.4)
                    function f (i : integer): real) : real;
var
    J : integer;
    Sum : real;
begin
    Sum := 0;
    for J := a to b do
        Sum := Sum + f(J);
    RealFunctionSum := Sum
end;
```

The parameters of the function f above are typed, but functions themselves are not types. If we wished to sum an integer-valued function, we would have to define a different function, IntegerFunctionSum, with parameter

```
function g(k : integer) : integer
```

Ada has broadened the notion of performing the same operations on objects of different types by providing *generic* procedures and functions.

There are practical situations where everything you need cannot be listed previously. One of these is in a linked list, where the "links" both point to and are part of records as shown in listing (2.5).

```
type                                        (2.5)

Link = ^ListNode;
ListNode =
    record
        Item : ItemType;
        Next : Link
    end;
```

This irregular feature with ListNode referenced before it is defined appears to be unavoidable. Ada cleans this up a bit, by writing the declaration shown in listing (2.6).

```
type ListNode;                  --Incomplete declaration    (2.6)
type Link is access ListNode;
type ListNode is
    record
        Item : ItemType;
        Next : Link;
    end record;
```

Requiring the incomplete declaration of ListNode allows the Ada rule that any data type mentioned must have been previously defined without exception. As long as we're looking at an Ada fragment, there are a few other things to notice as well. First, the keyword **is**, is just a nicety (syntactic sugar) for "=", which can be used interchangeably with **is** or **are**. The **end record**; is also optional, and a plain **end**; will suffice. However, the semicolons mark a change from Pascal, where they are used to *separate* statements. An Ada statement always ends with ";". One of the motivations for this change from the Pascal rule that semicolons be used to *separate* statements was the common Pascal programmer error of placing a ";" before an **else** in an **if...then...else** statement. We should be very clear here about the difference between separating and ending statements. For example, an **if...then...else** statement is defined as

```
if <expression>then <statement1> else <statement2>
```

No separation of statements is needed if both statement1 and statement2 are single statements because the **else** separates them. However, if we use semicolons to terminate statements, each of statement1 and statement2 will end with ";". The Ada designers also thought it closer to natural language, where statements represent sentences and should have some sort of punctuation.

By orthogonality, we meant the ability to combine independent language features freely. Obviously, Pascal functions are not orthogonal, since only scalar or pointer values may be returned. There are also limitations on parameters, with files always being passed by reference. What's more, the default parameter passing method is *by value* in Pascal, so **Procedure** P (f : FileType); will cause an error, while **Procedure** P (**var** f : FileType); will not.

Variable record structures

Records are the building blocks of data processing. We wish to make record definitions as descriptive as possible and group similar records into a single file. In the real world, similar records are not always structurally identical. Consider the size jump dictated by the American Kennel Club for dogs competing in the Open or Utility categories. Large dogs, such as Great Danes and Newfoundlands, are not expected to jump more than 36". Short-legged dogs, such as dachshunds or the Pekingese, must jump at least 8". For all other dogs, the jump is set at 1½ times their height from ground to withers (shoulder height). Obedience trials often involve a large number of dogs, and results must be announced promptly. It is desirable to define a single record type that will keep data on each dog, regardless of variations in the jump. If programming our dog show in Pascal, we could make use of the *variant record* for jumping. The Pascal form is shown in listing (2.7).

```
<record name> = record                                    (2.7)
   <fixed field list>
   case <variant-tag-selector> of
      <tag1> : <field list>;
         ...
      <tagn> : <field list>
end;
```

In Pascal the variant part comes last, but variants can be nested. Thus each variant could have a variant part, and so forth. Our record type declaration might be as shown in Figure 2.4.

Notice that there are nested variant records in both the Open and Utility classes, and that we repeated no field names. (JumpS, JumpM and JumpT are repeated, but in different type records.) To assign an open dog its jump size, we would make the assignments, Fido.Retrieve.JumpM := 22.

Notice also that we have made no assignment to Fido.Class or to Fido.Retrieve.Size, which is perfectly valid in Pascal. The compiler should be able to detect that the variants in use are Open and Medium because of the assignment to Retrieve.JumpM.

Regularity in a language means that there are no exceptions to rules. One irregular feature of Pascal is displayed above, where the **record** and the **case** statement are both terminated by the single **end**. One would expect (and in fact, one may use) two **ends**, one for each construct. A regular language is easier for programmers to remember and thus fosters efficient programming.

```pascal
type

Class = (Novice, Open, Utility);
Size  = (Short, Medium, Tall);
Dog = record
   AKCnumber, Breed  : packed array [1..8] of char;
   Height            : 0..50;
   TotalScore        : 0..200;
   case Class of
      Novice  :
         (Heel : record
                    OnLeashAndFigure8, Free    : 0..40
                 end;
          Stand, Recall, LongSitN, LongDownN   : 0..30);
      Open    :
         (HeelFreeAndFigure8                    : 0..40;
          DropOnRecall                          : 0..30;
          Retrieve : record
                        Flat                    : 0..20;
                        OverHighJump            : 0..30;
                        case Size of
                           Short :
                              (JumpS : 8..8);
                           Medium  :
                              (JumpM : 8..36);
                           Tall :
                              (JumpT : 36..36);
                     end;
          BroadJump                             : 0..20;
          LongSitO, LongDownO                   : 0..30;
         );
      Utility :
         (Signal                                : 0..40;
          Scent1, Scent2, DirectedRetrieve      : 0..30;
          GroupExamination                      : 0..30;
          Hurdle : record
                      OverHighJump              : 0..40;
                      case Size of
                         Short :
                            (JumpS : 8..8);
                         Medium  :
                            (JumpM : 8..36);
                         Tall :
                            (JumpT : 36..36);
                   end;
         )
   end;
```

Figure 2.4

Fido.Open

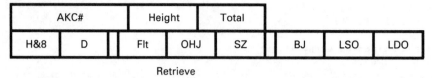

Retrieve

Fido.Utility

Hurdle

Figure 2.5

One of the criticisms of Pascal is that variant records are not necessarily strongly typed. For example, suppose we had a medium-sized dog, Fido, in the Open class. We would declare, Fido : Dog; and make the assignment, `Fido.ClassLevel := Open`. We would continue to make assignments to `Fido.HeelFreeAndFigure8`, `Fido.DropOnRecall`, `Fido.Retrieve.Flat`, etc. Now suppose Fido does well, and returns to the show ring competing in the Utility class. Fine! We're now dealing with `Fido.Hurdle.OverHighJump`, but where is it? Perhaps the two diagrams of the storage scheme shown in Figure 2.5 will help here.

Fido's jumping score was in the seventh field, OHJ, when he was an Open contender. In Utility, it is in the ninth field. If we try to access Fido.Hurdle.Over-HighJump before initializing it, an error will not be reported, but Fido's score from when he was a lowly Open class contender on the BroadJump will be returned. I suspect that your reaction is that such careless scorekeeping would never happen at AKC trials. Just attend one and watch all the dogs and handlers, both ruly and unruly.

This opening for undetected errors was, of course, closed in security-conscious Ada, where the tag fields (Level and Size) must *always* be specified and can be changed, e.g., from Open to Utility, only in combination with redefining every field.

EXERCISES

1. In the record structure of Figure 2.4, the variant structure for performance over hurdles was copied over for two classes, Open and Utility.

a. First, try to rewrite the record so that the information appears only once.

b. Can you think of a language design scheme that would let variant records share fields?

c. Dogs are asked to perform the various exercises in a specific order. In the Utility class, we were unable to reflect this order, where Group Examination comes last, because the variant part had to come last. Why do you think this design decision was made? ∎

2.4 ADA

Ada was designed at the behest of the United States Department of Defense (DOD) as a "common language for programming large scale and real-time systems" [ANSI-1815A, 1983]. It is a strongly typed algorithmic language with the usual control structures for iteration, recursion, branching, procedures, and functions. It also provides for modularity, where data types and procedures can be packaged and compiled separately. To facilitate real-time programming, Ada provides for modeling parallel tasks and handling exceptions without stopping program execution.

The DOD was concerned about program portability and supported the definition of a standard language definition [ANSI-1815A, 1983]. DOD held the registered trademark, Ada, and no compiler could be distributed under this name without valid conformance to the standard. It was written with "three overriding concerns: program reliability and maintenance, programming as a human activity and efficiency" [ANSI-1815A, 1983].

HISTORICAL VIGNETTE 3: Ada

In the mid-1970s the DOD, which is not known for its budgetary restraint, was spending approximately three billion dollars a year on software. We're all used to seeing such huge figures attached to the military, but in this case the cost was a bit too steep. Something had to be done to lower the software price tag. A large part of the problem was the fact that more than 450 different programming languages or incompatible dialects of the same language were being used by the military. This created problems of limited portability from machine to machine, limited reusability of procedures in subsequent programs and general confusion. The time had come to find a standard language in which *all* programs for the department would be written. Since about 56percent of the software purchased was used for embedded or mission-critical computer applications, it was decided that this standard language should be geared toward those applications. "Much of the computer programming done by the U.S. military is used for controlling military hardware—tanks, airplanes, nuclear bombs. To control such hardware, a computer program must operate in 'real-time,' that is, while the tank is rolling or the plane is flying. A navy fighter pilot can't wait for results to be returned from the computer center the next day" [Baron, 1986, p. 91]. Embedded real-time systems are embedded within a larger mechanical system, such as a robot or a pilotless plane.

In 1975, the DOD set up the Higher-Order Language Working Group (HOLWG) to find a standard language for embedded computer applications. HOLWG's first step was to develop a set of requirements for this language with input from the Army, Navy, Air Force, universities, and industry. From 1975 to 1979, as the set of requirements evolved and grew, the name given to the set changed from Strawman (1975), to Woodenman (1975), to Tinman (1976), to Ironman (1978), to Steelman (1979). This final Steelman set contains close to one hundred requirements. These requirements constrained the language "to have language constructs with specified characteristics in areas such as data types, control structures, modules, tasks, and exceptions. Certain global requirements on 'readability,' 'no excessive generality,' 'simplicity,' and 'verifiability' were also included" [Wegner, 1980, pp. vii–viii].

The next step taken by HOLWG was to study existing languages to see if any met the set of requirements. After an intensive study of the 26 existing candidate languages, it was decided that none filled all the requirements, and that a new state-of-the-art language would have to be developed. HOLWG recommended that one of ALGOL 68, Pascal, or PL/I should be used as a foundation for the design.

An international language design competition was held. Seventeen groups sent proposals, but only four were chosen for further development. These were funded for six months to produce a preliminary language design. Each group was given the name of a color to preserve anonymity and ensure fair evaluations. These groups were CII Honeywell Bull—Green, Intermetrics—Red, Softech—Blue, and SRI International—Yellow. It is very interesting that each of these goups chose Pascal as a base for their language design. At the end of six months, the Red and Green groups were chosen as finalists and given an additional year for development.

In 1979, the Green team was chosen winner. This team, led by Jean Ichbiah, renamed the Green Language, Ada. The name honors Augusta Ada Byron, the Countess of Lovelace and daughter of the English poet, Lord Byron. "She was the assistant, associate, and supporter of Charles Babbage, the mathematician and inventor of a calculating machine called the Analytical Engine. With the help of Babbage, she wrote a nearly complete program to compute the Bernoulli numbers, *circa* 1830. Because of this effort the Countess may be said to have been the world's first computer programmer" [Gehani, 1983, p. xi].

Jean Ichbiah's team completed the design of Ada in September of 1980, only after considering 7,000-plus comments and suggestions from language design experts in more than 15 nations. In January 1983, Ada became a military and American National Standard. Beginning in 1984, all embedded military software had to be programmed in Ada.

Even though a standard language had been developed, the problem of too many languages was not solved. The DOD realized that if subsets and supersets of Ada developed and were allowed to retain the Ada name, the portability problem would return. To ensure that this would not happen, the DOD took "the unprecedented action of registering the name 'Ada' as a trademark. This provides the ability to control the use of this name and to guarantee that anything called 'Ada' is the standard language. That is, subsets and supersets of Ada cannot legally be called 'Ada'" [MacLennan, 1987, p. 264]. In addition to this trademark, the DOD set up the Ada Compiler Validation project to develop a set of standard tests to determine if a compiler does in fact implement the standard language. This process includes more than 2500 tests. DOD has since dropped its trademark, although both defense and NATO contracts specify the use of validated Ada compilers.

Although designed for embedded processes, Ada is not restricted to these applications. Ichbiah sees a potential use for Ada in both business and education. "Several American universities are even experimenting with teaching Ada as a beginning programming language because of its high degree of structuring and its potential for revealing progressively more details of the language as students become increasingly proficient. Since Ada derives from Pascal, this move toward making Ada a general-purpose language is hardly surprising" [Baron, 1986, p. 10].

Ada has its problems and its critics. Although it is based on the small language Pascal, Ada is huge. It is more than three times the size of Pascal. This size has been cited as Ada's biggest flaw. A real-time language should be close to 100 percent reliable. Can a complex language like Ada meet this criterion? Tony Hoare, one of Ada's critics, states passionately, "Do not allow this language in its present style to be used in applications where reliability is critical, i.e., nuclear power stations, cruise missiles, early warning systems, antiballistic missile defense systems. The next rocket to go astray as a result of a programming language error may not be an exploratory space rocket on a harmless trip to Venus: it may be a nuclear warhead exploding over one of our own cities. An unreliable programming language constitutes a far greater risk to our environment and to our society than unsafe cars, toxic pesticides, or accidents at nuclear power stations" [Baron, 1986, p. 102].

Ada's acceptance will depend mainly on the decisions made by the DOD. Ada is presently used only for embedded programming applications. It is a young language, so it is too early to predict its impact. "It typically takes about 5–10 years for a language to become established, although the backing of the Department of Defense will speed the acceptance of Ada. Whether it will be Ada as now defined or some subset, it is almost inevitable that Ada will be an important milestone in programming languages" [MacLennan, 1987, p. 328].

Program Organization

An Ada program is composed of one or more *program units* that can be compiled separately. A unit may be a subprogram, a package, a task, or a generic unit. Each unit ordinarily has a *specification* and a *body*. The specification is public information needed to execute the unit, while the body may be hidden from the user and contains executable statements.

A subprogram may be either a **procedure** or a **function**. A program needs a main procedure to run, which will call other program units. For example, suppose we wished to print out the date, using a main procedure called Print_Date, as shown in listing (2.8).

```
with CALENDAR, INTEGER_IO, TEXT_IO;                          (2.8)
procedure PRINT_DATE is
   use CALENDAR, INTEGER_IO, TEXT_IO;
begin
   TEXT_IO.PUT("The date is: ");
   INTEGER_IO.PUT(MONTH(CLOCK)); TEXT_IO.PUT("/");
   INTEGER_IO.PUT(DAY); TEXT_IO.PUT("/");
   INTEGER_IO.PUT(YEAR);
end;
```

Three predefined packages are used with this procedure unit: CALENDAR, INTEGER_IO, and TEXT_IO. Part of the *specification* for CALENDAR is shown in listing (2.9).

```
package CALENDAR is                                          (2.9)
   type TIME is private;

   subtype YEAR_NUMBER  is INTEGER  range 1901 .. 2099;
   subtype MONTH_NUMBER is INTEGER  range 1 ..12;
   subtype DAY_NUMBER   is INTEGER  range 1 ..31;
   subtype DAY_DURATION is DURATION range 0.0 .. 86_400.0;

function CLOCK return TIME;

function YEAR    (DATE : TIME) return YEAR_NUMBER;
function MONTH   (DATE : TIME) return MONTH_NUMBER;
function DAY     (DATE : TIME) return DAY_NUMBER;
function SECONDS (DATE : TIME) return DAY_DURATION;
function TIME_OF (YEAR       : YEAR_NUMBER;
                  MONTH      : MONTH_NUMBER;
                  DAY        : DAY_NUMBER;
                  SECONDS    : DAY_DURATION) return TIME;

TIME_ERROR : exception;  --can be raised by TIME_OF;

private
   -- implementation dependent specification of the type for TIME
end;
```

This specification would be followed by an implementation-dependent package body defining each function in the specification. Notice that a group of related types and functions are packaged together in CALENDAR. Since TIME is a private type, it can be accessed only through the functions CLOCK, YEAR, MONTH, DAY, SECONDS, and TIME_OF. It is through private types that Ada supports abstract data types. The limited private type is even more restrictive

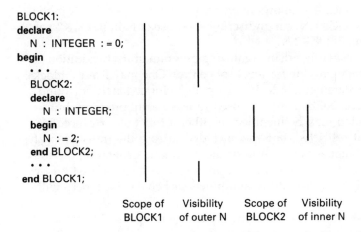

```
BLOCK1:
declare
   N : INTEGER : = 0;
begin
   • • •
   BLOCK2:
   declare
      N : INTEGER;
   begin
      N : = 2;
   end BLOCK2;
   • • •
end BLOCK1;
```

Scope of   Visibility   Scope of   Visibility
BLOCK1   of outer N   BLOCK2   of inner N

Figure 2.6

than the private type. Values may be assigned to private types, and variables may be tested for equality and inequality. If a variable is declared to be limited private, even these operations must be explicitly defined, as shown in listing (2.10).

```
package body CALENDAR is                              (2.10)

function CLOCK return TIME is
begin .. end;

function YEAR (DATE : TIME) return YEAR_NUMBER is
begin .. end;
...
end CALENDAR;
```

We leave the discussion of tasks until Chapter 4, where we will combine a consideration of distributed and concurrent programming paradigms.

Ada is block structured, with blocks being statements formed by

```
declare
   --type and variable declarations here
begin
   --statements go here
end;
```

As in ALGOL, blocks can be nested to any level. Thus variables declared in an outer block can be made invisible in an inner block if redeclared, as shown in Figure 2.6.

There is a difference between scope and visibility. A variable exists throughout its scope, but may not be accessible, i.e., visible. Although the outer N is invisible in BLOCK2, it does not cease to exist. Thus BLOCK2 is within the scope of the outer N. In fact, Ada allows reference to the invisible outer N in the inner block by using BLOCK1.N. An undiscriminated use of N in BLOCK2 has the same result as using BLOCK2.N.

Blocks serve purposes other than organizing program units. In addition to controlling visibility, they provide for levels of control. One may leave a block or a loop using a **goto** statement, or leave a loop to the immediately surrounding block using an **exit**. Neither may be used to leave a subprogram, but as many **return**s as wanted may be included in either a function or procedure. The **goto** is somewhat restricted, but was included to ease the translation of programs from other languages into Ada or the automatic generation of Ada programs. **goto**'s are very noticeable in Ada programs, as labels are set off by brackets, e.g., <<LABELX>>. Procedures and functions behave like blocks with their own scopes.

Packages and tasks interact differently. A package is a passive unit that is realized (called *elaborated* in Ada) in the scope where it is declared. Tasks depend on the block or subprogram in which they execute and must all be completed before the unit on which they depend is executed.

Types

Ada has both scalar and structured types as shown in Figure 2.7. Among the reals, there are two types: Floating, which can specify relative precision, and Fixed for situations requiring absolute precision. Relative accuracy is defined in terms of significant digits, i.e., 3.46 has the same relative accuracy as 0.000346 or 3,460,000,000,000, three significant digits. Declarations for floating type reals are:

```
type Area_Measure is digits 7;
type Person_Height is digits 4 range 0.5 .. 10.0;
```

Fixed reals are declared using the reserved word **delta**, which indicates the allowed range of error.

```
type Money is delta 0.005 range -1000.0 .. 10_000.0;
```

Computation with fixed reals is slower than with floating types, but necessary in some situations.

All of Ada's types are not built directly into the language. Types BOOLEAN, INTEGER, FLOAT, CHARACTER, NATURAL, POSITIVE, and STRING are defined along with operations on them in a package specification called STANDARD, which is implementation dependent but required as part of any Ada compiler. STANDARD is always available throughout the scope of any program.

Ada also has three anonymous types: *universal-integer*, *universal-float*, and *universal-fixed*. Literals and constants are of universal type, such as PI : **constant** := 3.141_592_65. If N is of float type, **digits** 7, then the assignment, N := 2 + PI; will convert both the literal, 2, and the constant PI from universal

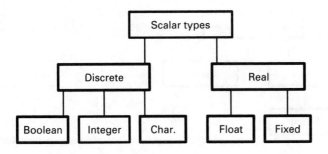

Figure 2.7

types to **digits** 7, and N = 5.141593 (notice that the result is rounded, rather than truncated). Automatic conversions are not allowed in Ada, thus the expression 3.6 + 5 would have to be written either 3.0 + FLOAT(5) or INTE-GER(3.6) + 5. In the first case, the result would be 8.6, and in the second, 9. However, universal-integers and universal-reals may be combined for the operations '*' and '/', with a result of universal-real. The result of either '*' or '/' operating on two fixed-types returns a universal-fixed value, with implementation-dependent accuracy, **delta**.

Ada includes several useful operators, called *attributes*, for scalars. If P is of type Person_Height, as declared previously, attribute P'First is 0.5, P'Last is 10.0, and P'Digits is 4. No set type is provided in Ada (see Figure 2.8), but built-in operators on arrays make the implementation easy, as shown in listing (2.11).

```
type SET        is array (POSITIVE range <>) of BOOLEAN;       (2.11)
subtype COLOR   is SET (1..3);
RED             : constant COLOR := (T,F,F);
YELLOW          : constant COLOR := (F,T,F);
BLUE            : constant COLOR := (F,F,T);
ORANGE          : constant COLOR := (T,T,F);
PURPLE          : constant COLOR := (T,F,T);
GREEN           : constant COLOR := (F,T,T);
WHITE           : constant COLOR := (F,F,F);
BLACK           : constant COLOR := (T,T,T);

C               : COLOR;
```

If we assign C := RED **and** YELLOW; the resulting color is C = WHITE. If we assign C := RED **or** YELLOW, we get C = ORANGE., **not** GREEN = RED, and ORANGE **xor** YELLOW = YELLOW, while ORANGE **xor** BLUE = WHITE. **or** represents set union; **and**, set intersection; and **xor**, set symmetric difference, the elements in one, but not both sets.

STRING is a predefined **array** type

```
array (POSITIVE range <>) of CHARACTER;
```

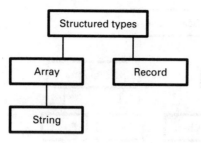

Figure 2.8

STRING may be used only for constants and determines the length of a constant string on assignment. Both STRING and POSITIVE are types defined in the package STANDARD. In addition to the required package STANDARD, a valid Ada implementation must also provide Library units, CALENDAR, IO_EXCEPTIONS, DIRECT_IO, LOW_LEVEL_IO, SEQUENTIAL_IO, SYSTEM, TEXT_IO, UNCHECKED_ CONVERSION and UNCHECKED_DEALLOCATION.

Ada's records are much like Pascal records, with a few bells and whistles added. As in Pascal, a record may have only one variant part, which must be the last component, as shown in listing (2.12).

```
type DEVICE is (PRINTER, DISK, DRUM);                    (2.12)
type STATE  is (OPEN, CLOSED);

type PERIPHERAL (UNIT : DEVICE := DISK) is  --DISK is the default
   record
     STATUS : STATE;
     case UNIT is                          --variant component
       when PRINTER =>
         LINE_COUNT : INTEGER range 1 .. PAGE_SIZE;
       when others =>
         CYLINDER  : CYLINDER_INDEX;
         TRACK     : TRACK_NUMBER;
     end case;
   end record;
```

PERIPHERAL is a *discriminated record*, with three possible subtypes depending on the discriminant UNIT, PERIPHERAL(PRINTER), PERIPHERAL(DISK) or PERIPHERAL(DRUM). All subtypes have the component STATUS in common. DISK and DRUM also have CYLINDER and TRACK in common, while PRINTER has a LINE_COUNT component. If a variable is declared to be of type PERIPHERAL, with no discriminant, DISK is the default UNIT value.

Ada arrays and records can also be assigned as *aggregates*. Our SET subtype could be given initial values using SET'(F,F,F) or SET'(1 .. 3 => F). PERIPHERAL could have three aggregates: PERIPHERAL'(PRINTER,0), PERIPHERAL'(DISK, 1, 0) and PERIPHERAL'(DRUM, 0, 0), as shown in listing (2.13).

Figure 2.9

```
A 3 X 3 dimensional array, could be declared:              (2.13)
A : array (0..2,0..2) of REAL := ((0.0,0.0,0.0),
                                  (0.0,0.0,0.0),
                                  (0.0,0.0,0.0));
or

A : array (0..2,0..2) of REAL := (0..2 => (0.0,0.0,0.0));

or
A : array (0..2,0..2) of REAL := (0..2 =>
                                    (0..2 => 0.0));
```

Slices of one-dimensional arrays can also be assigned, as in:

```
B : array (0..2) of INTEGER := (3, 4, 5);
C := B(1..2);
```

Here B′ FIRST = 0, while C′ FIRST = 1. But B′ LAST = C′ LAST = 2, where FIRST and LAST are array attributes. To avoid errors, Ada programs usually iterate over arrays from FIRST to LAST, rather than from 1 to N, as shown in Figure 2.9.

In addition to scalar and structured types, Ada provides an **access** type for storage location addresses. As with Pascal's pointer type, an access type must access storage for a distinct type, as shown in listing (2.14).

```
type NODE;                                                 (2.14)
type LIST is access NODE;
type NODE is
  record
    ITEM : STRING
    NEXT : LIST;
  end record;

GROCERY_LIST, JOBS_LIST, NAME_LIST, TEMP : LIST;
```

GROCERY_LIST, JOBS_LIST, and NAME_LIST will all have the initial value **null**. This is the *only* situation where Ada assigns initial values to variables without an explicit programmed assignment. Access types provide for dynamic allocation using the function **new**. Thus GROCERY_LIST := **new** LIST′ ("eggs"); will allocate a new storage location accessed by GROCERY_LIST, with GRO-CERY_LIST.ITEM = "eggs". We could have written GROCERY_LIST := **new** LIST′ ("eggs", **null**); with the same effect. Do you see why?

Consider the sequence of Ada statements shown in listing (2.15).

```
declare PRIOR, TEMP : LIST;                                   (2.15)
        GROCERY      : STRING(1..LENGTH);
        L            : LENGTH;
begin
  GROCERY_LIST := new LIST'("eggs");
  PRIOR := GROCERY_LIST;
  GET_LINE (GROCERY, L);            --L counts the length of GROCERY
  while (GROCERY /= "That's all") loop        --Make Grocery list
    TEMP := new LIST'(GROCERY);
    PRIOR.NEXT := TEMP;
    PRIOR := TEMP;
    GET_LINE (GROCERY, L);
  end loop;

  TEMP := GROCERY_LIST.NEXT;
  while TEMP /= null
        and then STORE_HAS(TEMP.ITEM) loop --Empty list
    BUY (TEMP.ITEM);
    PRIOR := TEMP;
    TEMP := TEMP.NEXT;
    PRIOR := null;
  end loop;
```

Ada does not include a deallocator such as Pascal's **dispose** function. Thus dangling pointers, i.e., access variables with no node to access, are eliminated. In listing (2.15), the nodes for the entire original grocery list are still allocated, even though after we BUY an item, access to it is set to **null**. Although not required, many Ada compilers include a *garbage collector* that periodically returns storage to which there is no access to the available storage pool. *But* (and this is a big *but*) one can turn off deallocation checking and manage storage oneself. The programmer who does this has no Ada guarantees and is thus on his or her own.

Interesting additions to Ada are the **and then** and **or else** operators, called *short-circuit logical operators*. In the example in listing (2.15), if TEMP /= **null** evaluates to FALSE, STORE_HAS (TEMP.ITEM); will never be evaluated, since the "and" expression is already known to be false. If we had used the **and** operator instead of **and then**, both would have been evaluated, no matter what the value of the left-hand expression.

The Generic Facility

The thesaurus included with a popular word processor lists *common*, *general*, and *universal* as synonyms for *generic*. We have already seen the flavor of Ada's generic facilities in the use of "<>", called *box*, for array bounds. We defined SET as a general array type, with indices to be determined as the need arose. STRING is also a predefined generic array type:

```
subtype POSITIVE is INTEGER range 1 .. INTEGER'LAST;
type STRING is array(POSITIVE range <>) of CHARACTER;
```

In Ada, when we use the reserved word, **generic**, we mean that the **type**, procedure or package, rather than the **range**, is yet to be determined. We could have specified SETS generically, as shown in listing (2.16).[8]

```
generic                                                      (2.16)
   type BASE is (<>);
package SETS is
   type SET is array (BASE) of BOOLEAN;
   type ELEMENTS is array (NATURAL range <>) of BASE;
   function CREATE_SET (A : ELEMENTS) return SET;
   function "*" (A, B : SET) return SET;   --intersection
   function "+" (A, B : SET) return SET;   --union
end SETS;

package body SETS is
   --define all the functions here
end SETS;
```

Ada is a strongly typed language, so a generic unit is not compiled when first encountered, but when instantiated. For our example above, we might instantiate COLOR as shown in listing (2.17).

```
type PRIMARY is (R, W, B);                                   (2.17)
package COLOR is new SETS (BASE => PRIMARY);
E : ELEMENTS;
C, RED, YELLOW, BLUE, ORANGE, PURPLE, GREEN, WHITE, BLACK : SET;
```

It is this reserved word **new** that triggers the compilation of the generic unit with the type PRIMARY filling in for <>. We could then assign E:= (R); RED := MAKE_SET (E); WHITE := MAKE_SET (()); and BLACK := MAKE_SET ((R, W, B));

The generic facility allows for the reuse of software and restricting visibility of program parts when combined with [**limited**] **private** declarations.

Exceptions

An *exception* is an unexpected event in program execution that would ordinarily cause an error. An *exception handler* is a program unit that is invoked only if the exception occurs. If you are familiar with PL/I, you have already seen exceptions handled by **ON** conditions. For example:

```
ON ENDFILE(SYSIN)
   MORE_DATA = NO;
```

The exception is ENDFILE(SYSIN), and MORE_DATA = NO; tells us what to do about it. Six PL/I **ON** conditions relate to I/O, and six more are for arithmetic operations, such as OVERFLOW and ZERODIVIDE.

Ada has five predefined exceptions:

---

8 A fuller version of a generic set definition can be found in [Barnes, 1982, p. 196].

```
CONSTRAINT_ERROR
NUMERIC_ERROR
PROGRAM_ERROR
STORAGE_ERROR
TASKING_ERROR
```

The first exception occurs if constraints are violated, such as exceeding array bounds or using the wrong variant component of a variant record. Numeric errors are such things as attempting to divide by zero or the inability of the system to deliver a sufficiently accurate value for a fixed type. Program errors occur when trying to call subprograms that have not been elaborated, and storage errors occur when memory is exhausted. Tasks may be executing concurrently. The most common error here occurs when two or more tasks attempt unsuccessfully to communicate. We'll reveal more of this in Chapter 4.

The designers of Ada extended the exception utility in two ways. First, one can define, raise, and handle one's own exceptions. Second, exceptions may be propagated up through the dynamic chain of execution until a handler is found, as shown in listing (2.18).

```
BLOCK1:                                                        (2.18)
declare
   M : INTEGER;
   function F return INTEGER is
   E : exception;
   N : INTEGER;
 begin
   ...
   raise E;                      --exception occurs here
   ...
   return N;
 end F;
begin                            --BLOCK1
   M := F;                       --call F
   ...                           --continue
   exception                     --exception handler here
     when E =>
       begin
       PUT("Trouble with E!");
       return 0;
     end exception;
end BLOCK1;
```

BLOCK1 begins executing by calling the function F, where an exception E is raised. F is terminated, and control returns to BLOCK1. Exceptions may be raised by the program itself as well as occur automatically. Notice that the handler includes a **return** statement so that M will have a value, and execution can continue at the code marked "continue." Of course, the handler could have been included at the end of the function F itself, where it would always be handled in the same way. In this example, it is handled as specified by BLOCK1, since F

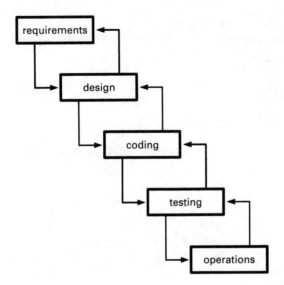

Figure 2.10

was called from BLOCK1. If called from a different environment, handling might have been different.

The Ada Programming Support Environment (APSE)

In addition to the successive language requirements documents Strawman, Woodenman, Tinman, Ironman, and Steelman, the DOD published Stoneman in 1980, which specified requirements for a programming support environment. It was the purpose of the APSE to "support the development and maintenance of Ada applications software throughout its life cycle, with particular emphasis on software for embedded computer applications" [Booch, 1986].

The most common model for this cycle is the *Waterfall Model*, first presented by [Royce, 1987] and shown in Figure 2.10. Each phase may involve different personnel, programming and debugging tools, machinery, etc. It was the desire of the DOD to standardize all these activities as much as possible to reduce costs and improve portability of both programs and programmers.

Figure 2.11 illustrates the various parts of the APSE. The innermost ring, past the host operating system, is the KAPSE, or kernel APSE. KAPSE interfaces with the host machine and will differ from machine to machine. Theoretically, a new KAPSE will be all that is needed to transport software to a different machine. The MAPSE is the minimum APSE, which provides common tools, including an editor, compiler, linker, peripheral interfaces, and various tools for run-time analysis. Any Ada system must provide these tools. The full APSE is

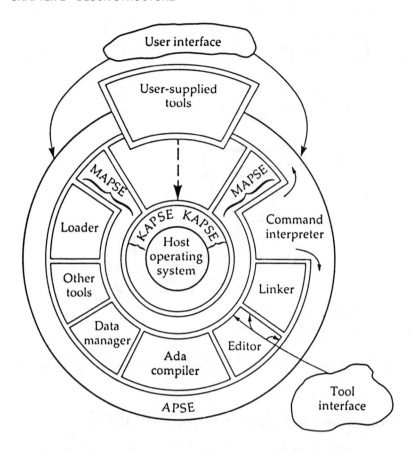

Figure 2.11 Reproduced with permission from Wolf, M. I., Babich, W., Simpson, R., Tholl, R., and Weissman, L. (1981). The Ada language system. *Computer* 14(6). © IEEE.

not defined precisely, but will include tools for managing databases, interfacing with graphics displays, and maintaining software, among others.

EXERCISES

1. The requirements for the STANDARD package suggest that additional real types be provided, such as SHORT_FLOAT and LONG_FLOAT. Many implementers also provide a type REAL. If you were writing an Ada compiler, what would you suggest for type REAL? Why?

2. Why does the result of multiplication or division of two fixed-reals result in a universal-fixed value, rather than a value of the same type as one of the operands?

3. Ada allows overloading of operators for various types. We could define set intersection using *"*"* as follows.

```
function "*" (A,B : COLOR) return COLOR is
begin
    return A and B;
end "*";
```

How could you define a set difference operator in Ada using **not, and, or,** and **xor**? (e.g., {1, 2, 3} − {2} = {1, 3}).

4. Describe the differences between and rationale for the three different ways of interrupting sequential execution: **exit, goto,** and **return**. How do these processes differ from an **exception**?

5. Suppose we wanted to redefine sets as linked lists, rather than as arrays. Why would we be better served having chosen a **limited private** type for a set, rather than a **private** type?

6. Following the declarations of listing (2.15), we created the first node of GROCERY_LIST, with the statement GROCERY_LIST := new LIST' ("eggs");. If NODE had been declared:

```
type NODE is
  record
    ITEM : STRING(1..4);
    NEXT : LIST;
  end record;
```

we could have assigned GROCERY_LIST := new LIST;, followed by GROCERY_LIST.ITEM := "eggs";. Why would this method of assignment have been invalid with ITEM declared STRING?

7. Can you think of an example where the short-circuit form **or else** works better than the usual **or,** where both expressions are always evaluated? When using A **or else** B, B is not evaluated if A evaluates to TRUE.

8. Consider the following recursive program, where an exception is raised [ANSI-1815A, 1983]:

```
function FACTORIAL(N : POSITIVE) return FLOAT is
begin
  if N = 0 then return 1.0;
    else return FLOAT(N) * FACTORIAL(N-1);
  end if;
  exception
    when NUMERIC_ERROR => return FLOAT'SAFE_LARGE;
end FACTORIAL;
```

If the call is FACTORIAL(100), and FLOAT'SAFE_LARGE = 2^{31} = 2 147 483 648.0, how many times will NUMERIC_ERROR be raised? What value will finally be returned?

9. A portable program is one that can run on various machines. What is meant by a portable programmer? ■

LAB III: Blocks: Ada/Pascal

OBJECTIVES

1. To explore the different blocks available, not including modules or packages (named, unnamed, block statements, procedures, functions, and system supplied).

2. To try out different schemes of local/global variables in nested blocks.

3. To trace a simple recursive procedure or function that employs both local and global variables.

4. To observe and handle exceptions occurring in an inner block, but propagated to the outer block if possible. (In Pascal, this will be an implementation-dependent interrupt handler.) ■

2.5 C

C has a different lineage from other ALGOL-like languages, as shown in Figure 2.12. We have discussed briefly the Pascal-Modula-Ada branch, and will consider the Simula-Smalltalk-C++ branch in Chapter 3. Here we will look at the ALGOL 60-CPL-BCPL-C branch.

Combined Programming Language (CPL) was devised in the decade following the ALGOL 60 report to provide a language closer to computing hardware. It was intended to be a means for solving *all* types of problems: numeric, nonnumeric, and systems. In contrast to the Pascal principles intended to encourage reliable structured programs, CPL was intended to allow as wide a range of applications as possible. Its successor, C, was kept small and flexible so

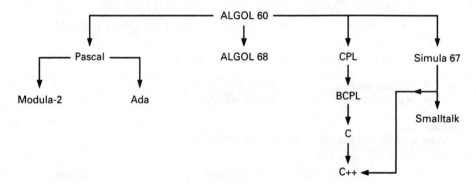

Figure 2.12[9]

9 Figure 2.12 indicates the major influences of ALGOL on subsequent languages. There are many variations on this diagram, e.g., see [Sammet, 1969], [Baron, 1986], or [Sethi, 1988].

that it could run on a variety of machines, with unimplemented features such as I/O and string processing developed easily onsite. While ALGOL-like languages are strongly typed, C comes from the typeless language CPL, where the store is viewed as bit strings, rather than as integers, reals, characters, etc.

HISTORICAL VIGNETTE 4:
The Dynamic Duo: Dennis Ritchie and Kenneth Thompson

C has become one of the most popular programming languages around town. It is famous for its amazing duality. It is both a high-level programming language and a low-level one. It is also both special and general purpose. Unlike some before him, such as the creators of ALGOL, Dennis Ritchie did not set out to develop a popular programming language. He wanted to design a better operating system.

Back in the 1960s, Ritchie was a Harvard physics major. After completing his undergraduate work, he specialized in the study of mathematics, like most computer science pioneers. In 1968, he went to work for Bell Labs and was teamed up with Ken Thompson. Thompson, who had grown up with ham radios and chess, received his undergraduate and graduate degrees in electrical engineering from the University of California at Berkeley. The two were given a compelling task: to think about interesting problems in computer science. The duo began to think about OS (operating systems).

At that time, scientists at Bell were experimenting with an operating system called multiplexed information and computing service (Multics). This multiuser, time-share system became the instant friend of programmers who were used to doing things the hard way. Instead of giving a stack of cards to an operator and waiting an hour or more for a printout of results, Multics allowed users to type commands at a keyboard and get an instant response. There was, however, one big problem. Multics was very expensive to run, everyone was using it, and that cost money. Bell Labs, to the dismay of many, decided to abandon Multics. But Ritchie and Thompson couldn't get used to doing things the old way again. They decided to design a system just for themselves and their fellow programmers at the lab. This operating system would soon be known to the world as UNIX®, a take-off on the Multics name.

Thompson, excited about the new project, turned in a proposal to his superiors. After the Multics financial disaster, they were wary of OS projects, and he was turned down. Refusing to be discouraged, he found a discarded, obsolete DEC PDP-7 and began work with Dennis Ritchie. The work was not easy, but the two soon had a complete OS on their hands. They knew it was unlikely that their work would be usable by others "as long as it ran only on an antiquated computer of which only a few existed [Slater, 1987, p. 279]. To get his hands on an up-to-date computer, Thompson sent in a proposal to develop an editing system for office tasks. It was approved, and Ritchie and Thompson had a PDP-11 to work with. In 1971, UNIX was completed, and its use inside Bell Labs began to grow, starting with the patent department. Problems developed, however. UNIX had been written in assembly language, which meant that it was not portable to machines other than the PDP-11.

In the 1960s, there were two types of languages. Low-level assembly languages allowed a programmer to control a particular computer, since he or she could manipulate individual bits of the store. High-level languages were easier to use and implemented on a variety of hardware. A programmer need not worry about messy low-level details and could concentrate on good algorithm design. A joint committee from the University of London Computer Unit and the University Mathematical Laboratory at Cambridge decided to design a language that was both high and low level. It would be high enough so that it wouldn't be tied to a particular computer, but low enough to allow the manipulation of specific bits. The resulting language was called Combined Programming Language (CPL). It was never popular, since it was a very large and difficult language, but a pared-down version, BASIC CPL (BCPL) attracts some users.

Back at Bell Labs, Thompson created an even smaller version of BCPL, called B (perhaps symbolizing that he only needed part of BCPL). Ritchie later transformed B into C by restoring some of the CPL features, such as rich data typing. UNIX was then rewritten in C. The resulting portability made UNIX a computer industry standard in the mid-1980s. Ritchie refuses to solve the mystery of C's name. He leaves it for us to decide "whether he was following Thompson in pulling out the next letter in the name BCPL or taking C as the next letter in the alphabet following B" [Baron, 1986, p. 159].

C, like its ancestor CPL, is both low and high level. It is a special-purpose language designed for systems programming, i.e., UNIX, and general purpose as well. Ritchie states that "C is a general-purpose programming language...Although it has been called a 'systems programming language' because it is useful for writing operating systems. It has been used equally well to write major numerical, text-processing, and database programs" [Kernighan, 1978, p. 1].

C is known as a programmer's language and was written by a programmer for programmers. This is apparent when you look at some of C's characteristics, which are short instead of pretty. For example, instead of "begin...end," brackets, {...}, are used. This makes for faster programming, but it also makes less readable code. Another example of C's orientation toward experienced programmers is its permissive data typing. If you make mistakes, you won't get neat error messages. You'll probably have to hunt down your own errors—no small challenge. Recent versions, however, do include a "lint" program that does error checking.

Ritchie and Thompson have collaborated on several editions of the ever-evolving UNIX. C also has undergone changes. Considering their past successes, the two are given almost unlimited freedom at Bell Labs. One can't help but wonder what they'll come up with next.

Basic CPL (BCPL)

CPL is typed and has four basic types: integer, real, complex, and index. It also has a Boolean type and a logical bit-string type. Structured types are limited to arrays and character strings, and there are no pointer types. ALGOL's two parameter-passing mechanisms, by name and by value, are extended to include by reference as well, where only the address of a variable is passed. CPL also provides an enlarged set of control structures. For example, the while loop has four variants:

```
while a do B            {evaluate a before executing B}
until a do B            {execute B at least once}
B repeat while a        {execute B, 0 or more times}
B repeat until a        {execute B 1 or more times}.
```

CPL is strongly typed, requiring explicit typing of parameters as well as functional results.

BCPL, designed by Martin Richards in 1967, is lower level than CPL, having only one type, the bit string. Working directly on bit patterns has the following effects [Richards, 1979, p. 3]:

1. There is no need for type declarations in the language, since the internal type of every variable is already known. This helps to make programs concise and also simplifies problems such as the handling of actual/formal parameter correspondence and separate compilation.

2. It gives the language nearly the same power as one with dynamically varying types, and yet retains the efficiency of a language (like FORTRAN) with manifest types. Although the internal type of an expression is always known by the compiler, its conceptual type can never be. It may, for instance, depend on the values of variables within the expression, such as the value of an index to an element of a vector, since such elements are not necessarily of the same conceptual type. It should be noted that in languages (such as ALGOL) where the elements of arrays must all have the same type, one needs some other linguistic device in order to handle dynamically varying data structures.

3. Since there is only one internal type in the language, there can be no automatic type checking, and it is possible to write nonsensical programs which the compiler will translate without complaint. This disadvantage has to be weighed against the simplicity, power, and efficiency that this treatment of types makes possible.

One of the design goals of BCPL was portability, or independence from any particular machine. Only four guidelines are given to BCPL programmers to ensure portability [Richards, 1979, p. 59].

1. Put all machine-dependent material in one module.

2. Avoid code that makes use of a particular representation for numbers or strings, e.g., a right shift may or may not divide by two on a particular machine.

3. The maximum size of integers or strings may differ. Provide careful documentation.

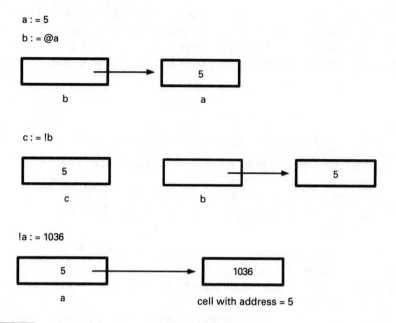

Figure 2.13

4. Avoid making assumptions about character sets and string size, as these may depend on word size. In particular, be sure a program will work when all lower-case characters are converted to upper-case.

One useful notion made operationally explicit in BCPL is that of left and right values. When we make an assignment, b := a, a and b are treated differently. A value is computed for a, and then an address is located for b. Finally, the value of a is copied into the storage location for b. The address of b (or any other identifier, for that matter) is called a left value, while the content of its memory cell is its right value. An expression such as 2x + 5 can have a right value, but not a left value. BCPL has two operators: @, which yields an l-value, and !, which produces an r-value.

Consider the assignments shown in Figure 2.13. This last assignment might seem a bit odd. !a selects the right value associated with a, but a is on the left, so this value is an address. The value 1036 is stored in a cell with address stored at the location associated with a.

As mentioned, BCPL has only one data type, a word of bits. One-dimensional arrays, or vectors, can be declared, however, using

```
LET v = VEC n
```

which reserves n + 1 words of consecutive memory for v. v itself is a pointer, as shown in Figure 2.14.

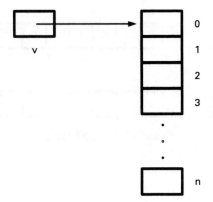

Figure 2.14

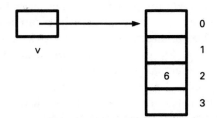

Figure 2.15

BCPL allows the use of the "contents" operator, !, as a binary operatory as well. `v!3 := 6`, will give the result shown in Figure 2.15. Since BCPL is typeless, any variable can be indexed. In our example of Figure 2.13,

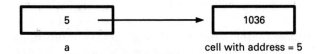

a!3 would provide the address 5 + 3 = 8 by equating the address in a, 5, with the 0th vector element. This is not possible in C, which is a typed language, where vectors are typed elements containing typed objects. C puns are possible, however, and we will look at some in Lab V.

BCPL's control mechanisms are conditionals:

```
IF t THEN c,
IF t GOTO label
TEST t THEN c1 ELSE c2;
```

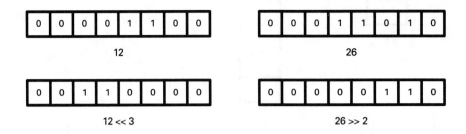

Figure 2.16

repeat and while loops, and a for loop with steps,

FOR n = e1 **TO** e2 **BY** k **DO** c.

It also kept ALGOL's switch statement,

SWITCHON e **INTO** c1, c2, ...,cn,

where e is evaluated and matched to one of the c_i, which is then carried out.

The notion of typeless variables carries over to labels, which can be added, indexed, or sent to routines as actual parameters. This leads to tricky programming that might be very hard to debug. An interesting feature of BCPL's routines (procedures) is that the number of actual parameters need not match the number of formal parameters. Thus VectorAdd(v, high, low), could be called by VectorAdd(a, 10, 5) or by VectorAdd(a, 10). In this second case, low might be assumed to be 0. This useful notion has been carried over to Ada.

BCPL has, in addition to ! and @, the four arithmetic operators +, *, –, and / and arithmetic comparators <, >, <=, >= and NE (not =). Most BCPL implementations provide a real type, either using single words or a vector of two words. This is achieved in a typeless fashion by providing new arithmetic operators, e.g., FADD, FMUL, FSUB, and FDIV.

BCPL also has two shift operators, Left shift, <<, and right shift, >>. 12 << 3 yields 96, and 26 >> 2 is 6. (See Figure 2.16.)

BCPL is a simplified typeless CPL. This simplification led to concise, fast code and fast compilers. It also has a small, but well-defined library of functions and routines. Since BCPL is typeless, almost any operation is valid, e.g., 7 + "A" works well, as does @x - 3.6. A BCPL programmer needs to act as if writing assembly language code. It requires logical control of both the program and the machine it will run on.

B

B, like BCPL, is typeless. BCPL is a statement-oriented language, while B is an expression language. An expression, such as x + y, always has a value. Assignment is treated as an operator, =, with the expression (x = 3 + 5) having the value 8. As a side effect, however, x is assigned the value 8. Consider a B program block to count the number of characters of input, as shown in listing (2.19).

```
{                                                            (2.19)
n = 0;
while ((c = getchar ()) != EOF)
  c != \0 || c != \n ? ++n : n;
}
```

Let's look at the two lines in the while statement. Remember that in an expression language, every expression yields a value. First, assignment of a character to c and comparison to EOF can all be done in the same expression. The value of the expression is either "true" or "false," but the variable c is assigned a value in any case as a side effect. The second expression is a conditional, signaled by "?." The expression, (e₁ ? a : b), yields the value a if e_1 is true, otherwise b. First, we compare c to \0 and \n. If it is not equal (!=) to either, the value of the conditional expression is n + 1 (++n). If it equals one or the other, the value is n. ";" is used to turn the expression into a statement. In expression languages, statements have no value, only side effects. The value of the expression is no longer needed, so it is thrown away. However, the side effect of increasing n has still occurred.

All the operators of B were carried over to C. They are (grouped in order of precedence), as shown in Figure 2.17.

Since B is typeless, there are no restrictions on these operators; addition of two pointers is just as permissible as of two integers. Typed C adds one operator and restricts usage to particular types.

As in C, there are only functions and no procedures. If a value is not **RETURN**ed, the functional value should be ignored. All parameters are passed by value, but reference calls are quite easily achieved by passing addresses.

B has an **if** and an **if..else** statement as well as **repeat**, **while**, **do..while..**, **switch**, and **for** statements, all of which have been carried over to C. An example of a C for statement is shown in listing (2.20).

```
for (i=0; i<5; i++) x=i;                                     (2.20)
```

The first expression gives a 0 start for the loop, it terminates when i==5, and i is incremented by 1 *after* it is used (i++). x will be assigned successively: 0, 1, 2, 3, and 4.

B is organized into modules of three types: manifest constants (macros), external variables (array and string initializations), and function definitions. These can be organized for separate compilation but may also reside on the same file.

Implementations of B also provide for obtaining extra memory when needed, using the function **getvec**(w), where w is the number of words requested. **getvec** returns a pointer to the first word of extra memory. This can

Primary

`()`	parentheses
`x[y]`	value of yth element of array x
`x->y`	value of y field of structure pointed to by x
`x.y`	value of y field of structure x

Unary

`!x`	not x; !x = 0 if x is nonzero, 1 otherwise
`~x`	1's complement of x. 0's become 1's and 1's become 0's.
`++x  (--x)`	x is incremented (decremented) before use
`x++  (x--)`	x is incremented (decremented) after use
`-x`	arithmetic negation of x
`*x`	value at address x
`&x`	address of x
`sizeof x`	# bytes in x

Multiplication

`x*y`	(x/y) product (quotient) of x and y
`x%y`	x MOD y

Addition

`x+y  (x-y)`	sum (difference) of x and y

Shift

`x<<y  (x>>y)`	x gets left (right)shifted y places

Relational

`x<y  (>,<=,>=)`	x less than y, etc. 0 if false, 1 otherwise

Equality

`x==y  (x!=y)`	x equal (not equal) y.

Bitwise (in order of precedence)

`x&y`	bitwise and of x and y 1&1 = 1, else 0
`x^y`	bitwise xor of x and y 1^0 = 0^1 = 1, else 0
`x|y`	bitwise or of x and y 0|0 = 0, else 1

Logical (in order of precedence)

`x&&y`	1 if both x and y are nonzero, else 0
`x||y`	1 if x or y are nonzero, else 0

Conditional

`x?y:z`	y if x is nonzero, z otherwise

Assignment

`x=y`	x gets the value of y
`xop=y`	x gets the value of x*op*y, where *op* may be +, −, *, /, %, >>, <<, &, ^, or |.

Figure 2.17

also be released using **risevec**(ptr, n), where "ptr" points to the beginning of the n words to be released. The corresponding functions in C are **calloc**(n,s), where n is the number of items of size s to be allocated and **free**(*ptr).

EXERCISES

1. In BCPL strings are constants. name := "Mary Jones" is an example, with name pointing to a bit string representing the characters in "Mary Jones." On a 32-bit BCPL compiler, with 8-bit characters, what would be the value of y := !name? of z := name!2? i := name + 4?

2. A BCPL vector always starts at the 0th location. Thus !v = v!0. What are the advantages of starting at 0 rather than 1? (Consider the meaning of v + 1, v + 7, etc.)

3. What are the values of 114 >> 3? 96 << 2? 8 >> 4? What is the relationship between ">>" and division by powers of 2? between "<<" and multiplication?

4. What values will x be assigned if we change the loop of listing (2.20) to **for** (i=0; i<5; ++i) x=i; ■

Data Types in C

Almost all of B has continued into C, but the designers felt the difference between a typeless and a typed language to be great enough to warrant a new name. C has two numeric types: **int** and **float**. A real can be **double float**, and an **int** may be **short**, **long**, or **unsigned**. There is a character type, **char**, but no Boolean type. In C, any nonzero value is considered to be true and 0 false. Since C is close to the machine, certain nonprinting character constants are available, such as \n for a newline, and \b for backspace.

Types derived from the simple types mentioned are:

Arrays   <element type><array name>[size]   ex: **char** name[25]

Functions   <value type><function name>(parameter list)
parameter definitions;
{
    local declarations;
    statements;
}

A functional value may be of any type except another function or an array. In functions returning integers, the value type may be omitted. A function returning no value is of **void** type.

```
ex: void swap(px,py)
       float *px; float *py;
       {...}.
```

One important difference between C and Pascal functions is that no type check-ing occurs on either the number or type of parameters when a function is called, if the function is defined as mentioned previously in the so-called *classic* style. More modern versions of C include a *modern* style, where parameter type infor-mation is included in the parameter list, and type checking can occur.

```
ex: void swap(float *px, float *py)
       {...}.
```

Another difference is that parameters are always passed by value, except for arrays. f(a[]) will pass a pointer to the first element of the array a.

Pointers   <type referenced>*<pointer name>
ex: **int** *pn

Structures   **struct**[10] [<structure name>]{<field list>}
ex: **typedef struct** {**int** dat, month, year}; date;
or, **struct** hire_date {**int** dat, month, year};

Using the **typedef** for date, We can then declare:

```
date hire_date;
```

and assign its fields, hire_date.day = 25;

```
hire_date.month = 9;
```

and

```
&hire_date -> year = 1990.
```

(Note here the combination &...→. → is a special symbol meaning "the field of the structure (union) pointed to by the variable on the left."

Unions   union[<union name>]{list of variants}. Unions are always dis-criminated, so no ambiguities can occur.

```
ex: typedef union {int iarg; float farg;} numeric_const;
numeric_constant pi, zero;
&pi -> farg = 3.141592; zero.iarg = 0.
```

Unions and structures are declared similarly, but in a **structure**, (C's record) storage is allocated for all fields, whereas in a **union**, storage is allocated for the largest variant, and only one is assigned to a union variable. Pascal's variant record can be created in C if desired, since a union can be a field of a record (and vice versa).

---

10 In syntax descriptions, the use of [...] usuallyindicates that the enclosed text is optional.

Type conversions and casts

C allows a small number of automatic type conversions. As Kernighan and Ritchie [Kernighan, 1978, p. 39] say, "The only conversions that happen automatically are those that make sense." **char**s and **int**s may be interchanged freely, with characters being converted to their ASCII valued **int**. The value of the expression

```
(c + 'a' - 'A')
```

is a lower-case character if c contains an upper-case **char**acter. **float** and **int** types may be combined, as in farg+iarg, with the **int** converted to **float**. In general, the conversion always is to the "higher type."

Any unstructured type may be converted to any other through the use of a *cast*. If n is an **int**, we can explicitly convert it to **float** by (**float**) n. The C terminology is that n is cast to **float**. In practice, casting pointers from one pointer type to another does not always work, although any pointer type p can be cast to (**char**) p. Casting is handy when calling functions, where parameters may be of a different type. For example, sqrt((double) n), will convert n to a long integer before sending it to the sqrt function, where it is automatically converted to **float** if necessary. We could, of course, have used a three-statement block

```
{long x; x = n; sqrt(x);}
```

to have achieved almost the same effect. In the first call to sqrt, n will remain a **long** int, while in the block, it remains an **int**.

The integer types are very flexible in C, and can be used for arithmetic, logical, or bitwise variables. As was mentioned before, any nonzero numeric value, integer, or real, is "true" while 0 is "false." Since C is an expression language, the statement in listing (2.21) is perfectly valid.

```
if (m -= 1){                                            (2.21)
   /* execute if m decremented by 1 is not 0 */
   statement_m1;
   if ( m -= 1)
      statement_m2;
}
else
   statement_m3;
```

C is a lean language, carrying no extra baggage. There are no predefined constants TRUE and FALSE. If one wants this feature, a macro can be defined at the beginning of a program:

```
#define FALSE 0;
#define TRUE  1;
```

C relations return values of 1 or 0, so the usual Boolean expression, such as (x < y), will evaluate to 1 if true and 0 if false.

An example of low-level bit operations

The following C program to pack characters into a list gives a little of the flavor of bit manipulations. The problem is a typical OS problem: to maintain strings (possibly error messages) in as little space as possible. For simplicity, we will assume that each message is composed of capital letters only, thus the ASCII codes start at 'A' = 65_{10} = $100\ 0001_2$, and end at 'Z' = 90_{10} = $101\ 1010_2$. Since we know each value is a character, we can throw away the 5th and 6th bits[11] and store our characters in 5-bit fields. The message OVERFLOW can thus be stored in 8 * 5 = 40 bits, or one 32-bit word plus an extra 8 bits.

The solution is in two steps:

1. Read a message character by character, adding the (packed) message to the message list, msg_list. Each message occupies a single line on an input file, terminated by the "end of line" symbol, \n.

2. Record the message number (msgnum), starting position (startptr), and length (endptr-startptr) on a dictionary (dic_list).

We will use two functions, add_msg and add_char, to implement step 1, and add_dic for step 2. add_msg returns the bit offset of msg_list following the just-added message, and add_char returns the bit following a just-added character. add_dic returns the bit of dic_list following an added entry. Line numbers have been added to facilitate discussion.

We will describe some C functions before looking at the program shown in Figure 2.18. & is the bitwise and operator. Thus 0000 0000 0001 1111 & c will mask out all but the last 5 bits of the value of c. We have defined CH_MASK = 0000 0000 0001 1111.

n/m is modular division with two integer arguments n and m, and n%m is n mod m.

| is the bitwise or operator, operating on two words. c|*l will append c to the list l, starting at the pointer position l. This works because C arrays are automatically initialized to 0, and l will be pointing to the word containing bits that have not been assigned new values.

<< is the left-shift and >> the right-shift operator. c>>5 shifts c 5 bits to the right.

Starting with an empty list, if we read in the characters, 'A', 'B', 'C', 'D', we would finish with what is shown in Figure 2.19. The main program (line 7) needs no explanation. It is just a driver that reads characters at the beginning of lines until end of file (EOF) is encountered and calls add_msg and add_dic.

---

11 In a word, bits are numbered 0 to 15, from right to left, with the low bit as 0th and the high bit, 15th. In an array, both bits and words are numbered from left to right, starting at 0.

```
1) #include<stdio.h>;      /* Standard I/O library routines        */
2) #define CH_MASK 0x1f;   /* CH_MASK is 0000 0000 0001 1111       */
3) #define WORD 16;        /* WORD length assumed to be 16 bits    */
4) unsigned dic_list[10]   /* pointer into dictionary for
                              coded messages                       */
5) unsigned msg_list[40];  /* pointer into Array of 40 words,
                              initialized to 0                     */
6) int char;              /* characters declared as integers       */
7) main()
   /* packs messages into msg_list, and stores message number,
      starting address and message length in dic_list.            */
     {
8) unsigned startptr;      /* bit pointer into msg_list;
                              start of message                     */
9) unsigned endptr         /* end of message                       */
10) unsigned msgnum        /* number of message                    */
11) startptr=endptr=msgnum=0;
12)    while ((char=getchar()!=EOF){
13)      endptr=add_msg(char,startptr,msg_list);
14)      dic_list=
            add_dic(dic_list,msgnum++,startptr,endptr-startptr);
       }
   }

15) unsigned add_msg(ch,s,lst){
16)    unsigned ch,s,*lst;
/* reads messages and stores characters in five-bit fields in
   the array, lst=msg_list                                        */
17)    {unsigned end=s;
18)      while ((ch!='\n'){
19)        end=add_char(ch,lst,end); ch=getchar();
       }
20)    return end;
   }

21) unsigned add_char(c,l,p)
   /* add character, c, to list, l, starting at offset, p          */
22)    unsigned c,*l,p;
23)    {unsigned b;           /* number of bits into list           */
24)    l+=p/WORD;             /* put list pointer at beginning
                                 of currently available word        */
25)    b=p%WORD;              /* starting position in current
                                 word for c                         */
26)    c = c & CH_MASK;       /* mask out all but last 5 bits       */
27)    if (b+5<=16)           /* c will fit in present word         */
28)      *l=c<<(16-b-5)|*l;   /* shift c left and append to l       */
```

Figure 2.18   (continued next page)

```
29)  else{                    /* c must be split up between the
                                current word and the next one.    */
30)     *l=c>>(b+5-16)|*l;    /* store high bits of c in current
                            word by shifting right & ORing with *l  */
31)     l+=1;                 /* make next word in l current       */
32)     *l=c<<(32-b-5)|*l;    /* put rest of c in next word of l   */
     }
33)  return(p+5);            /* current offset in l                */
}


34) unsigned add_dic(d,m,start,size){
        /* adds message number, m, start position and size to list, d  */
     ...
}
```

Figure 2.18   (continued from previous page)

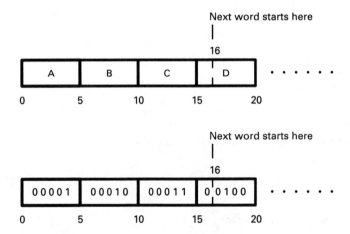

Figure 2.19

add_msg (lines 15–20) repeatedly calls add_char until encountering an end of line (\n) and returns a pointer to the next available location in msg_list. It is add_char that does the interesting work.

add_char(c,l,p) has parameters c, a character to be added to the array l, and p, the bit position in the array where storage for c is to start. b is a local variable that measures bits in the appropriate word of l. l was passed the name of an array, which is the address of its first element, i.e., the starting address of

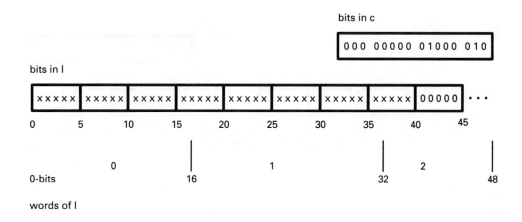

Figure 2.20

Figure 2.21

l[0]. Now suppose p is 40. Since WORDs are 16 bits long, the last message ended 8 bits into the third word of l, at bit 39. $p/WORD = 2$, and $p\%WORD = 8$. $l += p/WORD$; (line 24) puts us at the beginning of l[2]. Since $b+5 = 13 <= 16$, c will fit entirely in l[2] (line 27). Actually, c, coded into 5 bits, is to be placed in bits 40 through 44 of the array l. On entry to add_char, c is a 16-bit word, representing, say, 'B.' (See Figure 2.20.)

First, we mask out all but the last 5 bits of c (line 26), as shown in Figure 2.21. Next, we shift c left $(16 - 8 - 5) = 3$ bits so that the 'B' will be lined up with bits 40 to 45 in word 2 of l, as shown in Figure 2.22. The logical or of *l (word 2) and c (line 28) will leave word 2 as xxxx xxxx 0001 0000, with the 5-bit 'B' occupying the 3rd through the 7th bits. Bits 0 to 2 are then available for the left-most 3 bits of the next letter. The last 2 bits of this next entry will have to be stored in word 3, which we get to through the statement $l+ = 1$; (line 31). We leave diagramming the storing of this next letter as exercise 6. Notice that the array pointer l is incremented by words, while the bitpointers p and b shift left or right in bits. Notice also that we can use only the logical bit operations, & and |, with whole words. The next letter after that in the previous example will have

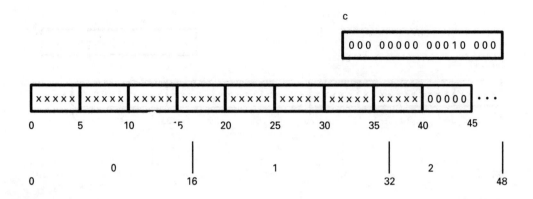

Figure 2.22

to be stored in two steps, with appropriate right (line 30) and left (line 32) shifts to line up the words correctly.

We have not provided code for add_dic, which adds the message number, starting address, and length to the message dictionary. If we want this to be "packed" as well, a similar strategy will do. However, here we will be dealing with numbers instead of characters, which will require 7-bit, rather than 5-bit codes. We would also need functions to retrieve, decode, and print out messages.

LAB IV: Combining Low- and High-Level Features: C

OBJECTIVES

1. To familiarize students with syntax of the C language.
2. To combine both low- and high-level features of C.
3. Illustrate the space savings gained by the use of low-level features. ■

Arrays, Pointers, and the "," Operator

Since C does not allow nested procedures and all parameters except arrays are passed by value, compilation and execution are fast. Programs tend to be composed of lots of little functions. When we declare an array, such as unsigned msg_list[40], the variable msg_list is assigned a pointer to the first unsigned integer element of the array. The value of the third element can be referenced as msg_list[2] or *(msg_list+2). The variable msg_list always references the begin-

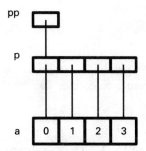

Figure 2.23

ning of the array, so msg_list++ is invalid. When an array is passed as a parameter, it is this pointer that is passed; the array is not copied. A straightforward example similar to one from *The C Puzzle Book*, [Feuer, 1982] is as shown in listing (2.22).

```
int a[]={0,1,2,3};          /* array with elements, 0-3    */   (2.22)
int *p[]={a,a+1,a+2,a+3};   /* array with pointer elements */
int *pp=p;
main(){
  printf("a=%d, *a=%d, p=%d, *p=%d, **pp=%d\n", a,*a,p,*p,**p);
                            /* "..." is a format directive */
}
```

The printout is a=<address of a>, *a=0, p=<address of p>, *p=<address of a>, **pp=0. Do you see why? Although somewhat inconsistent, it helps to remember that the array a==&a[0], the address of the 0th element of the array a, and that a[0]==*a, the value of the 0th element. (See Figure 2.23.)

C also supports pointer arithmetic. pp-p==0, and ++pp-p==1, since ++pp makes pp point to the second element of the array p, p[1]. Thus the value of pp is p+1, and pp-p= (p+1) -p=1.

We have already seen most of C's expressions and statements, as most are direct carry-overs from BCPL. One operator, however, is new to C: the "," operator. (a,b) is an expression that evaluates a and has the value of b. It is particularly useful for initialization, e.g.,

```
for(s=0,i=1;i<=10;s+=i,i++);
```

will end with s==55, the sum of the first 10 integers. There are two uses of "," here: first, in the initialization part, s=0, i=1; and in the reinitialization part, s += i, i++. The **for** loop evaluates s, but uses the value of the expression i during each iteration.

LAB V: Fun with C "Tricks"

OBJECTIVES

1. To demonstrate the effects of C's weak typing.
2. To pipe output from one C program into a second. ■

C and UNIX

As we have seen, C is intimately related to the UNIX operating system, which is written almost entirely in C. UNIX is composed of a kernel, one or more shells, and a large set of service routines. The kernel is small, about 10,000 lines of code, which creates a virtual machine that: (1) schedules, coordinates, and manages process execution; (2) provides system services such as I/O; and (3) handles machine-dependent hardware operations [Silvester, 1983]. All but the set of machine primitives tailored to the particular computer on which UNIX is running is written in C. The user rarely sees the kernel, but interacts with the set of procedures comprising one of the shells.

A UNIX system provides a variety of utilities such as editors, debuggers, and preprocessors as well as compilers for BASIC, FORTRAN, Ratfor, Pascal (at least in the Berkeley version), C, and Assembler. Source code in any of these languages is first translated into C intermediate code before being translated into Assembler, relocatable object, and finally executable machine-language code. Since all programs are first translated into C, new compilers are particularly easy to write. All one need do is design a translator into C, with no writing of Assembler code. This translator also enables the mixing of code written in different source languages and interfacing with applications such as databases, spreadsheets and graphics programs.

The Draft C Standard

The *de facto* standard for C has been Kernighan and Ritchie's book [Kernighan, 1978]. There is now, however, a standard from Technical Committee X3J11 of the American National Standards Institute [ANSI-X3J11, 1986]. All C compilers will now be expected to conform. A parallel committee of the International Standards Organization (ISO) is hoping to authorize a standard, identical except for locale-dependent features, e.g., comma or period for decimal point and month/day/year versus day/month/year or a different alphabetic sequence.

Committee X3J11 has been guided by several principles, the most important being "Don't make presently working code obsolete." That is, programs written in correct Kernighan/Ritchie code should still compile and run. Others advocate both portability and system-dependent C. The committee is trying to preserve C, pretty much as it exists and not "fix" it.

Advantages and Disadvantages

The main disadvantage of C is the difficulty of debugging programs due to automatic type coercions, pointer arithmetic, and side effects within expressions. It also fosters a terse programming style that is sometimes hard for anyone but the program designer to read. Thus it is often not the preferred language for business or scientific applications.

Its closeness to the machine, however, makes C ideal for writing operating systems and compilers. It is also very flexible for interactive programming, due to the variety of I/O facilities.

EXERCISES

1. Pascal allows automatic conversion of integers to floating types, but not characters to integers. Neither Modula-2 nor Ada allow either, and C allows both. How do Pascal, Modula-2, and Ada handle an expression like (r + i), where r is real and i an integer?

2. Why can one always cast a pointer to be a pointer to a character, but possibly not a pointer to an **int** or **float**?

3. Consider the following values of m on entry to the code of listing (2.21). Which statement(s) will be executed? (== is a C comparator, while = is the assignment operator.)

   a. `m==3`
   b. `m==2`
   c. `m==1`
   d. `m==0`

   Now, remove the block delimiters, "{" and "}", and answer (a) through (d) again.

4. In the function call

   ```
   add_dic(dic_list,msgnum++,startptr,endptr-startptr);
   ```

   of Figure 2.18, when is `msgnum` incremented? after, or before the procedure call? What will be the number of the first message?

5. What will be the starting address of the character 'E' if we add it to msg_list, as diagrammed in Figure 2.19? What value will the function add_char return?

6. Draw diagrams similar to those at the end of "An example of low-level bit operations," depicting the addition of the letter 'C' in bits 45 to 49 of msg_list.

7. Suppose we reverse the last two expressions in the loop at the end of "Arrays, Pointers, and the "," Operator," to: for(sum=0,i=1; i<=10; i++, s+=i);. What value will s have on completion of the loop?

8. Discuss the different collating sequences, other than the U.S. 26-letter alphabet and period for decimal, that might be used in non-American standard versions of C. ■

LAB VI: Tools from Pascal and C

OBJECTIVES

1. To investigate the programming tools provided with the version of Pascal or C available, especially string and graphics packages, editor, debugger, tracer, and browser.

2. To use and evaluate these tools for their intended purposes. ■

LAB VII: Using Tools in Ada

OBJECTIVES

1. To investigate the various tools provided with the Ada package being used.

2. To become familiar with the packages provided from the APSE. In particular to look at the various I/O packages included in the implementation being used. ■

2.6 SUMMARY

In this chapter, we have considered block-structured languages, which implement nested blocks and (recursive) procedures, beginning with ALGOL in 1957. We followed this development through its orthogonal cousin, ALGOL 68;

through its simplification, Pascal, on to Ada. This line of languages was also syntactically defined carefully through a formalization called the Backus Normal Form (BNF).

We also looked at the development of C from ALGOL 60 through CPL, BCPL, and B. As rules became stricter and the language higher level in the first group, things were relaxed in C so that a programmer could manipulate a machine's store directly.

Procedures may have formal parameters to which the values of actual parameters are passed. This can occur in several ways: by value, where the value of the actual is copied into a storage location for the formal parameter; by reference, where the address of the actual is passed to the formal parameter; by value-result, where the actual value is copied into the formal, and the formal value back into the actual on exit from the procedure; and by name, where the name of the actual is substituted for the name of the formal. Pascal implements the first two under programmer control, C passes all parameters except arrays by value, and Ada provides **in** or **out** parameters, which behave like value or value-result parameters respectively, but may be implemented differently, depending on the compiler writer.

Functions are procedures returning a single value. This value has been restricted to particular types by some languages. ALGOL 68 was the first to allow functions with values of any type. Ada also includes this feature and enforces value parameters.

Strong typing, where the values of a variable remain true to type throughout its usage, has been enforced in Pascal and Ada, but not in C. Free unions in Pascal are an exception to this notion, but resulting difficulties have been minimized in both C and Ada through insistence on discriminated unions only. The notion of generic functions and procedures, where types of both parameters and functional values can vary depending on use, has been provided in Ada.

The block-structured languages we looked at also provide for dynamic variables in two ways. First are local variables, which are created on entry and destroyed on exit from a block. The second sort are reference variables, which hold addresses of storage locations. These are called pointers in Pascal and C and **access** variables in Ada. Structures (records) can be defined recursively in Pascal, Ada, and C by including a pointer to a similar structure as one of the fields. If p is a pointer to such a structure, storage can be located for a new instance through the functions **new**(p) (Pascal, Ada) or **alloc** (C). Pascal and C also provide the functions **dispose** and **free**, respectively, to release previously allocated storage.

Programmer control over exceptions was first introduced in PL/I and expanded in Ada. PL/I also includes arrays of bits, which have been exploited more fully in C.

Both Ada and Modula-2 have provided higher-level modules, where variables and procedures can be grouped in self-contained units. In Ada these are packages and in Modula-2, modules. Ada also includes tasks to implement concurrency. Modula-2 has implemented coroutines, and UNIX has fork and join operations to implement concurrent C programs. We will look at these further in Chapter 4.

2.7 NOTES ON REFERENCES

To achieve a thorough understanding of block-structured procedural languages, one would do well to look at ALGOL 60 and ALGOL 68. [Naur, 1963] provides a good discussion and the entire, 17-page report. [Tanenbaum, 1976] is a tutorial on ALGOL 68, and [Branquart, 1971] provides a readable discussion of ALGOL semantics. Reading these three articles plus Knuth's summary of still ambiguous issues in ALGOL 60 [Knuth, 1967] would also give a reader a good idea of how hard it is to be precise.

Among the survey books, [Baron, 1986] describes programming languages to laypersons in a superficial, but interesting and competent way. More technical histories are [Sammet, 1969] and [Wexelblat, 1981]. [Horowitz, 1987] is a collection of important and easily read papers, originally written for publications as disparate as the *IBM Journal of Research and Development* and *BYTE Magazine*. This collection has been revised every two years since 1983, but a call to the publishers found no new edition planned.

The [Feuer, 1982b] paper in the *Computing Surveys* series from ACM compares Pascal and C, while [Smedma, 1983] considers Pascal, Modula, Chill, and Ada.

Two American National Standards Institute (ANSI) documents were mentioned in this chapter, ANSI 1815A83, which defines Ada, and ANSI X3J1186, the proposed standard for C. Pascal also has an American standard, ANSI/IEEE 770X3.79-1983. This was devised jointly by Committee X3J9 of ANSI and Project P770 of the Institute of Electrical and Electronics Engineers (IEEE). A Pascal international standard, DP7185 [ISO, 1980], differs somewhat from 770X3. Programs following the American standard will run in ISO Pascal, but the ANSI/IEEE standard does not include the conformant array of DP 7185. In ISO Pascal, **procedure** Process(A: **array** [start..finish] **of** SomeType); is perfectly valid, with "start" and "finish" conforming to the bounds of the actual parameter passed to the parameter A in "Process."

The Standard documents, which are very terse, are unsuitable for learning a language. The Ada "Bible" is [Booch, 1986]. Pascal manuals abound, with [Cooper, 1983] describing the standard to experienced programmers. [Kernighan, 1978] is still the most widely used C manual and [Plum, 1987] provides notes on the proposed standard, X3J1186.

[Marcotty, 1976] is a tutorial on formal language definitions. In addition to BNF and W-grammars, the axiomatic approach, the Vienna Definition Language, and attribute grammars are discussed plus a comparison and evaluation of the different methods.

3

OBJECT-BASED LANGUAGES

In dividing programming languages into two paradigms, imperative and declarative, each with three subparadigms, Wegner assigns *object-based* languages to the imperative paradigm and defines an object as a group of procedures that share a state [Wegner, 1988]. Recall that a program written in an imperative language involves a sequence of state transition commands. Booch [Booch, 1986, p. 47] speaks of an object as an entity that has a state, one that "is defined by the actions that it suffers, and vice versa" and is "an instance of a class of objects." Thus the state of computer memory is always prominent when considering objects.

Everything in Smalltalk is an object, with the class **object** being the superclass of all other objects. In CLU, objects are containers for data. Objects have *associated* operations and *values*. For example, if object S is a stack, and Push is one of its operations, the value of S after Push(S, 5) includes 5.

Blair asserts that there is no real consensus on what is meant by an object-oriented system and proposes that the key feature of anything called an object is that it be *encapsulated* [Blair, 1989, p. 12]. "An object is encapsulated if the notions of an operation set and a data set are incorporated in a single entity (i.e., the object). Furthermore, clients should be restricted to accessing the object only through the well-defined, external, operational interface."

This seems very similar to an abstract data type (ADT). We need some examples and some working definitions.

BRIEF THEORETICAL EXCURSION 3:
Objects: Abstraction, Encapsulation, and Polymorphism

In the real world, an *object* is a dynamic entity. It may change, but still remain the same object. A very complex object is a human being. A somewhat simpler object is a checkbook. It may (or may not, depending on how careful its owner is) represent the *state* of a bank account. It may balance or not, yet it is still the same checkbook. There are many checkbooks, with any particular one representing an *instance* of the *class* of all checkbooks. Sending a *message* to a checkbook to "Draw" itself makes no sense; however, it is reasonable to ask it to produce a current balance or record a $500 deposit.

An object may be as simple as an integer and its arithmetic operations or complex, such as a railroad train, including schedule, personnel, mechanical, and other objects in its definition. An object-oriented programmer approaches a problem by dividing it into interacting objects, while a programmer using a top-down style proceeds algorithmically, delegating responsibility for each step to a module. Objects are independent of each other, thus easier to verify and maintain than most procedures. They also facilitate the reuse of tested code. Robert Moskowitz [Moskowitz, 1989] claims that the provision of preprogrammed and user-modifiable objects "allows users who understand very little about computers to grasp and manipulate computer features, functions, and operations as easily as they grasp and manipulate tangible objects in the real world."

Definitions abound for the word *object*, other than CLU's "container for data." Perhaps the simplest is that of [Cox, 1984]. "Objects are private data and the operations supported on that data." Objects communicate by passing *messages*, which are "request[s] for an object to perform one of its operations." Object-based and object-oriented programming involve the support of objects plus other features, which vary somewhat from author to author and language to language.

Pascoe [Pascoe, 1986] describes an *object-oriented* language as one that supports information hiding, data abstraction, dynamic binding and inheritance. Wegner [Wegner, 1987, 1988, 1990] calls a language *object based* if it supports objects, *class based* if it also supports classes of objects, and *object oriented* if, in addition, objects can inherit features from their parent objects. Simonian and Crone [Simonian, 1988] list five requirements for object-oriented programming:

1. Information hiding (encapsulation)
2. Data abstraction
3. Message passing (polymorphism)
4. Dynamic binding
5. Inheritance

In this excursion, we will discuss object-based features, including 1, 2, and 3 above. Consideration of dynamic binding and inheritance will be deferred to Brief Theoretical Excursion 4. We also have discussed information hiding in our overview of concepts in Chapter 1. Procedure implementations and local variables of a module are hidden from the outside world. Changes to hidden objects are local and cannot affect a client program, as long as the interface remains the same. Modules that hide information are called *loosely coupled*.

Data abstraction is achieved through abstract data types, ADTs. An ADT is described in Theoretical Excursion 1 as the pair [objects, operations], where an object is considered to be a container for data. In a pure ADT, objects can only be known through their associated operations. The ADT Queue of Excursion 1 has the operations New, Add, Front, Remove, and IsEmpty?. We can use queues only through these five operations. No other access can be found to a queue or its elements. In CLU, if we declare the variable q to be of type Queue, we then create the ADT q through a function call of New(q). Implementation of the Queue operations, as well as the representation of the Queue object, may be hidden from the user. In this chapter, when we refer to an object, we will mean the entire pair [objects, operations], not just the data container. In the object-based sense, object = {data, methods}.

Message passing provides a means for objects to communicate with a client program and each other. A message is sent to an object where a *method* for responding is selected from those available. The message "Draw" sent to a rectangular object will elicit a different response than when sent to a circular object.

A procedure, as we have considered it so far, can call another procedure directly. This is not true, however, for methods. A method in Object1 cannot directly access a method in Object2, but must send a message to Object2, which will respond using its own methods. A procedure is controlled by the types of its parameters, whereas a method can also use information contained in its object's private data. Data contained in an object is accessible only to methods in the object and not outside. This private data is called the object's *state*. A state persists between invocations of methods. The notion of state harks back to ALGOL's **own** variables. Procedures as well as methods can access global data. These globals may be available to several procedures and are not part of any object's state.

In languages such as Modula-2, CLU, and Ada, data can be encapsulated along with associated operations in a **module** (Modula-2), **data type** (CLU), or **package** (Ada). So how does an *object*, in the object-based sense, differ from what we have seen? One way is that an object may include data and several data types with their associated operations. Another is what is known as *polymorphism*. An object receives a message, which is simply a name, such as "+" and reacts to it according to the methods included in the object. A different object may receive the same message and react to it differently. We are already familiar with functions that do different things when confronted with different data types. One example supported by most languages is the arithmetic "+." (1.5 + 3.246) is handled differently from (1 + 3) or from (1.5 + 3). "+" is a polymorphic (many form), or generic function. In object terms, "+" is a *message*, and different *methods* compute the sum in each of the three expressions. 1.5 and 3.246 are *instances* of real

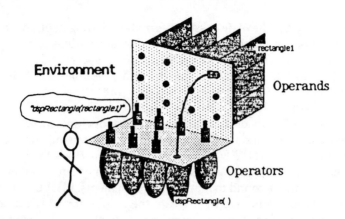

Figure 3.1   The operator/operand model. Reprinted with permission from *IEEE Software*, January 1984, p. 52. © IEEE.

objects, which include the method "+." Similarly, 1 and 3 are instances of integer objects, including "+." The 1.5 and 3 of the third expression are instances of mixed objects, also including a "+" operator. To keep everything clean, a language might designate the three different "+"s as real.+, int.+, and mixed.+ instead of asking the compiler to choose the right "+" by checking the arguments in the expression. When a language token like "+" has different meanings depending on the context, it is said to be *overloaded*.

Figures 3.1 and 3.2 from Brad Cox [Cox, 1984] may help make the difference between methods and procedures clear. In the first, we are using the procedure "dsp-Rectangle" to display a rectangle. It acts on whatever operand it is presented with, in this case, rectangle1.

The message/object model of Figure 3.2 assumes a layer of structure between the operation or message and the data. The command "display" can be passed to an object, which will behave according to its own methods. If the object represents rectangles and their associated operations, we might get the same result as that depicted in Figure 3.1. However, "display" could be meaningful to a variety of different objects. The message, or behavior, will be filtered through the object descriptors, to match up with whichever instance is presently being requested to display itself. We will see other properties of objects in a fuller diagram in the next Theoretical Excursion, when we examine classes, inheritance, and dynamic binding.

The term *message* is somewhat misleading, but so well established in object-oriented literature that it is likely to remain. A message suggests that objects are acting independently and concurrently, and indeed, *actor* languages, such as Pract and Acore [Agha, 1987], make these assumptions. In the languages we will consider here, a *method* is nothing more nor less than a function or procedure that has *state*. A *message* is the name of a method.

Environment

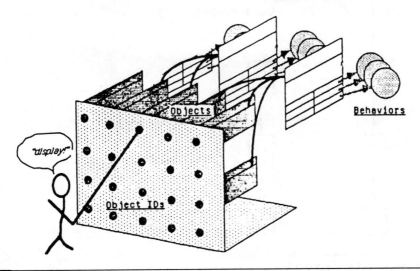

Figure 3.2   Reprinted with permission from *IEEE Software*, January 1984, p. 53. © IEEE.

EXERCISES

1. Procedures have local variables and constants. What is the difference between these local entities and the data private to an object?
2. Name two ways that messages differ from procedures or functions. ∎

3.0 EARLY NOTIONS OF OBJECTS IN SIMULA

Simula I originated at the Norwegian Computing Center in 1961 in the hands of Kristen Nygaard and Ole-Johan Dahl. Its purposes were to describe systems and program simulations [Nygaard, 1981].

A system, such as airport departures, was thought of as consisting of components of two different kinds: permanent active objects and passive objectives, acted on by the active ones. Passengers are examples of the first type, "grabbing and holding the passive counter clerks, fee collectors, etc." Abstract objects were thought of as nodes in a network. Figure 3.3 shows this relationship.

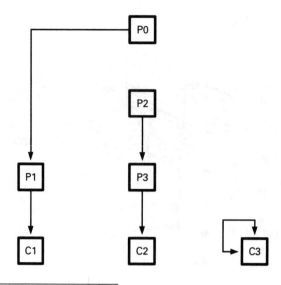

Figure 3.3   Passenger/Clerk network

Later work suggests that objects are better thought of as of one kind, which are sometimes active and sometimes passive, and that interacting processes form a better notion for objects than does a network. Simula I is an extension of ALGOL 60, with each process implemented as a stack. The diagrams from [Nygaard, 1981] in Figure 3.4 represent, on the left, the ALGOL 60 block structure, implemented as a stack, and, on the right, the SIMULA system as a nested collection of interacting blocks. Notice that the top level represents the ALGOL 60 portion of blocks.

At first, Simula was to be a preprocessor to ALGOL 60, with Simula code translated into ALGOL. This idea of objects being implemented on top of existing languages has been used in a preprocessor to Ada, InnovAda [Simonian, 1988], and in extensions to Pascal, Object Pascal [Tesler, 1985], and to C, C++ [Stroustrup, 1986].

Processes in Simula I are created and destroyed through a new data type, "process pointer," which is not a part of ALGOL 60. It is related to an ALGOL pointer, however, in that it contains the address of a memory location. Since processes can have their own private data, there was a danger in the ALGOL feature of variables being undefined until assigned a value. Thus all Simula variables are assigned neutral initial values. To do this, ALGOL itself had to be changed, as a preprocessor could not accomplish the task in the ALGOL portions of a program. This convention has been utilized in more modern languages as well, e.g., SETL's initial or assigned value of "OM."

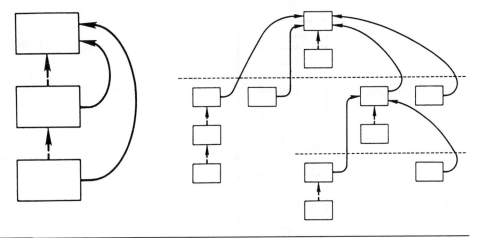

Figure 3.4 Reprinted with permission from Wexelblat, R.(1981), *History of Programming Languages*, p. 485. © Academic Press.

Simula's processes are *dynamic*, that is, they can be created when needed and later destroyed. Procedures (methods) in a process differ from the usual procedure block. They may run quasi-concurrently,[1] and contain statements requesting time delays. The early **pause**(<boolean expression>), which requested suspension of a currently active process until the expression became true, caused so much trouble that it was abandoned for the four directives, **passivate**, **activate**, **hold**, and **cancel**.

Simula I's successor, Simula 67, has *classes of objects* as its basic concept. Dahl and Nygaard had been working on a simulation of a bridge with a toll booth and a queue of trucks, busses, and cars. They noticed that a process for a truck included many of the same procedures as that for a bus or car. They developed a class called **link** that included all the queue operations, and made **car** a subclass of **link** and **truck** and **bus** subclasses of **car**, as shown in Figure 3.5.

The concept of classes of processes leans heavily on Hoare's notion of classes of records, with procedure as well as data fields. Each subobject *inherits* the procedures of the superclass. In the diagram above, **truck** inherits all the procedures of **link** and all those of **car**, with the exception of Toll, which is redefined for each of the **bus** and **truck** procedures. Simula 67 is more than an extension to ALGOL 60, although ALGOL is included as a subset and ALGOL programs can be run on a Simula compiler. A Simula program looks like one in ALGOL, with

---

1 Two or more procedures are quasi-concurrent if they can be active at the same time, and one is not a subprocedure of the other. Quasi-concurrency may be implemented through some form of single CPU time-sharing or multiple CPUs running in parallel.

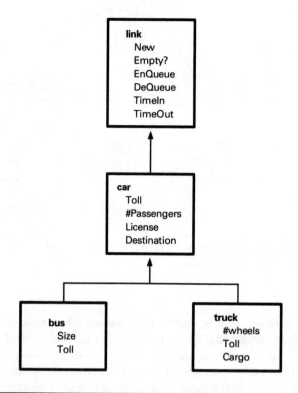

Figure 3.5   Class hierarchy for toll bridge simulation

```
SIMULA begin...end
```

marking a Simula block and providing access to the non-ALGOL simulation features. On exiting this block, control is returned to the ALGOL run-time stack.

By 1969, two Simula 67 compilers had been implemented, one for the UNIVAC® 1100 series of computers and one for the IBM 360/370 series. Although Simula has been largely superseded by other object-oriented languages, it still has an active group of users, mostly in Europe. There were 500 subscribers to the Simula newsletter in 1981, although research efforts at NCC had switched to the Simula successor languages, DELTA and BETA. BETA [Kristensen, 1987] has three kinds of objects: system, component, and item. A system object can be executed concurrently with other system objects. A component object is a coroutine and may alternate execution with other component objects. An item object is contained in either a system or component object and depends on its superobject for mode of execution. Object templates in BETA are called **pattern**s and may be used as classes, procedures, functions, or types.

3.1 OBJECT-BASED PROGRAMMING IN ADA

Two of the major goals in developing object-based software are cost reduction and security. The development of objects as reusable software units aids in the first, while information hiding promotes the second. When objects are created and destroyed dynamically, security requires special machine architectures. The design specifications for Ada did not require an object-oriented architecture, but that all type checking and allocation (binding) of storage for procedures be done at compile time. Thus we will not find Pascoe's last two requirements, dynamic binding and inheritance, in Ada.

Ada does provide, however, for information hiding and data abstraction. It also provides for a hidden state in an object. Thus an Ada object's procedures can rightly be called methods, which we shall do here, although you will not find any mention of methods in the Ada literature. An object is implemented in Ada through a **package**. If you recall from Chapter 1, an Ada package has two parts, the visible *specification* and the hidden **package body**.

Let us consider the robot object of Buzzard and Mudge [Buzzard, 1985] in listing (3.1).

```
package ROBOT is                                         (3.1)
  type ROBOT_ARM is limited private;
  type ARM_MODEL is (ASEA,PUMA);
  type POSITION is array (1..4,1..4) of FLOAT;

  procedure INITIALIZE_ARM (X: out ROBOT_ARM;
                            KIND: in ARM_MODEL);
  procedure MOVE (X: in out ROBOT_ARM; DESTINATION: in POSITION);
  procedure OPEN (X: in out ROBOT_ARM);
  procedure CLOSE(X: in out ROBOT_ARM);
  function GET_POSITION(X: ROBOT_ARM) return POSITION;

private     --not visible
  type ROBOT_ARM is record
    --The complete record contains a component of type POSITION,
    --a component of type ARM_MODEL and
    --a BOOLEAN component to indicate whether the gripper is
    --is open or closed.
    --In the actual Ada declaration, these fields would
    --be listed here.
end ROBOT;
```

A ROBOT consists of a single arm that can OPEN or CLOSE its gripper. Two models already in use are the ASEA and the PUMA, although more may be added. This package specification may be all a user will see, and can be compiled separately from either its body or a program using the package.

That ROBOT_ARM is **limited private** does not mean that the user cannot see the structure of its type. The record fields would be listed in the specifi-

cation, but a user would have no access to them except through the four procedures and the function listed above. A subprogram containing objects of type
ROBOT_ARM can use them only as parameters of the procedures and function.
A variable of type ROBOT_ARM has invisible POSITION and BOOLEAN
fields, which are its *state*. The state of this simple robot indicates where it is and
whether its gripper is open or shut.

In Turbo Pascal 5.5®, the object-oriented extension to Turbo Pascal, the
declaration would be:

```
unit ROBOT;                                                   (3.2)

interface

type
  ARM_MODEL = (ASEA,PUMA);
  POSITION = array [1..4,1..4] of real;
  ARM = record
    {fields listed here}
  end;
  ROBOT_ARM = object
    A : ARM;
    procedure INIT(KIND : ARM_MODEL);
    procedure MOVE(DESTINATION: POSITION);
    procedure OPEN;;
    procedure CLOSE;
    function GET_POSITION : POSITION;
  end;

implementation
...
end;
```

The declaration for an object looks pretty much like a record declaration,
and indeed it is. A Pascal object *is* a record, with procedures and functions as
well as data allowed as fields. Each of the procedures in the object ROBOT_ARM
operates implicitly on the ARM field A. If we declare:

```
MyRobot : ROBOT_ARM;
```

we can initialize MyRobot using `MyRobot.Init(ASEA);` move it with `My-
Robot.MOVE(ToSomeplace);` etc. Although these are called procedures in Pas-
cal syntax, they are really methods. They cannot be used with variables of type
ARM that have not been declared as part of an object of type ROBOT_ARM, and
they can only be activated through the object name.

Object Pascal has no facilities for restricting access to ROBOT_ARM. A user
can assign values to the fields of a variable of type ARM without using any of the
object's methods. The implementers assumed that those programming in an
object-oriented style will discipline themselves to use instances of objects only
through the methods included in the object definition. The inclusion of an INIT
method encourages this.

LAB VIII: Objects, Encapsulation, and Methods: Object Pascal/Ada

OBJECTIVES

1. To complete the `ROBOT` package or unit `queue` through suitable definitions for `ROBOT_ARM` and the associated procedures in object Pascal or Ada.

2. To consider the differences between the object implementation and an implementation using data types and procedures. Students should pay particular attention to the language in which they did *not* program. ■

3.2 CLASS-BASED LANGUAGES

We have given a good bit of consideration to modules, i.e., collections of related data, data types, and procedures. A *class* is a collection of procedures or modules, with one essential difference: an instance of a class may be *dynamic*, i.e., it may be constructed during run time and destroyed when no longer needed. We will first consider the language CLU (cluster), which remains largely experimental, but was the first to explore the class concepts. We will also look at generic packages in Ada, which are not true examples of classes, since they must be instantiated at compile time, not run time, and are never destroyed. They do, however, share some of the class notions. As our example of an implemented language supporting classes, we will look once again at Object Pascal.

The *class* notion comes from mathematical logic. A class is a set, but more closely structured. Georg Cantor's notion of a set as a collection of objects sharing certain attributes led to a number of paradoxes. For example, Bertrand Russell showed that if S is the set of all elements that are not members of themselves, a paradox occurs. A paradox is a statement that is both true and false. If S is defined as $S = \{X \mid \text{not } (X \in X)\}$, Russell proved that if $(S \in S)$ were true, then so was not $(S \in S)$, and vice versa. Mathematics, above all else, is assumed to be consistent and not lead to paradox, thus it was realized that some sets are not valid. The theory of *classes* was developed to build sets that would eliminate at least the known paradoxes.

In computer languages, *classes* are collections of elements, often called attributes, but are restrained to eliminate logical problems. In particular, if C is a class, then C cannot be an instance (member) of itself. A class is a collection of data and methods, where any instance includes the same methods, but may include different data values, or even different data types. When we consider subclasses and inheritance below, we will see that two subclasses may have different methods as well.

CLU

In Chapter 1, "Brief Theoretical Excursion 2: Modularization," we saw an example of a CLU **data type**, intset. It consists of six visible operation names or messages, the six corresponding methods, and one hidden method. There is also a representation, or **rep**, for the intset. In the example, the **rep** is an array of integers, but it could just as easily have been a linked list. No intset objects exist until an assignment such as i := intset$create(). If we subsequently assign j := intset$create(), the type intset contains two sets of integers, i and j, i.e., intset = {i, j}.

CLU also provides for **clusters**, which are classes of data types. A cluster for a set could include intsets, realsets, complexsets, etc. Its declaration would be as shown in listing (3.3).

```
set = cluster [t : type] is create, insert, delete, member, size,          (3.3)
        choose
    where t has equal : proctype(t, t) returns (bool)
    rep = array[t]
```

To make instances of realsets and complexsets, we would define the types and declare variables of these types:

```
realset = set[real]
complexset = set[complex]
r1 : realset
c1 : complexset
```

and then assign:

```
r1 := realset$create()
c1 := complexset$create()
```

Methods for a realset would include

```
member = proc (s : cvt, x : real) returns bool,
```

and

```
getind = proc (s : rep, x : real) returns real,
```

with parallel methods for complexsets.

Both realsets and complexsets are valid members of the class, set, since each has an **equal** function, as required by the **where** clause. We now have set = {realset, complexset}, realset = {r1}, and complexset = {c1}. This is in the spirit of mathematical classes, with realset and complexset being *first-order* classes, and set a *second-order* class. A first-order class may contain only individuals (objects), a second-order class may contain only first-order classes, and so on.

Notice that a CLU object does not exist until the **create** function has been called. Object-oriented programming favors the automatic creation of objects when they are declared.

CLU also provides for classes of procedures. Remember that a *procedure* can be called anywhere within its scope in a program, whereas a *method* can only be called indirectly through its object interface. In the example above, realset$<procedure name> provides the interface to a realset object. A generic CLU search procedure over an array of elements would be declared:

```
search = procedure [t : type](a: array[t], key: t) returns int.
```

To call search, the type of the array elements, name of the array, and search key must all be provided to the procedure. FoundIndex := search[**real**](a, 5.0) is a legal search, whereas Wrong := search(a, 5.0) is not. Search is called a *polymorphic* function.

Generic Packages in Ada

Ada provides for generic procedures and functions as well as generic packages. These are *classes* in the sense that a generic procedure or package provides the template for instantiating a collection of procedures or packages. They are not classes in the object-oriented sense of creating instances during run time. Let us look at procedures first, as they are somewhat simpler than packages. Squaring an item is a good candidate, as the process applies to several types of objects. Squaring X is X * X, where "*" may be interpreted differently for integers, reals, complex numbers, or vectors. A generic Ada subprogram begins with the reserved word, **generic**, as shown in listing (3.4).

```
generic                                              (3.4)
   type ITEM is private;
   with function "*" (X, Y : ITEM) return ITEM is <>;
function SQUARING (X : ITEM) return ITEM;
```

SQUARING has two generic parameters that must be supplied before an actual function is instantiated. The first is the type of the ITEM to be squared, and the second is the multiplication function, "*". The <>, called *box*, indicates that "*" will be matched with a previously defined function when SQUARING is instantiated, as shown in listing (3.5).

```
function SQUARING(X : ITEM) is                       (3.5)
begin
   return X * X;
end;
```

When an Ada compiler encounters a generic subprogram body, it *elaborates* it, which, for generics, has no other effect than establishing that the body can be used by other program units to obtain instances (see listing (3.6)).

```
type VECTOR is array (INTEGER range <>) of REAL;     (3.6)
function CROSS_PRODUCT (U,V : VECTOR) return REAL is
begin...end;
```

```
function SQUARE is new SQUARING(ITEM => VECTOR,
                                "*" =>  CROSS_PRODUCT)

SQUARE is new SQUARING (INTEGER);          --"*" of listing (3.5)

                                           --used by default
function SQUARE is new SQUARING (REAL);
```

The *class* SQUARING would now contain the elements SQUARE(INTEGER), SQUARE(REAL), and SQUARE(VECTOR). Note that the instantiation of SQUARE(VECTOR) assumes the existence of the function CROSS_PRODUCT. The instantiations of listing (3.6) can occur only in a program's declarative section where procedure and function declarations are permissible. Ada allows the overloading of procedure names, as can be seen from the three different uses of SQUARE above. Since SQUARING names a *generic* function, however, to avoid ambiguities, it may not be overloaded.

Ada allows nine different type forms to appear in a **generic** section. They are:

1. **limited private**, which matches any data type
2. **private**, matching any data type allowing assignment and tests for equality
3. **access**, providing a pointer to a specified type
4. <>, matching any discrete type
5. **range** <>, matching any integer type
6. **delta** <>, matching a fixed-point type with any degree of accuracy
7. **digits** <>, matching a floating-point type, accurate to any number of digits
8. **array** (ANY_INDEX_TYPE) **of** ANY_ELEMENT_TYPE
9. **array** (ANY_INDEX **range** <>) of ANY_ELEMENT_TYPE

Generic packages are declared and instantiated similarly. An abbreviated example for a generic stack package is shown in listing (3.7) and a package body STACK is shown in listing (3.8).

```
generic                                                        (3.7)
    SIZE : POSITIVE := 100;
    type ITEM is private;
package STACK is
    procedure PUSH (I : in ITEM);
    procedure POP  (I : out ITEM);
    OVERFLOW, UNDERFLOW : exception;
end STACK;
```

```
package body STACK is                                        (3.8)

    type TABLE is array (POSITIVE range <>) of ITEM;
    MY_STACK    : TABLE(1..SIZE);
    INDEX       : NATURAL := 0;

    procedure PUSH(E in ITEM) is
    begin...end PUSH;

    procedure POP(E out ITEM) is
    begin...end POP;

end STACK;
```

Recall that a package body may be hidden from the user. Thus STACK above is an example of an ADT, with the type of MY_STACK known only in the (hidden) package body. Notice also that INDEX is initialized in the declaration to 0. Stacks could be instantiated using:

```
package INT_STACK_100 is new STACK(SIZE => 25, ITEM => INTEGER);
package INT_STACK     is new STACK(ITEM => INTEGER);
--uses the default value of 100 for SIZE
package REAL_STACK_50 is new STACK(50, REAL);
```

The designers of Ada had security as one of their primary goals, so a compiled generic package specification may not be used by another program until the package body has also been compiled. Ada requires all types to be established (*elaborated*) at compile time, thus any vagaries of a generic package must be resolved before being incorporated in another program unit. To bring INT_ STACK into a procedure we would use a **with** clause.

```
with INT_STACK;          --INT_STACK specification made visible

procedure SOME_SUBPROGRAM is
--declarations
begin...end SOME_PROGRAM;
```

If you are familiar with the Pascal language, **with** allowed us to omit qualifications to records by using a **with** statement. In Ada, using PUSH or POP, rather than INT_STACK.PUSH and INT_STACK.POP, is accomplished with a **use** clause: **use** INT_STACK; The **with** attaches the package to the client program.

Classes in Object Pascal

Object Pascal is truly object oriented,[2] providing for classes of dynamic objects. Objects are also what are often called *first-class entities*, that is, they can be passed to procedures as parameters and returned as functional values. This pro-

---

2 Some authors have criticized Turbo 5.5 because it does not enforce data hiding. An object can be accessed directly as well as through its methods. A second complaint is that objects are not automatically constructed on declaration, but through a special procedure called a **constructor**.

cess is accomplished through pointers to objects, called *references*. In Object Pascal, all access to an object is through references, while in Turbo Pascal 5.5, objects may be passed as objects or references to objects. An entity of type object may not be returned by a function, but a reference to an object may. This should not surprise Pascal users, as pointers, but not structured types, may be functional values.

A Turbo 5.5 declaration for a stack might be as shown in Figure 3.6.

This is not very interesting as an object, since it provides only for Stacks with elements of a single type, in this case integers. Turbo does provide for generic objects through the inheritance and virtual facilities, however. Let's see how. First, we must provide a template for *items* to be stack elements, as shown in listing (3.9).

```
unit Items;                                              (3.9)

interface

  type
    ItemPtr = ^Item;
    Item = object
      procedure Display; virtual;
    end;

    RealPtr = ^RealItem;
    RealItem = object(Item)
      R : real;
      constructor Init(X : real);
      constructor CueR;
      procedure Display; virtual;
    end;

  IntPtr = ^IntItem;
  IntItem = object(Item)
    I : integer;
    constructor Init(J : integer);
    constructor CueI;
    procedure    Display; virtual;
  end;
```

Notice several points here. Each object class, except Item, has a **constructor**, which is needed for calling **virtual** methods. **Virtual** is Pascal 5.5's reserved word indicating that a procedure name (message) is polymorphic. There may be different procedures (methods) for processing objects of different types, but the message is the same. We will consider what the constructor does in Figure 3.7. Also notice that `RealItem` and `IntItem` are both `object(Item)` types.

A RealItem object is also of type Item, as is an IntItem. The reverse does not hold, however. Each has a virtual method table (VMT), which includes the

```
unit Stacks;

interface;      {visible}

const
   MaxSize = 1000;
type
   Item  = integer;
   Range = 1..MaxSize;
   Table = array [Range] of Item;

   Stack = object
      MyStack        : Table;
      Index, Size    : Range;

   procedure Init(S : Range);
   procedure Push(E : Item);
   procedure Pop(var E : Item);

end;

implementation     {hidden}
{-----------------------------------------------------------}
{              Stack's method implementations               }
{-----------------------------------------------------------}
procedure Stack.Init(S : Range);
begin
   Size  := S;
   Index := 0;
end;

procedure Stack.Push(E : Item);
begin
   if Index >= Size
      then Writeln('Error: Stack Full')
      else begin
         Index := Index + 1;
         MyStack[Index] := E
      end
end;

procedure Stack.Pop(var E : Item);
begin
   if Index := 0
      then Writeln('Error: Stack empty.')
      else begin
         E := MyStack[Index];
         Index := Index - 1
      end;
end.
```

Figure 3.6 An integer Stack object implemented as a unit

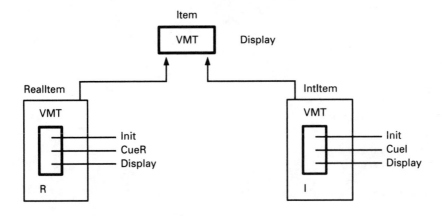

Figure 3.7   Hierarchy of Item objects

address of the constructor for the object, as well as addresses for any virtual methods. When confronted with a call to Display; the Object Pascal compiler checks to see what type object is involved in the Display, and then selects the appropriate method.[3] Item is a class that has no constructors. Thus there can be no instances of type Item. Such a class is called an *abstract class* and serves as a base class for RealItem and IntItem.

Notice how different this is from Ada's generics. Polymorphic Ada packages are declared at compile time, using the **NEW** function. There is no hierarchy of packages, and pointers to packages may not be passed as parameters. When we use **new** with an object in Pascal, we will be creating a pointer to a new object. The object itself, however, will not exist until the **constructor** is called. Recall that a Pascal record pointer "creates" a new record when **new**(Record-Ptr) is called, but does not initialize it. **New**(ObjectPtr) also reserves space, but a constructor is needed to set up the VMT as well as initialize any variables contained in the object.

Item's method implementations are shown in Figure 3.8. Figure 3.9 shows us how to incorporate Items in a stack.

A stack contains no objects other than those imported from Items. It does make sense to create it as a **unit**, though, to encapsulate stack data and procedures. We should mention that Pascal units do not enforce encapsulation of ADTs or objects. One can access a stack directly, not only through Init, Push, and Pop.

---

3 The method Display is included in object Item, even though we cannot construct an Item object. This is needed because the two descendants have methods called Display, and we wish to assign RealPtr's and IntPtr's to variables of type ItemPtr. A call to ItemP^.Display generates an error at compile time if ItemP is declared to be of type ItemPtr, unless there is a (potential) Display method defined for an Item.

implementation

```
{----------------------------------------------------------}
{   Item's method implementations                         }
{----------------------------------------------------------}

procedure Item.Display;
begin end;

{----------------------------------------------------------}
{   RealItem's method implementations                      }
{----------------------------------------------------------}

constructor RealItem.Init(X : real);
begin
  R := X
end;

constructor RealItem.CueR;
begin
  write('Enter a single real and press return:  ');
  readln(X)
end;

procedure RealItem.Display;
begin
  writeln(R:5:2)
end;

{----------------------------------------------------------}
{   IntItem's method implementations                       }
{----------------------------------------------------------}

constructor IntItem.Init(J : integer);
begin
  I := J
end;
constructor IntItem.CueI;
begin
  write('Enter a single integer and press return:  ');
  readln(I)
end;

procedure IntItem.Display;
begin
  writeln(I:5)
end;

end.
```

Figure 3.8   Implementation for Item methods

```pascal
unit Stacks;

interface

  uses Items;

  const
    MaxSize = 100;

  type
    Range = 0..MaxSize;
    Stack = record
      Table : array[Range] of ItemPtr;
      Max   : integer
    end;

  var
    Index    : Range;
    procedure Init(M : Range; var S : Stack);
    procedure Push(var S : Stack; E : ItemPtr);
    procedure Pop (var S : Stack; var E : ItemPtr);

  implementation

  procedure Init(M : Range; var S : Stack);
  var I : Range;
  begin
    S.Max    := M;
    Index    := 0;
  end;

  procedure Push(var S : Stack; E : ItemPtr);
  begin
    with S do begin
      If Index = Max
        then writeln('Error: Stack Full')
        else begin
          Index := Index + 1;
          Table[Index] := E
        end
    end
  end;

  procedure Pop(var S : Stack; var E : ItemPtr);
  begin
    if Index = 0
      then  writeln('Error: Stack Empty')
      else begin
        E := S.Table[Index];
        Index := Index - 1
      end
  end;

end.
```

Figure 3.9   Stacks unit

And finally, listing (3.10) shows a Pascal 5.5 program using both real and integer stacks.

```
program StackDemo;                                    (3.10)

uses Stacks, Items;

var
  RealStack     : Stack;
  IntStack      : Stack;
  AReal         : RealPtr;
  AnInt         : IntPtr;
  ItemP         : ItemPtr;

begin

{A RealStack example}

    Stacks.Init(10, RealStack);
    new(AReal, CueR);
    Push(RealStack, AReal);
    new(AReal, CueR);
    Push(RealStack, AReal);
    Pop(RealStack, ItemP);
    ItemP^.Display;
    Pop(RealStack, ItemP);
    ItemP^.Display;

{An IntegerStack example}

    Stacks.Init(5, IntStack);
    new(AnInt, CueI);
    {... with appropriate changes}
end.
```

This is not a very object-oriented way to implement a stack unit, since Stack itself is not an object. We'll see how to implement a Stack object in Section 3.3, after we have discussed Inheritance and Dynamic Binding.

EXERCISES

1. What meaning can you give to the position of the passenger object, P0, in Figure 3.3? Why couldn't a clerk object, such as C1, be "out of line"?

2. a. In the interface for the ROBOT unit of listing (3.2), what represents the *state* of an object of type ROBOT_ARM?

   b. What corresponds to the Pascal **interface** in Ada? to the Pascal **implementation**?

c. An Ada package specification can be compiled separately from the package body, where procedures are implemented. One advantage of this is that a main program using a package needs only the specification to compile properly, so work on a client program can proceed while a package is being completed. Object Pascal does not have this facility. The interface and implementation may be compiled separately from another program, but not from each other. How could you achieve the advantage stated above of Ada's separate compilation using Pascal?

3. Write generic declarations and a function body for VECTOR and CROSS_PRODUCT of listing (3.6) so that SQUARE will take vectors of any type, not just real vectors. Be careful about the sequence of instantiations.

4. Complete the coding for PUSH and POP of the STACK package of listing (3.8).

5. In Object Pascal, a **constructor** is needed to set up the VMT for an object. Suppose we have three instances of an object of type RealItem. Will each instance contain a table of pointers to the two functions, Init(X), and Display? If not, what will the VMT for an instance contain? If so, will these tables be identical or different?

6. Complete the IntStack example of listing (3.10).

7. In the StackDemo program, why did we have to qualify Stacks.Init, RealItem.Init, and IntItem.Init, but not Push or Pop? ∎

LAB IX: Polymorphism: Object Pascal/Ada

OBJECTIVES

1. To use the mechanisms available (Packages, units, objects) to encapsulate an ADT. In completing this lab, information hiding should be emphasized, even though the language may not enforce it.

2. To program a method already named in another object so that it acts differently on the new object. Overloading and/or virtual methods should be exemplified. ∎

HISTORICAL VIGNETTE 5: Smalltalk: Alan Kay

At first glance "smalltalk" seems like a strange name for any programming language to have. In society, smalltalk is the stuff of most gatherings. The word brings to mind conversation that is open to anyone. It can be understood and engaged in by people from various backgrounds and intellectual orientations since it deals with subjects that are universally understood and agreed on, e.g., the weather. Smalltalk is comfortable and easy with its traditional format. It doesn't delve into details. It skates along the surface of ideas. When Alan Kay developed Smalltalk as a language and philosophy of programming, his aim was to take the idea of "smalltalk" and bring it into the world of computing.

The story of Smalltalk, the computer language, begins when Alan Kay was in graduate school at the University of Utah in the late sixties. He was a man with a vision, which was to develop a notebook-sized portable computer that would have the capability of holding thousands of pages of information and execute millions of instructions per second. It would be programmed in a language nonspecialists could understand, utilize and learn from—unlike other programming languages of the sixties, which were geared toward specialists and applications that would not be used by others. The computer would have high-quality graphics that could make it more user friendly. It would have a keyboard, a CRT, and a mouse that would make it possible for areas of the screen to double as a keyboard.

"To appreciate how radical the hardware component of this vision was at the time, consider the state of computing in the 1960s. The personal computer had not yet been heard of. Keyboards and CRTs were still novelties in a world of punched cards, and the graphics capabilities of most mainframe computers were limited to printing pictures of Snoopy out of X's." [Baron, 1986, p. 358]. Kay envisioned the use of his computer and language as a tool that could reshape education with its ability to help students understand concepts and create new ones. This educational view was as radical as Kay's hardware visions. At this time, the only projected educational computer use involved drill and practice exercises.

Kay began working on a programming language called FLEX, a "flexible, extensible language." Kay incorporated ideas from the recently developed LOGO of Seymour Papert and his colleagues at MIT. LOGO was being used to teach programming concepts to children. Like LOGO, FLEX maintained an open, interactive dialogue between the user and the machine and allowed the user to create new discussions whenever needed.

After earning advanced degrees at the University of Utah, Kay went to work for the Xerox Palo Alto Research Center (PARC). There he continued working toward his vision. He organized the Learning Research Group to work to develop his computer, now called the "Dynabook," since it was based on the dynamic retrieval of information. Its software was named "Smalltalk™." An entire system was developed incorporating the special hardware and software. The first version of Smalltalk was completed and implemented in 1972. 1973 saw an "Interim Dynabook" completed for purposes of research. Smalltalk-72 and this Dynabook were used experimentally with more than 250 children aged 6 to 15 and 50 adults. Experience with Smalltalk has led to several revisions, including Smalltalk-74, -76, -78, and -80.

Smalltalk is intended as a language for everybody. There is a problem, however. It is very different from most other computer languages. It is a nightmare for lazy programmers, since learning a language based on unique concepts is harder than learning a language similar to others one knows. "As a language, Smalltalk offers a uniform and powerful metaphor: procedures and data that belong together are packaged in an 'object.' An object interacts with the rest of the system by singling out another object and sending it a message. Smalltalk's combination of good editors, a natural modularization of code, and a language based on a powerful idea forms a system that is at its best during construction and evolution of a large application program." [Kaeler, 1986, p. vii].

In 1980, Xerox Corporation began distributing Smalltalk-80. Companies chosen to review the language were Apple Computer, Digital Equipment Corporation, Hewlett-Packard, and Tektronix. Xerox wanted to expand both the communities of Smalltalk programmers and researchers, influence hardware designers to improve Smalltalk performance, and establish a standard for Smalltalk as an object-oriented, graphics-based programming language [Krasner, 1983].

By 1982, the review process was complete and it became possible to publish material about the Smalltalk system. In return for their help, the companies involved were given the right to use Smalltalk-80 in their research and hardware development projects. When Alan Kay left Xerox in the early eighties to work for Apple, he renamed his research group the Software Concepts Group, reflecting a change from the original educational focus.

Smalltalk as a production language never took off, but it has influenced other systems. The Apple Macintosh® mouse-controlled system of icons and overlapping windows was first pioneered by Kay for Smalltalk. He continues to work on perfecting his vision for the Dynabook. Unlike conversational smalltalk, the Smalltalk system has proved to be anything but trivial.

BRIEF THEORETICAL EXCURSION 4:
Objects: Inheritance and Dynamic Binding

We have already seen an example of *inheritance* in our Pascal classes, RealItem and IntItem, which inherit the Display procedure from the class, Items. We have also seen two *clients* of Items, the unit Stacks and the program StkDemo. Item is an *abstract class* because there is no Item `constructor`, thus there can be no Item instances. Its sole purpose is to implement polymorphic items with a method, Display. RealItem and IntItem each have one instance variable, R and I, respectively. The instance variable is initialized as part of the construction of a class instance, or object.

Smalltalk is a pure object-oriented language, where everything is an object descended from an abstract class called `Object`. Object has no instance variables, but does have 66 methods, which are inherited by all other objects. These, among others, define default methods for displaying, copying, and comparing objects and reporting errors.

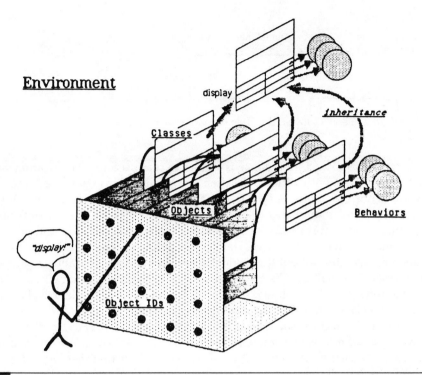

Figure 3.10   The message/object model including inheritance. Reproduced with permission from *IEEE Software*, January 1984, p. 53. © IEEE.

Let's fill in Cox's diagram as shown in Figure 3.2 to indicate inheritance of the method for a "Display" message—see Figure 3.10.

The little stick figure represents a client, while the shaded panels behind the wall are instances of object classes. Notice that each instance has a pointer into the class (the unshaded panels). In Object Pascal, this is a pointer into the VMT. The shaded circles represent the *behaviors* or *methods* of the various classes. When an object receives the message "Display," it checks to see if there is a method for answering the message. If there is not, it checks the class inheritance hierarchy as far as necessary to find one. In the figure, there is only one superclass to the class instance receiving "Display." It can be found in the background of the figure and has three behavior-producing methods.[4]

When discussing inheritance and the hierarchy of object types, an animal example is often used, as shown in the structure below [Digitalk, 1986].

---

4 Notice the active language when discussing objects. In actor languages, objects are viewed in just this way, as if they behaved and influenced other objects to act themselves. This is part of the object-oriented mindset.

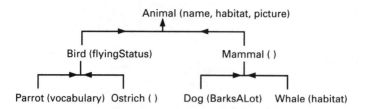

The tree structure for object inheritance is similar to that used for classification systems in the natural sciences, with which most users are familiar. This structure demonstrates the IS-A and HAS-A relations. A Bird IS-A mammal that HAS-A flyingStatus of true or false. Since a Bird IS-A mammal, it also HAS-A habitat. It inherits this attribute from the object Mammal. Attributes can be of three kinds (using Wegner's definition [Wegner, 1988]): redefined, virtual, or recursive. Habitat is redefined in the whale class, name and picture are recursive throughout the hierarchy, and flyingStatus, vocabulary, and barks-ALot are virtual. The attributes listed here are instance variables, but methods may also be recursive (inheritable), redefined, or virtual. In our Item example, Display is redefined in each subclass, while the constructors and variables are virtual.

This use of *virtual* does not conform to the Object Pascal **virtual** declaration. The English word *virtual* means proximate or having the same effect, as in, "My passing this course is virtually assured if I get an A on the next test." Virtual memory for a CPU is offline until needed. To the user it appears that this memory is virtually the same as central memory. A virtual computer is built on top of bytes and words so that users think they are dealing with higher-level objects, such as reals, integers, and characters. The old low-level machine behaves virtually the same as one with high-level features built in. Wegner's definition of virtual attributes in objects reflects another definition of *virtual*, listed as obsolete in some dictionaries: virtual = potential. The virtual attribute, flyingStatus, is potential for an animal, but actual if that animal turns out to be a bird. *And* we don't need to know whether the animal is a bird or not at compile time.

In Turbo Pascal 5.5, a **virtual** method is one that "is implemented using late binding, by defining it with the new reserved word, **virtual**. In practice, a virtual method shares an identical procedure or function header [message] with one or more methods within its object hierarchy." [Turbo 5.5, 1988]. In other words, Turbo's reserved word **virtual** is used to identify what Wegner calls redefined methods.

By now the notion of late binding shouldn't be too mystifying. When a source file is parsed and compiled, machine code for a static procedure is stored beginning at a particular memory address. Procedure calls found within the program are replaced with transfer instructions to that address. The call is *bound* to that beginning address. This is called early binding, since the call is bound at the earliest possible time. In contrast, a procedure call, such as ItemP^.Display (see Figure 3.10), cannot be bound at compile time because it will not be known until run time whether ItemP is pointing to an Item, a RealItem, or an IntItem. Thus the location where code for Display (the callee) is to be found must be bound late to the caller.

If a parent object has many descendants, and it is not known which descendants will be constructed during a program run, many virtual procedures and functions will never be called. However, object-oriented compilers as well as languages can remove any procedures that are never called by the program, generating code only for those that will potentially be used.

The object-oriented programming style demands familiarity with classes that are already available and then extending them to create other classes and objects specialized to the programming task at hand. Smalltalk-80 (from ParcPlace Systems) is shipped with more than 240 classes, while Smalltalk/V (from Digitalk) includes 110. Objective-C™ (Stepstone) includes 20, and C++ provides none. However, as is customary with C implementations, other vendors sell object libraries [Auer, 1989].

Ada lacks inheritance and dynamic binding of objects, and is thus not considered an object-oriented language. InnovAda [Simonian, 1988] has been designed at the Harris Corporation to preprocess class and object definitions into ANSI/MIL-STD 1815A Ada. The designers were motivated by a contract for the design of a space station. The specifications include expert system technology for communications and tracking systems. Harris does most of its artificial intelligence prototyping in object-oriented Flavors on a LISP machine or a Smalltalk machine. Final code had to be written in Ada, and manually translating classes and objects consumed too much time. InnovAda allows a programmer to define objects and methods, specify single and multiple inheritance, access an Ada compiler, linker, and debugger, and access all other VAX™/VMS™ tools and utilities. Objects are implemented as independent Ada packages. Recompilation of some client Ada units may be necessary during run time, since Ada requires that a package must be compiled before it can be **use**d in an Ada unit. This is, of course, slow but adequate for developing prototypes or experimental systems. The final programs will be solely in Ada.

Modula-2 provides for no automatic creation of objects and has a weak form of polymorphism. It does, however, offer separate compilation of definition and implementation modules, unlike Pascal. Modula-2 is still considered deficient in hiding implementation details, as is Object Pascal, since neither language enforces access to object variables solely through object methods. Bergin and Greenfield [Bergin, 1989] believe that extending Modula-2 to include objects would be both practical and useful, although not much progress has been made in that direction.

MULTIPLE INHERITANCE

So far we have seen classes providing for tree-structured inheritance, with descendants exhibiting an IS-A relationship with a parent. Some objects could rightly inherit from multiple parents, e.g., a BOOK IS-A NOVEL and a BOOK IS-A STORY make good sense. If BOOK, NOVEL, and STORY are all objects, the inheritance structure would be as shown in Figure 3.11.

The Eiffel language [Meyer, 1988], the Common LISP Object System (CLOS), and Version 2.0 of C++ [Shopiro, 1989] all support multiple inheritance. One must be con-

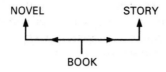

Figure 3.11   Multiple inheritance

ceptually careful when designing classes that inherit from multiple parents. First of all, the <descendant> IS-A <parent> relation should be maintained. IS-A restricts its descendants to be of the same object type as each of their parents, while a descendant extends the parent type to include new variables and methods. These notions must be preserved to keep designs understandable and clean.

One potential problem for a descendant object is name clashes among methods. What if NOVEL and STORY each have a method LIST_PLOT? This must be handled in the descendant, but is not difficult. Eiffel solves it by introducing a **rename** operator, as shown in listing (3.11).

```
class BOOK export...inherit                          (3.11)
    NOVEL;
    STORY
       rename LIST_PLOT as STORY_LINE
    feature
    ...
end                 --class BOOK
```

Multiple inheritance is new to C++, so there is little experience with it. Wiener and Pinson [Wiener, 1989] provide an example of a class IntegerArray inheriting from both Array and Integer classes, and Shopiro [Shopiro, 1989] discusses implemented, multiple inheriting classes from the Iostream library, which supplies I/O utilities. Ten interconnected classes have been designed to specialize the base classes shown in Figure 3.12 to files. This provides a good example of using inheritance to restrict general I/O to files and extend classes by providing specialized methods for files.

Iostream inherits from both istream, containing input methods, and ostream, which has output methods. It has no variables or functions at all, but inherits all its attributes from {ios, istream} or {ios, ostream}. Ios is an *abstract* class containing only *virtual* methods that are implemented in either istream or ostream. Streambuf is also a class to which *Streambuf points. Most of the real I/O work is included in Streambuf or other specialized classes. Ios decides whether Input or Output is occurring and makes the connection to Streambuf through a pointer, bp. Istream contains an input function, c = bp→get(), and ostream has an output method, bp→put(c).

So what is the advantage of being able to think of an iostream as either an input stream or an output stream? Before multiple inheritance there was only one kind of C++ stream. It was only at run time that an inappropriate operation, such as trying to write

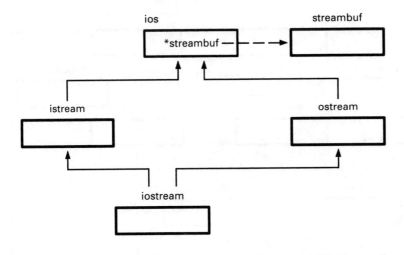

Figure 3.12   Multiple inheritance in C++

to an input stream, would be caught. Multiple inheritance allows the two kinds of streams to be separated into istreams and ostreams. This separation could have been accomplished without multiple inheritance only by copying over shared code for the two different stream types.

When these objects are specialized to files, however, the real utility surfaces, since there is more common code, as Figure 3.13 shows.

Shopiro [Shopiro, 1989] says that the C++ code implementing the objects of Figures 3.12 and 3.13, "is not quite a practical example of multiple inheritance in C++ because the facility it describes is too simple to be useful." Object-oriented programmers be warned!

EXERCISES

1. Redraw Figure 3.10 so that it conforms to the structure for Item, RealItem, and IntItem objects. Label each class and method with its message name.

2. Consider each of the variables and methods defined for the classes Item, RealItem, and IntItem, and classify each as recursive, redefined, or virtual using Wegner's definition.

3. Does the class IntegerArray satisfy the IS_A relationship with both its base classes, Integer and Array?

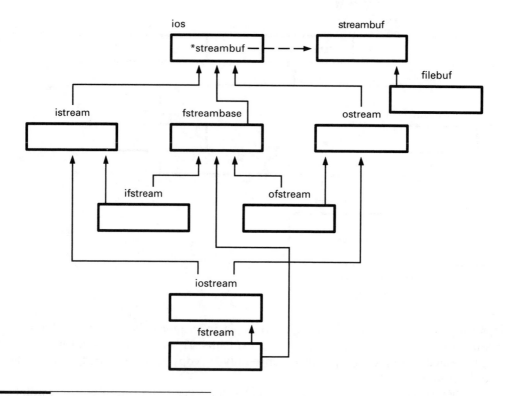

Figure 3.13 Specialization of ios to files

3.3 OBJECT-ORIENTED LANGUAGES

We are now ready to look at what are known as object-oriented languages, those supporting information hiding, data abstraction, message passing, dynamic binding, and inheritance.

Objects + Classes + Inheritance = Object Oriented

From Shopiro's comment above, it might seem that object-oriented programming isn't worth the trouble. It is inheritance that belies this conclusion. Even though tricky to write, classes are reusable. Once they have been verified, creating new classes and objects through inheritance should be easier than starting from scratch each time.

Learning an object-oriented language won't be a short task, however, as one must learn and understand class libraries to choose which ones to build on effectively. OOP languages are either pure, such as Smalltalk, or hybrid, like

C++ and Object Pascal. The hybrid languages have been built on top of existing languages and attract a coterie of programmers experienced in using the base language. Habits die slowly, and Object Pascal programmers will realize little improvement in productivity if they merely throw a few objects into a block-structured program. One must learn to think in terms of objects, rather than procedures.

OOP has some efficiency disadvantages. Classes use space to separate the virtual method tables and pointers from object instances into the VMT. Accessing methods through at least these two pointers also makes OOP programs run somewhat slower than their procedural counterparts. Researchers have also noticed something called the "Yo-Yo effect," where execution involving an object that inherits methods from ancestor classes keeps bouncing up and down the class hierarchy to find which method to use. This behavior suggests short ancestor trees or some sort of optimization so that the whole tree need not be traversed each time a distant method is accessed.

More Object Pascal

We will offer some suggestions for lending more of the OOP style to the Stack unit of Section 3.2. We'll start at the very beginning and let a Stack class inherit some of its methods from a more general List class. The object-oriented programming style includes reusing classes that have already been tested and debugged. Fortunately, Turbo Pascal 5.5 provides a List class called, obviously, List. Listing (3.12) shows this process.

```
uses                                              (3.12)
   Items;

type

NodePtr = ^Node;
Node = record
  Item : ItemPtr;
  Next : NodePtr
end;

ListPtr = ^List;
List    = object
  Nodes : NodePtr;
  constructor Init;
  destructor  Done; virtual;
  procedure Add(Item : ItemPtr);
  procedure Report;
end;

var
   ItemList : List;
```

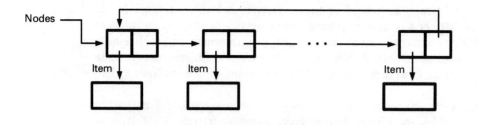

Figure 3.14   A circular List of pointers to objects

A List then is a list of pointers to nodes. In this case, each node contains two pointers, one to the Item on the list and the second to the Next Item, as shown in Figure 3.14.

As we have seen, Item objects can be polymorphic, thus the List above, pointed to by Nodes, can include Items, RealItems, and IntItems, or any other sort of items if we wish to create more descendants of Item.

We have already seen **constructors**, but a **destructor** is new. It does as the name suggests, destructs an existing object after we have finished with it. Just as **new** was extended to initialize objects, as in, **new**(RealItem, CueR); **dispose** can be used with **dispose**(ItemList, Done). A destructor cleans up any pointer fields in an object and any pointers inherited from ancestor objects. It also disposes of the VMT pointers and calls **dispose** to release storage occupied by the object. Implementation for a List destructor in Turbo 5.5 is shown in listing (3.13).

```
destructor List.Done;                                        (3.13)
var
  N : NodePtr;
begin
  while Nodes <> nil do begin
    N := Nodes;
    dispose (N^.Item, Done);
    Nodes := N^.Next;
    dispose (N);
  end
end;
```

In the second line of the **while** statement, we call **dispose**(N^.Item, Done). This "Done" refers to a **destructor**, Item.Done, not to List.Done, so we must add it to the Item **object**. In this case, the **destructor** need do nothing but the invisible operations of eliminating VMT pointers. Listing (3.14) shows this process.

```
type                                              (3.14)
  ItemPtr = ^Item;
  Item = object
    procedure Display; virtual;
    destructor Done;
  end;

  destructor Item.Done;
  begin  end;
```

List.Add adds a new Item to the front of the List, while List.Report takes care of output of Items. We will leave these for the Lab.

The List class is a template for Items of any type object. A client program must have access only to the type of Node:

```
Node = record
  Item : ItemPtr;
  Next : NodePtr
end;
```

We may not wish to change this record, so we can name an abstract class heading the objects we want to incorporate on our list, Item. The other alternative is to change the first field of Node to SomeOtherItem : SomeOtherPtr, which might require making changes to List methods. Pointing to OtherItems with a pointer called ItemPtr is probably as flexible as we can be.

LAB X: Classes and Inheritance: Object Pascal

OBJECTIVES

1. To complete the declarations for a List object, incorporating pointers to other objects.
2. To write some of the List utilities, such as DeleteFromFront, DeleteFrom-End, DeleteAfter, DeleteBefore, AddAfter, AddBefore, etc.
3. To complete the implementation of a stack of objects.
4. To sketch the implementation of a queue of objects.
5. To see how inheritance contributes to the value of reusable code. ■

C++

C++, like Object Pascal, is built on an existing language. That is, any C programs should run on a C++ compiler. With few exceptions, C is a subset of C++. One of the goals in writing C++ was efficiency. In part, C was written to eliminate the need for assembly language code. Bit manipulations are included in the language, providing for fast translation and compilation and the elimination of calls to assembly language procedures. C++ programs, although including higher-level features than C, can use the same run-time library developed for C.

Classes and structures

C++ adds the **class** type to C's simple and derived types. Continuing with our stack example, we will look at a declaration for a linked list in C++, which serves as an abstract class [Stroustrup, 1986]. First, we need to define an item type, a node class for objects holding an Item, and a pointer to the next link. As in our Pascal implementation, the first link field is a pointer to some object to be defined later. Listing (3.15) shows node class for a linked list.

```
typedef void* ItemPtr;                                    (3.15)

class node {
friend class list;
friend class list_iterator
  node* next;
  ItemPtr  e;
  node(ItemPtr a, link* p) {e = a; next = p;   }
};
```

Void serves as the base type for a pointer. Thus **void*** ItemPtr declares ItemPtr to be a pointer to any type we may want to use later. Node* points to a node. The function, node, is the constructor for node, and assigns a to the instance variable e and p to the node pointer, next. When a variable is declared to be of type, node, the constructor is called automatically.

```
real* x;              //x holds a pointer to a real
node a(x, 0);
```
[5]

initializes a to:

So far nothing looks different from our Pascal implementation, but this is misleading because the data fields, e and next, and the node constructor are not

---

5 In C, the token 0 is used for the null pointer as well as the number zero. Its use is determined by the context.

public information. e and next are known only through their **friend**s, list and list_iterator. The constructor is called on declaration of a node variable. C++ has three reserved words, **private, public**, and **protected**. Private class members are hidden from the user, and may be accessed only through **friend**s. Public members are known and can be accessed by any procedure, and protected members are known to descendants of a class. In the C++ literature, a descendant is called a *derived class*.

C supports a record type, called a **structure**. The default for **structure** fields is public, while the default for **class** fields is private. There is no other difference. Adding the reserved word **class** is little more than syntactic sugar in C++, as we could achieve the same results using structures with appropriate uses of **private** and **public**. Listing (3.16) shows class declarations for a linked list.

```
class list {                                              (3.16)
friend class list_iterator; // needs to be defined to get around

                            // the list in some applications
  node* last;               // last->next is head of list
public
  int insert(ItemPtr a);    //add a at head of list
  int append(ItemPtr a);    //add a at end of the list
  ItemPtr get();            //return and remove head of list

  list()          {last = 0;}                    //constructor
  list(ItemPtr)   {last=new node(a, 0); last->next=last;  }
                                                 //constructor
  ~list()         {clear();    }                 //destructor
};
```

The list **class** is not very useful, as all we can do with it is make linked lists of void pointers. It does, however, provide a reusable parent class for other useful structures. The C style includes combining many small files into the input for other programs. Thus we will store the list in a file, with a separate header, "list.h," containing a pointer to the executable code. We will **include** it in any programs requiring its methods. Listing (3.17) shows derived classes, list:stack and stack:realstack.

```
#include "list.h"                                         (3.17)

class stack : private list {
protected:
  virtual void push(ItemPtr a) {list :: insert(a); }
  virtual ItemPtr pop()        {return (ItemPtr) list :: get(); }

  stack();                     {}
  stack(ItemPtr a);            {}
}
```

```
struct realstack : stack {
  void push(real *a);              {stack :: push(a); }
  real pop();                      {return (*a) stack :: pop(); }

  realstack();                     {}
  realstack(real *a);              {stack :: stack(a); }
  ~realstack();                    {}

}
```

After list :: insert is suitably defined, the code: `{realstack rs; {rs.push`
`(1.0); rs.push(2.0); } }` will produce the stack,[6]

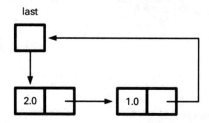

Notice that we declared all the methods of stack to be **protected**. Stack by itself cannot be used. It serves only as a template for various classes or structures derived from it. The methods of list are **private** in stack. So a call such as rs.get() would cause an error. In the spirit of ADTs, the only access to a realstack is through its methods, pop and push, its constructors and its destructor. Pop and push were declared **virtual** in class stack, so they will be redefined in derived classes such as realstack.

Multiple inheritance in C++

Although the first versions of C++ did not support multiple inheritance, Version 2.0 does. Problems involved storage for pointers to virtual functions, i.e., those that could be redefined in derived classes. C++ uses an implementation similar to Pascal's VMT to store pointers to its virtual functions. Consider three classes, a, b, and c.

```
class a {
  int i;
public
  virtual f1();
  virtual f2();
}
```

---

6 Keeping the list as a circular list enables easy access to either the front or the rear of a list. For details, see [Stroustrup, 1986, p. 203ff].

```
class b {
   int j;
public
   virtual f2();
   virtual f3();
}

class c: public a, public b {
   int k;
public:
   f2();
   f4();
}
```

The problem with multiple inheritance is setting up the pointers to virtual functions. In the Tau Metric C++ compiler [Ball, 1989], a class derived from only one ancestor would use only one virtual table. For example, class c : a would be stored as shown in Figure 3.15.

If we want class c to inherit from both a and b, two virtual tables are used, the first for c : a and the second for b, as shown in Figure 3.16.

Inheritance from more than two classes can be handled similarly, with an additional virtual table added for each new ancestor class.

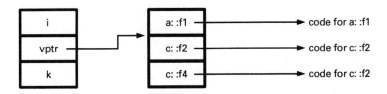

Figure 3.15   Class c derived from class a

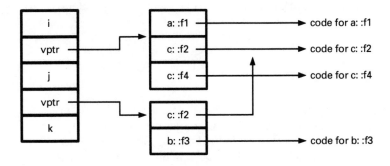

Figure 3.16   Class c derived from class a and class b

EXERCISES

1. Write C code for the get and insert functions of class list.
2. In the C++ code of listing (3.17), why are there parentheses around (Item-Ptr) and (*a)?
3. Redraw the diagrams of Figure 3.15 to represent class c : b, and Figure 3.16 to represent class c : b, a. ■

3.4 SUMMARY

In this chapter we have looked at object-based and object-oriented languages. Both languages support objects, which encapsulate data with state and operations on that data, called methods. Objects communicate with each other through message passing, where a message is the name of an object's method. In addition, object-oriented languages support dynamic binding, where an object can be created or destroyed at run time, and inheritance. Inheritance implies a hierarchy of classes, with objects in a subclass inheriting methods and/or data from a superclass. Inheritance can be single or multiple, in which case a subclass may inherit from more than one superclass.

Ada and CLU are object-based languages, while Object Pascal and C++ are object oriented, i.e., inheritance is supported. The first object-oriented languages were Simula and Smalltalk, which is a pure object language, in which every data type or aggregate is an object.

Programming with objects involves quite a different style from top-down procedural methods. Here a problem is envisioned as a collection of interacting objects. Objects in Simula were first thought of as either active or passive. Simula's successor languages have three sorts of objects that execute concurrently, as coroutines or subobjects. The notion of active objects has been implemented in actor-type languages that are assumed to be acting independently and concurrently.

3.5 NOTES ON REFERENCES

A good, although brief, summary of object-oriented languages is [Saunders, 1989]. He discusses and provides vendors for 16 languages categorized by type as Actor, concurrent, distributed, frame based, hybrid (C or LISP based), logical, Smalltalk based, idealogical extensions, and miscellaneous. Ada and other object-based languages are not included.

Several newsletters are attempting to publish the latest information in this rapidly developing field. Three of these are *The Journal of Object-Oriented Pro-*

gramming (JOOP), which publishes 10 issues a year, *Hotline on Object-Oriented Technology (HOOT)*, a monthly, and the *C++ Report*, published 10 times a year. *JOOP* contains articles plus regular columns on the Eiffel, Smalltalk, Actor, Common LISP Object System (CLOS), Objective C, and C++ languages.

Creating reusable classes that are practical and useful is hard work. [Johnson, 1988] follows a discussion of object-oriented toolkits and libraries with 13 good programming practice rules.

[Krasner, 1984] presents a good collection of papers describing the background of Smalltalk-80, experiences with implementing it for various computers, test results, and proposals for future development.

4

DISTRIBUTED PROGRAMMING: Language Constructs for Parallel Processing

If we divide up a job between two or more workers, it usually gets done faster, and sometimes better. Some real-world situations also imply activities going on concurrently. But too many cooks really can spoil the broth. Joint projects take coordination. In this chapter, we will look at languages that support more than one processor working on a problem. They may work independently and then communicate partial results to each other, or they may all work on the same project. The work may be done simultaneously or alternately. Whatever the system, three issues distinguish distributed from sequential programming [Bal, 1989]:

1. The use of multiple processors
2. Cooperation among the processors
3. The potential for partial failure

Labels have been intentionally omitted from Figure 4.1, since there is no unanimity in the literature for naming what each of the two diagrams represent. All agree, however, that both involve two or more CPUs which communicate with each other. The top shows each with its own memory and a communication channel between them. Here memory as well as CPUs are distributed. The

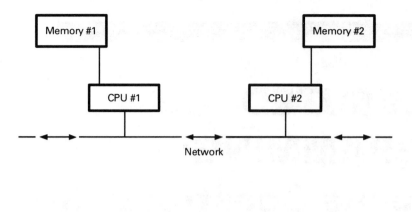

Network

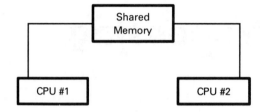

Figure 4.1

bottom diagram shows no communication channel, but shared memory. Only the CPUs are distributed.

Bal, Steiner, and Tanenbaum [Bal, 1989] call the top system *distributed*, and the bottom not, while Shatz and Wang [Shatz, 1989] consider them both to be distributed, since more than one communicating CPU is involved and work can be distributed over them. To complicate matters further, Shatz and Wang consider the top system to be *loosely coupled* and the bottom *tightly coupled*. Bal and his colleagues call only the top configuration coupled. To them, a loosely coupled system is one where the cooperating CPUs are physically far apart and communication may be unreliable. If the communication channel is a network, this is called a wide area network, or WAN. The closely coupled system is a local area network, or LAN.

In this chapter, we will look at both situations and not worry too much about the names. Where memory is unshared, CPUs communicate by sending and receiving messages. When shared, each cooperating CPU can initialize and/or update the same memory locations. A third configuration for multiprocessors provides for both message passing and memory sharing. In Figure 4.2 the shared memory is represented by a dashed-line box to indicate logical memory. It may physically be Memory #1, Memory #2, or some third block of Memory. When many processors are involved, sometimes thousands, a great

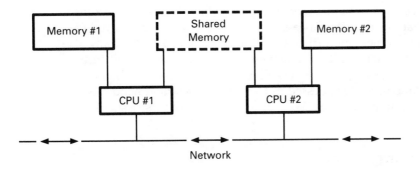

Figure 4.2

variety of architectures are possible. We will not consider these architectures here. The IEEE Computer Society has provided a very brief tutorial, with several good diagrams and guides to further reading in the February 1990 issue of *Computer* [Duncan, 1990].

Distributed systems are advantageous because:

1. They can speed up programs by running different processes in parallel
2. They can enhance reliability if two or more processors duplicate each other's jobs
3. They provide a natural avenue for system growth when additional processors are added
4. They facilitate naturally distributed tasks, such as electronic mail.

A word needs to be said about *processes* and *processors*. So far we have talked about CPUs or physical processors, hardware items that you can touch and see. In this sense, a process is a single sequential procedure running on a single physical processor. Processors can be logical, however. We encountered this notion when we looked at Modula-2's coroutines. On a single machine, coroutines execute alternately and one at a time, sharing the same CPU. In a multiple CPU architecture, a Modula-2 compiler could distribute the coroutines to different CPUs. This might well be an operating system function, with the user unaware whether coroutines were running in parallel or alternately. From a logical point of view, the processes and processors are the same. Some authors reserve the term *multiprocessing* for processes running in parallel and use multiprogramming to include either parallel or alternating execution of processes.

In Chapter 1, we saw two Ada tasks, DiskBuffer and Airplanes. The first provides for memory sharing, where communication occurs through the rendezvous. In the second, the several airplane tasks run in parallel without sharing memory.

Whether processes share memory or not or are loosely or tightly coupled, the probability that one or more processors will fail escalates when several are running at the same time. The further apart the processors are physically also contributes to system failure. Thus languages in this paradigm will include some mechanism for continuation of the still working processors and/or recovery from partial failure. You've guessed it! How do we raise and handle exceptions among cooperating processes? We will address each of these issues below.

4.0 MULTIPLE PROCESSES

A *process* is an abstract data type that can, although need not, run in parallel with another process. A *process unit* is the language construct capable of encapsulating a process. These units may also be called *units of parallelism*. In Modula-2, the unit is a coroutine; in Ada, a task; and in Concurrent Pascal, a process. The Occam language allows individual statements to serve as process units. A sequence of Occam statements preceded by **PAR** will execute in parallel. For example:

```
PAR i = 0 FOR 100
   A[i] := 0
```

will initialize an entire array to 0 simultaneously. This step may or may not save time, depending on how quickly the operating system can switch execution to the 100 separate processors. Objects can also serve as process units in languages that support them such as Concurrent Smalltalk or Emerald. Functional languages use expressions as process units, while logic-based languages use clauses. In some, although not all, of the literature, any unit of parallelism is called a process. We will observe this definition here.

ALGOL 68 includes the notion of *collateral clauses*, such as:

```
begin x := 3, y := 2, z := "bird" end
```

ALGOL statements are separated in most instances by semicolons, but in the collateral clause by commas. These statements can be executed in any order. As with most parallel execution schemes, which gets done first is not specified.

Collateral clauses do not communicate with each other. If we write:

```
x := 0;
begin x := 3, x := x + 1, z := "bird" end;
```

the value of x will be indeterminate after the collateral clause has executed, since we don't know which goes first. Is x = 3, or is x = 4? It is even possible that x = 1. Let's see how this could be. To facilitate discussion, we will call $x := 3$, c_1, $x := x + 1$, c_2, and $z :=$ "bird", c_3.

If c_1 completes before c_2 starts to execute, then c_2 will be $x = 3 + 1$, or 4. If c_1 executes after c_2 has completed, x will be 3. Now suppose the clauses are

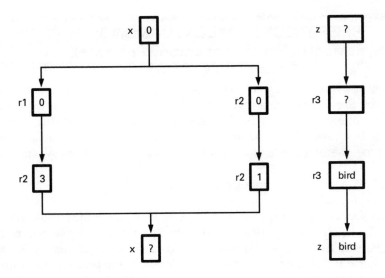

Figure 4.3

executing concurrently, and sharing the memory location for x. Execution of an assignment statement on a machine with registers usually involves three steps:

1. Load current value of x into a register, r.
2. Perform the right-side operation, leaving the result in r.
3. Store value of r in the location for x.

We will assume that c1 and c2 have associated registers r1 and r2. Now suppose c1 starts executing and stores 0 in r1. x = r1 = 0. c2 is also running, with x = r2 = 0. Now if c1 completes so that x = r1 = 3, c2 will not know about it. It has already performed the "read the value of x into r2" operation and proceeds to increment r2. The final "store r2 into x" will leave x = 1. (See Figure 4.3.)

Without some method for synchronization, we may make no assumptions as to how concurrent processes will be interleaved. Several issues arise here. Our three collateral clauses illustrate one: Who gets access to a shared resource, for how long and when?

Communication between processes can be handled through either message passing or data sharing. Message passing tends to be more reliable, but experience shows that the programs are harder to write than those for shared memories.

We will look at the synchronization of shared resources first. The excursion that follows makes little reference to existing languages, but discusses three synchronization mechanisms: semaphores, monitors, and rendezvous. We will discuss their implementations in Section 4.1.

BRIEF THEORETICAL EXCURSION 5:
Synchronization of Cooperating Processes

Two or more running processes may communicate partial results before continuing or may share resources. Resource sharing involves each process gaining access to the same memory locations, but only one at a time. Processes run at different speeds, so there is no guarantee that one process will have its results computed or relinquish shared resources by the time a second needs them. Thus the processes need to be synchronized in some fashion.

The Dining Philosophers is a famous example of potential problems with cooperating processes. (See Figure 4.4.)

The five philosophers sit around a table, with a bowl of rice in the middle and five chopsticks. Each alternately thinks and eats, and all five perform these two actions concurrently. Thus there are five processes in which P_i eats and thinks alternately. In order to eat, a philosopher must pick up two chopsticks, one from his left and one from his right. These are the shared resources. How can we schedule their actions so that no one is silent and no one starves?

Five problems should be avoided when scheduling cooperating processes. These problems are busy waiting, alternation, starvation, unfairness, and deadlock. We will describe each in terms of the Dining Philosophers.

Busy Waiting   One way to schedule the philosophers is to set up and test shared variables and test them repeatedly. For example, we could set up five $Hungry_i$ Booleans, one for each philosopher. If $Hungry_2$ were TRUE, then $Philosopher_1$ would be required to relinquish $Chopstick_1$ and $Philosopher_3$ to relinquish $Chopstick_2$ to $Philosopher_2$ in a reasonable amount of time. This schedule could easily be implemented using counters to monitor how long a particular philosopher had monopolized a particular chopstick.

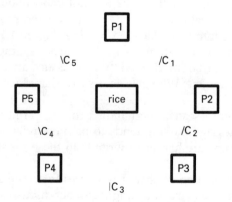

Figure 4.4

It is the repeated testing of the Hungry$_i$ variables that is called *busy waiting*. While a Philosopher waits for his two chopsticks, processes for Dining Philosophers are busily testing to see if a neighbor has signaled Hungry.

Alternation A simple solution would be to let P1 and P3 eat for a specified period of time, then P2 and P4, then P5 and P2, etc. However, the notion of concurrency includes response to random requests within a reasonable amount of time, not rigid scheduling of access. Each philosopher should be able to think when there is something to think about, and to eat only when hungry.

Starvation One possible scheme for scheduling the philosopher's eating is to let each check on the availability of the necessary chopsticks and eat only when both are available. Suppose P1 picks up C1 and C5. Then P2 and P5 must continue to think, whether or not they have anything interesting to think about. P3 could eat, however. P1 and P3 will finish eating eventually, but we still may starve one of the others. Only two can eat at a time, but the presence of five philosophers requires something more sophisticated than checking to see if both chopsticks are available.

Unfairness Unfairness results when one or more of the philosophers have to wait an unreasonable length of time either to think or eat. Somehow, the average waiting time should be the same for all five. One unfair, but easy solution would be to let philosophers eat (whether they wanted to or not) in the order: P1P3 P2P4 P5P2 and then start over. P2 would get fat or have to pass up some of his turns.

Deadlock Deadlock is a situation where two or more processes are waiting for events that will never happen. If each of our philosophers picks up the left chopstick and waits to eat until the right one is available, all will starve. The situation is *deadlocked*, as eating cannot proceed for anyone. Because each has indicated hunger, thinking will also cease, since it was to alternate with eating for each philosopher.

In all synchronization schemes for cooperating processes involving shared resources, provision must be made for mutual exclusion. A philosopher who is using a chopstick must be able to prevent his neighbor from grabbing it until he has finished eating. This step is accomplished in code through the use of *critical sections (CS)*. A process executing code in the CS will have exclusive access to shared resources until exiting the CS. What is more, once the critical code has been entered, it cannot be interrupted by a competing process until the CS is exited.

In some problems, multiple shared resources may be grouped into data *regions*, with only one process allowed into a region at a time. Do not confuse data regions with critical sections, which are portions of code.[1] We will not discuss these further, but will look later at a less expensive solution called a *monitor*.

---

1 The reader should be warned that in some of the literature, a critical section of code is called a *critical region*.

One way to manage CSs and eliminate busy waiting is the *semaphore*, first implemented in ALGOL 68. A semaphore acts very much like its namesake on the railroad. When it is down, execution is halted, and when it is up, a process may proceed. The actual workings of a semaphore, including its list of waiting processes, is usually implemented deep down in an operating system, with users accessing it through its two operations.

SEMAPHORES

A semaphore is a nonnegative, integer-valued variable S, on which two operations are defined, Wait and Signal.[2] S is initialized to 1 (up) so that some process can proceed.

```
Wait(S)
begin
   if S = up
      then S := down;  {Block other processes and enter the CS}
      else {put the calling process on the wait queue}
end {Wait};

Signal(S)
begin
   if {1 or more processes are waiting on S}
     then {let 1 proceed into the CS}
   else S := up
end {Signal};
```

For each of the five Chopsticks, we would need a semaphore, S_i. If P_i got hungry, he would execute Wait(S_i) and Wait($S_{(i-1) \mod 5}$). If both Chopsticks were available (S_i = up and $S_{(i-1) \mod 5}$ = up), he could enter a CS and start eating immediately. Otherwise, he will wait until the processes using the Chopsticks signal their availability.

For simplicity, we will consider the *binary semaphore*, which takes on only values of 0 (down) or 1 (up). If a process P1 executes a Wait(S) and finds the semaphore *up*, it is first put *down* to block other processes. P1 then executes its critical code and executes a Signal (S), putting the semaphore back up. Two processes, P1 and P2, wishing to execute code that modifies shared variables could be scheduled using:

```
var S : semaphore;

process P1:
   loop
      Wait (S);
         CS for P1
      Signal (S):
      Other non-critical code
   end {loop}
end {P1};
```

---

2 The Wait procedure was originally called P [Dijkstra, 1968a], the first letter of the Dutch word *passeren*, "to pass." Signal is V, standing for *vrygeven*, "to release."

```
process P2:
   loop
      Wait (S);
        CS for P2
      Signal (S):
      Other non-critical code
   end {loop}
end {P1};
```

Note that if P1 grabs its CS first, and P2 executes Wait (S), its execution will be suspended until P1 executes its Signal(S). Busy waiting is eliminated using semaphores, since a waiting process is picked off the wait queue when the CS becomes available. The Wait procedure "puts a process to sleep" if another process is using the shared resources, while Signal "wakes up a sleeping process" if there are any.

A semaphore can be used for a single purpose. S enforces mutual exclusion. Another could be used for time coordination. The producer-consumer relationship requires synchronization. A consumer cannot consume a resource until it has been produced. The simplest example involves a single producer and one or more consumers, with the producer producing a new resource only when the resource bin is empty, and a consumer consuming when it is full. This requires two semaphores: full, initialized to down; and empty, initialized to up.

```
full  := down;       {Nothing available to consume}
empty := up;         {Go ahead and produce something}

              Producer: loop forever
                      Wait (empty);
                         Produce something;
                      Signal (full);
                    end loop;

Consumer1: loop forever      Consumer2: loop forever
          Wait (full);               Wait (full);
            Consume resource;          Consume resource;
          Signal (empty);            Signal (empty);
        end loop;                   end loop;
```

We have assumed in both examples that a semaphore can take on one of only two values, up or down. This need not be the case. With minor variations, a semaphore can have any positive value. Our consumers would wait for full > 0. With Full initialized to 0 and Empty to 1, Wait and Signal would look like:

```
Wait(S : Semaphore)
begin
   if S > 0
      then S := S-1; {Block other processes and enter the CS}
      else {put the calling process to sleep on the wait queue}
end {Wait};
```

```
Signal(S : Semaphore)
begin
   if {1 or more processes are waiting on S}
     then {wake up 1 process and let it proceed into the CS}
   else S := S + 1;
end {Signal};
```

Semaphores cannot assure fairness or prevent starvation. In exercise 2, you will be asked to solve the Dining Philosophers problem using semaphores. Unfortunately, we cannot assure that a Philosopher will surrender his two chopsticks once he starts eating. Semaphores cannot eliminate greed!

MONITORS

A monitor is an interface between concurrent user processes and provides a set of procedures callable by the users, a mechanism for scheduling calls to these procedures if other concurrently executing processes request usage before the procedure has terminated, and a mechanism for suspending a calling procedure until a resource is available (**delay**) and then reawakening the process (**continue**). A monitor has no access to non-local variables and can communicate with other monitors only by calling procedures in them. Thus a monitor serves as a third-party policeman between two or more cooperating processes.

A *monitor* can be considered an abstract data type that includes a *shared data* structure and all the operations various (concurrent) processes can perform on it. These operations determine an initialization operation, access rights and synchronizing operations. Concurrent processes $P_1,...,P_n$ must be prevented from accessing the same data item simultaneously.

Other monitor functions must avoid mindless alternation of processes or starvation, where one or more processes run indefinitely, while another is never activated. Other synchronization operations must prevent *deadlock*, where all processes are suspended waiting for some event that never happens.

A monitor has the form shown in listing (4.1).

```
MonitorName monitor                                                    (4.1)

   var permanent variable declarations

   procedure operation₁ (parameter list₁)
   ...
   procedure operationₙ (parameter listₙ)

begin
   initialization code for permanent variables
end;
```

The permanent variables are maintained from invocation to invocation of the monitor. Thus a monitor, like an object, has a *state*. Processes can call a monitor's operations just like one would make a procedure call. Permanent variables can be accessed only through these calls.

Two operations, in addition to those defined in the monitor, are associated with each monitor. These are **wait** and **continue**, which are analogous to the semaphore's wait and signal. A monitor also has a queue in which to store requests for access. Thus execution of a **wait** enqueues a process, and **continue** dequeues the first waiting process and allows it to enter the monitor.

A monitor can be viewed as a module [Parnas, 1972], with most details hidden from the user. Its implementation will also be hidden in the operating system, so users will behave as if they were the only process running. An early use of monitors was in the BASIC time-share system. Interactive BASIC users do not run in parallel, but one at a time, sharing a single CPU. Their processes are suspended or allowed to run using monitor operations associated with two queues, one for suspended processes and another for terminated processes.

RENDEZVOUS

The *rendezvous* includes synchronization, communication, and execution of a block of code in one of two or more concurrently running processes. It coordinates what have been called *remote procedure calls* (RPCs), i.e., a procedure running on a remote processor calling a procedure located on a different processor. The calling procedure is a *client* of the accepting procedure, which functions as the *server*. Each kind of rendezvous in a server process is called a *transaction*. This word is suggestive of what actually happens. A client sends a message to a server, requesting service of some sort, and is blocked from further execution until the service has been performed. A rendezvous can be implemented with or without shared memory.

The rendezvous differs from a monitor in two fundamental ways. First, it is not a separate module coordinating running processes, but is achieved through the processes themselves. One process initiates a call and another accepts it. The call is processed by the receiver, which receives any parameters transmitted by the call and returns parameter values to the caller.

The second way in which it differs is that a process (called a **task** in Ada) can include several **entry**s, which other processes can call. Each entry maintains its own request queue, whereas a monitor has only one queue. A process gaining access to a monitor can call any of its procedures, whereas a process requesting a rendezvous must get in the queue for each entry it needs.

In addition to the production language Ada, rendezvous are implemented in Communicating Sequential Processes (CSP), an experimental language to explore concurrent programming facilities, and in Concurrent C.

EXERCISES

1. A cafeteria line is a good application for parallel processing. Customers are joining the line at the same time others are leaving it. This situation typifies a *producer-consumer* problem, where one cannot "consume" an item until it has been "produced," but consumers and producers can work in parallel. Write an informal algorithm to simulate a cafeteria line, with two processes, *MakeLunch* and *BuyLunch*, operating in parallel. Test it with some simulated customers. Try to avoid:

   1. Starvation: a buyer waits forever while lunches get made.
   2. Alternation: a second lunch does not get made until the first one is sold.
   3. Deadlock: a lunch preparer waits for a signal to make another lunch, while a buyer waits for a signal to buy one.

2. Use five binary semaphores, $Chopstick_1$ to $Chopstick_5$, and write a $Philosopher_i$ process that will run in parallel with the other four to implement the Dining Philosophers problem. The critical section will include the statement, Eat, and should be surrounded by Wait and Signal operations. Initially, each chopstick should be set "up" to indicate its availability.

3. To what does a process have access when it "enters a monitor"?

4.1 SOME SYNCHRONIZATION SOLUTIONS

Various solutions to either CPU sharing or parallel execution have been implemented. We will look at some of these below.

Semaphores in ALGOL 68 and C

ALGOL 68 was the first language with a built-in semaphore, and its two operations, **up** and **down**. ALGOL's **sema** mode (type) provides for several processes to execute in parallel, with a counter keeping track of how long to wait for communication from another process. Thus ALGOL 68 provides the possibility of avoiding deadlock from greedy processes. When the counter reaches some pre-assigned limit, a running process that had executed a **down** on a particular semaphore will be forced to execute an **up**, which will allow the next waiting process to access shared resources.

C running under the UNIX operating system has a semaphore and its operations provided in a library in three system files, with headers sys/types.h, sys/ipc.h, and sys/sem.h. Two of the operations are:

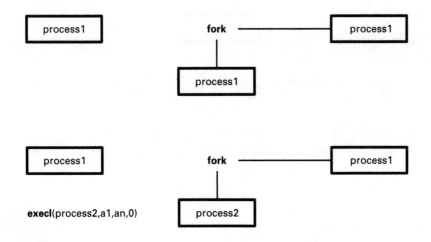

Figure 4.5 UNIX `fork` and `excel` operations to start two processes running concurrently

sem1 = **semget**(...), which creates a semaphore named sem1.

semctl(sem1,...,val), which resets sem1 to val.

The operations semaphore_send and semaphore_wait, implementing signal and wait, are accessed using **semop**. For example, **semop(semaphore_ send,...)** will execute a signal.

Semaphores written in C can be used with UNIX's **fork**, **execl**, and **wait** operations. C (and UNIX) manage memory in various ways. The **fork**, **execl**, and **wait** functions allow a running (parent) program to be suspended, while another program executes and uses the same memory locations. **fork** produces a new copy of the parent program, and **execl**(child_name,a1, a2,...,an,0) allows a new program called child_name to run in place of this copy. **wait** forces the parent to remain suspended until the child completes. A user can command UNIX to run two or more programs "simultaneously" using UNIX's **&** operator.

```
$ payroll hours employee payment & ed
```

will start payroll executing, but allow the editor to interrupt it if necessary. If more than one processor is available, these operators can administer parallel processing.

A child can run concurrently with its parent and can **fork** to its own child as well, as shown in Figure 4.5.

There is (theoretically) no limit to the number of processes that can be running concurrently on multiple processors or be swapped in and out on a single processor. In the latter case, UNIX overlays a parent's memory with that needed by the child. Thus large programs can be run "in relatively limited memory,

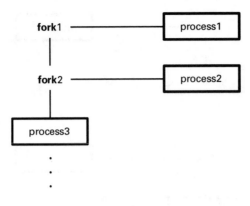

Figure 4.6   Hierarchy of concurrent processes

provided that it is possible to subdivide the program text and data in such a way that each and every executable [process] fits within the memory limitations of the machine" [Silvester, 1984, p. 76]. (See Figure 4.6.)

A *pipe* can be established through the shell so that output from one program is *piped* directly as input into another.

```
$ payroll | lpr
```

will pipe the output of the payroll program directly to the lineprinter. It accomplishes the same goal as the three commands:

```
$ payroll>scratch_file /* output of payroll to scratch_file */
$ lpr<scratch_file    /* send scratch_file to the line printer */
$ rm scratch_file     /* remove scratch_file from the system */

$ payroll | sort | lpr
```

will pipe payroll output to the sort program, and sort will pipe it to lpr for a sorted listing. All three programs would start executing simultaneously, with possible pauses for output from another program.

Monitor and Process Types in Concurrent Pascal

In Chapter 1, we saw the implementation of a disk buffer as an Ada task, with other tasks accessing the buffer through the **entry**, Send, to write data to the buffer, and Receive, which transfers data out of the buffer. Recall that a buffer is an area of storage on a disk used to store input and output data temporarily. It can also be implemented in Concurrent Pascal using a monitor.

As in Ada, there are two ways to enter the buffer. We have called them Send and Receive to make the comparison obvious. In the DiskBuffer monitor, the entries are procedures and are called from some process, which controls an input or output device. These controllers cannot access a VirtualDisk directly, only through a monitor procedure labeled **Entry**. Coordination of possibly concurrently running processes calling Send and Receive is accomplished within the monitor.

```
type DiskBuffer =                                    (4.2)³
    monitor(ConsoleAccess, DiskAccess : resource;
       Base, Limit : integer);
var                                    {shared data}
    disk: VirtualDisk; Sender, Receiver : queue;
    Head, Tail, Length : integer;

procedure entry Send(Block : Page);
{sends a page from a calling procedure to the disk buffer}
begin
    if Length = Limit then delay(sender); {buffer full, wait}
    disk.write(Base + Tail, Block);
    Tail := (Tail + 1) mod Limit;
    Length := Length + 1;
    continue(Receiver)
{transfers control to Receive if there is something in its queue, Receiver}
end;

procedure entry Receive(var Block : Page);
{returns a page to the calling process}
begin
 ...
end;

begin
    init disk(ConsoleAccess,DiskAccess);
    {initialization operation not described here}
    Head := 0;   Tail := 0;   Length := 0;
end;
```

Looking at the code in listing (4.2) from the top down, we first see that DiskBuffer is to be a **monitor** type with four parameters. The first two, ConsoleAccess and DiskAccess, will be variables of a system-dependent type, resource. The second two provide for a base address where the DiskBuffer starts and a Limit, which fixes its size. The VirtualDisk type is a Concurrent Pascal **class**, which includes both data and associated operations. Two of these operations are disk.write and disk.read. Our buffer data will be of this class.

Concurrent Pascal also includes a built-in **queue** that behaves when associated with a monitor as described in the excursion above. A calling process, if not delayed in the queue, will have exclusive access to the shared variables disk, head, tail, and length from the **begin** of the entry called until reaching the **continue** statement. Head is initialized to 0, the relative address of the start of the buffer. Tail, which is the relative address of the end (in pages) of the buffer, is also initialized to 0, indicating an empty buffer.

3 [Brinch Hansen, 1978]

The `Send` procedure includes three statements that must be executed before a calling process which has successfully gained entry to send without delay gives up shared data to a process entering the Receive procedure. These statements write to the buffer and increment `Tail` and `Length`.

Although the `DiskBuffer` monitor does not provide for it, Concurrent Pascal monitors can include calls to other monitors.

The Rendezvous in Ada and Concurrent C

Ada's program unit with potential for running in parallel with other units is called a *task*. It is syntactically similar to a **package** having a specification and a body, as shown in listing (4.3).

```
task T is          --specification                          (4.3)
...
end T;

task body T is     --body
...
end T;
```

Let's look in listing (4.4) at a simple example of tasks that might run concurrently. Suppose we're planning a party.

```
procedure PLAN_PARTY is                                     (4.4)
    task INVITATIONS;

    task body INVITATIONS is
    begin
       WRITE_INVITATIONS;
       MAIL_THEM;
    end INVITATIONS;

    task CLEAN;

    task body CLEAN is
    begin
       CLEAN_HOUSE;
    end CLEAN;

begin
    PREPARE_FOOD;
end PLAN_PARTY;
```

PLAN_PARTY is the *parent unit* for the two tasks, INVITATIONS and CLEAN. When **procedure** PLAN_PARTY is running, and the **begin** for this parent unit is reached, the two local tasks automatically start running as well. The **end** for PLAN_PARTY cannot be executed until all local tasks have terminated. In the schema above, three procedures, INVITATIONS, CLEAN, and PREPARE_FOOD run concurrently, but in no particular order. No communication takes place between them. Depending on the compiler and the hardware, these three procedures could run in parallel or on a single processor using some sort of time-sharing.

Now let's fancy up the party a bit so that the tasks can communicate with each other. In Ada, this is accomplished by one task (the callee) **accept**ing an **entry** into it when called by another task. An **entry** is a procedure call, but what gets done is determined by the task accepting the call. (See listing (4.5).)

```
procedure PLAN_PARTY is                                       (4.5)
    type NAME_LIST is array (INTEGER range <>) of STRING(1..50);
    task INVITATIONS is
        entry GUEST_LIST(NAMES : in NAME_LIST);
    end INVITATIONS;

    task body INVITATIONS is
        GUESTS : NAME_LIST;
    begin
        accept GUEST_LIST(NAMES : in NAME_LIST) do
            GUESTS := NAMES;
        end GUEST_LIST;
        WRITE_INVITATIONS;
        MAIL_THEM;
    end INVITATIONS;

    task CLEAN;

    task body CLEAN is
    begin
        CLEAN_HOUSE;
    end CLEAN;

    G : NAME_LIST;

begin
    PREPARE_FOOD;
    READ_LIST(G);
    INVITATIONS.GUEST_LIST(G);
end PLAN_PARTY;
```

Here, PLAN_PARTY is the caller to INVITATIONS. Since all three tasks begin simultaneously, INVITATIONS must wait to **accept** the entry GUEST_ LIST until it is sent by the main procedure. What happens during the **accept** . . . **do** . . . **end**; is called a *rendezvous*. When it is executing, the two tasks are said to rendezvous with each other.

A simple, but practical tasking example is that of an input/output buffer for a single character. Remember, we managed this job using an object hierarchy for streams in C++, with ios as an abstract object, and derived istream and ostream objects for input and output. That objects can act concurrently should not be surprising. We will look briefly at Concurrent OOP in the listing (4.6).

```
task CHAR_BUFFER is                                          (4.6)
   entry READ  (C : out CHARACTER);    --READ from buffer
   entry WRITE (C : in CHARACTER);     --WRITE to buffer
end CHAR_BUFFER;

task body CHAR_BUFFER is
   FULL : BOOL := FALSE;
   CH   : CHARACTER;
   loop
      select
         when FULL =>
            accept READ(C : out CHARACTER) do
               C := CH;
            end READ;
            FULL := FALSE;
      or
         when not FULL =>
            accept WRITE(C : in CHARACTER) do
               CH := C;
            end WRITE;
            FULL := TRUE;
      or terminate;
      end select;
   end loop;
end CHAR_BUFFER;
```

As usual, there are several points to notice here. First of all, CHAR_
BUFFER.READ(...) and CHAR_BUFFER.WRITE(...) will be called by other
tasks. Each entry has an associated queue, so if several tasks are trying to READ
or WRITE simultaneously, the calls will be queued and processed in first-in-first-
out (FIFO) order. We must, of course, have something in a buffer before it can be
READ from. Thus **accept** READ is guarded by the **when** FULL expression. The
select statement means that either of the **accept** statements may be chosen in
no particular order. In particular, if the buffer is empty and FULL = FALSE, the
CHAR_BUFFER task may **select** a call from the WRITE queue before accepting a
READ.

Another way to handle a read/write character buffer might be to set up
READ_CHAR and WRITE_CHAR as two tasks and start them running simultaneously, as shown in listing (4.7).

```
procedure BUFFER_TASKS;                                      (4.7)
   FULL : BOOLEAN := FALSE;
   pragma SHARED (FULL);
   CH : CHARACTER;
   pragma SHARED(CH);

   task READ_CHAR is
      entry READ(C : out CHARACTER);
   end CHAR_READ
```

```
task WRITE_CHAR is
   entry WRITE(C : in CHARACTER);
end CHAR_WRITE;

task body READ_CHAR_ is
begin
   loop
      when FULL =>
         accept READ(C : out CHARACTER) do
            C := CH;
            FULL := FALSE;
         end READ;
   end loop;
 end CHAR_READ;

task body CHAR_WRITE is
begin
   loop
      accept WRITE(C : in CHARACTER) do
         CH := C;
         FULL := TRUE;
      end WRITE;
   end loop;
end CHAR_WRITE;

begin
end BUFFER_TASKS;
```

An Ada **pragma** is a compiler directive. The SHARED **pragma**, to implement memory sharing, guarantees two things. First, if a shared variable, such as CH or FULL above, is read in a *critical section* (CS) in a task, it will not be updated by any other task until the CS is exited. In listing (4.6), such a CS occurs for CH between **accept** READ and its **end**. Second, if a shared variable is updated in a CS, it will not be either read or updated by any other task until the CS is exited. This step occurs between **accept** WRITE and its **end** for CH and in both **accept** statements for FULL.

Ada implements neither semaphores nor monitors, so these must be programmed in if we wish to avoid the synchronization problems discussed in Theoretical Excursions. Only simple or **access** (pointer) variables may be declared SHARED, so we must devise other means for protecting structured data. We will address this point in Lab IX, where we will construct a read/write buffer larger than a single character.

Ada's tasks may be dynamic as well as static. That is, they can be created or destroyed as a program runs. Suppose we wished to create CHAR_BUFFER tasks as needed in a program and also wanted the capability of having more than one such buffer at a time. To achieve this goal, we would add the reserved word **type** to the task declaration, and then create **access** type values pointing to the tasks, as shown in listing (4.8).

```
task type CHAR_BUFFER is                                    (4.8)
   entry READ  (C : out CHARACTER);
   entry WRITE (C : in CHARACTER);
end CHAR_BUFFER;

type BUFFER_PTR is access CHAR_BUFFER;
P, Q : BUFFER_PTR;

begin
   ...
   P := new BUFFER_PTR;
   Q := new BUFFER_PTR;
   ...
   P := null;
   Q := null;
   ...
end;
```

Ada does not destroy dynamically created objects through a procedure like Pascal's **dispose**. This was a design decision to eliminate "dangling pointers" that point to nonexistent data objects. Assigning an **access** variable the value **null** makes objects inaccessible. Their storage locations will be released when program execution exits the scope of the objects.

The C language has no constructs for concurrent processing, although we saw above how concurrently running procedures could be implemented using directives to the UNIX operating system. Concurrent C was developed to provide a **process** type and its associated operations as concurrent language features. It does not implement memory-sharing, but employs synchronous message passing with the client blocked until service has been received. It differs from Ada in several ways, of which we will mention four here. First, C's transactions are similar to function calls, whereas in Ada they are like procedures. This means that a call can appear anywhere that a function would be appropriate, whereas in Ada, a call is always a statement. C provides for user-specified process priorities, while in Ada they are always processed in FIFO order. C allows a transaction call with parameters so that only those calls meeting certain criteria are served. In Ada, when a main block with tasks is entered, its tasks are activated as well and terminated when the block is exited. In Concurrent C, one must activate each process, e.g.,

```
process buffer b;
b = create buffer(128);
```

It can also be terminated via **c_abort** (b) ; Other more subtle differences can be found in [Gehani, 1986].

Concurrent C has a type, **process**, which requires a specification (**spec**) and a **body** part. The specification is visible to other processes, while the body is not. A server process includes an **accept** statement to receive transaction (**trans**) calls. Let's look at the Dining Philosophers implemented in Concurrent C, as shown in Figure 4.7. Here, chopsticks are called forks.

```
process spec fork()
{
 trans void pick_up();
 trans void put_down();
};
process spec philosopher(
              int id, process fork left, process fork right);

#define LIFE_LIMIT 100000
process body philosopher(id, left, right)
{
   int times_eaten;
   for (times_eaten = 0; times_eaten != LIFE_LIMIT; times_eaten++)
     { /* think, then enter dining room */
       /* pick up forks*/
           right.pick_up();
           left.pick_up();
       /*eat */
           printf("Philosopher %d: *burp*\n", id);
       /*put down forks */
           left.put_down();
           right.put_down();
       /*get up and leave dining room */
     }
 process body fork()
 {
   for(;;)   /*forever */
     select
     {
       accept pick_up();
       accept put_down();
     or
       terminate;
     }
 }
 main()
 {
   process fork f[5];        /*array of five forks */
   int j;

   /*first create the forks, then create the philosophers */
   for (j = 0; j < 5; j++)
     f[j] = create fork();
   for (j = 0; j < 5; j++)
     create philosopher(j, f[j], f[(j+1) %⁴ 5]);
 }
```

Figure 4.7 Dining Philosophers in Concurrent C. Reproduced with permission from N. H. Gehani and W. D. Roome, *Concurrent C*. © 1986 by John Wiley & Sons.

---

4 Remember that "%" is the mod operator in C.

Each philosopher exists only until he has eaten 100,000 times. The forks go on forever. However, once all the philosophers have terminated, the forks have nothing else to do and so the **or** option of the **select** statement is chosen and each fork **terminate**s. Then, since all the processes have completed, the Concurrent C program **main** can also terminate.

EXERCISES

1. If `Head` is the relative address of the DiskBuffer of listing (4.2), what is the variable `Base`?

2. Complete the `Receive entry` for the `DiskBuffer` monitor.

3. Why is it necessary to include a **terminate** clause in the `CHAR_BUFFER` task, and why is it not listed as an entry?

4. What would happen if we left the updating of `FULL` outside the **accept** statements in the second buffer implementation, as we did in the first Ada fragment of listing (4.6)?

5. Write code for an Ada task with two entries to implement Dijkstra's binary semaphore.

6. The Dining Philosophers program of Figure 4.7 can lead to deadlock. When will this happen? Suggest how to avoid this problem. Notice also that output from the philosophers' processes can get mixed up if more than one tries to access standard output at the same time. How might this be resolved? ■

LAB XI: Simulation of Parallel Processing in Ada

OBJECTIVES

1. To experiment with different methods of synchronizing a buffer implemented through tasks.

2. To see what happens when the buffer is accessed by only one outside task or by several.

3. To devise a synchronization scheme for two client tasks using the buffer so that string code from the two clients does not intermix. ■

4.2 MESSAGE PASSING

Passing messages involves two issues: how sources and destinations are designated, and how processes are synchronized.

A source and a destination define a *communications channel*. The simplest designation is *direct naming*, i.e., send data to receiver or receive data from sender, where 'receiver' and 'sender' are the names of processes. When multiple processes are sending or receiving messages, buffering may be necessary to hold a message until a receiving process is ready for it. Such a buffer is often called a *mailbox*. In the particular case where there is only one receiver but many senders, the mailbox is called a *port*. A particular program may involve several ports, but a receive statement will designate a single port. The idea here is that all requests for a particular service go into a single mailbox, or port. Another channel notion is that of a *pipe*, where output from one process is piped as input into another. Both processes can be running concurrently, with the second process receiving input from the pipeline as it is produced by the first process. Pipes, however, flow only one way. We have already looked at the rendezvous notion, where messages can be sent in any direction.

Synchronization of message passing differs from that for shared resources, since no critical sections or regions need be maintained. Still, a process receiving a message must be ready to receive it, or the sending process must wait until the receiver is ready to process it. Waiting is usually managed by a queue or queues.

There are four basic message-passing models.

Point-to-point The simplest message-passing technique involves one process sending a message to another, which receives it. Some languages, such as SR and Concurrent C, provide for conditional receipt. For example, a request in Concurrent C to open a file if it isn't locked can be coded [Bal, 1989, p. 277]:

```
accept open(f) suchthat not_locked(f)
   {
      ... open process coded here...
   }
```

If the file f is locked, the request will not be accepted. Point-to-point schemes are *symmetric* if both the calling and receiving processes name each other. The schema above is *assymetric*, since the receiver does not name the sender. In this case, a sender requesting that a file be opened is willing for it to be opened by any process capable of doing so.

Point-to-point messages can be passed *synchronously* or *asynchronously*. In synchronous passing, the sending process is blocked until the receiver is ready to accept it. If passing is asynchronous, the sender continues to execute even though its message has not been accepted. In a synchronous system, there can be only one message pending from any process, while there may be several yet-to-be-answered messages from an asynchronous sender. Occam, the assembly language for transputers and a descendant of CSP, passes messages synchronously, while Network Implementation Language (NIL) is implemented asynchronously.

Rendezvous We have already discussed rendezvous, based on the three concepts: entry declarations, entry calls, and accept statements. The rendezvous is fully synchronous involving only two processes, the sender, which is suspended until accepted, and the receiver.

Remote Procedure Calls (RPCs) RPCs are much like the processes used to accomplish rendezvous. They are intended, however, to have exactly the same meanings as regular procedures. When this can be achieved, it permits the coding of concurrent processes in traditional procedural languages and allows conventional programs to be ported into the synchronizing system. RPCs have been discussed for use with Modula-2 and implemented in the V operating system and Concurrent CLU.

One-to-Many Message Passing One-to-many message passing is also called *broadcasting*, as it behaves much like a radio station, where all receivers hear the same message. One type is *unbuffered* so that a message sent can be picked up only by those processes ready to receive it. If messages are *buffered*, they can remain in the buffer indefinitely so that processes can receive them at any time. One language implementing one-to-many message passing is Broadcasting Sequential Processes (BSP), another descendant of CSP.

4.3 THE TUPLE-SPACE OF LINDA

Not all processes communicate through message passing or shared memory locations. Both of these methods suffer from some degree of unreliability due to the necessity of programmer-managed synchronization. Linda, developed at Yale University, is a language for parallel processing that implements a shared data space owned by none of the processes and called a *tuple space*. It acts like an associative memory that associates a base address with a key in a fast store. A tuple is an ordered collection of data items, e.g., ("hello world", 22, 2.17). There are four operations on tuples:

- `out`, places a tuple in tuple space
- `in`, matches a tuple and removes it from tuple space
- `rd`, matches a tuple and returns a copy of it
- `eval`, creates an active tuple (a new process)

`out`("hello world", 22, 2.17) creates a tuple and places it in tuple space. `in`("hello world", ?i, ?f) removes all tuples with first, coordinate "hello world"; second, any integer; and third, a float, assuming that i and f have previously been declared to be integer and float. `eval`(45, SomeFunction(x)) creates a new process which runs in parallel with the process that called **eval**. The tuple (45, SomeFunction(x)) is *active* as long as SomeFunction is running and passive when it terminates.

The idea, put simply, is that a process wishing to alter data will remove its tuple from tuple space using an **in**, process the data, and then return it to tuple space using **out**. Any other process will be blocked until the tuple is returned. Messages can also be sent using **out** and received using **in**.

Implementations of Linda include a preprocessor that uses queues and semaphores, among other techniques, to speed up tuple searches. The QIX operating system to implement parallel processing includes a Linda kernel. Its developers claim it to be more efficient than UNIX, while maintaining considerable compatibility with it. They also claim that it makes writing parallel programs easier and that they are independent of the particular architecture being used.

4.4 MANAGING PARTIAL FAILURE

When messages are passed, several things can go wrong.

1. The message can be lost by the network.
2. The reply is lost.
3. The server crashes before sending the reply.

One way to handle these situations is for the client to declare a pause for a specified period of time. If the desired reply is not received when the time expires, it is assumed that one of the three problems above occurred and remedial action is taken. This could be as simple as resending the request. In a situation like the second, however, this action may not be appropriate. Processes often have *state*, where variable values are maintained from invocation to invocation. For example, suppose the server incremented a counter, N, and remembered it. Resending a request would result in N being increased twice, even though only one reply was returned. One possible solution to this problem is to make the server atomic, that is, all or nothing. Either it replies successfully, or the previous state is restored.

Ada tasks are quite unrestricted and can lead to both sequencing and deadness errors. A sequencing error occurs when tasks communicate in an unanticipated order. A task is dead when it cannot proceed further. One particular possibility is *circular deadlock*, where each task has called the next task in the circle, which cannot accept it until it completes a rendezvous with the one ahead.

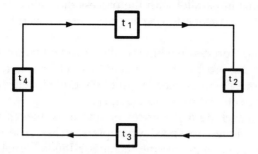

Concurrently running tasks are particularly hard to debug because they may run differently each time they are invoked. Debugging tools that are being developed are based on run-time monitoring, where a sequence of program "snapshots" is taken to pinpoint the states of selected running processes when one went dead.

Because of the inconsistencies that occur from one run to the next, an axiomatic proof system is particularly appropriate for validating concurrent processes.

4.5 OBJECTS AS UNITS OF PARALLELISM

Object-based or object-oriented programming is the hottest area in both programming language research and applications for the 1990s. Using objects as units of parallelism has thus received a fair amount of attention. Objects may be considered "independent abstract machines that interact in response to messages" [Caromel, 1989]. But most attempts to implement concurrently executing objects do not include asynchronous, randomly timed, message passing. Remote procedure calls, where one object calls a procedure in another object and waits for a reply is the preferred method. This is so in languages like Concurrent Smalltalk, ABCL/1, and Orient85. Emerald, developed at the University of Washington, also supports concurrent processes. It is not object oriented, but object based, as inheritance is not supported.

Caromel [Caromel, 1989] proposes a model for parallel object-oriented languages that fosters the strengths of objects—reusability, extendability, and highly readable programs. Experimentation with this model is currently being pursued in Nancy, France, using the object language Eiffel™. This implementation employs an object called PROCESS, with two methods, Create and Live. Create allows the creation of an instance of a PROCESS object, which proceeds to execute its Live routine. When this routine completes, the PROCESS dies. Eiffel supports multiple inheritance, where a single object can inherit from more than one superclass, thus any appropriate object could become a PROCESS by inheriting the PROCESS methods.

The focus of object-oriented concurrency is more to model situations where objects act together than to speed up program execution. This is a new and growing area of research including efforts to combine Concurrent C with its object-oriented cousin C++, as a single extension to C.

4.6 DECLARATIVE LANGUAGES SUPPORTING PARALLELISM

Not all theorists agree that procedurally oriented languages provide the best vehicle for implementing concurrency. The VonNeumann bottleneck, where only one word is transferred in or out of memory at each processor cycle still causes problems. We will look at notions for parallel processing using functions in Chapter 6 after you are more familiar with functional languages themselves. Processing logical clauses in parallel will be considered in Chapter 7.

4.7 SUMMARY

Distributed programming includes several models. All involve the use of multiple processors, cooperation among the processors, and handling the failure of one or more concurrently running processes while others continue. There are four main models:

1. Those based on shared memory
2. Those based on asynchronous (nonblocking) message passing
3. Those based on synchronous (blocking) message passing
4. A combination of message passing and shared memory

Ada implements the fourth model, while Concurrent C implements the third. No matter which model is chosen, cooperating processes must be synchronized if information is to be exchanged. Early mechanisms for synchronization were the semaphore and monitor. A semaphore controls access to a critical section of code, which cannot be interrupted until it terminates, once a process starts its execution. Monitors contain shared variables and any operations allowed on them. They communicate with other monitors but can be accessed by cooperating processes.

The rendezvous is a third mechanism for synchronizing processes. It is based on the client/server model, where a client requests service and then waits until it has been provided.

Several languages have been developed to experiment with concurrency on a single processor. This is sometimes called multiprogramming. Processes are thought of as operating concurrently, but actually implemented through being swapped in and out of a single CPU. ALGOL 68, C, Modula-2, and Concurrent Pascal are examples of such languages.

A fifth model for concurrency is the tuple space of Linda. Here processes and their associated variables are created and destroyed as tuples in a memory associated with, but separate from, the RAM of each process. Linda's creators find this model easier to imagine than message passing and shared memories.

4.8 NOTES ON REFERENCES

[Wegner, 1983] provides a good discussion of the differences between monitors and the rendezvous concept. He uses Ada and CSP as examples of languages implementing rendezvous. They implement a monitor in Ada using the monitor definition of Brinch Hansen [Brinch Hansen, 1978].

[Barnes, 1982] is a quite literate introduction to Ada written by John Barnes, one of the key members of the Ada design team. His special concerns included tasking.

A nice presentation of Concurrent C, with lots of elementary example programs is [Gehani, 1986]. It describes a version implemented under UNIX for a single processor. At the time the paper was written, a version for distributed systems was under development at Bell Labs.

For brief discussions of Linda, the reader is referred to [Leler, 1990] or [Carriero, 1989]. This second paper compares Linda to message-passing, object-oriented, logical and functional models for concurrent programming.

Four tutorials on parallel programming stand out, three from the ACM and the fourth from the IEEE. These are [Brinch Hansen, 1978], [Andrews, 1983], [Bal, 1989], and [Shatz, 1989]. Included in Shatz is a good discussion of debugging Ada tasks.

FORM AND STRUCTURE

CHAPTER 5:   FORMAL LANGUAGES

5

THEORETICAL EXCURSION 6: Formal Languages

An engineer friend of mine asked me what possible point there was in including a chapter on formal languages in a textbook such as this. When would computer scientists working in the real world ever have any use for such theoretical matters? His is a good question, which has given me a lot of trouble. A quick, concise answer is not forthcoming.

The computer science discipline has been criticized by those in the other natural sciences for being too applications oriented. Claims are made that beginning students of biology, chemistry, and physics are taught classic theory such as the laws of motion and work on laboratory assignments to substantiate these results. Computer science students see the theory of computation only as upper-level or graduate students, if at all. Emulating the other sciences is not enough reason, however, for including a little theory here.

Lewis and Papadimitriou [Lewis, 1981] believe that students should be exposed to theory early in their education, "because of the deeper insights it yields on specific topics in computer science, and because it serves to establish essential mathematical paradigms." Daniel Cohen [Cohen, 1986] claims that "Every interesting career a student of computer science might pursue will make significant use of some aspects of [theory]." In particular, he believes that two of the most important skills an undergraduate student will learn are the ability to recognize and manipulate context-free languages and understand recursion.

From my perspective, I find theory interesting. I have always been plagued by unstated questions of "Why?" So for those of you who will benefit from a brief excursion into the foundations of formal languages, and for those who find satisfaction in some sort of unification of seemingly diverse topics, this chapter is included.

A programming language does not originate like Athena—sprouting fully developed from the head of Zeus. It reflects the experience of practitioners with other languages. Chapter 1 dealt with abstraction, the distillation of a language construct to its stripped-down essential form. It is in that spirit that we will study formal languages. It may come as a surprise that languages aren't as different as one might think. At least syntax can be reduced to a few notions. After all, a computer is basically very simple. It has a memory composed of sequences of electrical signals (symbolized by 0 or 1), and a programming language facilitates the changing of 0's into 1's or 1's into 0's.

Computers, although essentially binary strings, can also be thought of as virtual machines specialized to individual programming languages. For example, block-structured languages are implemented as a single stack, while concurrent imperative languages require several stacks with associated queues. In this chapter, we will look at the most basic of these virtual machines and comment on their essential links to language types.

When we speak of a *formal language*, we mean the form or *syntax* of valid words, expressions, and statements in the language. We are not concerned with what it means, i.e., its *semantics*. If *work* and *house* are legal words, and one of the word-formation rules says that the concatenation of two words is also a word, then *workhouse, housework, househouse,* and *workwork* are all words. The first two are meaningful in English, although their semantics are different, but the last two make no English sense. No matter! In a formal language with a concatenation rule, all four are equally valid. Numbers are not as ambiguous as English words. If 3 and 17 are numbers, then 317, 173, 33, and 1717 are all meaningful.

The formal rules for generating and recognizing computer languages are almost all syntactic rather than semantic, with the semantics described in some natural language, in our case, English. The semantics of valid strings will not be of concern here, although much of language theory addresses the notion that proper syntax captures intuitive meanings, and that statements which are inexpressible may well be meaningless.

Formal languages are particularly useful in analyzing programming languages, which is one thing a compiler has to do. Different levels of analysis apply, from the recognition of syntax errors to the understanding of which programs always terminate with correct solutions to the problem at hand. Formal languages and the theoretical machines that recognize them are useful throughout, from the earlier levels of language element recognition to the higher levels of proving program correctness.

You may be surprised to know that there are essentially only four basic language forms. That communication at its fundamental levels is not as various as one might think has attracted the attention of investigators in diverse fields. Languages of each form have definitive properties. They are suitable for particular computing devices, for one thing. The amazing thing is that the relationship between language and theoretical machine is one-to-one. By this we mean that if a certain machine recognizes a language, the language is of a particular type. The opposite holds as well. But more on that point later. First, we need to see just what a formal language is.

5.0 FORMAL LANGUAGES AND LANGUAGE HIERARCHIES

To define a formal language, L, we will need two things:

1. An *alphabet*, Σ, of individual symbols
2. A set of rules to determine which strings of symbols from Σ are legal words of L

Using this definition, a *language* is nothing more than a set of legal strings from an alphabet. Taken together, the alphabet and rules for forming strings are called a *grammar*.

For example, suppose our alphabet, Σ = {0 1}, has just two symbols. Strings are such items as 0, 1, 01, 10, 000, etc. '0'[1] and '1' have length 1, while 000 has length 3. A string of length 0 contains no symbols at all and is usually denoted by the Greek letter Λ. The set of all possible strings from Σ is Σ^*, called the *closure* of Σ. 1^* is the set of all strings containing 0 or more 1's and no other symbols.

$$1^* = \{\Lambda, 1, 11, 111, 1111,...\}^2$$
$$= \{1^0, 1^1, 1^2, 1^3, 1^4, ...\}$$
$$= \{1^n : n = 0, 1, 2, ...\}$$

Formal grammars constitute a hierarchy based on the form of the rules. Various researchers have worked on these forms to generate languages of a particular type, raising several questions. Just what restrictions are essential and which can be eased up? With a given class of grammars, what sorts of problems can be solved? Given a language, what sort of machine can recognize properly formed strings and reject those that are invalid? For what sorts of languages will a machine always be successful in recognizing valid strings? Can a machine recognize potentially infinite strings? For what applications are particular languages best suited?

It is interesting to note that although investigators worked independently on formal language theory, their various formulations eventually fell into four distinct classes, starting with grammars formed of unrestricted rules through increasingly more rigid formation rules. Machines that recognize unrestricted grammars can, of course, generate solutions to a large class of problems, but

---

1 A string can be denoted as abc or as 'abc'. Where there is no confusion, we will omit the single quotes.
2 This raised * is called the Kleene star after its originator, Stephen Cole Kleene.

they cannot recognize problems they can't handle. Machines based on stricter grammars can guarantee the generation of solutions, but to a more limited class of problems presented.

5.1 THE CHOMSKY HIERARCHY

We will look at the formal language types described by the linguist Noam Chomsky. These languages form a hierarchy, in that any type 3 language is also type 2, any type 2 language is also type 1, and those languages of type 1 are also type 0. Thus type 0, the most general, includes all the other three types.

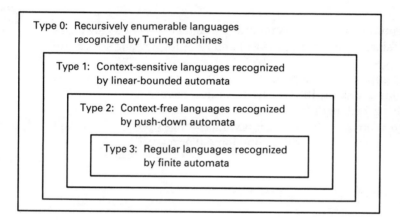

In the following sections we will describe as briefly as possible three aspects of languages of each type:

1. The set of rules or grammar for languages of the type
2. The theoretical machine that recognizes legal words of the languages
3. What differentiates the type from the next lower type

But first, let's look at just who Noam Chomsky is.

HISTORICAL VIGNETTE 6: Language Classifications: Noam Chomsky

We've all heard of the romance languages, but rarely do we hear of an individual who has had a lifetime romance *with* languages. Noam Chomsky is such an individual.

His deep interest in the study of linguistics began when he was only 10 years old. He was fascinated with the proofs he read in his father's edition of a thirteenth-century grammar. These proofs were informally written and did not conform to the traditional structural school of linguistics. Chomsky's informal introduction to the study of languages colored his future work in that field. One can't help but wonder whether he would have become the revolutionary linguist that he did if his first introduction to the field had been more traditional.

In 1945, Chomsky entered the University of Pennsylvania where he majored in linguistics. Here his life-long interest in political change also began to surface. He was particularly attentive to developments leading to the establishment of the state of Israel.

In 1951, he received an M.A. degree from Pennsylvania with a thesis called "Morphonemics of Modern Hebrew," based on efforts to develop a system of rules that could be used to characterize every sentence structure in a language. He received a Ph.D. in linguistics from the University of Pennsylvania in 1955.

At first Chomsky had a very difficult time publishing any of his work, which was too revolutionary for the established linguistic community. He not only exposed the inadequacy of structuralist grammars, but he criticized more modern linguistic practice as well. The structuralist school contended that language is primarily behavioristic, depending on an individual's response to his or her external environment. Chomsky felt that the structural explanation did not take account of linguistic creativity in humans. About behaviorism, he said, "Skinnerian-type training is appropriate only for industrial-type workers who need to develop complex technical skills. Is growing up and learning no more than the shaping of behaviors? If that's what education is all about, authoritarian figures shaping people, then maybe we don't need it" [*Newsweek*, August 26, 1968]. He also felt that modern linguistics "has not explicitly recognized the necessity for supplementing a "particular grammar" of a language by a universal grammar if it is to achieve descriptive adequacy. It has, in fact, characteristically rejected the study of universal grammar as misguided, and...it has not attempted to deal with the creative aspect of language use. It thus suggests no way to overcome the fundamental descriptive inadequacy of structuralist grammars" [Chomsky, 1965, p. 6].

To support his theories, Chomsky relied heavily on mathematics and published his first book in 1957. By then he was a professor of linguistics at MIT. In *Cartesian Linguistics* [Chomsky, 1966], he divides the study of linguistics into three main categories:

1. Investigations that focus directly on the nature of language, including descriptions of syntax, semantics, phonology (the study of sounds), and their evolution

2. Studies dealing with the use of language and the abilities and mental organization that it presupposes, such as the language learning processes of both children and adults and language as used in literature

3. Background sociological studies placing the various approaches to the study of language in appropriate historical and intellectual settings

Although considered a genius in the linguistics field, Chomsky never minimized its difficulties. He once claimed, "It may be beyond the limits of human intelligence to understand how human intelligence works" [*Time*, February 16, 1968].

Chomsky's political interests resurfaced around 1965 when he began protesting the Vietnam War. He became a leader in peace organizations such as Resist, a national draft-resistance movement. He taught undergraduate courses dealing with political change and published widely on his pacifist views. Once again he was openly challenging the authorities. Israel Shenker wrote in the *New York Times* (October 27, 1968), "In his twenties, Noam Chomsky revolutionized linguistics. In his thirties he has been trying to revolutionize society." His writings continue to the present. *The Culture of Terrorism* [Chomsky, 1988] protests U.S. policies in areas such as Central America and Iran. He states [p. 7], "even in a largely depoliticized society such as the United States, with no political parties or opposition press beyond the narrow spectrum of the business-dominated consensus, it is possible for popular action to have a significant impact on policy, though indirectly. That was an important lesson for the Indochina wars. It is underscored, once again, by the experience of the 1980s with regard to Central America. And it should be remembered for the future."

His present-day influence continues in fields other than linguistics and political activism. His legacies are very apparent in computer science. His development of a mathematical theory of natural languages and description of four different classes of languages have made the analysis of the syntax and grammar of programming languages possible. "This has had important practical benefits, since it has permitted the development of automatic parser-generators, thus automating what had been one of the more difficult parts of compiler writing." [MacLennan, 1987, p. 167].

Type 3: Regular Grammars

A grammar of type 3 is called *regular*. We will define a regular grammar in two steps. The first is to define a *regular expression*, e, over an alphabet, Σ.

1. Λ (the null string) is a regular expression.
2. If $x \in \Sigma$, then x is a regular expression.
3. If e_1 is a regular expression, then so is (e_1).
4. If e_1 and e_2 are regular expressions, then so are $e_1 + e_2$, $e_1 \cdot e_2$, and e_1^*.

That Λ is a regular expression needs no explanation. Rule 2 says that each symbol of Σ is a regular expression. Note that regular expressions are closed under three operations, + (union), · (concatenation) and * (Kleene star). The parentheses of rule 3 need a little explanation. Neither "(" nor ")" is a symbol in Σ, but they may be used freely to make expressions clear. Symbols such as "(" and ")" that may be used in expressions, but are not part of the language itself, are called *metasymbols*.[3]

---

3 In some texts, symbols of Σ are written in boldface to separate them from metasymbols, e.g., **(x)(yy)**.

To understand rule 4, we will consider an example. Suppose that $\Sigma = \{x\ y\}$. Rule 4 states that x + y is regular. Here, x + y means x or y, or the set union of x and y if x and y are sets. $x \cdot y$ (usually written xy) is also a regular expression, as are xx, xxx, ..., yx, yy, yyy, xxy, xyy, etc. We may write xyy as (x)(yy) to indicate the concatenation of x and yy.

With regular expressions defined, we are ready to list the rules of a regular grammar used to build a regular language, L, from a regular expression, e. We will write L(e) to indicate the language L defined by e.

1. If e = x, then L(x) = {x}. That is, the only word in the language L is x.
   $L(\Lambda) = \{\Lambda\}$.
2. If $L(e_1) = L_1$, and $L(e_2) = L_2$, then
   a. $L(e_1e_2) = L_1L_2$
   b. $L(e_1 + e_2) = L_1 + L_2$
   c. $L(e_1^*) = L_1{}^*$

Some examples are in order. Suppose $L_1 = \{x\}$ and $L_2 = \{y\}$, where $e_1 = x$ and $e_2 = y$. That is, each language has exactly one word in it. Then:

a. L(xy) = {xy}, a single word, xy
b. L(x + y) = {x} + {y} = {x\ y}
c. $L(x^*) = L^* = \{\Lambda\ x\ xx\ xxx\ ...\}$

Also $L(x^*y) = L(x^*)L(y) = \{y\ xy\ xxy\ xxxy\ ...\}$

To be a little more practical, consider the language B of binary decimals including 0, but less than 1, correct to two places. The alphabet $\Sigma = \{0.\ 0\ 1\}$. B = {0.00 0.01 0.10 0.11}. B can be constructed from the two languages

$L_1 = \{0.\}$ and $L_2 = \{00\ 01\ 10\ 11\}$
   $= L(0.)$ $= L(0 + 1)(0 + 1)$
                     $= L((0 + 1)^2)$

Then $B = L((0.)(0 + 1)^2) = L_1L_2$. B is generated by the regular expression $((0.)(0 + 1)^2)$.

Finite automata (FAs, NFAs, and DFAs)

Now that we know how to generate a regular language, we are faced with the opposite problem. Given a particular language such as B above, and a string from its alphabet, how can we recognize whether a particular string is valid or not? We want a recognizing machine, RM, so that RM(0.11) = True, and RM(10.) = False. For regular languages, such a machine is called a *finite automaton* or FA for short. The recognizer will process one symbol at a time from left to right. For our language, B, an FA looks like the diagram shown in Figure 5.1.

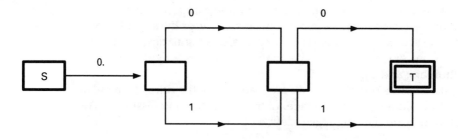

Figure 5.1   Transition diagram for the FA for language B

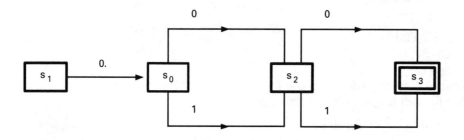

Figure 5.2   Transition diagram for B including states

If a word is processed beginning at the start arrow labeled S, it is recognized by the FA if processing eventually terminates at the node marked T. Words that are not recognized are said to be rejected or to fail. A *finite automaton* is:

1. A set of States, S, where s_0 is the starting state and s_n is the terminal or stopping state. The states in Figure 5.1 are s_0 plus the boxed nodes.

2. An alphabet, Σ. In our case, $\Sigma = \{0. \ 0 \ 1\}$.

3. A set of transitions, T. In the *transition diagram* above, the transitions are represented by arrows. Figure 5.2 shows a state diagram for the same finite automaton.

A transition diagram can also be represented by a transition table. One is free to use whichever representation is the clearest. The transition table for the FA for language B is as shown in Figure 5.3.

Note how this works. If the FA is in state s_0 and recognizes an input of 0., the transition is to s_1. If it is in state s_1, the transition is to s_2 if a 0 or a 1 is recognized, and similarly from s_2 to s_3, the terminating state. The transitions marked F represent failure to recognize a legal word of the language B.

The finite automaton described above is also called a *deterministic finite automaton*, or DFA, because there is only one possible transition from each state,

Inputs

states	0.	0	1
s_0	s_1	F	F
s_1	F	s_2	s_2
s_2	F	s_3	s_3

Figure 5.3   Transition table for the language B

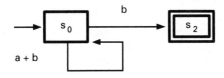

Figure 5.4   NFA transition diagram for the language L

given a particular input. If other choices are offered, the FA is called a *non-deterministic finite automaton*, or NFA. The diagram in Figure 5.4 is for an NFA because there are two transition choices from s_0 on recognizing the letter b. What language does it recognize?

The transition marked a + b is called a loop. One can go around it 0 or more times. Work by Kleene and others has shown that any language which can be defined by an NFA can also be defined by a (probably more complicated) DFA. The DFA for the NFA above is shown in Figure 5.5.

When processing has progressed to the termination state, s_1, it may either stop, loop through 0 or more b's, or return to s_0. The language L contains an infinite number of words, since one can go around the loops any number of times. L is still regular, since its words can be recognized by an FA. It has also been shown that any language with a finite number of words can be recognized by a finite automaton. The converse is, of course, not true. We refer the interested reader to [Cohen, 1986].

Production systems

Formal grammars can also be generated using *production systems*. Each system requires two alphabets plus a set of rules for forming legal strings. The first alphabet, T, is a set of terminal symbols, and the second, NT, is composed of nonterminals. NT contains a special symbol, S, indicating "start here." A sequence of 0 or more rules is called a *derivation*. A production rule allows for

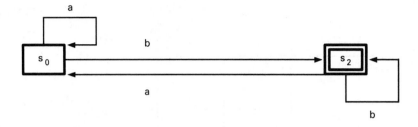

Figure 5.5 DFA transition diagram for the language L

the replacing of symbols from the second alphabet with symbols from the first or second alphabet.

Let's look in listing (5.1) at a production system of binary decimals for our language B.

$$T = \{0. \ 0 \ 1\} \quad\quad\quad (5.1)$$
$$NT = \{S \ S_1 \ S_2\}$$

Production rules are:

$$S \ => 0.S_1$$
$$S_1 => 0S_2 \ | \ 1S_2 \quad \{\text{Here } | \text{ means "or"}\}$$
$$S_2 => 0 \ | \ 1$$

The start symbol S can be replaced by $0.S_1$. (We say that S *produces* $0.S_1$.) Now S_1 can be replaced by either $0S_2$ or $1S_2$. So we produce $0.0S_2$ or $0.1S_2$. Finally, S_2 can be replaced by either 0 or 1. (Notice the connection between the nonterminals and the states of the FA of Figure 5.1.)

A derivation producing 0.01 is written:

$$S => 0.S_1 => 0.0S_2 => 0.01, \text{ or } S => \dots => 0.01$$

Production rules for regular languages are of two kinds:

1. $N_T \rightarrow t$, where N_T is a nonterminal, and t is string of one or more terminals.

2. $N_{T1} \rightarrow tN_{T2}$, where t is a single terminal and N_{Ti} is a nonterminal.

Applications

We have seen a group of languages, called regular, that are generated by regular expressions and whose words can be recognized by DFAs (NFAs). In fact, any language that can be recognized by an FA is equivalent to a regular language. Since a language with a finite number of words can be generated as a regular language, text processors can be written using DFAs. As we saw in Figure 5.5 above, a DFA may be more complicated, hence, slower to process than an NFA, so text processors have been influenced more by NFAs.

Compilation of a language involves several steps, the first of which is *lexical analysis* (scanning) or the recognition of legal tokens and symbols. A special language called LEX [Lesk, 1975] has been implemented to produce a DFA from source code. Some compilers implement a DFA for the first pass over source code. For an example of how LEX produces a DFA scanner for FORTRAN arithmetic statements see [Aho, 1979].

EXERCISES

1. Construct a transition table and an FA for a language with two symbols, $\Sigma = \{a\ b\}$, where L contains words comprised of a string of at least 2 a's. Some words of L are aa, aaab, baa, and bbaaaaa.

2. You probably built an NFA for number 1 above. If so, construct the equivalent DFA.

3. Construct a production system for your language of numbers 1 and 2. ∎

Type 2: Context-Free Grammars (CFGs)

There are languages that cannot be recognized by NFAs and are not regular. One of the simplest of these is the language

$$LN = \{a^n b^n: n = 1, 2, ...\} = \{ab\ aabb\ aaabbb\ ...\}$$

The proof that LN is not regular uses the fact that if it were there would be a finite automaton that recognizes legal and rejects illegal strings, and that the existence of such an FA leads to a contradiction. The proof can be found in [Cohen, 1986, p. 202]. Thus there are other language types. The next most general type includes context-free languages. As before, we will characterize languages of Chomsky Type 2 by describing the grammars (CFGs) that generate their legal strings and the theoretical machines that recognize them.

A production system for a context-free grammar is like that for a regular grammar except that the right side may include any combination of terminals and nonterminals. CFGs are called *context-free* because replacements can be made wherever they occur and not in the context of other surrounding symbols. For example, a context-free rule might allow the replacement of "the" with "this" in any English sentence, i.e., The dog barked → This dog barked. A context-sensitive rule might be to replace "the" with "an" if the following word begins with a vowel, otherwise replace it with "a". The dog barked → A dog barked, while The otter barked → An otter barked.

Our production rule for strings $a^n b^n$, is a single one.

S => aSb | Λ

The rule S => Λ is called an "erasing rule," since it allows for the erasing of the symbol S. If we want to produce $a^1 b^1$, we would use the productions:

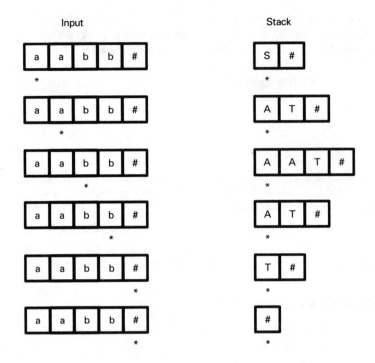

Figure 5.6   PDA to recognize words from LN

S => aSb => ab

where the final production erases the S. Notice that S => Λ is also a valid production, including the empty string Λ in the language. Erasing can lead to trouble, so various strategies have been developed to eliminate erasing rules. Here, we could have used:

S => ab | aSb

Push-down automata (PDAs)

Just as the words of a regular language can be recognized by a finite automaton, words of a context-free language are recognized by a push-down automaton (PDA). The converses are also true—any language recognized by an FA (PDA) is regular (context-free).

A PDA is composed of two tapes (possibly infinitely long). The first is an input tape containing the word to be recognized. The second is a push-down stack, initially containing the start symbol S and a termination symbol, #. Let's see how this works when recognizing a^2b^2 from our language LN. The action is to stack the a's and pop them off as we find corresponding b's. The '*' below each tape marks the position pointer. (See Figure 5.6.)

A PDA can be defined as a set of rules for two tapes, $(r, s_1) \to (n, s_2)$. r lists what is read from the input tape, and s_1 lists what is on the top of the stack. s_2 replaces s_1 on the stack, while the read-pointer advances one character (denoted by ε). We are not confined to reading only one symbol from the stack, but may read as many as are needed. Rules for the PDA above follow. The first rule can be read as "If you see an 'a' on the input tape and an 'S' on the stack, advance one character in the input and replace the 'S' with 'AT'."

$(a, S) \to (\varepsilon, AT)$ {Rewrite S as T, and push A on Stack}

$(a, A) \to (\varepsilon, AA)$ {Push A on the Stack}

$(b, AA) \to (\varepsilon, A)$ {Pop A from the Stack}

$(b, AT) \to (\varepsilon, T)$ {Pop Stack}

$(\#, T\#) \to$ Success!

Cohen [Cohen, 1986] provides an extensive treatment of PDAs relating them to flow charts, rather than rule pairs. This method for specifying PDAs can be found in a 1965 paper by Griffiths and Petrick [Griffiths, 1965].

Applications

Context-free grammars have many practical uses, as much of the syntax of programming languages can be specified using them. The first to do so was ALGOL 60, followed by FORTRAN, Pascal, BASIC, PL/I, and finally, Ada, among others. Each of these languages has noncontext-free constructs, however. One such is the header for a procedure with parameters. Parameters only make sense in the context of a procedure, thus are not context-free. Compilers are particularly amenable to CFGs with their implementations as stacks.

EXERCISES

1. Why is the rule S => aSb not allowed for producing a regular language?

2. Suppose the language with words, $a^n b^n$, is restricted to n < 1000. Call it L_{1000}. Since any language with a finite number of words is regular, L_{1000} is regular. Construct production rules to generate words of L_{1000} and an FA for recognizing words of L_{1000}.

3. Consider the following context-free grammar to generate English sentences.

   $S \to NP\ VP$ $DET \to$ the | a

   $NP \to DET\ N$ $N \to$ man | boy | ball

   $VP \to V_T\ NP$ $V_T \to$ hit | saw

   $VP \to V_S\ S$ $V_S \to$ said | believed

   Is "The ball believed the man hit the boy." a valid sentence? If so, rewrite the CGF to eliminate it. ■

Normal forms

Normal forms are methods of language description following certain rules. One of their important uses is in constructing proofs about language properties. For many languages, we may assume they are specified in normal form and confine our proof to these constructs. Normal forms may not be particularly easy to read or understand, but they are easier to analyze than more casual language descriptions.

Any context-free language can be described by any one of the normal forms below.

Chomsky Normal Form (CNF)   A grammar is said to be in Chomsky Normal Form if all its production rules are of one of two forms.

1. $N_{T1} \rightarrow N_{T2}N_{T3}$, where N_{Ti} is a nonterminal
2. $N_T \rightarrow t$, where N_T is a nonterminal, and t is a single terminal.

Let's write our CFG for LN in CNF. Remember that LN is the language of words of the form $a^n b^n$, and its context-free grammar is the two rules, (1) $S \rightarrow aSb$, and (2) $S \rightarrow ab$. An equivalent CNF for this grammar is:

1. $S \rightarrow AC$
2. $C \rightarrow SB$
3. $S \rightarrow AB$
4. $A \rightarrow a$
5. $B \rightarrow b$

And a derivation of $a^3 b^3$ is

$$\overset{1}{S} \rightarrow \overset{2}{AC} \rightarrow \overset{1}{ASB} \rightarrow \overset{2}{AACB} \rightarrow \overset{3}{AASBB} \rightarrow \overset{4}{AAABBB} \rightarrow \overset{4}{aAABBB} \rightarrow \overset{5}{...} \rightarrow$$
aaabbb

(A number above an arrow indicates which rule was used to produce the right side from the left.)

CNF makes language analysis particularly easy, as you have to worry only about words produced through productions of two kinds. The two-rule CFG for LN was rewritten into five CNF rules. This is usually the case, so CNF grammars tend to be very long.

Backus-Naur Form (BNF)   A more readable normal form is Backus Normal Form, (BNF). BNF is also called Backus-Naur Form, recognizing the contributions of Peter Naur as the editor of the ALGOL 60 report, which was written in BNF.

BNF is a *metalanguage* used to describe production systems to generate context-free languages. For each language generated it includes a set of terminals, a set of nonterminals, and a list of productions. Terminals are indicated variously in different language references. We will use a boldface lower-case string. Nonterminals are enclosed in angle brackets. The metasymbols of BNF (as used in this text and in the minimanuals) are shown in listing (5.2).

Symbol	Meaning	
::=	is defined to be	(5.2)
|	alternatively	
<something>	nonterminal	
something	terminal	

As time has passed, BNF has been extended to EBNF to make language descriptions more readable by replacing some recursive definitions with iterative ones, as shown in listing (5.3).

[something]	0 or 1 occurrences of something, i.e., optional	(5.3)
{something}	0 or more occurences of something	
>	has an alternative definition	
(this | that)	grouping; either of this or that	
	end of definition	

The recursive BNF definition for a Pascal identifier is:

<letter-digit> ::=
<letter> | <identifier><letter> | <identifier><digit>

In EBNF we could write nonrecursively:

<identifier> ::= <letter> | <letter>{letter | digit}

The Ada EBNF definition for an if-statement is:[4]

if_statement ::=
       if condition **then** sequence_of_statements
       {**elseif** condition **then** sequence of statements}
       [**else** sequence of statements]
end if;

In CNF, it gets quite long. We could start out:

IS → I TP
I → **if**
TP → C TS
etc.

Let's look at LN defined in BNF.

---

4 In the *Ada Language Reference Manual*, terminals are written in lower-case bold, and nonterminals in plain text.

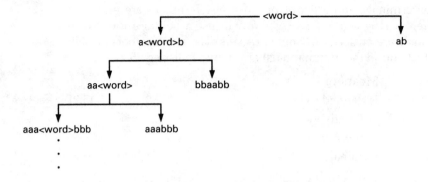

Figure 5.7

<word> ::= **ab** | **a**<word>**b**

Notice the recursive use of <word>. To derive a^3b^3, we would use the definition three times:

<word> → a<word>b → aa<word>bb → aaabbb,

with the final substitution for <word> being the terminator ab.

BNF has an advantage other than making definitions precise and aiding in language analysis. It imposes a structure on words that aid in constructing a recognizer, as shown in Figure 5.7.

Methods for traversing trees are well developed. To recognize a^3b^3, we could traverse the tree from the bottom aaabbb up to the top <word>, or from the top down. Such trees are called *parse trees* due to their use in determining the structure of language elements.

LAB XII: EBNF

OBJECTIVES

1. To use EBNF form as a language generator, employing EBNF definitions for an existing language such as Pascal or Ada.

2. To rewrite the EBNF definitions as a context-free grammar.

3. To build a push-down automata (PDA) to recognize the language fragments generated by number 1.

4. To program number 3, if the instructor wishes it and there is time. ∎

Syntax Diagrams Normal forms can still be hard to read and understand for those untrained in mathematical logic. Syntax diagrams equivalent to the forms can be used by even novice programmers. A syntax diagram for a^nb^n is shown in Figure 5.8.

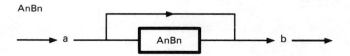

Figure 5.8

Notice the recursion here. We are defining AnBn, as listed in the heading to the diagram, and AnBn occurs in the diagram itself. It's not hard to see that AnBn is taking the place of the start symbol S of the production rule S → ab | aSb.

EXERCISES

1. Finish the CNF definition for an Ada if_statement. For the sake of brevity, omit CNF definitions for conditions and a sequence_of_statements.
2. Construct a syntax diagram for an Ada if_statement. ■

Type 1: Context-Sensitive Grammars

Some languages are not context free. One of the simplest words that cannot be generated by a CFG is $a^n b^n c^n$. The proof is beyond the scope of this brief introduction, but can be found in [Cohen, 1986] beginning on page 462. Productions, x → y, for context-sensitive grammars are like those for context-free languages except that

1. The left side, x, can contain more than one symbol as long as at least one is a nonterminal.
2. The length of x is less than or equal to the length of y.
3. There are no erasing rules.

These last two restrictions prevent dead ends where what is to be replaced (x) may become longer than the word so far generated. A CSG grammar for words of the form $a^n b^n c^n$ is:

1. S → aSBC
2. S → aBC
3. CB → BC
4. aB → ab
5. bB → bb
6. bC → bc
7. cC → cc

and the production of $a^3b^3c^3$ is:

$$\begin{array}{cccccc} 1 & 1 & 2 & 3 & 3 & 3 \end{array}$$
$$S \rightarrow aSBC \rightarrow aaSBCBC \rightarrow aaaBCBCBC \rightarrow aaaBBCCBC \rightarrow...\rightarrow$$
$$aaaBBBCCC$$

$$\begin{array}{cccc} 4 & 5 & 5 & 6 & 7 & 7 \end{array}$$
$$\rightarrow aaabBBCCC \rightarrow...\rightarrow aaabbbCCC \rightarrow aaabbbcCC \rightarrow...\rightarrow aaabbbccc$$

The only difference between these production rules and those for a CFG is the presence of two symbols on the left sides of rules 3 through 7. These symbols provide the *contexts*. 'B' may be changed to 'b' when preceded by 'a' (rule 4) or 'b' (rule 5).

HISTORICAL VIGNETTE 7: Alan Turing: What Can't Machines Do?

The title of Andrew Hodges's biography of Alan Turing [Hodges, 1983], *Alan Turing: The Enigma*, is a pun. Enigma, meaning a mystery or perplexing problem, is also the name of an ingenious machine used to generate German codes during World War II. Turing was a mathematical genius who cracked the Enigma code in 1942, was convicted of "gross indecency" in 1952, subjected to a demeaning course of hormone therapy to control his homosexuality, and committed suicide by eating an apple dipped in cyanide in 1954. It is of such stuff that legends are made, and indeed, Hodges's book was made into a successful Broadway play in 1988.

Alan Turing was born in 1912 to parents in the Indian Civil Service of Great Britain. In 1933, he entered Cambridge University to read mathematics. It was a heady time, as two important questions about the nature of mathematics, whether it is complete and/or consistent, had been answered negatively, while a third remained open.

In 1931, Kurt Gödel had shown that any worthwhile mathematical system could not be complete without being inconsistent. A complete system is one in which any true statement can be proved, while a consistent one is one in which no false statement can be proved. Gödel had shown that any mathematical system complex enough to include multiplication and division contains true statements that make the system inconsistent if proven. One such statement in the Theory of Integer Arithmetic is "This statement cannot be proven." If a proof is provided, the statement is false, making the theory inconsistent, and if the statement is true, no proof can be found, so the theory would be incomplete. Such statements are called "self-referent" because they talk about themselves.

In 1933, a still-open question was whether there could be any "mechanical" method to determine which statements are decidable or not, i.e., can it be decided in advance which sorts of problems will lead to answers and which will lead to endless indecisive computing? A "mechanical" method is one that follows rules, but may or may not be realized in a physical machine.

Alan Turing chose to address this problem of decidability. First, he had to make precise just what is meant by a "machine." This question resulted in a theoretical machine which could be expected to solve any problem that any other machine, or human being, following specified rules, could solve. He was able to find seven questions such a machine cannot answer.

1. Given an arbitrary problem-solving machine, M, and an arbitrary problem, P, can M solve P?

2. Given a particular machine, M, can M solve an arbitrary problem, P?

3. Given M, can the machine recognize a nonproblem when it sees it?

4. Given M, can it solve any problems at all?

5. Given M, can it solve all problems?

6. Given two machines, M_1 and M_2, can they solve the same problems?

7. Given a Turing machine (TM) is the language TM accepts regular? context-free? decidable?

We will look at just what a "Turing machine" is below.

World War II interrupted Turing's theoretical studies, when he was assigned to the Government Code and Cypher School (GCCS) at Bletchley Park, just halfway between Oxford and Cambridge Universities. The Germans were using a machine with four rotors to generate codes for transmissions to, among other things, submarines. With 26 characters and four rotors, a code could have $26 \times 26 \times 26 \times 26 = 456{,}976$ different configurations, and the Germans changed the code daily.

By 1940, the British had designs for the Enigma machine, obtained by Polish agents, but determining just what the state of the rotors was remained a problem. What was needed was a machine to analyze Enigma codes and decipher them quickly. Turing's interests in number theory, mathematical logic, and probability theory plus the engineering necessary to build a practical machine paid off.

In 1942, GCCS built a machine, called a "Bombe" because of its loud ticking, capable of deciphering Enigma codes. Alan Turing was the brains behind the endeavor. It is not an overstatement to say that this effort changed the course of the war. The British were now able to determine the exact location of every German submarine in the various seas.

After the War, Turing returned to his investigation of the capabilities of the "Turing machine" at the National Physical Laboratory and the University of Manchester. His promising career came crashing down with his conviction for "gross indecency," a euphemism for homosexual activity in 1952. His death in 1954 was assumed by most to be a suicide, but sloppy police work was never able to eliminate the possibility of an accident. Some commentators feel this was subterfuge, intended by Turing to spare his family the ignominy of a suicide. They were free to believe what they wanted.

In his brief life, Alan Turing dealt with some of the most profound questions presented by computers. Can a machine be as "intelligent" as a human? Is free will compatible with a mechanistic view of the world? Are emotion and reason the same or different? Can machines understand human experiences? love? frustration? suffering? despair? He also tried to combine mathematics, philosophy, and engineering—scoffed at during his lifetime, but taken seriously now, 27 years after his death.

Linear-bounded automata (LBAs)

A recognizer for a context-sensitive language is a deterministic Turing machine (TM) called a *linear-bounded automaton*, or LBA. It requires only one tape, whereas the PDA, which recognizes context-free languages, uses two. A TM requires six things [Cohen, 1986, p. 553]:

1. An alphabet, Σ, of input symbols
2. A tape divided into cells, labeled 1, 2, 3, ...
3. A read-write head that can move left or right one cell, read what it finds, and write or erase this information. We do not allow the head to go left from cell 1, since there are none preceding it.
4. An alphabet, Γ, of characters that can be written onto the tape. Γ may include Σ, but need not.
5. A finite set of states, including start (S) and halt (H)
6. A set of rules called a *program*. Each rule is of the form, (state$_1$, read-char, write-char, direction, state$_2$). If the current state of the TM is state$_1$, the head reads read-char in cell$_i$, then it writes write-char in the same cell and moves either right or left. The new state is then state$_2$.

Let's look at a fairly extensive example of an LBA to recognize strings of the form, $a^n b^n c^n$. The input language $\Sigma = \{a\ b\ c\ \#\}$. Here '#' marks the end of the input. $\Gamma = \{A\ B\ C\ T\}$. 'T' is a temporary symbol used to replace B's. The string 'aabbcc' will be transformed into 'aabbcc' → 'AATTcc' → AABBCC. The T's take care of context; the extra transformation is needed because the b's are in between a's and c's. The TM will have recognized a correct string when all the lower-case letters have been changed to upper-case; the end symbol, '#', has been reached; and the machine is in state 5.

States are:

s_0: When the read-write head, '*', is at cell$_i$, and the machine is in s_0, all cells before cell$_i$ are correct and need no further processing.

s_1: An 'a' has just been changed to an 'A', and we are looking right for a 'b' to match it.

s_2: A 'b' has just been changed to a 'T', and we are looking left for the next 'a' to change.

s_3:   A 'T' has just been changed to a 'B', and we are looking right for a 'c' to match it.

s_4:   A 'c' has just been changed to a 'C', and we are looking left for the next 'T' to change.

s_5:   HALT

Figure 5.9 shows the processing of 'aabbcc'!

We have seen the execution of a successful program, so now it's time to see the program itself. Each instruction applies to the current state, reads, writes, moves, and then changes state.

$(s_0\ a\ A\ R\ s_1)$	{Start processing here}
$(s_0\ T\ B\ R\ s_3)$	
$(s_0\ C\ C\ R\ s_0)$	{Looking for '#' to HALT}
$(s_0\ \#\ \#\ R\ s_5)$	HALT
$(s_1\ a\ a\ R\ s_1)$	{Looking forward for a 'b' to match an 'A'}
$(s_1\ T\ T\ R\ s_1)$	
$(s_1\ b\ T\ L\ s_2)$	
$(s_2\ T\ T\ L\ s_2)$	{Looking back for the next 'a'}
$(s_2\ a\ a\ L\ s_2)$	
$(s_2\ A\ A\ R\ s_0)$	
$(s_3\ T\ T\ R\ s_3)$	{Looking forward for a 'c' to match a 'B'}
$(s_3\ C\ C\ R\ s_3)$	
$(s_3\ c\ C\ L\ s_4)$	
$(s_4\ C\ C\ L\ s_4)$	{Looking back for next 'T'}
$(s_4\ T\ T\ L\ s_4)$	
$(s_4\ B\ B\ R\ s_0)$	

The last rule, $(s_4\ B\ B\ R\ s_0)$, is similar to others, where the symbol read, in this case 'B', is the same as the one written. Some descriptions of Turing machines offer the option for moving without writing. We chose to rewrite a symbol just to make the presentation easier.

A deterministic linear-bound automaton is a Turing machine that is deterministic and halts in a finite amount of time, i.e., for each pair of instructions, if $(s_1\ X\ Y\ Z\ s_2)$, $(s_3\ A\ B\ C\ s_4)$, if $s_1 = s_3$ and $X = A$, $Y = B$ and $Z = C$, then $s_2 = s_4$. This means that the next step is always completely determined by the state and the input. If we input a string, the TM can decide whether it is a legal string or not in an amount of time proportional to the length of the string. Of course, it will take longer to process $a^{2346}b^{2346}c^{2346}$ than $a^2b^2c^2$, but some function of the TM will tell us how much longer it will take. Our final group of languages will not have these guarantees.

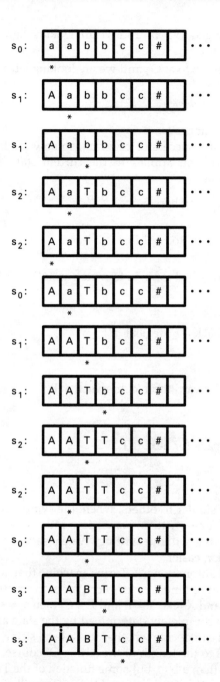

Figure 5.9 (continued next page)

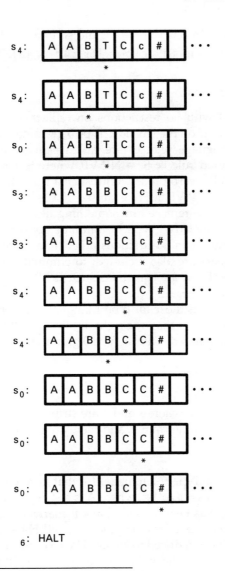

Figure 5.9   (continued from previous page)

1. Let $|a|$, $|b|$, and $|c|$ indicate the number of 'a's, 'b's, or 'c's in an input string. Using the TM above, try test strings to show that:

   a. The TM halts in s_0 or in s_5 if $|a| = 0$.

   b. The TM halts in s_1 if $|a| > 0$, and $|b| = 0$.

c. If $|a| > 0$ & $|b| > 0$, it halts in s_3 if $|a| < |b|$, and s_1 if $|a| > |b|$.

d. If $0 > |a| = |b|$, the TM halts in s_0 if $|c| > |a|$ or if $|c| < |a|$. ∎

Type 0: Unrestricted Grammars

Type 0 grammars are constructed with no restrictions on replacement rules except that a nonterminal must appear on the left side. Type 0 grammars where nonterminals represent natural language phrases are called *phrase-structured grammars*. A typical phrase-structured rule is: S → NP VP, where S denotes a sentence, NP a noun phrase, and VP a verb phrase. With such a rule, strings of the form X S Y can be replaced by X NP VP Y. For example, if X is "The tiger," and Y is "ate the lady," X S Y could be replaced by something like "The tiger, who was behind the first door, ate the lady." Type 1 grammars are sometimes called *restricted phrase-structured* grammars. Restrictions other than those listed above for context-sensitive grammars are also included, to eliminate features not occurring in natural languages. These are constructs such as NP → NP S or VP → V VP, where V indicates a verb.

Type 0 productions are the same as those for type 1 languages except that rule 2, that the left side must be no longer than the right, is eliminated. Rule 3, which forbade erasing, may also be ignored. Thus a Type 0 grammar is:

1. An alphabet Σ of terminal symbols

2. An alphabet Γ of nonterminals

3. A set of production rules, x → y, where x and y are strings from $\Sigma \cup \Gamma$, x contains at least one nonterminal, and there are no restrictions on y.

Now we need an example of a Type 0 language, L_0, that is not Type 1. Legal strings of L_0 will be of the form s = #A#B#, where A is a string of a's and B is a string of b's, but the B-string has been erased. (Here # marks the beginning or end of a string.) Input to recognizer for L_0 might be #aaa#bbbb#, which will halt when the input string has been reduced to #aaa#. The recognizer's first job will be to find the second '#', marking the end of the A-string. The difficulty is that the A-string may never terminate. Our TM recognizer is shown in Figure 5.10.

For the corresponding Type 0 grammar, we will use as terminals Q_i, corresponding to the q_i (i = 0..4) above, to relate it quickly to the TM of Figure 5.9. Our grammar is shown in Figure 5.11.

Σ = {a b #}
Γ = {Q_0 Q_1 Q_2 Q_3 Q_4}

$(q_0$ # # R $q_1)$	{Start}
$(q_1$ a a R $q_1)$	{Go right over the a's}
$(q_1$ # # R $q_2)$	{End of A-string}
$(q_2$ b b R $q_2)$	{Go right over the b's}
$(q_2$ # _ L $q_3)$	{Erase end mark for B}
$(q_3$ b _ L $q_3)$	{Erase b's, one by one}
$(q_3$ # # R $q_4)$	{End mark for A-string}
q_4 HALT	

Figure 5.10   TM for recognizing strings from L_0

Productions

1. $Q_0 \rightarrow$ #Q_1 {Start: write #}
2. $Q_1 \rightarrow$ aQ_1 {write in the a's}
3. $Q_1 \rightarrow$ #Q_2 {write the end-mark for the A-string}
4. $Q_2 \rightarrow$ bQ_2 {write in the b's}
5. $Q_2 \rightarrow$ #Q_3 {write the end-mark for the B-string}
6. #$Q_3 \rightarrow Q_4$ {erase the end-mark for B-string}
7. b$Q_4 \rightarrow Q_4$ {erase the b's}
8. #$Q_4 \rightarrow$ #   {stop erasing at end-mark for A-string}

Figure 5.11   Type 0 grammar for generating L_0

Grammars for Natural Languages

Human beings communicate in natural languages, but no natural language can be characterized precisely enough to define a grammar that generates all valid sentences. Arbitrary statements cannot always be parsed either, to facilitate understanding. However, in addition to phrase-structured grammars, both context-free and context-sensitive techniques have proved useful in understanding natural languages in some fairly restricted settings. It is the ambiguousness of unrestricted everyday language that hinders the development of practical speech-recognition devices.

Closely related to the finite automata (FAs) we described as recognizers for regular languages are *recursive transition networks* (RTNs). These can be used as context-free language generators equivalent to a CFG. They differ from FAs in that they allow arc labels which refer to other networks. For example, the CFG to generate strings of the form $a^n b^n$ is S $\rightarrow$ ab | aSb. An equivalent RTN is shown in Figure 5.12.

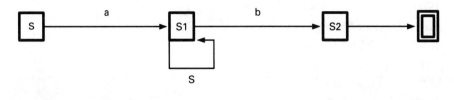

Figure 5.12   RTN to generate a^nb^n

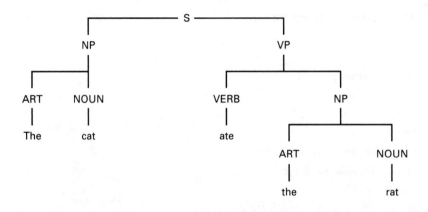

Figure 5.13   Sentence parse tree

The difference here from an NFA is that the arc labeled S occurs in the middle of the RTN. It means that the entire S network is to be inserted for the label S. You will be asked to investigate a related NFA in exercise 2 below.

A simple CFG for generating English sentences is the following:

$$S \leftarrow NP\ VP$$
$$VP \leftarrow VERB\ NP$$
$$NP \leftarrow NAME$$
$$NP \leftarrow ART\ NOUN$$

where S stands for Sentence, VP for Verb Phrase, NP for Noun Phrase, and ART for Article. Sentences such as "The cat ate a rat" can be generated with it, but so can "A cats ate a rats" or "Cats meowed dogs." A good bit more information is needed to generate meaningful sentences. Notice that the arrows in the grammar rules are reversed from what we have seen before. This reversal suggests bottom-up sentence parsing, which is one of the first steps in the mechanical understanding of natural language (See Figure 5.13).

One method that has proved useful in automatic language understanding is the *augmented transition network* (ATN). Here the RTN is augmented by tests on each arc, which guarantee agreement between nouns and adjectives, subjects and verbs, verbs and auxiliaries, etc. A transition network must also be augmented to handle verb compliments, such as adverbial and infinitive phrases.

ATNs can be used to generate and recognize grammatically correct sentences, but meaning is another complex activity. Consider the various meanings of "broke":

1. Alex broke the glass with a rock.
2. The rock broke the glass.
3. The glass broke.

Add an adverb to number 1, "Alex intentionally broke the glass." Does "The rock intentionally broke the glass" or "The glass intentionally broke" make sense? Semantic networks have been developed to deal with questions such as these and many others. Only animate entities can have "intention." We will deal with some of these relationships when we discuss declarative languages in Part VI.

EXERCISES

1. a. Follow the grammar of Figure 5.11 to generate a string with 3 a's followed by 2 b's.
   b. Submit your string to the TM of Figure 5.9 to see if it is recognized.
   c. What happens if we submit an infinite string of a's to the TM?

2. What is the language generated by the NFA below? How does it differ from the RTN of Figure 5.12? What category of language is generated?

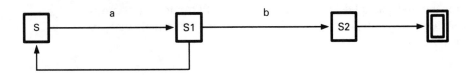

3. Parse the three sentences using the verb "broke" in a manner similar to that of Figure 5.13.

4. Below are three ambiguous English phrases. Can you find at least two meanings for each? Do the two meanings parse differently?
   a. "I hate visiting relatives."
   b. "5 * 3 + 2"
   c. "Here's to my last wife!" ■

5.2 SUMMARY

We have looked at four formal language types. Type 0 is the most general and includes all the others. Type 0 languages are also called *recursively enumerable* (r.e.), which means that there is some function f(n) from the natural numbers to the alphabet Σ that will generate valid strings. Strings may be infinite in length. Grammars to generate such languages are called *phrase structured*. It is widely held by mathematicians that any function which can be effectively computed is r.e. Strings of Type 0 languages can be recognized by Turing machines.

Type 1 languages are generated by context-sensitive grammars. There are no restrictions on the form of production rules except that if $\alpha \to \beta$ is a rule, then the length of α must be less than or equal to the length of β. They can be recognized by *linear-bounded automata*, which will halt in time proportional to the length of an input string.

Context-free languages (CFLs) are of Chomsky Type 2. They can be generated using production rules with a single nonterminal on the left side. These are the most important for the construction of parsers for compilers, since many computer languages can be almost completely defined by a context-free grammar. Although we have not discussed it here, the construction of parse trees from PDAs is straightforward. Backus Normal Form and its extension are equivalent to context-free grammars. BNF and EBNF (Extended Backus Normal Form) are widely used to specify context-free language rules. The Ada Standard is written in EBNF with those portions that are not context free described in ordinary English. Context-free languages are recognized by push-down automata (PDAs).

Regular languages are context free, but can be generated by production rules of the form $N_T \to t$, or $N_{T1} \to tN_{T2}$. Any language with a finite number of words is regular, and can be recognized by finite automata. Some parsers are based on FAs for the first-pass checking for valid tokens,[5] PDAs for the second-pass checking statement syntax, and some other process for statements that are neither regular nor context free.

5.3 NOTES ON REFERENCES

Treatment of formal languages has been very brief here. A course in theoretical computer science would consider proofs of much that we have mentioned. A good elementary treatment is [Cohen, 1986]. Lewis and Papadimitriou's text [Lewis, 1981] has long provided a somewhat more advanced handling. Hopcroft and Ullman [Hopcroft, 1979] also provide a good treatment. The classic book on recursive function theory is [Rogers, 1967].

---

5 A token is a valid string in a language such as an identifier, an assignment indicator, :=, reserved word, IF, comparator, <, etc.

Turing machines are considered in many mathematical logic texts, e.g., [Mendelson, 1979]. Using Turing machines to build context-free recognizers continues to receive attention. See [Griffiths, 1965] for earlier work and [Graham, 1980] for something more recent. Both articles contain extensive bibliographies. Hodges's [Hodges, 1983] biography of Alan Turing is notable in its combination of sensitive commentary on a troubled life with correct scientific exposition. For a brief, but meritorious review of Hodges, see [Hofstadter, 1985b].

Natural language understanding is often the purview of linguists. A good place to get started in the literature is through the Synthese Language Library published by D. Reidel. One collection surveying current trends is Volume 15, *The Nature of Syntactic Representation* [Jacobson, 1982].

PART
IV

DECLARATIVE LANGUAGES

6

LOGIC PROGRAMMING

Logic is the science of reasoning and as such includes formal methodologies that have been found useful for solving problems other than those resolved by intuition, leaps of faith or compromise. Such nonlogical methods are used to arrive at workable solutions to many social problems, but often cannot be translated into algorithms usable for computer programs.

THE PROPOSITIONAL CALCULUS

The first known logical system, attributed to Aristotle during the fourth century B.C., included laws of deduction based on statements of four possible forms. "All students work hard" and "Some students eat a lot" represent two of the forms. The deduction rules then allow us to state that "Some who eat a lot work hard."

He was the student of Plato, tutor to Alexander the Great, and a prolific author who wrote on virtually every field of study known in his time. His works dealt with such diverse topics as logic, politics, economics, biology, physics, meteorology, ethics, psychology, and theology. His name is Aristotle, and he was one of the greatest philosophers of the ancient Greek world.

Aristotle was born in the Ionian colony at Stagira in Macedonia in 384 B.C. Randall [Randall, 1960] notes that "all the major Greek philosophers, with the exception of Socrates and Plato, had been Ionians." Although Aristotle's father is listed as Nicomachus, physician to King Amyntas, it was rumored that his real begetter was the god of healing and medicine and his grandfather, Apollo, god of reason and light [Randall, 1960].

Aristotle was sent at 17 to Athens to study at the Academy. There he was trained in philosophy by Plato and quickly established himself as "the mind of the school" and "the reader." Aristotle disagreed with some of Plato's doctrines, but was influenced greatly by Plato's work, especially during his early years. His writings during this period reflect Plato's own on such topics as the immortality of the soul, rhetoric, justice, and the idea of pure good.

However, Aristotle was sharply critical of the instructor Isocrates. "He shared Plato's contempt for Isocrates' poverty of thought and for his elevation of oratorical success over the pursuit of truth" [Ross, 1923]. This criticism made him the enemy of the Isocratean school.

When Plato died in 348–7 B.C., he left the direction of the Academy to his nephew, Speusippus, even though he considered Aristotle to be his best student. Some say this is why Aristotle left the Academy. Others claim it was because of Speusippus's stressing of mathematics, while still others hypothesize that Aristotle had not been fully accepted socially.

Aristotle spent several years studying plants and animals along the coast of Asia Minor before traveling to Macedonia to assume the post of tutor to King Philip's 13-year-old son Alexander. When the boy became king, Aristotle returned to Athens to establish his own school in the Lyceum. The school was called "the Peripatetic" because Aristotle often walked and talked with his students in the Lyceum gardens. Mornings were devoted to logic and afternoons given to rhetoric, politics, and ethics. Aristotle stated that logic, originally called analytics, is "not a substantive science, but a part of the general culture which everyone should undergo before he[/she] studies science; and which alone will enable him[/her] to know for what sorts of proposition he[/she] should demand proof and what sorts of proof he[/she] should demand for them" [Ross, 1923]. Aristotle's inspiration to develop logic was a desire to lay down the mathematical pattern present in all sciences. He defined science as "a series of incontestably true statements for which it can be maintained that they fall into two classes. To the first class belong the basic principles or axioms, i.e., the remarkable propositions whose truth is so evident that they are neither capable of nor in need of proof. To the second class belong the propositions or theorems, i.e., the propositions whose truth can be demonstrated on the basis of the truth of the axioms" [Scholz, 1961]. The model for these propositions was Greek geometry. Aristotle's greatest work in the field of logic is the *Organon*, which is comprised of several volumes. The main body of the work deals with different types of statements and their logical properties and relationships.

When Alexander died in 323 B.C., anti-Macedonian feelings ran rampant. Aristotle's Macedonian connections, along with the enmity of the Isocrateans, made him a likely scapegoat. He retired to Chalcis where he died the following year at the age of 62.

THE CALCULUS OF STATEMENTS

Aristotle's rules of deduction were found to be inadequate for many statements, and a somewhat different logical system was formalized later. It is known as the propositional

Truth	Values	Defined for OR
p	q	p OR q
1	1	1
1	0	1
0	1	1
0	0	0

Figure 6.1

calculus (PC), since it provides rules for calculating the truth values of propositions, which are simply declarative sentences, or statements. In this system, any proposition must be assigned the value TRUE or FALSE. There are no MAYBEs. For example, from the two propositions

  p: Brutus killed Caesar.
  q: Cassius killed Caesar.

we can construct the proposition

  r: p OR q

expressing the notion that either Brutus or Cassius killed Caesar, or possibly both. Then the truth value of r would be calculated in PC as TRUE, (Value (r) = TRUE), if either Value (p) = TRUE or Value (q) = TRUE. These truth values can be determined using the method of truth tables. We usually let 1 represent TRUE and 0 represent FALSE, to save ink. Another reason will be explored in exercise 3 at the end of this section.

The value of a proposition containing OR is defined by the table in Figure 6.1. It is called the *inclusive-or*, since Value (p OR q) = 1 includes the case where Value (p) = 1 and Value (q) = 1. Whether Brutus or Cassius or both killed Caesar is called an *instance* of the proposition p OR q, with "Brutus killed Caesar" being substituted for p, and "Cassius killed Caesar" substituted for q. We could just as well substitute "The Sparrow killed Cock Robin" for p. "The Sparrow killed Cock Robin or Cassius killed Caesar" would then be a different instance of the proposition p OR q. An *interpretation* of p OR q is an assignment of truth values to the proposition variables p and q. The various possible interpretations of p OR q are displayed in Figure 6.1.

There are three logical connectives: OR, AND, and →. p → q can be read, IF p THEN q. p → q is TRUE except in the case where the antecedent p is TRUE and the succedent q is FALSE. The notion here is that a true premise (p) can lead only to a true consequence (q). However, if we interpret p to be "The moon is made of green cheese," then q can be any statement whatsoever. Suppose q is "Many college sophomores win Nobel Prizes." Then p → q is considered TRUE. This is justified (logically) by the notion that anyone who believes the moon is made of green cheese might believe anything else as well including many sophomores win Nobel prizes.

When formalizing logic, the first step is to describe what constitutes a legal proposition. This step is done recursively with three formation rules, as follows:

FR1: A single letter of the alphabet is a proposition.

FR2: If p is a proposition, so is NOT(p) ($\neg$p).

FR3: If p and q are propositions, so is p OR q.

(FR4): If p and q are propositions, so are p AND q, and

   $p \rightarrow q$.

As will be seen in exercise 2 at the end of this section, rule 4 above is not needed. We can get by using only NOT and one of OR, AND, or $\rightarrow$, with the remaining two defined as abbreviations of longer expressions.

A *theory* includes all legal statements. Some of these statements are called *axioms* and are assumed to be true without proof. A *thesis* is a true statement that is either an axiom or derivable from the axioms using the rules of inference of the theory. Many formulations of the theory for the propositional calculus have been shown to be equivalent. The two requirements for any such set of axioms is that they be *complete* and *consistent*. A theory is said to be complete if all statements that are TRUE are theses. It is consistent if no statement that is FALSE can be derived. PC can be shown to be both complete and consistent [see, for example, Mendelson, 1979]. One of the best-known sets of axioms for PC is that of Whitehead and Russell's *Principia Mathematica* (PM) [Whitehead, 1910].

A1: $(p \text{ OR } p) \rightarrow p$

A2: $q \rightarrow (p \text{ OR } q)$

A3: $(p \text{ OR } q) \rightarrow (q \text{ OR } p)$

A4: $(q \text{ OR } r) \rightarrow ((p \text{ OR } q) \rightarrow (p \text{ OR } r))$

Two rules of inference in PM are:

R1 (Uniform Substitution): If p is a thesis, and q is a statement derived from p by substituting every occurrence of a letter, x, by another letter, y, then q is a thesis.

R2 (Detachment, or *Modus Ponens*): If p and p $\rightarrow$ q are both theses, then q is a thesis also.

Using R1 and A1, we would have that (s OR s) $\rightarrow$ s is a thesis of PM, by uniformly substituting the letter s for p. However, (s OR p) $\rightarrow$ s may not be a thesis, since we did not substitute s for *all* occurrences of p. The substitution was not uniform.

We can test the validity of statements using truth tables, or we can construct a proof listing all the true statements as premises and then derive the statement we wish to prove through repeated use of the two inference rules.

PROOF BY CONTRADICTION

Another proof method known as *reductio ad absurdum* is more applicable to computer solutions. Here we assume the statement to be proved is FALSE and derive a contradiction. We will demonstrate this method to show the validity of A4 by assuming Value (A4) = 0.

Step 1:   (q -> r) -> ((p OR q) -> (p OR r))
                        0

We place a value of FALSE (0) under the "$\rightarrow$" indicating that we must show this implication to be false. Given the meaning of "$\rightarrow$," the value occurs only when the antecedent is TRUE and the succedent, FALSE. Thus:

Step 2:   (q -> r) -> ((p OR q) -> (p OR r))
                1   0   0

We can do no more with the antecedent (q $\rightarrow$ r) at this time, so we consider how to make the succedent FALSE. This truth value occurs once again with a true antecedent and false succedent.

Step 3:   (q -> r) -> ((p OR q) -> (p OR r))
                1   0   1   0   0

Now (p OR r) has a truth value of 0 only when Value(p) = 0 and Value(r) = 0

Step 4:   (q -> r) -> ((p OR q) -> (p OR r))
                1   0   1   0   0 0 0

We must now make Value(p) = Value(r) = 0 uniformly.

Step 5:   (q -> r) -> ((p OR q) -> (p OR r))
                1 0   0   0 1   0   0 0 0

Next, we assign the necessary values to q. Value (q) must be 0 so that Value ((q $\rightarrow$ r)) = 1, as determined in step 2.

Step 6:   (q -> r) -> ((p OR q) -> (p OR r))
                0 1 0 0   0 1   0   0 0 0

Value (p OR q) = 1 (step 3) and this can only occur with Value (q) = 1, since Value (p) = 0 (step 5).

Step 7:   (q -> r) -> ((p OR q) -> (p OR r))
                <u>0</u> 1 0 0   0 1 <u>1</u> 0   0 0 0

We have underlined the two values here, since they represent a contradiction. Thus we "reduced to the absurd" our original claim in step 1 that Value (A4) = 0. In logic, a contradiction is a statement that is both TRUE and FALSE. Contradictions do not occur in a consistent theory. However, in a complete theory, every legal statement is either TRUE or FALSE, so A4 must be TRUE.

We write the entire reduction in a single line by placing the steps above and the truth values below the statement.

Steps:
```
            6 2  5  1    5  3 7  2    4  3 4
            (q -> r) -> ((p OR q) -> (p OR r))
```
Truth Values: 0 1 0 0   0 1 1 0   0 0 0

EXERCISES

1. Construct truth tables to define the logical connectives AND and NOT.

2. a. Using the identity $p \rightarrow q \equiv$ NOT(p) OR q, rewrite the PM axioms using only NOT and OR.

   b. Using the identity p OR q $\equiv$ NOT(NOT(p) AND NOT(q)), rewrite the PM axioms using only NOT and AND.

   c. Rewrite the axioms using only NOT and $\rightarrow$.

3. Substitute ordinary multiplication (*) for AND, ordinary addition (+) for OR, and negation ($\neg$) for NOT. Show that each of the PM axioms has a value ≥ 1.

4. Use the *reductio* method in "Proof by contradiction" to show the validity of:

   a. p OR NOT(p)   (Law of the Excluded Middle)

   b. NOT(p & NOT(p))

   c. $(p \rightarrow q) \rightarrow ((p \rightarrow r) \rightarrow (p \rightarrow (q \text{ AND } r)))$ (Composition)

   d. $((p \rightarrow q) \rightarrow ((q \rightarrow r) \rightarrow (p \rightarrow r))$

   e. $((q \rightarrow r) \rightarrow ((p \rightarrow q) \rightarrow (p \rightarrow r))$ ((d) and (e) are the Laws of Syllogism)

   f. (NOT(NOT(p))) $\leftrightarrow$ p ($\leftrightarrow$ means "if and only if" (iff)). A proof involves two parts: a proof of (NOT(NOT(p))) $\rightarrow$ p and one for p $\rightarrow$ (NOT(NOT(p))).

5. Using the PC theses of exercise 3, make appropriate substitutions for the statement letters p, q, and r to model in PC the following statements:

   a. One either dies of the flu or gets better; there are no two ways about it.

   b. If I pass this course, it means I really studied. There might be a bit of luck involved too.

   c. All men are mortal. Socrates is a man, therefore, Socrates is mortal. ∎

THE PREDICATE CALCULUS

The predicate calculus is nothing more than the statement calculus with quantifiers added: FORALL and EXISTS. For example, (FORALL X)(IF X is a dog THEN X barks) and (EXISTS X)(X is a dog) are statements of the predicate calculus. "Dogs bark" is in the statement calculus, but has no quantifiers. We will look at these differences more closely below.

Relations

The propositional calculus lacks expressive power, in that statements are indivisible. We cannot use the same statement in different instances. For example, we might not know who killed Caesar, but we do know he's dead and need a statement saying that "Someone killed Caesar." Then we could substitute either Brutus or Cassius for *Someone*. Brutus or Cassius is related to Caesar by the relation KILLED. KILLED (Brutus, Caesar) and KILLED (Cassius, Caesar) are two instances of the two-place relation KILLED. (Notice, we still don't know who did it. That depends on an interpretation, or assignment of truth values to the two instances of the KILLED predicate.) In mathematics, a two-place (or binary) relation is simply a set of ordered 2-tuples. An example is the relation LESS-THAN, (or <), which includes (2,3) and (5,7), but does not include (2,2). Other relations may be functions, such as TIMES (*), which is a three-place relation or set of 3-tuples. (3,2,6) belongs to TIMES but (3,2,5) does not. Relations are often written with their names appropriately between the arguments, e.g., 3 * 2 = 6, 2 < 3, or Brutus KILLED Caesar.

A *predicate* is a relation that can (potentially) be assigned a truth value. It consists of a predicate symbol, such as TIMES, <, or KILLED, and arguments, which may be either variables, constants, or functors. Thus TIMES (3,2,X) is a predicate, which is FALSE if 5 is substituted for X and TRUE if we substitute 6. We may also write TIMES (3,2,(1 + Y)) if we allow expressions such as 1 + Y to be substituted for variables. What substitution for Y makes this last relation TRUE? That (3,2,6) belongs to TIMES constitutes a proof of the statement "There exists an X and (TIMES (3,2,X))." In the PROLOG language, this existential statement would be written `WHICH(X : TIMES(3,2,X))`, `which (_x (times 3 2 _x))` or `?- TIMES(3,2,X)`, depending on the dialect being used. It is the job of the PROLOG interpreter or compiler to prove that the variable X may be replaced by 6.

To add predicates to our PC statements, we use formation rules FR1 through FR3, as in "The calculus of statements," and add:

FR4: If p is a formula and X is an individual-variable, then (FORALL X) p is a formula.[1]

---

1 Note that we have changed the designation of a statement from "proposition" to "formula." In many discussions of logic, statements written correctly according to FR1 through FR4 are called well-formed-formulas, or WFFs.

Just as we were able to define p AND q as NOT(NOT(p) OR NOT(q)) (see exercise (b) above), we can define (EXISTS X) p as NOT(FORALL X)(NOT(p)). In order to say, "There exists a yellow cat," we could use the convoluted statement, "It is not true that all cats are not yellow." (You were forewarned against the double negative by your high-school English teachers for matters of style, not meaning.)

In `IS-A(X, Yellow, Cat)`, X is said to be "free." In `WHICH(X: IS-A(X, Yellow, Cat))`, X is "bound"[2] by the quantifier `WHICH` (exists).

Inference rules R1 and R2 still apply to the predicate calculus, and we add two new rules to handle the variables.

R3 (Uniform Substitution of Variables): If X is an individual variable, and p is any legal formula, and if q is a formula differing from p only in that all free occurrences of X have been replaced by Y, then (FORALL X) p → q is a thesis, provided the Y did not become bound in q when it replaced X.

R4 (Universal Generalization): If X is any individual variable and p and q are formulas, then if p → q,is a thesis, so is p → (FORALL X) q.

These *substitution rules* are quite tricky. A simple example due to Hughes and Cresswell [Hughes, 1968, p. 138ff.] demonstrates the trouble you can get into if you ignore the proviso in R3. Suppose p is the statement (EXISTS Y)(X is-a-child-of Y). This statement, in effect, states that whoever X is, he has a parent (most likely true). Note that X is free in p, while Y is bound. Now q is (EXISTS Y)(Y is-a-child-of Y), which is false, at least as far as we know. This substitution of Y for X violates the proviso, since it allowed the free occurrence of X to become bound by the (EXISTS Y). The statement (FORALL X) (EXISTS Y)(X is-a-child-of Y) → (EXISTS Y)(Y is-a-child-of Y) surely cannot be a thesis, since the antecedent is true, but the succedent, false. Fortunately, logic programmers usually need not concern themselves with such problems, but the developers of a language based on logic, such as PROLOG, worried about bindings and scope a great deal.

THE FIRST-ORDER PREDICATE CALCULUS

The order of a logical system depends on what values the individual variables, such as X and Y, may have. That is, when we say (FORALL X) p, just which X's did we have in mind? In a first-order theory, we may either replace X with a different variable name, as prescribed in R3, or we may replace X with a constant, called an individual. That is, in the statement IS-A(X, yellow, cat)), X may be replaced only by Fluffy, Tiger, or Magnifi-Cat, not by some other formula, such as OWNS(Tommy,X). In other words, IS-A(OWNS(Tommy, X), yellow, cat) is not a legal first-order substitution.

This should not be surprising here, since in the predicate OWNS(Tommy, X), we are looking for some value for X that makes OWNS(Tommy, X) TRUE. If Tiger is substituted for X, and Tommy does indeed own Tiger, then in the IS-A formula, we would

---

2 You struggled with bindings when you programmed functions and procedures. Variables are either global or local to a procedure and, if local, are "bound" to the procedure where they are declared.

have IS-A(OWNS(Tommy, X), yellow, cat) replaced by IS-A(OWNS(Tommy,Tiger), yellow, cat), which would evaluate to IS-A(TRUE, yellow, cat). We would like some mechanism to get from the fact that Tommy OWNS Tiger to the fact that Tiger IS-A yellow cat. We, of course, have this mechanism at hand and will use implication. That is, IF OWNS(Tommy, X) THEN IS-A(X, yellow, cat). To use the proof system known as resolution, which is the basis for PROLOG and will be discussed in the next section, we would write this statement backward, as IS-A(X, yellow, cat) ← OWNS(Tommy, X).

PROOFS

Resolution

In 1965, Julia Robinson published an article in the *Journal of the Association for Computing Machinery* (JACM) demonstrating a new principle called *resolution*, which is a single process including no axioms and a complete and consistent first-order logical system. It bears similarities to the *reductio* method of "Proof by contradiction." In its simplest form, resolution works like this: Suppose we are still interested in the fact KILLED (Brutus,Caesar) OR KILLED(Cassius,Caesar). This statement can be *resolved* to p: KILLED(Brutus,Caesar) if we also have the fact ¬q: NOT(KILLED(Cassius,Caesar)). Here, KILLED(Brutus,Caesar) is called the *resolvent*. This resolution can be written symbolically in three equivalent ways:

$$
\begin{array}{ccc}
\dfrac{p \text{ OR } q}{\neg q} & \dfrac{\neg p \to q}{\neg q} & \dfrac{(p \text{ OR } q) \text{ AND } \neg q}{p} \\[2ex]
p & p &
\end{array}
\qquad (6.1)^3
$$

We say that q is a logical consequence of facts $p_1, p_2, ..., p_n$, if whenever all of the p_i are interpreted as TRUE, so is q.

The theorem applicable to resolution as used for logic programming is:

Resolution Theorem   q is a logical consequence of $p_1, p_2, ..., p_n$, if (¬q AND p_1 AND p_2 AND ... AND p_n) is FALSE.

If we rewrite this in the OR form, we have: q OR ¬p_1 OR ¬p_2 OR ... OR ¬p_n is TRUE. This last statement, which contains n + 1 disjuncts, only one of which is positive, is called a *Horn clause*. If, in addition, we allow the universal quantifier, FORALL, statements are said to be in "extended Horn clause form." It is the resolution of extended Horn clauses that forms the basis for pure logic programming, of which PROLOG is an enhanced implementation.

Let's look at an example from Doug DeGroot [DeGroot, 1984] of a list of Horn clauses and their resolution. For ease of understanding, we will write the clauses in "←" form. Writing the implication arrows backward has become customary in logic pro-

---

3 We use the abbreviation "¬p" to represent NOT(p).

gramming to emphasize the goal of a proof, i.e., that which is to be proved on the left by implication from premises on the right. Thus A ← B & C should be read, "A is true if both B and C are true."

C1: HAPPY(Tom) ← WATCHING(Tom,football) & HAS(Tom,supplies)
C2: HAS(Tom,supplies) ← HAS(Tom,beer) & HAS(Tom,pretzels)
C3: WATCHING(Tom,football) ← IS-ON(tv) & PLAYING(cowboys)
C4: IS-ON(tv)[4]
C5: PLAYING(cowboys)
C6: HAS(Tom,beer)
C7: HAS(Tom,pretzels)

If we wish to find out if Tom is happy, we have to show that HAPPY(Tom) is a logical consequence of C1 through C7. We know from the resolution theorem that if ($\neg$HAPPY(Tom) & C1 & C2 & ... & C7) resolves to FALSE, then HAPPY(Tom) is TRUE. We thus add a new clause called a QUERY.

Q: $\neg$HAPPY(Tom)?	
C8: $\neg$WATCHING(football,Tom) OR $\neg$HAS(Tom,supplies)	Q & C1
C9: $\neg$HAS(Tom,supplies) OR $\neg$IS-ON(tv) OR $\neg$PLAYING(cowboys)	C8 & C3
C10: $\neg$HAS(Tom,supplies) OR $\neg$PLAYING(cowboys)	C9 & C4
C11: $\neg$HAS(Tom,supplies)	C& C5
C12: $\neg$HAS(Tom,beer) OR $\neg$HAS(Tom,pretzels)	C11 & C2
C13: $\neg$HAS(Tom,pretzels)	C12 & C6
C14: FALSE	C13 & C7

Since we have derived FALSE from $\neg$HAPPY(Tom)? and C1 through C7, we may conclude that Tom is indeed happy, by the resolution theorem. Notice the order in which the resolution chain proceeded. First, the QUERY was resolved with the first clause on the list. If this were not possible, we would next try to resolve Q with C2, C3, etc. In each step after the first, resolution of the new resolvent is attempted with the next clause down the list. Notice also that resolution is not confined to single disjuncts, as shown in listing (6.1). The general resolution principle is shown in listing (6.2).

S_1 OR q OR S_2 (6.2)
S3 OR $\neg$q OR S4   resolves to:
$\overline{S_1 \text{ OR } S_2 \text{ OR } S_3 \text{ OR } S_4}$ for any S_1, S_2, S_3, and S_4.

Also note that:

P
$\underline{\neg P}$

resolves to: FALSE.

---

4 C4 through C7 are Horn clauses, each with an empty set of negative disjuncts. A Horn clause necessarily contains a single positive disjunct, but may have any finite number of negative disjuncts, including none.

EXERCISES

1. Recalling that r ← p & q ≡ r OR ¬p OR ¬q, resolve the following:

    a. r ← p & q
        ¬r
    b. q OR r
        ¬q OR ¬r
    c. s ← p & q & r
        p
        q
    d. s OR ¬p OR ¬q OR ¬r
        p
        q

2. Consider the clauses below, and use resolution to answer the queries following:

    C1: IN-JAIL(Mary) ← COMMITTED(Mary,Crime) & CAUGHT(Cop,Mary)
    C2: CAUGHT(Cop,Mary) ← SAW(Cop,crime)
    C3: SAW(Cop,crime) ← ON-DUTY(Cop)
    C4: COMMITTED(Mary,crime) ← TOOK(Mary,wallet)
                                & BELONGS-TO(wallet,Jane)
    C5: TOOK(Mary,wallet) ← HAD(Mary,opportunity)
    C6: ON-DUTY(Cop)
    C7: HAD(Mary,opportunity)
    C8: BELONGS-TO(wallet,Jane)
    Q1: COMMITTED(Mary,Crime)?   Q2: IN-JAIL(Mary)?

3. Suppose that in a resolution chain, the first predicate to the right of a "←" must be resolved before trying to match any of those further to the right. For example, in number 3 above, when Q2 is resolved with C1 to ¬COMMITTED(Mary,crime) OR ¬CAUGHT(Cop,Mary), the next resolution would necessarily involve the COMMITTED predicate, even if an instance of CAUGHT were encountered earlier on the list. Redo the HAPPY(Tom)? query, following this matching rule. Does it make any difference? Which method would make a more efficient algorithm: (1) Resolve the rightmost predicate first; or (2) Check all predicates in a clause, and resolve with the first match you find on the list. Might this depend on the length of the clause list? ∎

UNIFICATION

Just as we wished to extend the propositional to the predicate calculus to include general formulas containing variables and quantifiers, proofs by resolution should apply to such statements as well. These proofs require a process known as *unification*.

Suppose we change clause 1 to

C1′: HAPPY(x) ← WATCHING(x, football) & HAS(x, supplies)

This new statement suggests that anyone, not just Tom, who is watching football and has supplies is happy. A first step in resolving C1′,C2 through C7, with the QUERY, ¬HAPPY(Tom)? is to *unify* the QUERY with the leftmost predicate of C1′. We need to find bindings for any variables in the two expressions, which will make them look alike, except for sign. If we substitute Tom for x in C1, the two expressions match. The substitution must be uniform, resulting in C1″: HAPPY(Tom) ← WATCHING(Tom, football) & HAS(Tom,supplies). Q and C1 are unified by the substitution sets, { }[5] and {x/Tom}.

Let's rewrite our conditions for happiness again, allowing a few more choices.

D1: HAPPY(x) ← WATCHING(x,football) & HAS(x,y)
D2: HAS(x,supplies) ← HAS(x,y) & HAS(x,z)
D3: HAS(x,beer)
D4: HAS(x,pretzels)
D5: WATCHING(x,football) ← IS-ON(tv) & PLAYING(y)
D6: IS-ON(tv)
D7: PLAYING(cowboys)

The resolution and unification, if queried with ¬HAPPY(Tom)?, would proceed as follows (as before, explanations are found in the right-hand column):

D8: ¬WATCHING(Tom,football) OR ¬HAS(Tom,y)   Q,{x/Tom},D1
D9: ¬HAS(Tom,y) OR ¬IS-ON(tv) OR ¬PLAYING(y1)
                                           {y/y1},[6] D8,{x/Tom},D5
D10: ¬HAS(Tom,y) OR ¬PLAYING(y1)   D9,D6
D11: ¬HAS(Tom,y) OR ¬HAS(Tom,x) OR ¬PLAYING(y1)
                                           {y/supplies},D10,{x,Tom},D2
D12: ¬PLAYING(y1)   {y/beer,x/beer}D11,D3
D13: FALSE   {y1/cowboys},D11,{y/cowboys},D7

In this resolution, we never used the clause HAS(x,pretzels), since we substituted beer for both x and y in D12. For Tom, beer seems to be enough. You'll be given a chance to think about this in exercise 3.

---

5 The query Q has an empty substitution set, { }, because it contains no free variables. Such a clause is called a **ground** clause.
6 The substitution y/y1 is needed in D8, since the y in D5 need not represent the same constant as the y in D8.

EXERCISES

1. Unify the following terms, or state why they cannot be unified:

   a. A(x,3); A(2,3)

   b. A(x,3); A (y,y)

   c. MOTHER(Rhea, X); MOTHER(Y, Jupiter)

   d. FATHER(Saturn, X); FATHER(Y, Y)

   e. SON(Jupiter, Saturn); SON(Y, Y)

   f. P(x,y); P(z,z)

2. Write an algorithm for a function UNIFY (Term1, Term2), which returns Term3 or FAIL. A term is defined recursively:

   a. If c is a constant, then c is a term.

   b. If x is a variable, then x is a term.

   c. If P_N is an n-place predicate symbol, and $t_1,..,t_N$ are terms, then $P_N(t_1, ..., t_N)$ is a term.

3. The unification and resolution of D1 through D13 in "Unification" above assumed that we used D3 twice, once to unify and resolve with HAS(Tom,y) and then to unify and resolve with HAS(Tom,z). Suppose we desired the process to continue as follows:

   D11: ¬HAS(Tom,y) OR ¬HAS(Tom,x) OR ¬PLAYING(z)
   D12: ¬HAS(Tom,x) OR ¬PLAYING(z)   {y/beer},D12,D3
   D13: ¬PLAYING(z)   {x/pretzels},D12,D4
   D14: FALSE   {z/cowboys},D13,D7

   a. Suggest two ways to disallow the substitution of beer for both y and z in D2. One way could modify D2 and the other could modify the search rule for resolution clauses.

   b. If one always tries to unify and resolve a clause with D2 before trying D3 or D4, what would happen when querying D1 through D7 with ¬HAPPY(Tom)? How could you prevent this?

4. Listing (6.2) provides the resolution rule for two clauses in what is called disjunctive normal form. That is, the only logical connectives are OR and NOT. The resolution examples we have seen involved Horn clauses, written in the form $A \leftarrow B_1 \& ... \& B_n$.

   a. Prove that a clause in the $A \leftarrow B_1 \& ... \& B_n$ form is a Horn clause as defined in "Resolution."

   b. State a resolution rule equivalent to listing (6.2) for Horn clauses in the $A \leftarrow B_1 \& ... \& B_n$ form that does not first translate clauses into OR form.

   c. Using your rule from (b), suggest a clause form for a query to clauses in $A \leftarrow B_1 \& ... \& B_n$ form. ■

LAB XIII: PROLOG I

OBJECTIVES

1. To become acquainted with entering and executing PROLOG programs.
2. To use some of the tools provided with the PROLOG you are using, particularly EDIT, TRACE, and DEBUG.
3. To see in action the way your PROLOG backtracks.
4. To gain some experience with the differences order has when entering the various instances of a relation. ■

SEARCHING

Proof through resolution involves searching through a list of clauses for unifiable terms and resolvable clauses. In our examples so far, we started at the top of the clause list and successfully matched the query with the first clause, and so on down the list until FALSE was obtained. Things don't always work out so well. Suppose we add the clause C0 to the front of C1 through C7, in "Resolution," where:

> C0: HAPPY(Tom) ← WATCHING(Tom,football) & HAS(Tom,dinner)

An attempt to resolve the query, ¬HAPPY(Tom)? is:

C15: ¬WATCHING(Tom,football) OR ¬HAS(Tom,dinner)	Q & C0
C16: ¬HAS(Tom,dinner) OR ¬IS-ON(tv) OR ¬PLAYING(cowboys)	C15 & C3
C17: ¬HAS(Tom,dinner) OR ¬PLAYING(cowboys)	C16 & C4
C18: ¬HAS(Tom,dinner)	C17 & C5
FAIL	

Our failure certainly can't mean that we proved Tom to be unhappy. We already know that the QUERY is resolvable with C1 through C7, so it should surely resolve with C0 through C7. We need to undo the resolutions already complete and start over, trying to resolve Q with C1 instead of C0. This step is accomplished through a technique called *backtracking*.

Backtracking

The situation of our example can be drawn as a tree, as shown in Figure 6.2. We delete C18 and backtrack to C17. Since C17 could resolve with no clause other than C5, we delete them and look at C16. Our choice tree now looks like the one shown in Figure 6.3. We are ready to choose a clause different from C4 to resolve with C16.

The only other clause possible is C5, which resolves to: C19: ¬HAS(Tom,dinner) OR ¬IS-ON(tv). This leads to the new resolution chain shown in Figure 6.4.

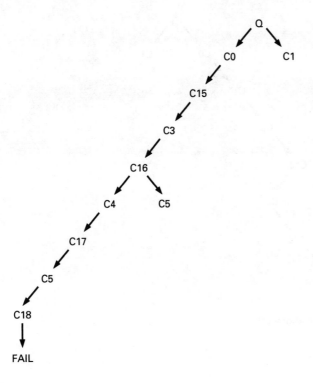

Figure 6.2

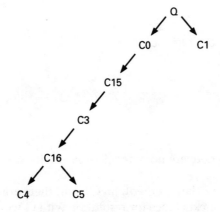

Figure 6.3

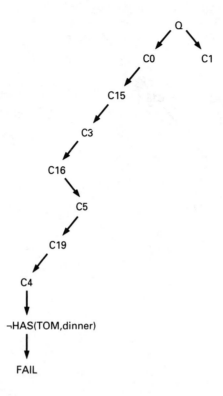

Figure 6.4

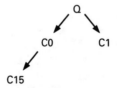

Figure 6.5

Since we again failed, and there are no other choices at C16, we backtrack to C15, as shown in Figure 6.5.

C15 will not resolve with any clause other than C3, and there are no other choices at C0, so we backtrack to Q. Our next choice for resolution with Q would be C1, which we know results in success. (See Figure 6.6.)

A situation related to the lack of pretzels to go with Tom's beer occurs if we query D1 through D7 with ¬HAS(Tom, x)? and expect as a solution a list of all the things Tom HAS. Our resolution trees would be as shown in Figures 6.7 through 6.11.

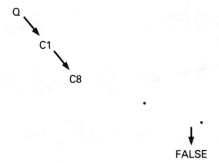

Figure 6.6

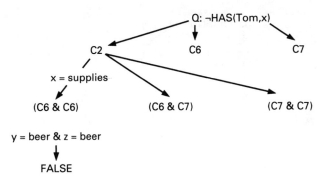

Figure 6.7

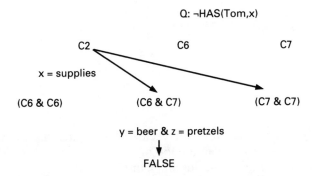

Figure 6.8

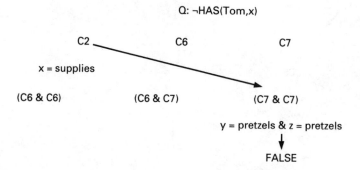

Figure 6.9

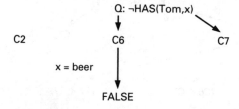

Figure 6.10

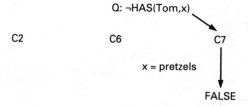

Figure 6.11

Unifications would occur in the order represented by Figures 6.7 through 6.9, assuming we examine clauses in order from the top of the list to the bottom. This was Robinson's assumption in presenting the resolution method, but other optimizations are possible. See, for example, [Genesereth, 1985]. Notice also that HAS(Tom,supplies) is derived three separate times when backtracking, and that HAS(Tom,beer) is repeated four times.

Facts, Goals, and Conditions

As we noted above, statements can be written as conditionals in the form "if A then B" or "B if A," where B is a single statement or clause, and A is zero or more clauses. If A has no clauses, then B is a *fact*, i.e., true under any conditions whatsoever. These facts are called proper axioms in logic and function in the same way as the logical axioms A1 through A4 in "The calculus of statements." If B contains one or more clauses, then A is called the *goal* and the conditions of B the *subgoals*. As we move through a resolution chain, each subgoal becomes a goal. When all these subgoals have been resolved with the facts, the principle goal, A, has been proved.

Backward and Forward Chaining

When we begin a resolution chain with a goal, A, as in demonstrating the goal, A = Happy(Tom), we chain backward from the goal to the facts. As with proof by contradiction, we start with what is to be proved, rather than with what is known, i.e., the axioms or facts. When there is only one or possibly a few choices for clauses to resolve with a goal, backward chaining is effective. However, if there are many choices (two are shown at some of the decision points in Figures 6.2 through 6.6), backward chaining can become inefficient because of all the backtracking necessary to undo fruitless resolution paths.

For certain problems, forward chaining from facts to goals is more efficient. If there are more rules than facts, forward chaining will probably work better. That is, if we chain from the smaller to the larger set of statements, we may encounter fewer wrong paths. Another situation where forward chaining proves preferable is when there are fewer choices at each decision point when reasoning from the facts. This, of course, may be hard to know in advance. Forward chaining may also be more effective when a user wants to see a justification for each step in a proof and naturally thinks from the known to the unknown.

The language PROLOG, which we will discuss in "PROLOG," uses resolution with backward chaining as its problem-solving strategy. Other languages, such as OPS-5, rely on forward chaining. PROLOG itself can be used, however, to implement an interpreter that uses forward rather than backward chaining [Malpas, 1987, Section 5.3].

Representing Negative Facts

Negative statements have often caused trouble for logicians and mathematicians. As an example, consider the following folk query: "In a small Transylvanian town, there is a barber who shaves all those residents who do not shave themselves, and only those. The query is, 'Who shaves the barber?'"

Translating this situation to Horn clauses gives us:

C1: NOT(SHAVES(X,X)) ← SHAVES(Barber, X)
C2: SHAVES(Barber, X) ← NOT(SHAVES(X, X))

Now suppose we query, Q: SHAVES(Barber, Barber)? Q will resolve with the goal of C2 if we unify X with Barber. Thus Q and C2 resolve to

C3: ¬NOT(SHAVES(Barber, Barber).

Two negatives make a positive (as we saw in the exercise section in "Proof by contradiction,") so we have

C3: SHAVES(Barber, Barber)

C3 resolves with C1, with resolvent

C4: ¬SHAVES(Barber, Barber)

which is equivalent to our original query, Q. Thus Q produces an infinite loop in our resolution chain.

Now suppose we approach the problem from another side, by querying,

Q': NOT(SHAVES(Barber, Barber)?

Q' and C1 resolve, producing

C5: ¬SHAVES(Barber, Barber)

which resolves with C2, giving

C6: SHAVES(Barber, Barber)

etc., etc., etc.,...

What's the problem here? It turns out that Barber is not an allowable substitution for X in this situation. To prevent such problems, negative clauses are allowed only if the domain has been specified for each variable in the scope of the NOT in question. We could rewrite our little story as:

C1': SHAVES(X, X) ← NOT(Barber = X) &
                          NOT(SHAVES(Barber, X))
C2': SHAVES(Barber, X) ← NOT(Barber = X) &
                          NOT(SHAVES(X, X))

If we try to resolve SHAVES(Barber, Barber)? with C1' or C2', X will be unified with Barber *before* the term NOT(Barber = X) is encountered. At that point NOT(Barber = Barber) will FAIL, so the query itself will fail. Failure, in this case, indicates that using the facts we have, we don't know what the Barber does. Consideration of the facts we have in the database, and only those, is called the closed-world assumption, or circumscription. It means that our world of facts is comprised of exactly those things we know from our fact list plus anything derivable using logic from the rules we have listed. Truth is circumscribed to just what we know.

EXERCISES

1. Consider the set of rules and facts below, and construct a resolution tree similar to those in Figures 6.2 through 6.6, starting with the query

    a. Q: North-of(Chicago, NewYork)?

    C1: North-of(X1, X2) ← Location(X1, Y1, Z1) &

            Location(X2, Y2, Z2) &

            Less(Y2, Y1)

    C2: Location(NewYork, 41, 74)

    C3: Location(Chicago, 42, 88)

    C4: Location(Tokyo, 35, 140)

    C5: Location(Oslo, 60, 11)

    C6: Location(Quito, 0, 80)

    C7: Location(Cairo, 30, 30)

    b. Now construct a tree starting with the query

    Q': North-of(X, NewYork)

    Be sure you backtrack to explore *all* the possible substitutions for X.

2. Construct a resolution chain for HAPPY(Tom) using clauses C0 through C7 of "Proofs" and "Searching," but chain forward from the facts C4 through C7, rather than backward as in the examples shown.

3. a. Why would backward chaining be preferable when trying to determine a travel route from home to an unknown destination (the goal)?

    b. Suppose facts determine which words are verbs, nouns, adjectives, etc., and rules describe what comprises an English sentence. For simple sentences, the following three rules suffice:

    R1: Sentence(NP, VP) ← NounPhrase(NP) & VerbPhrase(VP)

    R2: NounPhrase(A, N) ← Article(A) & Noun(N)

    R3: VerbPhrase(V, NP) ← Verb(V) & NounPhrase(NP)

    If our goal is to parse a given sentence, would forward or backward chaining be preferable? Try a few sentences to see which seems more natural.

    c. In a medical diagnosis problem, the facts are symptoms, and the goal is to match these symptoms with a disease. Would forward or backward chaining be more reasonable here?

    d. In a game of tick-tack-toe, the goals are winning configurations of the 3 × 3 grid. How many are there for a single player? (Be careful about this calculation: Remember that a configuration involves all nine squares, not just the winning row, column, or diagonal.) How many

total configurations are there? (A blank grid is one!) Would forward or
backward chaining find a winning solution more easily? Why?

6.0 PROLOG

HISTORICAL VIGNETTE 9: PROLOG: Colmerauer and Roussel

A look at the history of PROLOG is another look at the history of logic itself, and its
future. Originally developed by Alain Colmerauer, Philippe Roussel, and their colleagues of the *Groupe d'Intelligence Artificielle* (University of Marseilles) to be a theorem-
proving language, PROLOG has entered the fourth generation as a good language for
database management and into the fifth in the field of artificial intelligence.

PROLOG's beginnings date back 22 centuries to Aristotle's traditional logic. One
of the problems of that system is that it is entirely static. A statement can have only one
value, True or False, and once established can never be changed. The first dissatisfac-
tions surfaced during the nineteenth century, when DeMorgan, an English mathematician, began the development of a formal system, more representative of mathematical
reasoning than natural language. Gottlob Frege's contributions in the latter half of the
century firmly established symbolic logic as a branch of mathematics, only sometimes
tied to philosophy.

During the 1960s, there was great interest in automatic theorem proving. Robert
Kowalski, working at the University of Edinburgh, concentrated on logic programming,
the use of computers to make controlled logical inferences.

Colmerauer and Roussel, a Canadian student, developed with others the first logic
programming language. They called it PROLOG, an abbreviation for *programmation en
logique*, following a suggestion of Roussel's wife, Jacqueline.

Given the close ties to mathematical logic and theorem proving, it may seem surprising that PROLOG is becoming known as an artificial intelligence language. "Artificial intelligence requires a computer language which in turn represents the things we
use human language to talk about. Yet logic was originally designed for just these purposes" [Baron, 1986, p. 323]. There was little interest in PROLOG in either the United
States or Europe until the early eighties, when Japan's Institute for New Generation
Technology announced plans to produce a fifth generation of computer hardware that
would accept natural-language input and process large quantities of information. Their
chosen language was PROLOG. At first scientists in the U.S. laughed at Japan's move,
quickly assuming that a big mistake was being made, but the laughter died down as
reports of Japan's success with its fifth-generation projects began to spread.

Today PROLOG is widely used in the U.S. as well as in Japan for theorem proving,
relational database design, software engineering, natural-language processing, knowledge representation in artificial intelligence, and expert-systems programming. Perhaps

PROLOG's greatest feature is that it is a step toward nonprocedural programming, where less programming is involved as more gets done automatically. The user can concentrate more on what needs to be done than on how to do it.

The future of both PROLOG and logic programming is unclear. PROLOG is to logic programming what FORTRAN was to modern computer programming: a beginning. The Japanese are already developing a new logic programming language called KL. For the present, most PROLOG programmers are computer enthusiasts who want to learn more about AI programming. Several versions of PROLOG are available for microcomputers. Perhaps PROLOG will be left behind as a production language and remain as an AI teaching tool, as newer languages are developed.

Conversing in PROLOG: Facts, Rules, and Queries

PROLOG has been described as relational [Malpas, 1987], descriptive [Genesereth, 1985], or declarative. Both the relational and descriptive views consider the organization of the database, or set of PROLOG facts. PROLOG is considered declarative in that one describes to it what one wants to accomplish, such as, "sort([5,3,7,2],Answer)!", with little regard to the procedure for accomplishing the sorting task, which returns "Answer = [2,3,5,7]". Of course, we must describe further just what is meant by "sort."

PROLOG is also called a language for programming in logic [Calingaert, 1988; Ghezzi, 1987]. This last may be the most accurate classification, but PROLOG itself is only logic based and does not produce all the same proofs possible from methods using the full power of the predicate calculus.

PROLOG comes in several dialects [Sosnowski, 1987]. The original version of Colmerauer and Roussel is Edinburgh syntax, also called DEC-10 PROLOG, due to its early implementation on DEC-10® computers running on the TOPS-10 operating system. Micro-PROLOG, another dialect, is available for microcomputers, although "Core PROLOG," a subset of the DEC-10 version, appears to have become the de facto standard for micros, minis, and mainframes. We will use the "Core PROLOG" syntax, since it is widely available for both 32-bit and 16-bit machines, although learning PROLOG on one's own is still most easily accomplished using Clark and McCabe's manual for micro-PROLOG [Clark, 1984].

The main difference between Edinburgh and micro-PROLOG is in the form of a clause.

```
happy(tom) -| watching(tom,football),has(tom,supplies).
```

is an Edinburgh clause, while

```
((happy tom)(watching tom football)(has tom supplies))
```

is the same clause in micro-PROLOG syntax. Each clause means that Tom [is] happy [if] Tom [is] watching football [and] Tom has supplies.

Some differences arise in the evaluation of arithmetic and some other expressions as well. Once you have mastered one, it is not hard to shift to the other dialect. Either syntax is fairly easy to learn. Writing efficient PROLOG programs, however, requires a fairly sophisticated understanding of both logic and the execution of an abstract PROLOG machine.

Syntax

A PROLOG program is a list of statements called facts or rules that is entered through a query. The general form of a statement is: HEAD :- BODY., where HEAD is a single structure, and BODY is comprised of 0 or more structures, called subgoals, separated by commas, meaning "and" or semicolons meaning "or". A fact is a statement with no body, while a rule contains both a head and a body. A query is a fact preceded by "?-", and returns either true or false. If a query contains variables, values are printed that make the query true.

The form of a structure is just that of a PROLOG fact, FUNCTOR(TERM$_1$, ..., TERM$_n$). A TERM may be either a constant, variable, or a structure.

Functors are predicate symbols, operators, or relation names. A predicate symbol generally takes on the values true or false. `<=(2,4)` is true, whereas `<=(4,2)` is false. Some operators built into PROLOG are those for integer arithmetic. Thus `+(+(X,Y),Z)` can be written `X+Y+Z` and `+(X,*(Y,Z))` as `X+Y*Z`. A PROLOG user may declare functors to be operators by specifying the name, the precedence, and the type, where types may be infix (X + Y), prefix (–2) or postfix (5!). Precedence and associativity must also be specified for operators, and those for arithmetic obey the standard rules, e.g., * precedes +.

A constant is thought of as naming a specific object or relation and is either an atom or an integer. A constant atom is a string of letters and digits beginning with a lower-case letter and containing no signs other than the underscore. `john_alden`, `x`, `y`, and `map2` are all constants, but 2X, Mary, and gambier-ohio are not. However, any character may be used to form a constant between single quotes. Thus `'Gambier-Ohio'` is a constant.

An atom may also be composed entirely of signs, but these are reserved for special purposes. Two of these special atoms are ":-", which means "if" and "?-", signaling a query.

The signs are: { + - * \ / ^ < > ~ : . ? @ # $ & }. A RELATION-NAME is also an atom, e.g., the "<" in `<(2, 4)` or the "has" in `has(tom,beer)`.

A VARIABLE is an atom preceded by either a capital letter or the underscore. `Who`, `Salary_Amt`, `X`, and `_2_brothers` are variables, while Last-Name and 2ndBase are not. PROLOG also has a special anonymous variable, "`_`". The query, `?- has(tom,_).`, will return all atoms satisfying the "has" relationship, with "tom" as the first term. As we saw in "Resolution," beer, pretzels, and supplies satisfy the `has` relation for tom. (Notice that a query, a fact, or a rule is terminated by a period ".")

If you recall, we did not allow is_a(owns(tommy, X), yellow, cat), as a legal first-order term in "Unification." However, if `is_a(owns(tommy, tiger), yellow, cat).` is a fact in the database, the query `?-is_a(owns(tommy,X),yellow,cat).` will produce tiger as a substitution for X, which might represent the fact that Tommy owns a yellow cat named Tiger. Remember that PROLOG is logic based, and not a pure implementation of the first-order predicate calculus.

Data structures

The only data sructure built into PROLOG is a relation for a list, "`./2`". The period, "`.`", is the functor name, and the 2 represents its arity, or the number of terms expected. When using any functor, the arity is omitted. `.(broccoli, [])` is a list with a single element, "broccoli". The "`[]`" is a special symbol representing the empty list. `.(broccoli, .(potatoes, .(milk, [])))` is a three-element list. For convenience, PROLOG allows writing this same list as `[broccoli, potatoes, milk]`. A list of indeterminate length can be written as `[broccoli, potatoes|X]`, where X is a variable representing the tail of the list.

Listing (6.3) shows a PROLOG program to append two lists.

```
append([],L,L).                                        (6.3)
append([X|L1],L2,[X|L3]) :- append(L1,L2,L3).
```

Now suppose we query, `?- append([],[1,2],X)`. PROLOG will return

```
X = [1,2].
No.
```

The "No" means that there are no more solutions. If we name the program's two clauses C1 and C2 and the query Q, our resolution proceeds as shown in Figure 6.12.

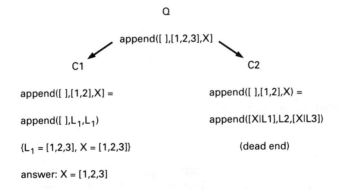

Figure 6.12[7]

---

7 Whenever a rule is tested in a resolution chain, its variables are renamed so that there are none in common with already existing variables.

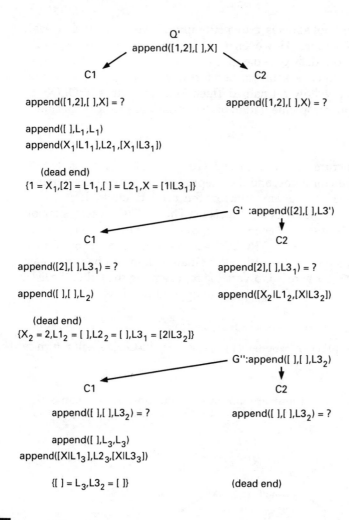

Figure 6.13

Now suppose we change the query a bit to:

```
Q': ?- append([1,2],[],x).
```

Figure 6.13 shows the results.

The resolution is complete, so now we backtrack all the way up the tree, substituting constants for variables as we go. The un-unified subgoals are G', which we now replace with:

G': append([2],[],[2 | []]),

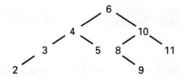

Figure 6.14

and the main goal, Q, which we unify to

Q: append([1,2],[],[1,2 | []])

or

append([1,2],[],[1,2]).

Recursion is usually implemented using a stack. The stack for the variable X in Figure 6.13, would have been as shown in listing (6.4).

$$[1,2 | []] \qquad\qquad (6.4)$$
$$[1,2 | L3_3]$$
$$[1,2 | L3_2]$$
$$[1,L3_1]$$
$$X$$

For the append procedure, there is no need to build and empty this stack at all. We could have noted that X was the variable to be evaluated and then replaced X with $[1,L3_1]$, $[1,2,L3_2]$, $[1,2,L3_3]$, followed by $[1,2 | []]$. Such a procedure is called *tail recursive*, and will be discussed in "Control." Notice that the append procedure lists as its first clause, append([],L,L). This clause used at the bottom of the recursion, before backtracking up the recursive stack (if there is one). Omission of a recursion-terminating clause at the beginning of a recursive procedure leads to infinite loops. PROLOG doesn't care, but you'll probably get a "no space left" notice after such a procedure runs for a while. Try reversing the order of the two clauses and see what happens with your PROLOG version. In a language with pointers, such as Pascal or C, recursive structures are often kept as records, with one field holding a pointer to the next record. For example:

```
Tree = ^TreeNode;
TreeNode = record
   Data : DataType;
   Left,Right : Tree
end;
```

declares a Pascal binary tree structure. An example of such a tree might be as shown in Figure 6.14.

In PROLOG, we can accomplish the same thing with

```
%      tree(LeftTree, Info, RightTree)
```

(The "%" sign signals a comment. Some implementations enclose comments between "/*" and "*/".) The PROLOG data for the search tree of Figure 6.14 could be the fact:

```
tree(tree(tree(tree(End,2,End),3,End)),4,tree(End,5,End)),6,
     tree(tree(end,8,tree(end,9,end)),10,tree(end,11,end))).
```

Notice that the data appears, reading the fact from left to right, as an in-order traversal of the tree. If we wanted to keep data in pre-order, the fact could be:

```
% pre(Data,LeftTree,RightTree)
pre(6,pre(4,pre(3,pre(2,end,end),end),pre(5,end,end)),
    10,pre(8,end,pre(9,end,end)),pre(11,end,end))).
```

Core PROLOG has no built-in structures for arrays, sets, or strings, but some implementations are extended to include strings and string manipulation operators. Several implementations contain extensions for writing top-down parsers.

EXERCISES

(If possible, it is best to do most of these exercises at a terminal. However, think each one through first and then see what actually happens.)

1. Read "PROLOG Dialects: a déjà vu of BASICs" [Sosnowski, 1987] and compare the merits of Edinburgh, Turbo, and micro-PROLOG.

2. What answers would you expect to the queries:
   a. `?-append(X, [2], [1,2]).`
   b. `?-append(X,Y, [1,2]).`
   c. `?-append(comanche, [], Z).` Could you fix up this query so that PROLOG won't accept this input?

3. Write a PROLOG query to append the Address, State, and Zip to the name, `'Donald Trump'`.

4. Consider a PROLOG procedure to reverse a list.
   ```
   reverse([],[]).
   reverse([X|Y],Z) :- reverse(Y,Z1),
   append(Z1,[X],Z).
   ```

a. Construct a resolution tree for ?- `reverse([1,2],Z)`.

b. Construct stacks for X, Y, and Z. Is this procedure tail recursive?

5. Now consider a different procedure to reverse a list:

```
reverse2(L1,L2) :- reverse3(L1,[],L2).
reverse3([],L1,L1).
reverse3([X|L1],L2,L3) :- reverse3(L1,[X|L2],L3).
```

(reverse2 is introduced for the sole purpose of making the call more natural. The second variable of reverse3 is used to accumulate partial results.)

a. Trace the execution of ?-`reverse2([1,2],R)`.

b. Is this procedure tail recursive?

6. ?-**findall**(X,p(X),List). will return the List of all values satisfying X. What value would you expect PROLOG to return for List if p(X) is has(tom,X), from the database in "Unification."

7. A PROLOG function for computing N! is:

```
factorial(0,1).
factorial(N,M) :- N1 is N - 1,
                  factorial(N1,M1),
                  M is N * M1.
```

a. Build the resolution tree and stack for ?-factorial(3,X).

b. Is this procedure tail recursive?

c. If your answer to (b) is no, can you write a procedure factorial2(N,M) that is tail recursive?

8. The Fibonacci series is {1,1,2,3,5,...}, where each term after the 0th and 1st is the sum of the two previous terms, i.e., Fib(i) = Fib(i–1) + Fib(i–2). A PROLOG procedure for Fib is:

```
Fib(0,1).
Fib(1,1).
Fib(N,M) :- N1 is N - 1, N2 is N - 2,
            Fib(N1,M1),Fib(N2,M2),
            M is M1+M2.
```

This procedure is not tail recursive. Can you make a new procedure, Fib2(N,X,M), which uses X to store partial results, and which is tail recursive?

9. Write a PROLOG fact, post(LeftTree, RightTree, Data), which represents the binary tree of Figure 6.14 in post-order. ■

Built-in functors

In addition to the **not** predicate, PROLOG provides several comparators, operators for control of execution and debugging and for determining types. We will look briefly at a few of these here. PROLOG does not include equality in the usual sense. If the term X = Y is encountered, PROLOG attempts to unify the X with Y. Thus `butter = butter` succeeds, and `butter = guns` fails, but `butter = W` succeeds, as does X = Y. As a side effect, W will have the value butter and Y the same value as X. Two structures are equal if they have the same functor and number of arguments, and all the arguments are equal. A second equality operator, "==/2", is stricter than =. X==Y will not try to unify Y with X. Thus if either of X or Y is an uninstantiated variable, X==Y will fail. However, if we follow X=Y by X==Y, both X=Y and X==Y succeed. (See listing (6.5).)

```
X                                                             (6.5)
Y
?- X==Y
no

?- X=Y
yes
X                               X₁
Y
X==Y
yes
```

One very useful functor is "=../2", called *univ*. If we query

```
?-son_of(julio,juan) =.. List.,
```

PROLOG will return

```
List = [son_of,julio,juan]
```

Similarly,

```
?-Term =.. [son_of,julio,juan].
Term = son_of(julio,juan).
```

Such switching between **lists** and terms allows the **modifying** of programs while they are running. Thus programs can be made to learn while they execute. One use of univ is in constructing the function mapcar, which is one of the mapping functions built into LISP. (See listing (6.6).)

```
mapcar(_,[],[])/?                                           (6.6)⁸
mapcar(Foo,[X|Args],[Y|Answers]) :-
        Foobar =.. [Foo,X,Y],
        call(Foobar),
        mapcar(Foo,Args,Answers).
```

---

8 The functors "foo" and "foobar" have been used traditionally by applicative and logic programmers as in jokes. "foo" stands for "fu," an acronym for "fouled-up" and "foobar" for "fouled up beyond all repair." (The two o's are to improve pronunciation.) You will see these acronyms scattered through many texts and papers.

The application of mapcar(func,list₁,list₂), will return as list₂, the result of applying func successively to the elements of list₁.

```
?-mapcar(upper-case,[a,b,c,d],X).
```

will return

```
X = ['A','B','C','D'],
```

assuming upper-case has been appropriately defined.

Terms can be tested for type using the predicates "**var**/1", "**nonvar**/1", "**integer**/1", and "**atom**/1". **atom**(X) is true for noninteger constants.

Arithmetic If PROLOG encounters X = 1+2, it will try to unify X with the term 1+2. To have X assigned the value 3, we must use "**is**/2". X **is** 1+2 performs the desired arithmetic and instantiates X to 3. If we want to test arithmetic equality, we query ?- X =:= 3., since X = 3 behaves differently as discussed above. "**=\=**/2" tests arithmetic inequality. "**<**/2","**>**/2","**>=**/2", and "**=<**/2" behave as one might expect. (Notice the "=<", rather than the usual "<=".)

Only integers are built into PROLOG. Real-number arithmetic is not supported, although floating-point capabilities are an extension in some versions. ?-X **is** 5/2 will normally return X = 2. However, where floating-point numbers are supported, / may mean real-number division and // integer division.

Input/Output I/O is usually the most nonstandard part of a programming language, as it is often tailored to particular equipment. In addition to "**get0**/1", and "**put**/1" for characters, and "**read**/1" and "**write**/1" for terms, PROLOG has various predicates for file control. Although there can be only one current input stream and one current output stream, each can be changed through "**see**/1" or "**tell**/1". Most implementations also provide some version of "**consult**/1", which allows various files to be consulted as needed.

EXERCISES

1. Write in PROLOG what might be a definition for the "=" predicate. Must it be recursive? Why?

2. What might happen if we allow the substitution {Y/f(Y)} in a PROLOG implementation? Consider the query ?-Y=f(Y). Try this query, using any functor for f, with your version of PROLOG and see what happens.

3. Why is the list ['A','B','C','D'] returned when using mapcar listing (6.6) with the functor **upper-case** instead of [A,B,C,D]?

4. Read "The British Nationality Act as a Logic Program" [Sergot, 1986] and write a review and/or report to your class on this very interesting use of PROLOG to sort out a complicated bit of British law. ■

Control

Because PROLOG performs exhaustive depth-first searches when trying to unify its variables, program execution can be very inefficient in both speed of execution and use of memory. Thus it is up to the programmer to write procedures that minimize both search time and memory usage.

Tail Recursion We have already seen examples of *tail recursion* in the append procedure and the exercises in "Conversing in PROLOG: Facts, Rules, and Queries." A tail-recursive subgoal can be recognized at the time it is called, and some PROLOG implementations automatically apply tail-recursive optimization. As we saw, a tail-recursive procedure saves stack space, since intermediate results need not be saved on the recursive stack. Such a recursive subgoal is characterized by the following: (1) At the time it is called, all previous subgoals have been determined; (2) There are no further subgoals after the recursive subgoal. When writing a rule, it is guaranteed to be tail recursive if it is of the form:

$$R(t_1,\ldots,t_n) \; :- \; C_1,C_2,\ldots,C_m,R(t_1',\ldots,t_n').$$

where each of the C_i are subgoals satisfied by a *single* solution or if C_m is a cut (!). We will discuss the effect of *cut* in the next section. If there is no C_i, as in the append procedure, the condition is, of course, satisfied. For examples of how to change procedures into equivalent tail-recursive ones, see [Clark, 1984].

A form of recursion always to be avoided is left recursion. Consider the following rule and fact:

```
R: ancestor(X,Z) :- ancestor(X,Y) & ancestor(Y,Z).
F: ancestor(gaston,ferdinand).
```

If we query, Q: ?-ancestor(X,Y), PROLOG will match Q: with the head of R: and activate the subgoal, ancestor(X,Y). This query will again match the head of R:, and a new subgoal, ancestor(X,Y) will be activated, which will match R:, and so on. This infinite circling through R: will continue until a "no space left" error appears. Our problem is that we keep recursing from the right to the left of R:, with identical goals to be satisfied, and never reach the fact F.

Cut, Fail, and Not The built-in predicate cut, !/0, always succeeds and prevents reevaluation of any clauses that precede it. If your PROLOG version does not provide tail-recursive optimization, you can do some of the job using cut. PROLOG searches for all possible solutions to a query. If you know there is only one, cutting off further search after the single solution has been found saves both time and space.

Since append2 stops when the first clause is reached, we will place a cut there, as shown in listing (6.7).

```
append2([],L,L) :- !.                              (6.7)
append2([X|L1],L2,[X|L3]) :- append2(L1,L2,L3).
```

PROLOG will stop the search the first time it satisfies append2([],L,L). Such a one-solution procedure would be useful if we always were to use it with two ground clause lists as the first two arguments, as in

```
?-append2([1,2,3],[4,5,6],L)
```

However, if we want to find all possible sublists, as in

```
?-append2(X,Y,[1,2,3,4,5,6])
```

PROLOG would return only one answer:

```
X = []; Y = [1,2,3,4,5,6]
```

The cut would prevent any further search.

Fail is a predicate that always fails. Suppose we want to determine whether an individual is a British citizen—not an easy task in a colonial nation. An individual who has renounced his citizenship in the United Kingdom, such as Guy Burgess, is clearly not a British citizen. Thus we might have a rule:

```
citizen(X) :- renounced(X,UK), !, fail.
citizen(X) :- born_in(X,UK);...
```

where the ... indicates all the myriad conditions allowing citizenship. Then ?-citizen(Burgess). would return "no".

We need the cut here to prevent any further search for a rule that would give citizenship to Burgess, but we also need the fail to return a negative answer to our query.

The cut/fail combination can always be replaced by the use of **not**. Our definition above would be:

```
citizen(X) :- not(renounced(X,UK)).
citizen(X) :- born_in(X,UK);...
```

In more complicated definitions, using "**not**" may require deeply nested parentheses, which makes a program less readable to some.

Programs that Modify Themselves PROLOG has predicates that can delete or add clauses to the database while a program is running. Below is a program that queries a user about drug allergies and adds the information to the database.

```
drug(penicillin).
drug(sulfadiazine).
drug(aspirin).
drug(carbromal).
drug_quiz :- write('Please enter your last name: '),
             read(Patient),
             write('After each drug is listed, answer yes'),
             write(' or no if you are allergic or not.'),nl,
             drug(DrugName), write(DrugName),nl,
             read(yes),assert(allergic(Patient,DrugName)),
             fail.
```

The **fail** is used here to force PROLOG to backtrack through all the drugs in the database. **nl** causes a carriage return in the output stream.

EXERCISES

1. Consider the following set of gardening facts:

```
flower(phlox).        type(phlox,perennial).
flower(petunia).      type(petunia,annual).
flower(rose).         type(rose,bush).
flower(daisy).        type(daisy,perennial).
                      type(daisy,annual).
```

   a. Use your PROLOG **debug** and/or **trace** utilities to trace the execution of ?-perennial_garden(X) ., if perennial_garden is the rule:

```
perennial_garden(F) :- flower(F),type(F,perennial).
```

   b. Add a cut to the rule in (a) and trace again.

   c. Which rule could produce a list for the entire perennial garden? Which is faster?

2. Consider the following definition using cut [Clocksin, 1984]:

```
number_of_parents(adam,0) :- !.
number_of_parents(eve,0) :- !.
number_of_parents(X,2).
```

   a. What will be the response of PROLOG to:

```
?-number_of_parents(betty,N).
?-number_of_parents(X,Y).
?-number_of_parents(eve,2).
```

   b. Clocksin and Mellish fix this up as:

```
number_of_parents(adam,N) :- !, N = 0.
number_of_parents(eve,N)  :- !, N = 0.
number_of_parents(X,2).
```

   i. Can you think of another way to do this, perhaps by modifying the last clause, rather than the first two?

   ii. Will either of these ways work properly for

```
?-number_of_parents(X,Y)?
```

3. Rewrite the following rule using cut/fail to an equivalent rule using **not**.

```
marriageable(X,Y) :- (first_cousins(X,Y);
                      same_sex(X,Y);
                      siblings(X,Y)),
                     !,fail.
    marriageable(X,Y) :- !. ■
```

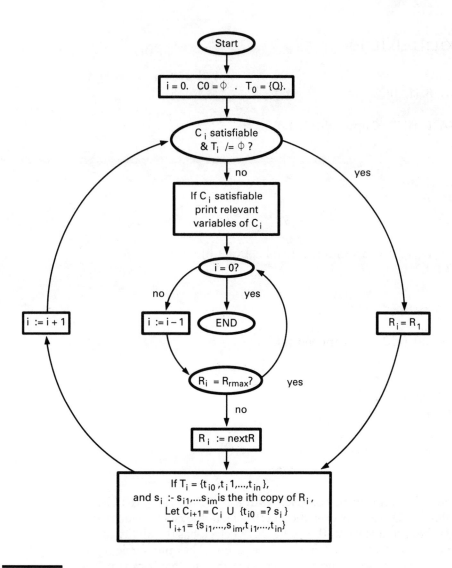

Figure 6.15

PROLOG Implementations

A theoretical machine

The execution of a PROLOG program can be described by the theoretical machine of Figure 6.15. Colmerauer [Colmerauer, 1985] calls it "the PROLOG Clock," since its main function is to keep track of time.

R1: append([],L,L)
R2: append([X | L1],L2,[X | L3])
i := 0
$C_0 = \phi$
$T_0 = \{append(A_1,B_1,[1,2])\}$
$R_0 = R1$
$C_1 = \{append(A_1,B_1,[1,2]) =? append([],L_1,L_1)\}$
$T_1 = \phi$

i := 1
$A_1=[]$, $B_1=L_1$, $L_1=[1,2]$
print answer1:   A = [], B = [1,2]

i := 0
$R_1 := R2;$
$C_1 = \{append(A_2,B_2,[1,2]) =? append([X_1 | L1_1],L2_1,[X_1L3_1])\}$
$T_1 = \{append(L1_1,L2_1,L3_1)\}$

i := 1
$A_2 = [1 | L1_1]$, $1 = X_1$, $B_2 = L2_1$, $[2] = L3_1$
$R_1 := R1$
$C2 = C_1 \cup \{append(L1_1,L2_1,[2]) = append([],L_2,L_2)$
$T_2 = \phi$

i := 2
$L1_1 = []$, $L2_1 = [2]$, $[2] = L_2$
print answer2:   A = [1], B = [2]

Figure 6.16   (continued next page)

A computer clock, not to be confused with a real time clock (RTC) that measures the time of day, counts execution cycles. Here the clock value is that of the variable i above and starts at 0. The PROLOG clock has the ability to run backward as well as forward, thus it is two clocks in one. The outer circle represents the forward-running clock, and the inner circle, the one that backs up. The C_i are *constraints* and represent attempts to match PROLOG terms (T_i) with others in the database. R_i represents the rule we are testing for a match at clock = i, and the s_{ij} and t_{ik} are the terms still to be matched at succeeding times.

In Figure 6.16, let's follow through the execution of

```
?-append(A,B,[1,2])
```

following Figure 6.15 at the various clock times, i.

i := 1
R_1 = R2
C2 = {C_1 U {append($L1_2$,$L2_2$,[2]) =? append([X_2 | $L1_3$],$L2_3$,[X_2 | $L3_3$]}
T_2 = {append($L1_3$,$L2_3$,$L3_3$)}

i := 2
$L1_2$ = [2], L22 = L23, 2 = X2, [] = L33
R2 := R1
C3 = C2 U {append(L13,L23,[]) =? append([],L3,L3)}
T3 = ϕ

i := 3
$L1_3$ = [], $L2_3$ = [], [] = L_3
print answer3:   A = [1,2], B = []

i := 2
R_2 := R2
C_3 = C_2 U {{append($L1_4$, $L2_4$,[]) = append([X_3 | $L1_5$],$L2_5$,[X_3 | $L3_5$])}
T_3 = {append($L1_5$,$L2_5$,$L3_5$)}

i:=3
dead end

i := 2
i := 1
i := 0
END

Figure 6.16   (continued from previous page)

Parallel architectures

PROLOG is admirably organized for parallel processing. If a rule is t_0 :- t_1, t_2, ..., t_n, with goal t_0, and we have n-processors available, why not resolve all n subgoals simultaneously? This sort of parallel execution is called *AND parallelism* because in a clause such as A :- B,C, we will attempt to prove B AND C concurrently in order to prove A. Unfortunately, PROLOG programs work from left to right, and often the order of the terms is important. For example, suppose we define a descendant relation as:

```
R1: descendant(Y,X) :- parent-of (X,Y).
R2: descendant(Y,X) :- parent-of(X,Z), descendant(Y,Z).
```

This works just fine, but now consider:

```
R2': descendant(Y,X) :- descendant(Y,Z), parent-of(X,Z).
```

R2' contains the same information as R2, but reverses the order of the two sub-goals. As we saw in "Control," R2' is left-recursive and will produce an infinite loop. The resolution of descendant(Y,Z) requires that parent-of(X,Z) already be resolved.

AND parallelism requires that subgoals be independent of each other, or that some other method of avoiding variable clashes be devised. For example, in Concurrent PROLOG, the clause A :- B(X),C(X?) restricts assigning X a value to B(X). C(X?) may only read X, not write to it. There is also a hidden advantage in assignment restrictions. A variable can be used as a communication channel with processes such as C(X?) waiting until X has received a value.

OR parallelism, which eliminates backtracking, is substantially easier. If we look again at Figure 6.16, and if all the processing at a given time occurs in parallel (i.e., the assignment i := i – 1 of the inner clock never happens), we would have an example of OR parallelism. AND parallelism involves concurrent processing across different time levels. OR parallelism works concurrently on clauses such as:

```
A :- B
A :- C
```

Here we can prove A true by either proving B OR C. Thus we work concurrently on both B and C, stopping when A is resolved. The proof of A is thus indeterminate. When PROLOG announces that A is true, we may not know or care whether B or C is also true. "Don't know" nondeterminism is a feature of closed systems, where only successful resolutions are visible to the user. PROLOG is often implemented as a reactive system, where the user can see partial results as a computation progresses. This system requires "don't care" nondeterminism, also called *indeterminism*. A subgoal may fail, but the application doesn't care as long as the primary goal can be shown.

The development of parallel processors and compilers to take advantage of them is receiving much research attention at this time. For example, see [Proc. SLP, 1986]. A good exposition of the complexities of parallel execution using Parlog86 can be found in [Ringwood, 1988].

Garbage collection

Parallel execution can speed up processing, but PROLOG programs still consume large amounts of memory. To keep variables separated, each time a rule is invoked, its variables must be given new names. When a particular resolution has completed, these variables may still exist. Reclaiming storage locations that are no longer needed through a memory reorganization is known as *garbage collection*. The theoretical machine of Figure 6.15, is much simplified from an actual PROLOG compiler. The *Warren Abstract Machine (WAM)* [Warren, 1988] has become generally accepted as a basis for implementations. Data is kept in three areas: the code area containing the program; the control area, made up of machine registers; and three stacks. The first stack keeps track of recursion, the second contains structures, lists, and variable values, while the third, called the trail, refers to variables that will be undone on backtracking. Various methods for garbage collection during execution of the WAM have been proposed, e.g., see [Appleby, 1988].

Types and modules

Besides space and time inefficiencies, PROLOG has other shortcomings [Genesereth, 1985]. One of these is that the logic used relies on complete (closed-world) systems and cannot be used to generalize knowledge beyond the database, reason from analogies, or make deductions from uncertain data. The ability to write, debug, and maintain large programs is also limited due to a lack of data typing and modularity. When we speak of data typing, we don't mean just integer, real, or character, but the ability of the user to define and maintain abstract data types, *along with their associated operations.*

Goguen and Meseguer [Goguen, 1984] have suggested a revision and extension of PROLOG, called *Eqlog*. It includes genuine equality, as in 3 + 4! = 27; user-defined types, called **sorts;** modules, such as integer sets with definitions for membership and union; and a mechanism for defining generic modules. We won't discuss just what a generic module is here, but give Goguen's example for a quasi-ordered set instead. (A quasi ordering is reflexive and transitive, but not every two elements need be comparable.)

```
theory QUOSET is
sorts elt
preds  _=<_ : elt,elt
vars A,B,C : elt
axioms
   A =< A.
   A =< C :- A =< B, B =< C
endtheory QUOSET
```

A user can then ask to have an Eqlog object, X, "certified" as being of generic sort QUOSET. If such certification is successful, X must be quasi ordered. A module, including predicate, function, and variable definitions, and a group of axioms using sort QUOSET could be:

```
module INTSORT[T::QUOSET] using INTSET = SET[INT]
...
endmodule INTSORT
```

EXERCISES

1. Consider the following Hamburger database:

```
condiment(ketchup).      veggies(onion).
condiment(mustard).      veggies(lettuce).
cheese(cheddar).         cheese(swiss).
cheeseburger :- condiment(X), veggies(Y), cheese(Z).
```

   Trace the execution of ?-cheeseburger. through the PROLOG clock of Figure 6.15.

2. Program the append procedure in a procedural language you know, such as Pascal or FORTRAN. Comment on the differences between this program and the PROLOG one regarding:

   a. Ease of programming

   b. Speed of execution

   c. Versatility

   d. I/O differences

3. The Missionaries and Cannibals problem involves three missionaries, three cannibals, one boat, and one river. The problem is to get all six across the river, with there never being more cannibals than missionaries on either side. The boat holds only two people. Look at the Eqlog solution to this problem in [Goguen, 1984], pp. 204 through 206, and trace its execution. ■

Applications

Artificial intelligence

Artificial intelligence is a loosely defined term encompassing activities carried on by computers that are ordinarily thought to require some sort of human intelligence. These activities include understanding written and spoken natural language, learning new information, recalling previously learned facts, scientific analysis, planning, and problem solving, and various physical feats, such as navigating a room without bumping into the furniture. PROLOG is being used in all these areas.

Another area is the so-called expert system. For some systems, such as MYCIN, which is used to diagnose and recommend therapy for infectious diseases, a trained knowledge engineer extracts information from medical experts and then incorporates it into a computer program that would provide the combined wisdom of the experts. MYCIN was not written in PROLOG, but in LISP, which is generally acknowledged to be harder to learn. Some developers believe that knowledge engineers will no longer be needed when user interfaces to expert systems, called *shells*, become easier to use. As is noted below, the Japanese are relying on PROLOG to develop such shells.

Relational databases

Without question, the most prevalent use of computers is the construction and maintenance of databases. Every enterprise with more than a very few employees has to keep records for payroll and tax purposes. Every manufacturing or retailing business must provide for inventory control. The amount of data kept by local, state, and federal governments is monumental, including information on health, crime, taxes, etc. Thus it is not surprising that developing new and better ways to manage this information has been and will continue to be an area of interest.

Once a database is established, it is quite difficult to reorganize or shift to a new and better database manager. The relational database, with its theoretical basis in the relational algebra (operations for manipulating relations), has become the style of most promise. PROLOG, which is itself based on the relation concept, is thus an ideal language for these applications.

The fifth generation

The adoption of PROLOG by the Japanese as the core language for its "fifth-generation" effort has spurred interest from industry and universities alike. Japan plans to package and sell knowledge as other nations market wine or clothing. To do this, their computers must be intelligent, i.e., able to "learn, associate, make inferences, make decisions, and otherwise behave in ways we have always considered the exclusive province of human reason" [Feigenbaum, 1983, p. 12].

In "PROLOG Implementations," we discussed implementation of the PROLOG language itself. The Japanese envisage a computer system using PROLOG as its core language, as diagrammed in Figure 6.17. As one can see, PROLOG is to be built into the hardware itself.

Applications range from resource exploration through medical diagnosis and library functions to weapons systems. Research areas are roughly organized under problem-solving and inference, knowledge-based, human-machine interface, development support, and basic applications systems. An amazing feature of the Japanese effort is its 10-year implementation plan, with inter-industrial, university, and governmental cooperation. The United States is just beginning to respond to this challenge.

Fifth-Generation Computer Systems

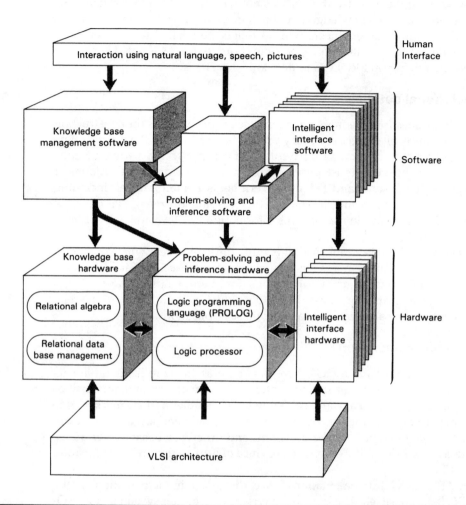

Figure 6.17 Reprinted with permission from Feigenbaum & McCorduck, *The Fifth Generation: Artificial Intelligence and Japan's Challenge to the World* (Reading, MA: Addison-Wesley, 1983)

LAB XIV: PROLOG II

OBJECTIVES

1. To see examples of well-written and well-documented PROLOG program(s).

2. To see an appropriate example of a program that solves an interesting, nondeterministic problem.

3. To see a good use of relation addition and/or removal through the use of **assert** and **retract**.

4. To monitor run time before and after making changes to the programs provided. ■

Strengths and Weaknesses

PROLOG has several features whose combination is unique from those encountered in other languages [Cohen, 1985]. These are (1) Each parameter to a procedure can be either input or output at each invocation, as the user wishes; (2) Procedures may return results with unbound variables, thus presenting partial or generic solutions to a problem; (3) Multiple solutions may be found using built-in backtracking. Cohen also lauds the logic base of PROLOG in the interests of effective problem specification, the potential for parallel processing, and the conciseness of PROLOG programs—estimated at 5 to 10 times smaller than those written in a procedural language.

There are, however, recognized shortcomings, other than those mentioned in [Goguen, 1984; Cohen, 1985; Feigenbaum, 1983]. It is not very easy for the uninitiated to read or write information using the first-order predicate calculus (PC). But once that is done, PROLOG takes over and makes inferences on its own. Some see this too as a serious flaw, since experienced programmers can improve the efficiency of program execution if they can control the method of solution. As it now exists, PROLOG has no mechanism for specifying parallel execution, no block structure, no methodology for documentation, and no type checking. It is, however, an evolving language, being less than 15 years old and undergoing rapid development and experimentation.

6.1 SUMMARY

The foundation for logic programming is the predicate calculus, an extension of the logical systems of Aristotle. Aristotelian logic is used to find new information from a given database following the rules of deduction. One of these rules is called *reductio ad absurdum*, where we assume that a statement to be proved is false and derive a contradiction. A version of the *reductio* method of proof called resolution is the basis for the logic programming language, PROLOG. The resolution theorem states that q is a logical consequence of $p_1, p_2, ..., p_n$ if ($\neg$q AND p_1 AND p_2 AND ... AND p_n) is FALSE.

q :- $p_1, p_2, ..., p_n$ (meaning that the truth of p_1 and p_2 ... and p_n implies the truth of q as well) is resolved in PROLOG, by first proving all the subgoals, p_1 through p_n, and then deriving a contradiction from the inclusion of NOT(q). If goals include variables, e.g., $p_i(x)$ and $p_j(y)$, substitutions are sought to unify the two goals, making both true. This might mean substituting z for both x and y, (p_i(z) and p_j(z)), and finally KingTut for z (p_i(KingTut) and p_j(KingTut)).

PROLOG, which exists in several dialects, is logic based and includes facts, rules, and queries. Rules produce derivations of new facts from old ones, while a query asks whether a given statement is true or false, according to the existing facts, e.g., `?-(which(x (lives_in(Montana, x)))).` would check the two-place lives_in relation to see which people in the database live in Montana.

PROLOG, as it exists, is inefficient in both time and storage usage, but it is the first fully functional logic-based language, with others being developed rapidly. Some of these languages include facilities for parallel execution. PROLOG forms the basis for Japan's "fifth-generation" project to mechanize and disseminate information rapidly.

6.2 NOTES ON REFERENCES

The late Julia Robinson writes beautifully while explaining basic theory. Her original presentation [Robinson, 1965] of resolution is quite comprehensible. For her view of the future, see [Robinson, 1983]. An extended discussion on the relationship of logic to programming can be found in Hoare and Shepherdson [Hoare, 1985].

Several journals are either devoted to or regularly publish articles on PRO-LOG. A guide to these can be found in [Cohen, 1988] and [Poe, 1984]. Also check issues of *PROLOG Digest* for current controversies.

The January 1988 issue of the *Communications of the Association for Computing Machinery* (CACM) contains good historical articles on PROLOG [Cohen, 1988], [Kowalski, 1988]. An earlier issue (December 1985), is also devoted to PROLOG. For a good introduction to the underlying ideas, application areas, and a manual of DEC-10 PROLOG itself, see [Malpas, 1987]. Clocksin and Mellish [Clocksin, 1984] and Clark and McCabe [Clark, 1984] are the standard beginners' references to Edinburgh- and micro-PROLOG respectively and are often included with a compiler or interpreter purchase.

The Warren Abstract Machine (WAM) is not the only model for PROLOG compilation. PROLOG has been compiled into intermediate languages that are known to be reasonably efficient and are implemented on several machines. Work has been done using Pascal and C, among others [Weiner, 1988].

Expert systems are only one application of what is generally called rule-based systems or RBSs. For an overview, see [Hayes-Roth, 1985]. If you're not familiar with the series *Computing Surveys*, now is the time to become so. These quarterlies are written for students and provide surveys of important research areas or tutorials. For an excellent treatment of logic and databases in this series, see [Gallaire, 1984].

The *ACM Computing Surveys'* special issue on programming language paradigms [Wegner, 1989] discusses parallelism in logic programming in two articles. The first [Bal, 1989] is easy to understand and discusses both AND and OR parallelism in the context of concurrency in general. The second [Shapiro, 1989] is devoted entirely to logic parallelism, and is hard to read, but thorough. He includes a discussion of all the current implementations: GHC, PARLOG, FGHC, P-PROLOG, ALPS, FCP, Concurrent PROLOG, and CP.

7

FUNCTIONAL (APPLICATIVE) PROGRAMMING

Peter Wegner [Wegner, 1989] states that "The primary distinguishing features of the functional paradigm are higher-order functions, lazy evaluation, data abstraction, and equations with pattern matching." Among their advantages is simplicity. The symbols needed plus a description of what comprises a legal expression and what it means can be written very briefly. Functional language advocates also claim that programs can be written more quickly, are closer to traditional mathematical notation, are easier to verify, and can be executed more easily on parallel architectures than in traditional imperative languages [Hudak, 1989]. John McCarthy's original description of LISP [McCarthy, 1960], including a motivating preface and a description of an interpreter for the IBM 704, took up only 12 pages. More important than an economical language manual, however, is that the semantics or meanings of legal expressions are very simple. Thus proofs of program correctness are quite possible. There is, of course, a price for this conciseness, which is that an algorithm written in a functional language does not look much like the English language we are used to. It looks like, and is, mathematics. For example, the expression M+N is written in the lambda calculus as $(\lambda a(\lambda b(Ma((Na)b))))$, eliminating the "+" symbol from the calculus. It is simpler, in that there are fewer defined constructs, but more complex in building up functions from the few symbols needed.

We discussed relations in the last chapter, as ordered tuples. A function can also be thought of as a relation, $f = (x_1, x_2, ...x_n, y)$ where the last coordinate y, called its value, is uniquely determined by the first n, $x_1, x_2, ..., x_n$, called its arguments. A functional relation is often written $f(x_1, x_2, ...x_n) = y$. A function is

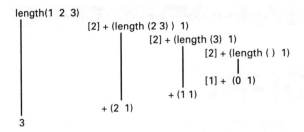

Figure 7.1

first-order if it takes individuals as arguments, i.e., such things as numbers, strings, names, etc., and returns an individual value. It takes two steps to evaluate a function such as f(x). First, a suitable individual must be *substituted* for x, e.g., the substitution of 2 for x yields f(2) = y. Next, f(2) is *evaluated* according to some defining rule for f. If f(x) is defined to be x + 3, then f, when applied to 2, evaluates to 5, i.e., f(2) = 5.

A higher-order function can take other functions as arguments and return functions as values. We say that such functions are *first class*. They can be assigned wherever any other objects may be. An argument to a first-class function can be an array value, a record field, or part of any other data structure. Furthermore, a function such as ChangeF(f1) can return another function, say f2, as its value, where f2 is a modified version of f1. Such functions are said to *learn* as execution proceeds.

So far, we have seen functions evaluated whenever they are called. Lazy evaluation (sometimes called call-by-need) means that a function or parameter is evaluated only when and if necessary. As a simple-minded example, suppose a potentially infinite array, A, is an argument of a function sum, where sum(A,i) = A(0) + A(1) + ... + A(i), and that A(0) = A(1) = 1, and A(n) = A(n − 2) + A(n − 1). (Does A look familiar?) With lazy evaluation, A(j) will never be computed unless needed by sum(A,i), that is, where j ≤ i.

We have already seen abstract data types in Chapters 2 and 3. This binding of operations to data has also been implemented in functional languages, in particular, Haskell.

An example of equations with pattern matching is the following function to determine the length of a list:

[1] length ( )   = 0
[2] length (x ls) = (+ (length ls) 1)

An argument passed to length will first be compared with ( ), the empty list. If the match fails, matching will proceed to the second equation. For example, suppose we ask length((1 2 3)) to be evaluated, as shown in Figure 7.1.

We will discuss each of these features in this chapter, but first we will look at the mathematical foundations of functional programming, the lambda calculus of Alonzo Church [Church, 1941].

BRIEF THEORETICAL EXCURSION 8: The Lambda Calculus

The λ-calculus (lambda calculus) was developed by Church to formalize intuitive notions about functions. If we write the expression $(x + 1)$, it can be thought of as either a rule for computation, or as a variable numeric expression. As a number, $(x + 1) = (y + 1)$ will be true just in case $x = y$. However, if we wish to express the notion that the *rule* is the same, no matter what values may be substituted for x or y, we need a new notation, $\lambda x(x + 1) = \lambda y(y + 1)$. The notation λx indicates that x is *bound* in the expression that follows, i.e., $(x + 1)$ is a function of one variable, x. Since $\lambda y(y + 1)$ differs only in that the single bound variable has been renamed, from x to y, the two expressions represent the same function. A λ-expression, $(\lambda x(E))$, is called an *abstraction*, since it generalizes the expression E for any value substituted for x. The other sort of λ-expression is called an *application*. For example, $(\lambda x(x + 1)\ 4)$ indicates that we are to apply the function $(x + 1)$ with 4 substituted for the bound variable x. When this function is evaluated, the result will be 5.

SYNTAX AND SEMANTICS

The syntax of the λ-calculus is simplicity itself. It has three *improper symbols*: λ, (, and), and an infinite list of *variables*; a, b, c, ..., x, y, z, a_1, b_1, ..., a_i, b_i, ... A formula is any finite combination of improper symbols and variables. There are four rules for combining the symbols and variables into well-formed formulas (WFFs), and three transformation rules. The WFF rules are:

1. A variable, x, is a WFF, and the occurrence of x in this WFF is free.
2. If F and A are WFFs, then so is (F A). An occurrence of a variable in either F or A or both is free (or bound) in (F A) if it is free (or bound) in F or A.
3. If F is well formed and contains at least one free occurrence of a variable, x, then (λxF) is well formed. All occurrences of x in (λxF) are bound. If y is another variable occurring in F, and y is not x, then y is bound or free in (λxF), depending on whether it is bound or free in F.
4. A formula is a WFF and variables occurring in it are free or bound only when this follows from rules 1 through 3.

Given the formation rules above, λ-expressions involve deeply nested parentheses. As we saw above, M + N is $(\lambda a(\lambda b(Ma((Na)b))))$. This is often abbreviated as $\lambda a.\lambda b.Ma(Nab)$, when no ambiguity may occur.

Any function of the λ-calculus may always be considered a function of a single variable, using one of two devices. Suppose we have a λ-expression λx.λy.(+ x y) representing ordinary integer arithmetic with the function + applied to the variables x and y. This function can be rewritten as ((+ x) y), where (+ x) is a function that adds x to its single parameter y. The other device is to consider (+ x y) as (+ p), where p = (x y) is a single argument consisting of a pair of variables. These devices simplify proofs about properties of the λ-calculus, since we may assume that all λ-abstractions are single parametered.

Transformation rules depend on whether variables are bound or free, as described above. The three rules are called α-conversion, β-conversion, and η-conversion. α-conversion allows us to change variable names to avoid name conflicts. We will use the notation [y/x]E to mean "Substitute y for every free occurrence of x in expression E."

α-conversion: $\lambda x.E \underset{\alpha}{\leftrightarrow} \lambda y.[y/x]E,$

where y is not free in E.

β-conversion allows us to *apply* a function, (λ-abstraction), to a particular argument. For example, the expression ((λx. + x 1) 4) reduces to (+ 4 1). The rule is:

β-conversion: $(\lambda x.E_1)\, E_2 \underset{\beta}{\leftrightarrow} [E_2/x]E_1.$

The final conversion rule is η-conversion, which can sometimes remove unnecessary λ-abstractions. For example:

$(\lambda x. + 1\ x) \underset{\eta}{\leftrightarrow} (+ 1)$

since the left and right sides describe the same function. Both β- and η-conversions are called reductions when converting from the left to the right side.

A few examples are in order. Suppose we want to reduce (λx.{λx. + (– x 1)}x 3) 9 [Peyton Jones, 1987], using β-reduction (we have used both ( ) and { } for clarity). (See listing (7.1).)

```
(λx.{λx. + (- x 1)} x 3) 9                              (7.1)
->   {λx. + (- x 1)} 9 3)          [9/x] in (...)
->         + (- 9 1) 3             [9/x] in {...}
->         +  8      3
->        11
```

The next example shows how three fundamental LISP functions can be written as λ-abstractions. LISP is an acronym for "list processing," with its basic structure the list. The three fundamental LISP functions on lists are **CAR**, **CDR**, and **CONS**. (**CONS** a b) returns the dotted pair a · b. If lyst is a list, (**CONS** head lyst) returns a new list, with the element, head, appended to lyst as the first element. (**CAR** lyst) returns the first item of lyst, and (**CDR** lyst) returns everything on lyst but the first element. Thus if lyst = (a b c), the value of (**CAR** lyst) is a, (**CDR** lyst) is (b c), and (**CONS** head lyst) is (head a b c). Now, if you recall our earlier discussion of abstract data types, a data type such as a list can be defined by functions, which are appropriately related. If we specify that

(**CAR** (**CONS** head lyst)) = head, and (**CDR** (**CONS** head lyst)) = lyst, any functions will do as long these relations are maintained. Now suppose we define λ-abstractions:

```
CONS ≡ (λa.λb.λf.f a b)
CAR  ≡ (λc.c (λa.λb.a))
CDR  ≡ (λc.c (λa.λb.b))
```

Let us check that in fact, after β-reductions, (**CDR** (**CONS** head lyst)) = lyst, as shown in listing (7.2).

```
(CDR (CONS head lyst))                                      (7.2)
= (λc.c (λa.λβ.b)) (CONS head lyst)
->       (CONS head lyst)(λa.λb.b))
=        (λa.λb.λf.f a b) head lyst (λa.λβ.b)
->           (λb.λf.f head b)  lyst (λa.λβ.b)
->           (λf.f head lyst)      (λa.λb.b)
->              (λa.λb.b) head lyst
->                 (λb.b) lyst
->                    lyst
```

So **CDR** is related correctly to **CONS**. We leave **CAR** as an exercise.

This is but one example showing that we really don't need special built-in functions at all, but could get along with λ-abstractions. This in fact is one of the major advantages of the λ-calculus. Church's thesis, which is accepted as true, but not proven, states that any effectively computable function can be represented as a λ-abstraction. What has been proven, however, is that the Turing-computable functions and recursive functions are equivalent to the λ-calculus, as are the systems of Markov [Markov, 1954] and Post [Post, 1943]. It is generally believed that any one of these systems includes all functions that can be computed in finite time.

The λ-calculus has other advantages. One of these is that any recursive function is equivalent to one that is nonrecursive. Another advantage is that evaluation of λ-expressions can be done in any order. What this means is that if a function has several interrelated parameters, say $f(g_1(D)\ g_2(D)\ ...\ g_n(D))$, the g_i can be evaluated in any order without affecting the result of f. In particular, all the g_i could be computed simultaneously, in parallel, returning results to f for the final computation. This is in sharp contrast to the sequential execution of imperative languages. What makes this possible is the lack of *side effects* in functional languages. The parameter D, which is shared by all the g_i, will not be affected when any g_i is applied to it, nor when $g_i(D)$ is evaluated.

EXERCISES

1. Which of the following are legal λ-abstractions?

   a. $\lambda x.x$

   b. $\lambda y(\lambda x.x)$

   c. $\lambda x(\lambda y.x)$

   d. $\lambda x(y\ (\lambda y(+\ x\ y))\ x)$

   e. $\lambda x.(+\ x\ y)$

   f. $\lambda x.\lambda y.\ (+\ x\ y)$

2. Make the following applications and evaluate the resulting λ-expression where possible:

   a. $(\lambda x.x)\ z$

   b. $(\lambda y.\lambda x.x)\ 6$

   c. $(\lambda y.(\lambda x.x)\ 6)\ 2$

   d. $\lambda x.(y\ (\lambda y.(+\ x\ y))\ x)\ 2$

   e. $(\lambda x.(+\ x\ y))\ 5$

   f. $(\lambda x.\lambda y.\ (+\ x\ y))\ 2\ 5$

3. An abstraction $\lambda x(\lambda y(E))$ can be written: $\lambda x.\lambda y.E$, as we have seen. It can also be abbreviated: $\lambda x\ y.E$. Rewrite the expressions of exercises 1 and 2 in this abbreviated form.

4. Show that (CAR (CONS head lyst)), β-reduces to head. (See listing (7.2).)

■

COMPUTABILITY AND CORRECTNESS

A function is a rule or method for computing a value, given a (single) parameter. A function is computable if the method terminates, with a single result. Church's thesis holds that all computable functions are part of the theory of the λ-calculus. The converse, however, is not true. Just because a particular function is λ-definable, does not guarantee that it is computable. Attempts to evaluate λ-abstractions that are not computable never terminate. An example of a nonterminating function is the λ-application,

$(\lambda x.x\ x)(\lambda x.x\ x).$

Substituting $(\lambda x.x\ x)$ for each x in the first expression, we get the nonterminating result:

```
(λx.x x)(λx.x x)
=>(λx.x x)(λx.x x)
=>(λx.x x)(λx.x x)
=>...
```

It has been shown that there is no test, Halts?(f), that returns YES if a computation of f terminates and NO otherwise. Even so, the λ-calculus has some nice properties that make it particularly suitable as a basis for functional programming languages:

1. Any recursive function that is expressible in the λ-calculus is equivalent to a nonrecursive λ-abstraction.

2. If two functions are equivalent, they can be reduced through α-, β-, and η-reductions to the same form, called a *normal form*.

3. For any expression that can be reduced to a normal form, there is a normal order reduction that will produce the form.

The second property is concerned with normal forms, which are just λ-expressions that cannot be reduced further. The third property tells us how to obtain this form if it exists. A *normal order reduction* starts at the left of an expression, reducing from left to right where possible. An *applicative order reduction* reduces the innermost expression first, wherever it may occur. Although normal order may not be the most efficient reduction, it is guaranteed to produce a normal form if one exists. Nonterminating applications, such as (λx.x x)(λx.x x), have no normal forms. The existence of normal forms and the elimination of recursion makes semantic proofs about the λ-calculus particularly straightforward.

Recall that *semantics* are involved with what a language means, in contrast to *syntax*, which is what it looks like or can be transformed into. Two operators are built into the λ-calculus, **APPLY**(E₁ E₂), which we have already seen in working with applications, and **EVAL**(E), which evaluates a user-defined expression. **APPLY**((λx.+ 1 x) 2) is (+ 1 2) = 3; **EVAL**(Add1 5) is 6, where Add1 is a user-defined function that adds 1 to its single argument. For Add1, the effect of **EVAL** would be:

$$\text{EVAL}(Add1\ 5)$$
$$\Rightarrow \quad \text{APPLY}((\lambda x.+\ 1\ x)\ 5)$$
$$\Rightarrow \quad (+\ 1\ 5) = 6$$

In practice, one of the first extensions to the λ-calculus is always a list of constants containing at least 0. Given this enhancement, λ-expressions mean different things in different environments. A λ-variable is assigned at most one value in any environment. However, the same variable *name* may have different values in different environments. You won't be too far off if you think of an environment as a procedure block, with all parameters passed by value. Thus a name, x, should be thought of as x_{e1}, x_{e2}, etc., where e1 and e2 are different environments. Given the existence of environments, the semantics of λ-expressions can be summed up as shown in listing (7.3).

EVAL(k) $_e$	= constant k in environment e	(7.3)
EVAL(x) $_e$	= x_e	
EVAL(E₁ E₂) $_e$	= (EVAL (E₁)$_e$) (EVAL(E₂) $_e$)	
EVAL(λx.E) $_e$	= EVAL(E) where x=a, an arbitrary	
	element of e.	
EVAL(E)	= ⊥ where E has no normal form[1]	

In practice, constants and built-in functions are the same in all environments. For example, **EVAL**(0) = 0, **EVAL**(+) = +, **EVAL**(TRUE) = TRUE, **EVAL**(FALSE)= FALSE and **EVAL**(IF) = IF. Similarly, **EVAL**(IF TRUE a b) = a and **EVAL**(IF FALSE a b) = b.

We will also insist that if two expressions, E₁ and E₂, reduce to the same form, E, then **EVAL**(E₁) = **EVAL**(E₂) = **EVAL**(E). For example, we noticed above that λx(x + 1) = λy(y + 1), and introduced the α-conversion rule to substitute one variable for another. However, two functions may return the same values, but not be reducible to each other. For example, λx.(* x x) and λx.(expt x 2), where (expt x 2) is x^2, return the same values.

---

1 The symbol ⊥ is called "bottom" and is assigned as a value to noncomputable functions.

EVAL(λx.(* x x)) = **EVAL**(λx.(expt x 2)), but there is no common normal form to which both expressions reduce.

EXERCISES

1. Show that given an arbitrary element a,

   APPLY(λx.(* x x)a) = **EVAL**(expt a 2))

2. Show that, using η-conversion, λc.λa.a, reduces to λa.a, and λc.λa.c reduces to λc.c.

3. (hard) Show that if TRUE = λx.λy.x, FALSE = λx.λy.y, and the conditional is **COND** = λp.λa.λb.(p a b) then **EVAL**(**COND** TRUE) = λa.a and **EVAL**(**COND** FALSE) = λb.b. Thus, **COND** can be rewritten as IF p THEN a ELSE b. (Hint: Use the result of number 2 for the final steps.) ■

Implementing Functional Languages

Compilers for functional languages are easy to implement since programs can be translated into a language intermediate to the machine code, the λ-calculus, as shown in Figure 7.2.

Any compiler can be built if the second step, translation from the lambda calculus to machine code, has been specified for a particular machine. How one translates a higher level functional language into the lambda calculus is beyond the scope of this book, and the reader is referred to [Peyton Jones, 1987].

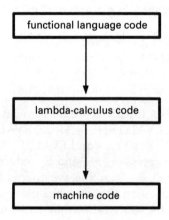

Figure 7.2

CAR   CDR

Figure 7.3

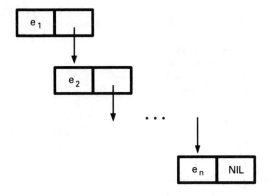

Figure 7.4   List implemented as dotted pairs[2]

There are several concerns. One is that functional languages are generally typeless. However, if '0' is the constant zero, it should not also be the name of a function. If **CONS** is defined as a function, it should not also be a variable. (+ **CONS** 2) makes sense if **CONS** has been assigned a numeric value. But then we will have lost the usual meaning, where (**CONS** a (b c)) returns the list (a b c). Usually, the functional programmer need not specify the types of variables, but a smart compiler must be able to differentiate the various meanings. Thus type checking must occur automatically. In particular, an error must be reported if an expression is meaningless, e.g., (+ 'this' 5).

McCarthy's original basis for LISP was the S-expression, standing for "symbolic expression." An atomic symbol is either a string, a variable name, or a number. An S-expression is then defined recursively as:

1. An atomic symbol
2. If e_1 and e_2 are S-expressions, then so is ($e_1 \cdot e_2$). This second expression is called a dotted pair. A list can be implemented as

   ($e_1 \cdot (e_2 \cdot (\ldots(e_n \cdot \mathbf{NIL})\ldots)))$,

   where **NIL** is an atomic symbol for the empty list. Implementation of the dotted pair on the IBM 704 was the binary, or CONS cell, as shown in Figure 7.3. A list is then as shown in Figure 7.4.

---

2 In most LISP implementations, the CAR cell contains a pointer, rather than a value. Thus each atom is stored only once, and it is referenced through a pointer.

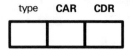

Figure 7.5

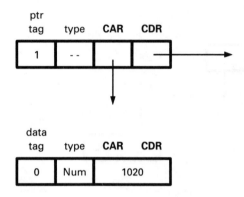

Figure 7.6

This dotted pair implementation does not take typing into account. Some implementations append a third cell onto each binary pair with the (implied) type of the element, as shown in Figure 7.5.

The entry in the type cell will be a code for a Number, Built-in function, Character, or a Structure, such as a nonempty list, called a CONS cell, or empty list, NIL. In addition, some languages, notably SKIM (1980) and NORMA (1985) also add to each dotted pair a bit that marks it as a pointer or data cell, as shown in Figure 7.6.

Lazy vs. Strict Evaluation

We have already mentioned lazy evaluation as the computing of argument values only if needed. For example, in the expression (IF p THEN q ELSE s), q need only be evaluated if p is TRUE. Similarly, s is evaluated only if p is FALSE. In a strict evaluation, p, q, and s would all be evaluated before executing the conditional expression. Lazy evaluation also involves evaluating an expression as few times as necessary. For example, $\lambda x.(+x\ x)(2*10)$ reduces to $(+\ (2*10)(2*10))$, given the λ-calculus' β-reduction rule and normal-order reduction. To complete the computation, $(+\ 20\ (2*10)) \rightarrow (+\ 20\ 20) \rightarrow 40$, would involve two computations of 2*10. If we used applicative-order reduction, where the innermost reduction is made first, we would have:

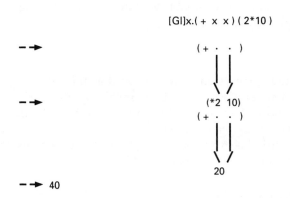

Figure 7.7

$$\lambda x.(+x\ x)(2*10) \rightarrow \lambda x.(+x\ x)(20) \rightarrow (+\ 20\ 20) \rightarrow 40,$$

eliminating one computation. Remember, however, that applicative-order reductions do not guarantee reaching a normal form if there is one. As usual, everything has its price.

The case for lazy evaluation includes more than eliminating unnecessary computations. Another advantage is that potentially infinite data structures can be implemented, with only that portion needing evaluation. The argument against lazy evaluation is execution speed. Determining just which computations can be either avoided or postponed is expensive and involves the efficient implementation of "thunks," which we discussed in Chapter 2, "Concepts from ALGOL 60." Functional languages like ML and Hope have made a compromise, with strict evaluation being the norm unless lazy evaluation is called for by the programmer. The SCHEME dialect of LISP has two built-in operators, **delay**<exp> and **force**<exp>, to implement lazy evaluation. A delayed expression is set aside (as in a thunk) and not evaluated until a **force** is executed. What SCHEME's **delay** and **force** do, as in other lazy evaluation schemes, is to decouple execution from the apparent structure of a program. It's as if all procedures existed at the same time and were evaluated only when necessary.

Another method for speeding up lazy evaluation is through graph reduction with normal evaluation rather than the usual string reduction used with the lambda calculus. Our example above, if reduced through graphical methods, would yield [Hudak, 1989, p. 384] the results shown in Figure 7.7.

Note that this method takes the same number of steps as applicative-order reduction, where the (2*10) was evaluated first, but is otherwise a normal-order resolution.

Scope and Bindings

LISP, which we will discuss below, looks like the lambda calculus and allows λ-expressions to represent unnamed functions. An expression like (λx.(+ x x)(2*10)) can never be used again, since there is no name to reference it. To save computing an expression more than once, we can use a LET clause. The variable y retains its value throughout the body of the LET, as shown in listing (7.4).

```
(LET ((y ((LAMBDA(x)(+ x x))(* 2 10))))                              (7.4)
     <body involving y> ...)
```

The value of the lambda expression 40 will be used as the value of y throughout the LET expression, i.e., wherever y occurs in <body involving y> ... . The LET above is thus easier to read and a more efficient way to evaluate (<exp>(LAMBDA(x)(+x x))), equivalent to an applicative evaluation of (e_1 e_2).

We could also accomplish this evaluation using two LET expressions, with the second within the scope of the first, as shown in listing (7.5).

```
(LET ((x (* 2 10)))                                                 (7.5)
     (LET ((y (LAMBDA(x)(+ x x)))
          <exp>...))
```

A LET allows the assignment of several variables, as in:

```
LET ((y (LAMBDA(x)(+ x x))(* 2 10))
    (w 22)
    (z (- 16 3))
    <expression involving y, w, and z>
```

In this LET expression, w will be assigned 22 and z, 13. This behavior conforms to the evaluative independence of functional arguments. w, y, and z are all parameters to the LET, and we may make no assumption about which gets evaluated first. If <expression> is (+ y w z), the LET above is equivalent to $(\lambda z.\lambda w.\lambda y.<exp>)(\lambda x.(+ x x)(* 2 10) 22 (- 16 3))$. Which is easier to read is a matter of taste.

SCHEME allows the use of LET* to assure an ordered evaluation so that previously assigned variables may be used in succeeding expressions.

```
(LET* ((x (* 2 10))
      (y (LAMBDA(x)(+ x x)))
     <exp> ...)
```

is equivalent to the two LETs of listing (7.5).

LETREC (recursive LET) can be used in place of **LET***, but is more powerful. The following example from the *SCHEME Reference Manual* [TI, 1987] shows the definition of two mutually recursive functions, even? and odd?, both of which recurse down to 0.

```
(LETREC ((even? (LAMBDA(n)
                   (IF zero? n)
                   #T
                   (odd? (- n 1)))))
        (odd?   (LAMBDA(n)
                   (IF zero? n)
                   #F
                   (even? (- n 1))))))
       (even? 88))
```

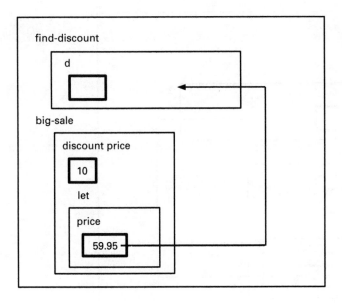

Figure 7.8

The final expression, `(even? 88)`, takes the place of <exp> in the other examples and is a call to `even?` returning a value `#T`.

As we have seen, variables can be either free or bound in a lambda expression. It is how the free variables are bound to values that is of concern to us here. Suppose we define a function as follows:

```
(define find-discount (LAMBDA (d)
                        (* d price)))
```

Notice that d is bound and price is a free variable in find-discount. In a dynamically scoped language, a call to find-discount would evaluate price in the environment in which it was called. For example, suppose we define a new function, big-sale.

```
(define big-sale (LAMBDA (discount)
                  (LET ((price 59.95))
                       (find-discount discount))))
```

A call to (big-sale .10) will return 5.99, even though big-sale is defined in an environment entirely different and subsequent to the environment where find-discount is defined. We have been able to pass a value for the free variable, price, from big-sale's environment into the environment of find-discount using the LET. Or put another way, we have transported the definition of find-discount to the environment of big-sale, as shown in Figure 7.8.

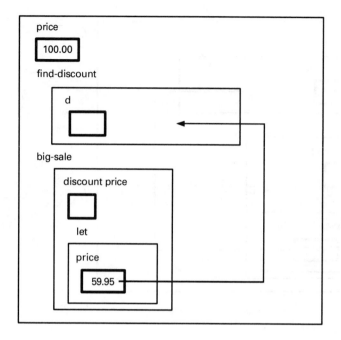

Figure 7.9

Dynamic scope can lead to errors, as keeping track of variable names and environments can become hopelessly confusing to a programmer. It also violates the "black-box" notion for a procedure that we do not meddle with its internal workings and are guaranteed correct results if we pass appropriate actual parameters. We will look at two of these problems, the so-called FUNARG problems.

The FUNARG Problems   LISP is the first language to treat functions as first-class variables. Functions can be passed to or returned as values of other functions. For example, a LISP function, `(mapcar func args)`, can be defined that produces a list of values for func(arg). `(Mapcar sqr (1 2 3))` will return the list (1 4 9), i.e., ((sqr 1) (sqr 2) (sqr 3)). We pass the function, `sqr`, and a list of arguments as parameters to `mapcar`. No problems arise with the argument func, since mapcar does not involve free variables.

There are, however, two problems discussed in the LISP literature when free variables are present: the *downward funarg problem* and the *upward funarg problem*. The downward problem occurs when a procedure captures free variables in another environment.

Suppose the environment in which find-discount was defined included a variable named price with a value of 100.00, as shown in Figure 7.9.

When (big-sale .15) is called from another environment, .15 is passed to discount in the function big-sale, which passes it on to find-discount. So far, so good. But when 59.95 is passed as a value for price, the variable price that contained 100.00 is "captured"

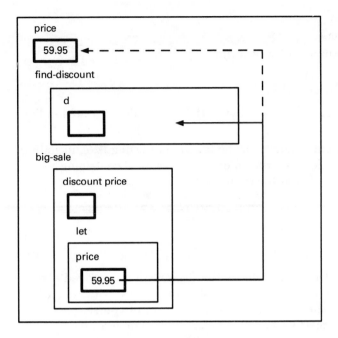

Figure 7.10

by big-sale's price and reassigned, as shown in Figure 7.10. This capture may be a shock to the program's user.

The upward problem occurs when a procedure is returned as a value and loses the bindings of its free variables. Abelson and Sussman [Abelson, 1985] give the exercise shown in listing (7.6) to illustrate the problem.

```
(DEFINE (make-adder increment)                          (7.6)
        (LAMBDA (x) (+ x increment)))
```

LET ((add3 (make-adder 3))) will return the function add3, defined as (**LAMBDA** (x) (+ x 3)). A subsequent call of (add3 4), within the scope of the **LET** expression, will return 7. However, if we try to evaluate make-adder directly, as in ((make-adder 3) 4) in a dynamically scoped LISP, the 3 will get lost if there is already a variable named increment in the calling environment. This time, the existing variable will "capture" make-adder's increment and substitute its value for the intended 3.

EXERCISES

1. Evaluate the following expressions using:
    a. Normal evaluation (left to right)
    b. Applicative evaluation (innermost expression first)

c. Lazy evaluation

d. Graph reduction.

Keep track of the number of substitutions.

a. λx.(λy.(+ y y) x) (3*20)

b. λx.λy.x λx.x (λs.(s s) λs.s)

2. How would a language like Pascal view the scope rule illustrated in Figure 7.8?

3. Draw an environment diagram for the function of listing (7.6), including the call to ((make-adder 3) 4) from another environment containing a variable increment = 25. What is the result of this call?

7.0 LISP

The fundamental data element of LISP is the S-expression described above. Pure LISP allows no side effects and does not support lazy evaluation, data abstraction, or pattern matching. Data abstraction can, of course, be implemented by choosing suggestive names for functions. For example, a LISP implementation for rational numbers could be defined with the eight functions [Abelson, 1985] shown in listing (7.7).

```
(make-rat (lambda n d))      returns (n.d)                      (7.7)
(numer      (lambda x))       returns n, where x is (n.d)
(denom      (lambda x))       returns d, where x is (n.d)
(+rat (lambda x y))     returns x + y, where x and y are rationals
(-rat (lambda x y))     returns x - y, where x and y are rationals
(*rat (lambda x y))     returns x * y, where x and y are rationals
(/rat (lambda x y))     returns x / y, where x and y are rationals
(=rat (lambda x y))     returns TRUE or FALSE
```

LISP, especially the SCHEME dialect, is easy to learn, and gives a good flavor of functional languages. It is also interesting historically, as the first implemented functional language. It is notable for its implementation of the conditional (IF..THEN..ELSE) expression, use of lists and higher-order operations over lists, and use of dotted pairs, garbage collection, and S-expressions. As an example of operations over lists, we might consider the mapcar function, which repeatedly maps the CAR of a list onto a functional value. If a list, lyst has 25 elements; (mapcar fun lyst) will return another list of 25 values for these elements. We already saw an example of its use in "Implementing Functional Languages." Mapcar can be defined in LISP as shown in listing (7.8).

```
(DEFINE (mapcar fun lyst)                                        (7.8)
      (IF (null? lyst)
          NIL
          (CONS (fun (car lyst))
                (mapcar fun (CDR lyst)))))))
```

Suppose we evaluate the expression, `(mapcar sqr ' (1 2 3))` as shown in listing (7.9).

```
(CONS (sqr 1)                                              (7.9)
      (mapcar sqr (2 3)))
            (CONS (sqr 2)
                  (mapcar sqr (3)))
                        (CONS (sqr 3)
                              (mapcar sqr ()))
                                    (null ()) NIL)
                        (9)
                  (4 9)
      (1 4 9)
)
```

Notice the recursion that repeatedly calls mapcar until the null list is encountered, at which time the whole chain can unwind constructing the list of values. This is often called "consing up a list." This behavior causes problems for the beginning LISP programmer, who sometimes creates infinite recursive calls.

HISTORICAL VIGNETTE 10: LISP: John McCarthy

> Artificial intelligence (AI) is the part of computer science concerned with designing intelligent computer systems, that is, systems that exhibit the characteristics we associate with intelligence in human behavior—understanding language, learning, reasoning, solving problems, and so on [Jackson, 1986, p. 2].

LISP is a programming language with a purpose. It was developed specifically for AI programming in the late 1950s by John McCarthy, then a professor at Dartmouth. The seeds of LISP were sown in McCarthy's mind, back in the summer of 1956 when he attended the first major workshop on AI at Dartmouth. He realized that existing languages would not meet the needs of AI programmers. Languages such as FORTRAN dealt with numbers. An AI language, if it were truly to mimic the human brain, would need to encode words and concepts.

McCarthy worked to develop LISP for the next two years. The language is a combination of four elements—two existing languages, mathematics, and the last from McCarthy himself. LISP borrowed algebraic syntax from FORTRAN and methods of symbol manipulation from Information Processing Language (IPL). In mathematics, McCarthy found two equivalent systems—Kleene's recursive function theory and the lambda calculus, a convenient notation for LISP's anonymous functions. Its inventor, Alonzo Church, had been McCarthy's thesis advisor at Princeton. Although inspirational, the λ-calculus was not followed slavishly. The last elements are McCarthy's own: the use of lists to represent information, the representation of programs as data, and the creation of garbage collection to round up and make available memory locations that were no longer needed [Baron, 1986, p. 225].

Like FORTRAN, the first implementation of LISP was for the IBM 704. It had only a few primitives and used punched cards in batch mode. An interactive LISP system developed in 1960 has the honor of being one of the earliest examples of interactive computing. Still, the growth of LISP use was slow. AI was a relatively new field that needed large computers with massive memories.

Interest in AI grew with interest in LISP, which became the primary experimental AI language. "It is a characteristic of artificial intelligence applications that the problem is not well understood. Indeed, often one goal of the research is to understand the problem better...LISP is very [well] suited to this kind of problem" [MacLennan, 1987, p. 435]. LISP is good for ambiguous problems because of its dynamic type system and flexible data structures, which encourage an experimental approach to problem solving.

Of course, not every aspect of the LISP picture has been rosy. Early systems were all interpreted rather than compiled, making programs run SLOW. Today, most LISP systems provide compilers with speed optimizers, but its reputation as a slow language remains. Also, LISP makes much use of recursion, which many programmers find difficult to grasp. And finally, LISP programs require very large central memories to run. Thus the development of better garbage collectors remains an active research area.

AI can be divided into three research areas: natural-language processing, robotics, and knowledge engineering. It is this third area where LISP excels. "Knowledge engineering focuses on both the development of software for expert systems and on the analysis of ways in which human experts solve problems. Knowledge engineers interact with human experts to help them describe their knowledge and inference strategies in terms that will allow the knowledge to be encoded. Thus, a knowledge engineer combines a large measure of cognitive psychology with symbolic programming techniques to develop expert systems" [Harmon, 1985, p. 8].

Expert systems focus on two types of knowledge. The first, *public knowledge*, is the sort found in textbooks. A human expert in a field has a firm grasp of factual information. Expert systems can surpass human experts in retrieving pertinent information, given an adequate database. The second is *private knowledge*, which might be called intuition or common sense. "This private knowledge consists largely of rules of thumb that have come to be called *heuristics*. Heuristics enable the human expert to make educated guesses when necessary, to recognize promising approaches to problems, and to deal effectively with errorful or incomplete data. Elucidating and reproducing such knowledge is the central task in building expert systems" [Hayes-Roth, 1983, p. 4]. When it comes to private knowledge, humans usually beat the machines.

Examples of expert systems written in LISP and in use today are DENDRAL, MACSYMA, EXPERT, and MYCIN. DENDRAL is used to analyze mass-spectographic, nuclear, magnetic resonance, and chemical experimental data to infer the plausible structure of an unknown compound. MACSYMA performs differential and integral calculus symbolically and excels at simplifying symbolic expressions. EXPERT is used to build consultation models in endocrinology, ophthalmology and rheumatology. MYCIN diagnoses infectious blood diseases and prescribes treatment.

The number of expert systems continues to grow as AI programming methods are improved and refined. Thus LISP's position is secure for now.

Pure LISP

Pure LISP allows only function calls and has no side effects. All data structures are built from S-expressions, so addressing efficiencies cannot be implemented. For example, array elements may or may not be stored in consecutive locations. A program consists of a function, which calls another function, which calls another, etc. The only built-in functions are **CONS**, **CAR**, **CDR**, **EQ**, and **ATOM**. We have already seen the first three. (**EQ** A B) tests whether the atoms A and B are the same or not. (**ATOM** A) returns **T** if A is an atom and **F** otherwise. **T**, **F**, and **NIL** are built-in atoms, as are the capital letters of the alphabet and the digits 0 through 9. In pure LISP, **NIL** represents the empty list. In other LISPs, () may be used. These atoms are not, however, reserved for their particular functions. A user can very well use **T** as a variable and override its use as the Boolean value, true.

McCarthy used the five basic functions to define APPLY, EVAL, and EVALQUOTE, which in effect built an interpreter for LISP. This is another example of an interpreter or compiler written in the language it is to translate to machine code. We already looked at another, the C language. APPLY evaluates each of its two arguments, and then applies the first, which should be a function, to the second, which is a list of arguments. (APPLY (QUOTE **CAR**) (QUOTE (A B C)))[3] returns A, the first element of the list (A B C). EVAL handles forms, which may have functional values. Suppose we

```
(SET (QUOTE X)(QUOTE (CONS (QUOTE A) (QUOTE (B C)))))
```

X now has the value (**CONS** A (B C)). Then (EVAL X) will return the evaluation of (**CONS** A (B C)), which is (A B C). EVAL includes a call to APPLY after evaluating X. EVALQUOTE invokes both EVAL and APPLY, and implements reading from and writing to a terminal. Thus EVALQUOTE is in fact a pure LISP interpreter.

The EVALQUOTE function has another feature worth mentioning, just to warn the user of various LISP dialects. We have been writing our LISP functions as S-expressions, surrounded by parentheses, e.g., (**CONS** A (B C)). When using an evalquote interpreter, this could be entered in more functional notation as **CONS** (A (B C)). That is, f(x y), instead of (f x y). This practice has been largely abandoned, as it is inconsistent with most LISP syntax. However, you may see **cons** (A (B C)), (**cons** A (B C)), (**cons** A, (B, C)), **cons** (A; (B, C)), or other

---

3 The function (QUOTE **CAR**) returns the atom CAR, and (QUOTE (A B C)) returns (A B C).

variations in different interpreters or compilers. LISP 1.5 was also case sensitive, so that a and A represented different variables.

Note that no arithmetic functions are built into pure LISP. These, as everything else, must be built by the programmer. For example, assuming we have already written the functions `pred` (predecessor) and `succ` (successor), where $pred(x) = x - 1$, and $succ(x) = x + 1$, addition can be defined as shown in listing (7.10).

```
(DEFINE (plus num1 num2)                                    (7.10)
        (COND ((zero? num1) num2)
              (#T (plus (pred num1) (succ num2))))))
```

The **COND** expression is a conditional,

```
COND ((C1 E1)
      (C2 E2)
       ...
      (Cn En))
```

Execution starts at the top, evaluating the Ci until one evaluates to true. The value of the corresponding Ei is returned. If none of the Ci are true, the result is ambiguous—possibly an error or possibly an infinite looping through the expressions. In `plus`, if `num1` is 0, the value of `num2` is returned. Otherwise we proceed to the second alternative, where C2 = **T**. E2 = (plus (pred num1)(succ num2)) will always be evaluated if num1 is not 0, since its *guard* is always true.

Literally all working LISP systems have extended pure LISP to include arithmetic functions, number comparisons, real numbers, and commonly used list operators.

Lists as data structures

Lists, however, are amazingly flexible for developing data structures. An employee record could be the list (name (address city state zip)) job (salary (retirement-deductions health-deductions))). The ordered binary tree, shown in Figure 7.11, is (((0) 1 (2)) 3 ((4) 5 (6))), in list form. Notice that each subtree is itself a list: the left subtree appearing to the left of the root node and the right to the right.

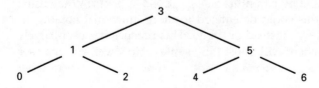

Figure 7.11

McCarthy's LISP 1.5 [McCarthy, 1965] and various other implementations incorporate many side effects and some built-in data types, whereas SCHEME [Sussman, 1975] is closer to the lambda calculus. For example, the `append` function is definable in all LISP systems and **constructs** a *new* list from its two arguments. `(append (RED HOT) (PO TATO))` returns, as its value, the new list `(RED HOT PO TATO)`. LISP 1.5 also has a function, **nconc**, which returns the same value as append but has the *side effect* of altering the first list. Perhaps the diagrams in Figures 7.12 through 7.14 will make the difference clear.

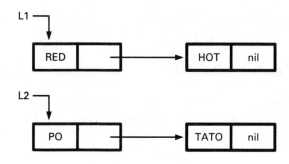

Figure 7.12   Original two lists, L1 and L2

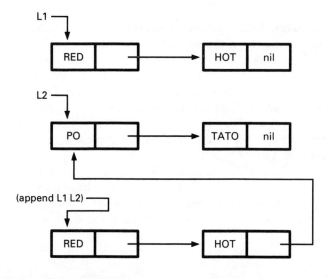

Figure 7.13   After (append L1 L2)

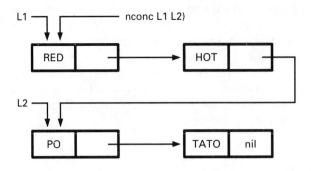

Figure 7.14 After (nconc L1 L2)

Notice that L1 has been copied over, and that the original L1 has not been altered. (See Figure 7.13.)

After an `nconc`, the first list, L1, has been altered so that its last cell points to L2. Not only does this save space, but the time required to copy over L1. We have, however, violated the no-side-effects rule of the lambda calculus. The SCHEME dialect of LISP passes all parameters *by value*. Thus SCHEME has no nconc function.

To avoid confusion, from here on we will use the syntax of SCHEME for LISP expressions.

We have seen a variety of data structures, which will all be expressed as lists in LISP. For example, a one-dimensional array is just a simple list, and an nXm array of two dimensions is a list of lists, (ROW1 ROW2...ROWm), where each ROW is an n-dimensional list. A three-dimensional array is (A1, A2, ...Am), where each Ai is a two-dimensional array, etc. Suppose A = ((1 2 3) (4 5 6) (7 8 9)), a 3 x 3 array. SCHEME (and most other LISPS) have special functions to find individual elements quickly. (**car** A) is the list (1 2 3). But suppose we want A[1,1] = 1 or (**car** (**car** A)). This is abbreviated (**caar** A). A[2,1] = 4 is (**caadr** A), and A[3,1] = 7 is (**caaddr** A), or (**car**(**car**(**cdr**(**cdr** A)))), which is (**car**(**car**(**cdr** ((4 5 6)(7 8 9)))))), which is (**car**(**car** ((7 8 9))))), or (**car** (7 8 9)) = 7. All these abbreviations start with c, end in r, and have as many a's or d's as we need **car**'s or **cdr**'s.[4] Get it?

As one more data structure, consider the queue. We can enqueue an item to the end of a queue using (append q (item)). Dequeuing is a little trickier, since we want both the first item and an altered queue returned. This can be achieved by returning the pair ((**car** q) (**cdr** q)). We leave the stack as an exercise.

---

4 Most LISPs limit the length of a c...r operator. In PC SCHEME, it is cxxxxr, where each x may be **d** or **r**.

Lists as programs

A LISP *form* is an S-expression that is meant to be evaluated. The number 2 is a form that evaluates to 2. (+ 3 5) is also a form that evaluates to 8, as is (**LAMBDA**(x) (+ 3 x) 5) and (**DEFINE** Plus3 (**LAMBDA** (x)(+ 3 x))) Each form could be considered a program.

In practice, a program is saved for repeated use and is a collection of function definitions. For example, the program for the SCHEME "help" facility begins with the definition of a function to access the various aspects of the facility.

```
(DEFINE help
    (LAMBDA subject⁵
        (If (null? subject)
            (show-help-topics)
            (fetch-help (CAR subject)))
    *the-non-printing-object*))
```

The call (help) will invoke the first clause of the conditional, show-help-topics, which of course is another function. (help 'x) invokes fetch-help, which provides information on the status of the variable x. Help is a function, so must return a value, which in this case is the special SCHEME atom, *the-non-printing-object*, which prints nothing to the screen. There must be at least two other defined functions, show-help-topics and fetch-help. These functions, in fact, invoke still other functions, which invoke others, etc.

When help is loaded, evaluation puts the body of each of the help system functions in the current environment and makes them available to respond to function calls from the terminal. The help facility is composed of 22 defined functions, with access through (help).

A SCHEME program could also include other expressions to be evaluated. For example, we could end the help file with the function call (help). Then loading the file would result in the help topics being listed automatically. Probably not a good idea, but possible.

One aspect of LISP not shared by other languages is that programs (S-expressions) and data are indistinguishable. Just as a program can modify the values of variables, so can it modify other programs or even itself. Function definitions, environments, programs, and files are all first-class LISP objects that can be passed to functions and returned as values.

---

5 We have seen (**LAMBDA**(x) ...) binding x to the succeeding S-expression. In PC SCHEME, (**LAMBDA** x ...) without parentheses surrounding x allows a parameter list with any number of parameters. In the help example, using (**LAMBDA** subject ...) permits a call to help with 0 or more parameters. A call of (help) binds subject to (), and a call of (help x) binds subject to (x).

Recursion and control

As we saw in Chapter 1, control abstractions can be divided into branching, iteration, and procedures. In LISP, the **COND** expression controls branching, with

```
(COND ((boolean1 exp1)(boolean2 exp2)...(booleanN expN))),
```

implementing both if..then..else's and case statements. Iteration and procedural control in SCHEME, as in all LISPs, is largely through recursive function calls. Each call sets up a new environment, with the results from the bottom of a recursion being passed all the way back to the top, as a value for the original function. Using that old standby, factorial, let's once again see how this works, implementing its definition as shown in listing (7.11).

```
factorial (n) =    if (n = 0) then 1                        (7.11)
                   else (n * factorial(n - 1))


(define factorial
  (lambda (n)
    (if (zero? n)
    1
    (* n (- n 1)))))
```

A call to `(factorial 3)` will produce four nested environments before arriving at any value, and partial results must be passed all the way back to factorial, as shown in listing (7.12).

```
(factorial₁ 3) => ?                                         (7.12)
   (factorial₂ 2)     => ?
      (factorial₃ 1)      => ?
        (factorial₄ 0)       => 1
      (factorial₃ 1)       => (* 1 1) = 1
   (factorial₂ 2)      => (* 2 1) = 2
(factorial₁ 3) => (* 3 2) = 6
```

A more efficient computation is $(N * (N - 1) * (N - 2) * ...* 1)$, with a temporary variable acting as an accumulator for the partial sums. (See listing (7.13).)

```
(define factorial2                                          (7.13)
  (lambda (n)
    (let f2 ((i n) (a 1))
      (if (zero? i)
          a
          (f2 (- i 1)(* a i)))))))
```

Here, the action is as shown in listing (7.14).

```
factorial2  => ?                                            (7.14)
   (f2₁ 3 1)      => ?
      (f2₂ 2 3)       => ?
         (f2₃ 1 6)        => ?
```

```
            (f2₄ 0 6)        => 6
        (f2₃ 1 6)         => 6
      (f2₂ 2 3)       => 6
    (f2₁ 3 1)       => 6
factorial2   => 6
```

Notice that the final value is obtained at the bottom of the recursion, in environment₄. This behavior is *tail recursive*. In such a case, the 6 need not be passed through the entire recursive stack, but can be returned directly to the top. What's more, we don't even need to maintain environment₁ through environment₃, as any information needed is passed on to the next environment. Thus an optimal implementation for factorial2 would be as shown in listing (7.15).

```
factorial2   => ?                                    (7.15)
    (f2₁ 3 1)       => ?
        (f2₂ 2 3)       => ?
            (f2₃ 1 6)       => ?
                (f2₄ 0 6)        => 6

factorial2   => 6
```

Implementations of SCHEME, as well as Common LISP, are built to recognize tail-recursive calls and optimize both speed and storage usage.

EXERCISES

1. Consider the `mapcar` function of listing (7.8). Suppose L1 is a circular list where the last cons cell points to the beginning of the list. Show how `(mapcar sqrt L1)` will work if L1 is:

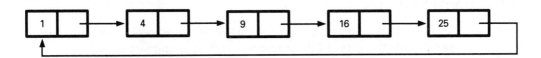

2. a. Draw figures similar to that of Figure 7.11 for the lists:
   1. (((J) I) M (M (Y)))
   2. (((My) Dog) has (fleas))
   b. The trees of "Lists as Data Structures" and the two above are listed in in-order. What would the list representation be for the same lists if traversed in pre-order? post-order?
3. Following the pattern of listing (7.10), write a LISP function for TIMES.
4. a. Why does passing all parameters by value prevent side effects?
   b. Why do read and print functions produce side effects?

5. What c...r abbreviations would we use to find the second elements of each of the rows in A = ((1 2 3)(4 5 6)(7 8 9))?

6. How could we implement a stack as a list, and how would its operations be written in LISP? ■

LAB XV: LISP 1

OBJECTIVES

1. To familiarize students with the SCHEME (or other LISP) system they have available, including the Help facility.

2. To enter and execute simple SCHEME expressions interactively, noticing how both errors and successful evaluations are reported. ■

LAB XVI: LISP 2

OBJECTIVES

1. To design, write, save, and execute a larger SCHEME program involving several functions.

2. To design, write, save, and execute a SCHEME program dealing with file input and/or output as well as screen I/O.

3. To use the SCHEME editor Edwin to enter and save a short program. ■

Nonfunctional Features

The lambda calculus is pretty sparse, using only variables, parentheses, commas, and the special symbol, λ, plus four formation and three transformation rules. Thus designers of languages quickly insert abbreviations instead of all those parentheses. Pure functional (λ-calculus) programming is also slow, relying on recursion and taking no advantage of space- or time-saving economies.

Iteration

Recursion is the means by which LISP iterates over a data structure. Some LISPs, including Common LISP, provide program functions, that evaluate a list of forms, returning the value of the last form, throwing away earlier results. For example,

```
(progn   (setf x 1)
         (setf y 2)
         (values x y))
returns (1 2) as a result.
```

Progv can establish new bindings. It also returns as a value the evaluation of the last form.

```
(progv (list a b c)(list 1 2 3)
       (list x y z)(list 4 5 6)
       (values x a b))
```

will return 4 1 2, and a,b,c,x,y, and z will retain their bindings of a = 1, b = 2, c = 3, x = 4, y = 5, and z = 6.

Using one of the prog functions, LISP programs can be written much in the style of imperative languages like Pascal or Ada. A program to make change could be written as:

```
(defun make-change (
       (progn   (read 'cost)
                (read 'money)
                (setf 'change (- money cost))
                (princ change)
)))
```

This is not in the functional style, and Pure LISP does not implement progs. SCHEME does, however, have the **let** expression, which is somewhat similar, binding variables at the beginning and returning the value of the last in a list of expressions.

Vectors and strings

One disadvantage of the list is that it can only be accessed from the front. To get to the Nth element, we have to **cdr** down N – 1 times and then take the **car** of the remaining list. More modern LISPs have added other data types, in particular vectors and strings. In SCHEME, a vector is like a fixed-length array, with indices starting at 0. It is like a list, however, in that its elements can be of any type. One can access a particular element using the function **vector-ref** and modify it using **vector-set!**.

Strings are of specified length and created using **make-string**. Individual characters can be modified with **string-set!**, or accessed with **string-ref**.

SCHEME also includes a **list-ref** function that finds the Nth element of a list. It behaves semantically like **vector-ref**, but is implemented differently. **Vector-ref** calculates the address of the desired item and returns the element at that address, whereas **list-ref** uses N – 1 **cdr** operations to find the Nth element.

Objects and packages

LISP has been extended to support object-oriented programming, notably through Flavors [Moon, 1986] and LOOPS [Bobrow, 1983]. SCHEME also has an object-oriented extension, SCOOPS, written entirely through SCHEME macros. Macros are user-defined special forms, where special forms are expressions distinguished by a leading *keyword*, such as (+ x y), where "+" is the keyword known to the SCHEME system. When the SCHEME interpreter encounters a macro expression, its *expansion* is copied directly into the SCHEME program, where it is evaluated. Just how an expression is expanded depends on the interpreter or compiler. One method is to translate it into the lambda calculus, including an expansion for each recursive call, if there are any. The user will not be aware of this expansion when running SCOOPS, but the expansions may appear in a print-out of a program that has been run. In any case, once defined, macros will behave like any other special form.

SCOOPS implements classes, instances of classes or objects, class variables, instance variables, methods, and mixins. Mixins are superclasses inherited by a class being defined. SCOOPS includes the macros **define-class**, **classvars**, **instvars**, **mixins**, and **define-method** to define classes and **make-instance** to create objects. We will leave further discussion of SCOOPS for Lab XVII.

Although the core for Common LISP, which we will discuss below, is a small language, it incorporates many extensions. One of these is packages, which we looked at in Ada. LISP packages were first developed for ZetaLISP and incorporated into Common LISP. A LISP package is essentially a name space. If NewAdd is a function in package1 and also in package2, a name conflict will not occur. One can think of NewAdd as package1.NewAdd and package2.NewAdd (much as in Ada). Packages must be manipulated with care to avoid subtle bugs, but they do provide modularization, allowing several programmers to work on a large system without stepping on each other's turf.

LAB XVII: LISP 3

OBJECTIVE

1. To use SCHEME's iterative looping structure, **do.** ■

Dialects

SCHEME was developed as a part of research and teaching efforts at the MIT Artificial Intelligence Laboratory in 1975. A SCHEME chip was built in 1981, that incorporated an innovative compiler. The language was further developed for special courses at Yale and the University of Indiana, and language variants or dialects began to confuse users. A student who learned SCHEME at, say Indiana, and then went to MIT for graduate work, might not even be able to read programs written there. Thus SCHEME's originators, Harold Abelson and Gerald Sussman, along with a baker's dozen of assistants, took on the task of defining the language [Rees, 1987]. SCHEME was the first LISP to be lexically scoped, treat procedures as first-class objects, and to rely solely on procedure calls to express iteration, rather than relying on nonfunctional loops and goto's. It also incorporates first-class escape procedures. Some of these features have been incorporated into the production language, Common LISP. There have been many other dialects of LISP, where features were added when problems became apparent. SCHEME started over from the beginning, using the definition of Pure LISP, overcoming many of the previous LISP's shortcomings.

The two most common experimental LISPs used during the 1970s were MacLISP (MIT) and its West Coast cousins, Franz LISP (UC Berkeley) and UCI-LISP (Stanford). InterLISP is a commercial product from Bolt, Beranek and Newman, Inc., and Xerox. ZetaLISP was also developed at MIT to take advantage of a special LISP machine. These different locations were all research organizations, so the languages changed to fit particular interests of the researchers involved. One could usually, with some effort, rewrite programs from one dialect into another, but not always. This is fine if programs rarely travel off location.

Common LISP

Common LISP [Steele, 1984] is a large commercial product, incorporating all the features anyone might want. As Guy Steele, one of its 63 developers puts it, "Common LISP is to LISP as PL/I was to FORTRAN and COBOL," that is, the sort of language where you go down the hall and ask someone how to do what you want to do, rather than try to find it in the huge manual. It's not usually the best choice for one's first LISP encounter.

By 1980, LISP implementations had begun to diverge due to their environments—ZetaLISP and Spice LISP for personal computers, NIL for commercial time-shared computers, and S-1 for supercomputers. Common LISP is intended to be compatible with ZetaLISP, MacLISP, and InterLISP, in that order, i.e., a program written in the Common LISP core should run in any of the other systems, with non-Common LISP features considered as extensions. Common LISP also has extensions, such as an implementation of packages, but these are not part of the core.

Common LISP is intended to be portable, eliminating features that cannot be implemented on a large number of machines. Efforts have been made to make it consistent, expressive, efficient, and powerful. It is also intended to be stable, when completed, so that later implementations will be extensions to the unchanging core.

One real plus for Common LISP has been the Department of Defense's interest in it, or some extension, as the basis for a very high-level language for developing prototypes [Gabriel, 1989]. If, as has been suggested, the DOD accepts programs written only in Ada or Common LISP, these languages will surely prosper, as DOD is the United States's largest software consumer. (At least it has been up until Perestroika!)

LAB XVIII: Tracing and Debugging in SCHEME

OBJECTIVES

1. To investigate the tools available with SCHEME.
2. When presented with a buggy program, to use the various tools to find and eliminate the bugs.
3. To monitor execution of a program with and without the PCS-DEBUG-GER-MODE on. ■

7.1 APL

APL is not a purely functional language, but is an example of a language with functional features not built on the λ-calculus. Where LISP's primary data structure is the list, APL's is the array. It has influenced other functional languages, notably FP [Backus, 1978], where the primary data structure is the sequence. The Functional Array Calculator (FAC) of Tu and Perlis [Tu, 1986] is based directly on APL, but includes infinite as well as finite arrays. FAC, of course, relies heavily on lazy evaluation to achieve this power.

HISTORICAL VIGNETTE 11: APL: Kenneth Iverson and Adin Falkoff

APL is a very simple name, short for "A Programming Language." APL does not, however, have a reputation as a simple language. Its code is said to be highly complex and basically unreadable. Still, this child of two mathematicians, Kenneth Iverson and Adin Falkoff, continues to grow in popularity.

In the late 1950s, Iverson was an assistant professor of applied mathematics at Harvard University. He was working under Professor Howard Aiken, who was organizing a new graduate program in automatic data processing, and Iverson was appointed to teach some courses in it. He became aware of a need for some type of notational tool that could be used in the classroom and elsewhere to analyze data processing problems.

This notation would eventually evolve into the APL language. Given Iverson's background, APL had strong mathematical roots from the beginning. Mathematics and computers are a duo with history. FORTRAN, the first high-level language, was designed for making scientific calculations. Most of the pioneers in computer science started out as mathematicians. Programs for applications that seem very removed from the world of mathematics, such as those that allow one to print newspapers or draw pictures, are often quite mathematical, although the user may well be unaware of this.

Iverson cites the tremendous influence Professor Aiken had on his mathematical development and on the development of APL. Aiken always stressed simplicity and practicality, two of the guiding principles in APL's design. Iverson remembers how Aiken, when he didn't understand a student's presentation on some topic, would say, "I'm a simple man. I don't understand that. Could you try and make it clear?" [Wexelblat, 1981, p. 682]. Iverson also remembers Aiken's practicality. "Aiken was raised an engineer. Although he had a very theoretical turn of mind, he always spoke of himself as an engineer. And an engineer he characterized as being a man who could build for 1 buck what any damn fool could do for 10" [ibid].

Iverson went to work for IBM in 1960, when Harvard decided not to reappoint him since he had published nothing but one little book. There are those who feel that Harvard forgot that what Iverson lacked in literary quantity, he more than made up for in the creative quality of his work. At IBM, he continued to work with Falkoff. That APL began as a notation system and not a programming language gave the two an advantage. They didn't have to make APL fit a particular machine. They were free to experiment. Other languages, such as Pascal, BASIC, and Ada, are said to be the children of other languages, but APL stands alone.

In 1962, Iverson published *A Programming Language* [Iverson, 1962]. The name APL would later be derived from the title of this book. During that same year, Iverson and Falkoff began the description of a complete computer system, the IBM 360, written in the APL notation.

By 1964, APL was sufficiently well defined to begin work on its implementation as a computer programming language. Implementation involved some problems, not the least being APL's character set. APL contains special characters, some devised by Iverson and some common mathematical symbols. Part of APL's beauty is that single symbols can be used to perform complex operations on sets of data. For example, 2 φ 'ABCDEFG' produces the result, CDEFGAB. Here, 2 and 'ABCDEFG' are arguments to the rotation function φ. The first 2 characters of the string are rotated to the end. APL programs of a single line might need 20 or 30 lines of code in other languages. To use APL requires a special keyboard to accommodate the special characters. Even then it is not all smooth sailing. Many APL characters can be formed only by typing in one character, backspacing, and striking a second character to print on top of the first. "Contemplating the APL keyboard, you may well be asking whether Iverson has achieved but a Pyrrhic victory: attaining the goal of simplicity of operators at the cost of an arcane symbol set that is not available on the average computer keyboard and that requires special effort to use even when it is available" [Baron, 1986, p. 129]. It is this strange character set that is partially responsible for its image as a language that is impossible to understand. The character set did have to be modified a bit when APL was implemented. For one thing, the language had to be linearized, i.e., things like superscripts and subscripts were no longer permitted.

During the implementation phase of APL, Iverson and Falkoff kept two ideas in mind:

1. The implementation was to be experimental, with efficiency considerations subordinated.

2. It was to be compromised as little as possible by considerations about machines on which it was eventually to run.

They wanted the mathematics of APL to "work like you thought it did in high school." This may sound easy, but in fact it proved to be enormously complex. For example, if $Y = 2/3$, and $X = 3*Y$, they wanted the comparison $2 = X$ to be true. Computers being limited, rounding errors led to other results. This problem was solved by the introduction of comparison tolerances called "fuzz."

Another important APL feature is the concept of a *workspace*. The notion is not unlike pages in a notebook holding both data and functions. Workspaces can be stored and retrieved from a library of workspaces.

By 1968, the APL system was debugged and running. Falkoff states,

A user of early APL systems essentially had what appeared to be an 'APL machine' at his disposal, but one which lacked access to the rest of the world. In more recent systems...this isolation is overcome and communication with other users and the host system is provided for by *shared variables*. Two classes of shared variables are available in these systems. First, there is a general shared variable facility with which a user may establish arbitrary, temporary interfaces with other users or with auxiliary processors. Through the latter, communication may be had with other elements of the host system, such as its file subsystem, or with other systems altogether. Second, there is a set of system variables which define parts of the permanent interface between an APL program and the underlying processor. These are used for interrogating and controlling the computing environment, such as the origin for array indexing or the action to be taken on the occurrence of certain exceptional conditions [Falkoff, 1976].

Although APL is well suited for data processing with its sorting capabilities and ability to perform operations easily on all the data in a particular file, it has not yet come close to presenting a challenge to COBOL, the most common business language. Falkoff, however, believes APL's use will continue to grow, since it represents a new trend: the combining of standard mathematical notation and programming. Other languages are also rooted in mathematics, but APL is closer than most others.

The continued success of the cumbersome COBOL over graceful APL brings to mind a story Iverson told about Professor Aiken. "I don't know what the occasion was, but one of his graduate students was becoming a little paranoid that somebody might steal one of the fantastic ideas from his thesis, so he was stamping every copy 'Confidential.' Aiken just shook his head and said, 'Don't worry about people stealing your ideas. If they're any good, you'll have to ram them down their throats'" [Wexelblat, 1981, p. 682].

Functions and Functional Notation

Since APL's primary data structure is the array, many of the built-in functions manipulate arrays. To assign an array to the variable A, we could use:

```
□←A←2 3 ρι6
```

The symbol □ is known as quad or window, and indicates that we want the output of the expression to the right printed to the terminal. ι6 asks for the integers from 1 through 6, and the 2 3 ρ indicates that the dimensions of A are 2×3. Here,

```
1 2 3
4 5 6
```

would be printed.

If we define a second matrix B as B←3 2ρι6, then the *inner product* of A and B is,

$$C = \begin{bmatrix} 1\,2\,3 \\ 4\,5\,6 \end{bmatrix} \times \begin{bmatrix} 1\,2 \\ 3\,4 \\ 5\,6 \end{bmatrix} =$$

$$\begin{bmatrix} (1 \cdot 1 + 2 \cdot 3 + 3 \cdot 5) & (1 \cdot 2 + 2 \cdot 4 + 3 \cdot 6) \\ (4 \cdot 1 + 5 \cdot 3 + 6 \cdot 5) & (4 \cdot 2 + 5 \cdot 4 + 6 \cdot 6) \end{bmatrix} = \begin{bmatrix} 22 \ 28 \\ 49 \ 64 \end{bmatrix}$$

In APL this is accomplished using `C[I;J]←+/A[I;]×B[:J]`, or even more succinctly, `A+.×B`.

At first, APL seems very arcane with its 20 special symbols, each having a particular functional meaning. But when one's work primarily involves matrices, as in statistical analysis, it can be very quick and easy once the syntax is mastered.

Many APL implementations also include graphics functions, such as HIST, which prints a histogram with horizontal ordinate; PLOT, with vertical ordinate; and CURVE, which prints a line graph. Working interactively with data, checking graphical representations when wanted and easily making changes, is the heart of exploratory data analysis [Tukey, 1977]. Francis Anscombe [Anscombe, 1981] has written an interesting advanced introductory statistics text with APL as its primary pedagogical tool.

EXERCISES

1. Suppose we allow "fuzz" of .001. That is, $X = 2$ will be true if $|X - 2| <$ .001. Suppose we round $Y = 2/3$ and $X = 3*Y$ appropriately so that $X = 2$ is "true." Will the same "fuzz factor" work for the sequence $Y = 2/3, Z = Y*5$, $W = Z/5, X = 3*W$?

2. Write as short a procedure as possible in Pascal or any other imperative language for the rotation function of two arguments, ϕ. Write it again in LISP. What can you say about economy of code in each of the three versions? ∎

7.2 SUPPORTING PARALLELISM WITH FUNCTIONS

Pure functional languages, where side effects are not allowed, have been thought to be naturals for parallel processing. A function, $f(e_1, e_2, ..., e_n)$, could be processed by assigning each of its n parameters to a different processor and returning their values to the processor working on f. Research has proceeded along the lines of automatic detection and assignment of parallel processes by a compiler.

In "Lazy vs. strict evaluation," we provided a brief example of lazy evaluation using graph reduction. Graph reduction is the main method for introducing parallelism into functional language processing, where strict evaluation is (at least initially) assumed. Suppose we have a function, $(+ e_1\, e_2)$. '+' is strict (not lazy), since both its arguments must be evaluated. Its graph is shown in Figure 7.15. The @'s mark nodes in the graph. A compiler detecting nodes that are candidates for initiating parallel processes would find the two marked with '#'. There should be no problems evaluating e_1 and e_2 concurrently since they cannot affect each other or any global variables.

Conditionals are expressions where lazy evaluation would be appropriate. `if <test-exp> <then-exp> <else-exp>` is the if-then-else statement in SCHEME. There are three expressions, all of which could be evaluated in paral-

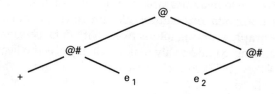

Figure 7.15

lel, only one of which, <test-exp>, is strict. A conservative compiler would evaluate only <test-exp>, and then one of <then-exp> or <else-exp>. A speculative compiler would evaluate all three in parallel and use what is needed. Several issues arise here. Not all the expressions may terminate, so speculative parallel processing might unnecessarily use up CPU time. Some schemes do start processing all three expressions, but kill those which eventually become unneeded.

Although functional languages are usually made concurrent by the compiler rather than the programmer, the same issues that we saw in Chapter 4 are involved. Should we distribute expressions at every possible node or only major program segments?[6] Which expressions should be assigned to which processors? Should memory be distributed or shared?

The advantages claimed for the functional approach, with parallelism detected by a smart compiler, are based on the fact that programmers are producing mathematical expressions, rather than worrying about parallelism. The programs produced are thus completely portable from machine to machine, more conducive to formal verification than traditional imperative programs, and easier to debug. Programs are also shorter and more elegant, thus easier to understand by those comfortable with mathematical methods. D.A. Turner writes in "Recursion Equations as a Programming Language" that a basic difficulty of programming languages which are not functional is that "they are very long winded, in terms of the amount one has to write to achieve a given effect" [Carriero, 1989, p. 453].

The problem is that the programmer has no control over the granularity (see footnote 6) of the parallelism. Programmers often experiment with different versions of a program to make it more efficient. Usually, coarse-grained parallelism runs faster than fine-grained, as the expense of synchronization is minimized. A smart compiler cannot decide on a program-by-program basis whether it is more advantageous to divide a function into many small expressions, assigning each to a different processor, or to assign fewer but larger program segments to fewer processors.

There are several experimental programs to develop parallel graph reduction. One is the Rediflow project at the University of Utah, which distributes memory over a collection of processor/memory/switch units called Xputers. A function graph is distributed over all the Xputers involved. Another is Applicative Language Idealized Computing Engine (ALICE) at Imperial College, London. Here the entire graph is held in shared memory, although processors also have individual memories. A group at Yale is working on the Distributed Applicative Parallel Systems (DAPS) project and a group at University College, London, is developing Graph Reduction in Parallel (GRIP). References to these systems can be found in [Peyton Jones, 1987].

---

6 Just how much gets done by each of the processors working in parallel is called *granularity*. Fine-grained parallelism partitions an expression into many small segments to be evaluated in parallel, while coarse-grained parallelism assigns larger program segments to fewer processors.

7.3 OTHER FUNCTIONAL LANGUAGES

John Backus's FP was one of the first functional languages other than LISP. The designer of FORTRAN wrote an eloquent treatise on the advantages of functional programming in his 1978 Turing Award Lecture [Backus, 1978]. In it he discussed the inadequacy of imperative languages for the computing needs of the future. The essential problem is that program execution proceeds by altering the store one computer word at a time. No provision is made for multiple concurrent actions in any single instant of time. FP is not based on the λ-calculus, but on a few rules for combining functional forms. Backus felt the power of the λ-calculus to express all computable functions was broader than necessary and could easily lead to chaos.

At the same time that FP was being developed in the U.S., ML appeared in the U.K. Unlike LISP, ML is strongly typed although a user need not declare types, as the compiler determines types by inference. ML allows polymorphic functions, i.e., parameters of any type may be passed to a single function. It also provides for user-defined abstract data types.

Among the λ-calculus-based languages are SASL, KRC, Haskell, and Miranda, which is perhaps the only commercially marketed functional language. See [Hudak, 1989] for a summary of these languages, features, and an extensive bibliography.

7.4 SUMMARY

Functional languages are based on the notion of a mathematical function, which, given a list of actual parameters, returns a single value according to some rule. Pure functional languages allow no side effects. That is, the values of parameters are never changed during a function call. Parameters are never passed by reference, name, or value-return, only by value.

Functional languages form a good basis for parallel execution, since a program is nothing more than a single function, $p(a_1, a_2, ...,a_n)$, where each parameter a_i is also a function, returning a value to p. Each of the a_i can be assigned to a different processor and computed independently.

The first, and still most common, functional language is LISP, based on the λ-calculus of Alonzo Church. The calculus is formally very simple and includes two types of form, λ-abstractions and λ-applications. The first form provides for the association of formal parameters with rules, and the second for the evaluation of functional forms with actual parameters.

Simplicity of definition can lead to complicated expressions involving deeply nested parentheses. Thus LISP implementations such as Franz LISP, ZetaLISP, InterLISP, and Common LISP provide many extensions and abbreviations. The SCHEME dialect is closer to the λ-calculus than these other implementations. Languages other than LISP that are based on the λ-calculus are SASL, KRC, Haskell, and Miranda.

APL is also a functional language, not based on the λ-calculus, but on mathematics. The fundamental data types of LISP are the S-expression and the list. The fundamental data type of APL is the array. APL is very concise and uses esoteric symbols not found on most computer keyboards. Modern languages influenced by APL, but without the unusual characters, are FP and ML.

A second group of functional languages is based more on common mathematical notation than on the λ-calculus. The pioneer of these languages is APL. Its fundamental data type is the array, with its associated operations, rather than the list. The most promising successor to APL is the language FP.

Advocates of the functional style claim that it produces shorter programs that are easier to debug and verify than is the case with procedural languages. Mathematics and its methods of proof have been around for centuries. Functional languages, which build directly on this experience, can take advantage of this large body of research.

7.5 NOTES ON REFERENCES

Douglas Hofstadter wrote a delightful series of three articles on LISP for *Scientific American* when he was writing the "Metamagical Themas" column. These are reproduced in [Hofstadter, 1985a] and provide a pleasant romp through such LISP functions as HOTPO followed by TATO. The final column presents a solution to the Towers of Hanoi problem. Another "painless" introduction to LISP is *The Little LISPer* [Friedman, 1987], which includes many diagrams and humorous programs.

There are several SCHEME manuals, including [Dybvig, 1987]. The reference manual and tutorial [TI, 1987] are quite adequate if one is using PC SCHEME. The 40-page report defines the language [Rees, 1987]. Abelson, Sussman, and Sussman [Abelson, 1985] is a remarkable first course in programming, using SCHEME throughout. It reportedly works well for MIT freshmen, but is tough going for most other beginners.

The Fall 1989 volume of *Computing Surveys* [March, 1989] is devoted to programming language paradigms. The article by Paul Hudak, [Hudak, 1989] provides a good, although not elementary, discussion of the history and possible future of functional languages.

An interesting book from Colorado State University by Robert Mueller and Rex Page is *Symbolic Computing with LISP and PROLOG* [Mueller, 1990]. The authors discuss declarative programming through typical applications, with solutions in either LISP, PROLOG, or both. It is quite suitable for self-study.

8

336

LANGUAGES
FOR DATABASES

A database is a more or less permanent file that has structure. In its simplest form, it is a file of records or *entities*, such as a library card catalog. It is *persistent* in that both its entities and the relationships between them are preserved from one usage to the next. Almost all languages support persistence in the form of files, but very little structure remains offline after a program has terminated. Pascal, for one, does support files of typed data with its `file of` declaration, but not relationships between the data objects.

Languages for manipulating databases must support a description of these relationships and entities and also means for changing both. These are sometimes called data system languages, or DSLs. DSLs often support two sublanguages, the data description language, or DDL, and the data manipulation language, or DML. The DDL describes the structure and relationships between data entities, while the DML supports (at least) operations to lookup, insert, delete, and modify data. In addition, sometimes the DML has as a subset a query language, which is user friendly, screen oriented, interactive, and relatively easy to use. Both the DDL and the DML may be embedded in a host language, such as Pascal (Pascal/R), COBOL (SQL), or FORTRAN (DL/I).

A database can be viewed in several ways. At the lowest level is the *physical view*, which describes the actual physical disks or drums where data is stored. At the next higher level of abstraction is the *storage view*, which gives structure to the physical data itself. The most common storage structure for large databases is the B-tree (height-balanced tree), with indexes, indexes to indexes, etc. Database administrators and programmers, but not the user, may interact with this view.

The next higher abstraction is the *conceptual view*, which describes how the data is organized. Finally there are several possible *external views* to a database. These views are seen and used by the user, often through the query language. Taken together, the host language plus the DSL, and the external, conceptual, and physical views comprise a *database management system*, or DBMS.

HISTORICAL VIGNETTE 12: The 4GLs: James Martin

James Martin is the world's best-selling author of computer books. His background includes working 19 years at IBM, and acting as a high-level advisor to several governments and a member of the first joint American-Russian committee to study possible exchanges of computer expertise. Martin conducts a biannual seminar that is one of the most highly attended in the computer industry. A major focus of his research has been in the area of the 4GLs. He produces "The James Martin Report on High-Productivity Languages," which is available by subscription, and comments on recent developments. He also writes a regular column for *PC Week*, the weekly newspaper directed to corporate users of personal computers.

The first three generations of programming languages are machine languages, assembly languages, and high-level languages such as FORTRAN and Pascal. Fourth-generation languages were designed for a special purpose: defining and manipulating databases. If you recall from Chapter 0, Gary Hansen [Hansen, 1988] mentioned five properties of 4GLs: provision for database structures, data dictionaries, good visuals, accessibility by novices as well as experienced programmers, and an interactive programming environment. They are included among declarative languages, since the user is to concentrate on *what* the problem to be solved is, rather than *how* to solve it.

A user of a fully functional 4GL can query a database with a simple command such as:

```
LIST BY CUSTOMER AVERAGE (INVOICE TOTAL)
```

One can plot these results using:

```
PLOT AVERAGE (INVOICE TOTAL) BY CUSTOMER
```

Reports can then be generated quickly, incorporating the results of queries. In the IDEAL code below, `INV-RPT` refers to a predefined form.

```
<<CUST-DATA>> PROCEDURE
    FOR EACH CUSTOMER
        WHERE (COUNT (INVOICE) > 5)
        SET INV-AVG = AVERAGE (INVOICE TOTAL)
        PRODUCE INV-RPT
    ENDFOR
ENDPROCEDURE
```

Data can also be analyzed statistically or by spreadsheet techniques, such as the calculation of column entries as a function of several other columns.

Any of these activities can be carried out using a procedural language such as COBOL or Ada. A 4GL, however, has the procedures built in. Martin calls a 4GL "fully functional" if its functions include all the power of a traditional procedural language. The 4GLs that are fully functional in comparison with COBOL and included in his two-volume work, *Fourth-Generation Languages* [Martin, 1985 and 1986] are MANTIS, IDEAL, NATURAL, and APPLICATION FACTORY. These are necessarily very large languages. Other languages, such as SQL or QBE, are more limited in function. In 4GLs, picking the language to suit the application becomes an issue.

One of the directions from generation one to four has been maximizing user friendliness. Martin [Martin, 1985, p. 15] summarizes the main principles of 4GLs as:

- *Minimum Work*—That is, maximal work for computers and minimal for users.
- *Minimum Skill*—Users should be able to use computers without long years of esoteric training.
- *Avoiding Alien Syntax and Mnemonics*—Syntax should be as close to natural language as possible.
- *Minimum Time*—Computers should be usable without lengthy delays for application development.
- *Minimum Errors*—The probability of human error should be minimized, and those errors that do occur should be caught automatically, if possible.
- *Minimum Maintenance*—4GL mechanisms should make applications easy to change, in contrast to the expense of reprogramming 3GL applications.
- *Maximum Results*—Computer applications should be as powerful, useful, and interesting as possible. 4GLs should enable users to employ complex tools for decision support, command and control, automated design, and so on.

Adherence to these principles has made 4GLs popular among businesspeople who were increasingly frustrated with the difficulty involved in writing, changing, and debugging programs. Martin includes among 4GLs languages for manipulating spreadsheets and languages for statistical analysis as well as those used with databases.

8.0 DATABASE MODELS

The historical first of the conceptual views is the *hierarchical model*, where data is viewed as a tree. One DDL for the hierarchical model is IBM's Information Management System (IMS), with its accompanying DML, DL/I. In the library the DDL might describe the hierarchy shown in Figure 8.1.

A typical database request is:

```
get all PUBLISH.NAME where AUTHOR = 'Kurt Vonnegut'.
```

The difficulty with the hierarchical model is that access to data records is always from the top down. Finding the publisher's name for a particular

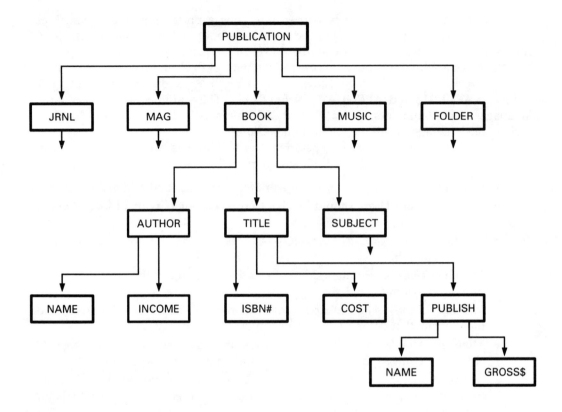

Figure 8.1 Publications hierarchy

AUTHOR NAME would involve traveling down the tree through AUTHOR to NAME and then climbing back up to the BOOK level, and traversing back down through the SUBJECT and PUBLISH levels to NAME. There are ways to connect a hierarchy across levels, but it is not easy for database users to use these methods.

The obvious solution is to model the database as a graph, where connections can be made between any nodes in any direction. This is called the *network model*. An example is shown in Figure 8.2.

The Data Base Task Group (DBTG) of the Conference on Data Systems Languages (CODASYL), which was responsible for the standardization of the business language COBOL, has made a series of proposals for a standard network language. Three languages have been proposed, starting in 1971: a DDL, DML, and a language for defining different views of the DDL. Manipulation of the database is still at the record level, as in the hierarchical model, but making connections is somewhat easier.

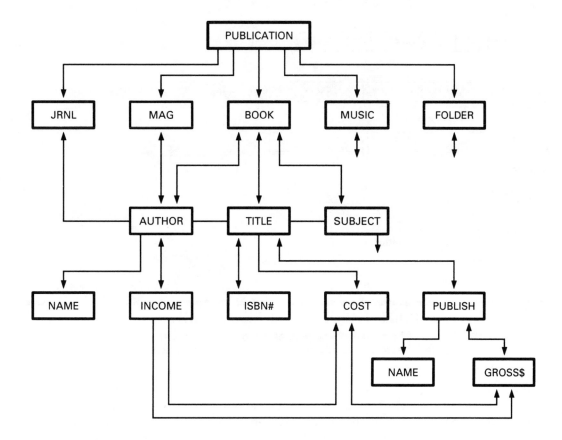

Figure 8.2 Publications network

Neither hierarchies nor networks provide much structure to the database itself. Form is added in the relational view. As we have mentioned, databases are often used by those with little knowledge of computers or mathematics. When most people think of data it is in the form of a table with rows and columns. A relation instance is then a row in a table. Some possible relations from our PUBLICATION database are shown in Figure 8.3.

Notice that we have built-in fields to connect one relation to another. BOOK itself is composed of three *keys* that refer us to the subrelations. AKEY and SKEY are called *foreign keys*, since they are keys to relations other than BOOK. ISBN# is both a *primary key* for BOOK and a foreign key, since it is the primary key for the TITLE relation as well. There are several relational languages, of which the most pervasive is Structured Query Language (SQL).

BOOK

AKEY	ISBN#	SKEY

AUTHOR

AKEY	NAME	PKEY

TITLE

ISBN#	NAME	AKEY

PUBLISH

PKEY	NAME

Figure 8.3   Publications relations

BRIEF THEORETICAL EXCURSION 9:
Manipulating Relational Databases

As with other languages we have seen, mathematical systems of long standing underlie the structure of relational query languages. There really is nothing new under the sun. In this excursion, we will view a database as a set of relations, where a relation is a set of tuples (a table). An instance of a relation is a *k-tuple*, where k is the *arity* of the relation. The symbol $t^{(k)}$ is used to indicate an arbitrary k-tuple. For the PUBLISH relation of Figure 8.3, k = 2, and for the other three, k = 3. We will use the sample library database in Figure 8.4 as an example of the manipulations possible on a database of relations.

So far, we have looked at data descriptions, but not at data itself. Individual records conforming to a particular description are called *instances*, and a collection of instances is a *database*.

The AUTHOR-1 relation of Figure 8.4 has three 3-tuples, or instances, AUTHOR-2 has two 3-tuples, PUBLISH has two 2-tuples, and TITLE has 5 3-tuples.

THE RELATIONAL ALGEBRA

An algebra is a set with operations defined on it. The relational algebra is defined by the operations allowed on sets of relations. The system for the example above is: <{AUTHOR-1, AUTHOR-2, PUBLISH, TITLE}, Union, Set Difference, Cartesian product, Projection, Selection>. S = {AUTHOR-1, AUTHOR-2, PUBLISH, TITLE} is the set of relations, while *Union, Set Difference, Cartesian product, Projection*, and *Selection* are the operations on S. We will define these operations below.

AUTHOR-1

1001	Smith	MH
1002	Jones	MH
1003	Cohen	MH

PUBLISH

MH	McG-Hill
BA	Bantam

TITLE

0-013	Cats	1002
1-025	Dogs	1002
0-036	Birds	1003
1-324	Cows	1001
2-066	Sheep	1003

AUTHOR-2

1003	Cohen	BA
1004	Brown	MH

Figure 8.4 Library database

Union   Union(A, B) is the set of tuples that occurs in A or in B or in both. **Union**(AUTHOR-1, AUTHOR-2) is:

1001	Smith	MH
1002	Jones	MH
1003	Cohen	BA
1004	Brown	MH

Set Difference   The **Set difference** of two relations A and B is A – B, the set of relations in A but not in B. **Set difference**(AUTHOR-1, AUTHOR-2) is:

1001	Smith	MH
1002	Jones	MH

Cartesian Product   The **Cartesian product** of two relations A and B is the relation A X B, whose first coordinates are those of A and last, those of B. Thus if A has k_1-arity and B has k_2-arity, then A X B has $(k_1 + k_2)$-arity. AUTHOR-2 X PUBLISH is:

1003	Cohen	BA	MH	McG-Hill
1004	Brown	MH	MH	McG-Hill
1003	Cohen	BA	BA	Bantam
1004	Brown	MH	BA	Bantam

The Cartesian product is not too useful, since we get duplicate columns (PKEY) and some nonsense relations. For instance, Cohen's publisher is McGraw-Hill, not Bantam. Two variations are implemented for relational databases. The first is the *equijoin*, where only those relations are joined that have equal entries in a specified column. For example, the **equijoin**_PKEY of AUTHOR-2 and PUBLISH is:

		PKEY	PKEY	
1003	Cohen	BA	BA	Bantam
1004	Brown	MH	MH	McG-Hill

The *natural join* eliminates the duplicated column from the equijoin. The natural join of AUTHOR-2 and PUBLISH is:

		PKEY	
1003	Cohen	BA	Bantam
1004	Brown	MH	McG-Hill

Projection   A **projection**, π, produces a new relation from an existing one, with only a subset of the components or with components rearranged. For example, $\pi_{3,2}(\text{TITLE})$ is:

1002	Cats
1002	Dogs
1003	Birds
1001	Cows
1003	Sheep

Only columns 2 and 3 remain, rearranged from 2,3 to 3,2 order.

Selection   Selection, σ, as the name implies, selects out those tuples satisfying some condition. For example, $\sigma_{[\text{NAME} = \text{'Cats'} \wedge \text{NAME} = \text{'Cows'}]}(\text{TITLE})$ is:

0-013	Cats	1002
1-324	Cows	1001

Operations other than the equijoin and the natural join can be defined from these operations as well.

Intersection $A \cap B$ is shorthand for $A - (A - B)$

Quotient $A \div B$ is the relation that factors out tuples from B occurring in A. For example (taking a little liberty with the notation), $(a, b, c, d, e) \div (b, c) = (a, d, e)$.

A purely algebraic relational language is Information System Base Language (ISBL) developed by IBM in Britain for use in an experimental system, the Peterlee Relational Test Vehicle. Its better features have since been combined in the SEQUEL language (also known as SQL), which we will look at below, combining both the relational algebra and the relational calculus.

THE RELATIONAL CALCULUS

The relational calculus is really two calculi, the tuple calculus and the domain calculus. We already know a good bit about the tuple calculus from Chapter 6, since it is nothing more than the predicate calculus applied to tuples. Variables will represent tuples. A formula such as $(\text{EXISTS } (t^{(k)})) A(t^{(k)})$ means, "Is there a k-tuple, $t^{(k)}$, such that $A(t^{(k)})$ is true?" The tuples will, of course, need to be part of some relational database.

The Tuple Calculus

If you recall from Chapter 6, atomic formulas are simply letters such as p and q, or p(x) and q(x). We shall specialize these to relational databases, but otherwise, the predicate calculus remains the same. Remember that a formula of the predicate calculus, or the relational calculus can be either TRUE or FALSE. For the relational calculus, atomic formulas are:

1. R(t), where R is a relation and t is a tuple.
2. t[i] <comparator> u[j], where <comparator> is a comparison operator such as =, <, or >. t[i] represents the ith component of the tuple, t.
3. t[i] <comparator> C, where C is a constant.

We will give as examples relational-calculus formulas representing the operations of the relational algebra. These are given as sets. The set will be assigned a TRUE value, just in case its members fulfill the condition used in its description. Capital letters such as R or S represent relations, while lower-case letters such as t or u represent tuples. $u \in R$ means that the tuple u belongs to the relation R.

Union: $R \cup S = \{t \mid R(t) \text{ OR } S(t)\}$
Difference: $R - S = \{t \mid R(t) \text{ AND NOT}(S(t))\}$
Cartesian product: $R \times S = \{t^{(r+s)} \mid \text{EXISTS}(u \in R) \text{ EXISTS}(v \in S)$
$\qquad (t[1] = u[1] \text{ AND } ... \text{ AND } t[r] = u[r] \text{ AND}$
$\qquad t[r+1] = v[1] \text{ AND}...\text{AND } t[r+s] = v[s]) \}$
Projection: $\pi_{i1...ik}(R) = \{t^{(k)} \mid \text{EXISTS } (u) \text{ AND } R(u) \text{ AND}$
$\qquad t_1 = u[i_1] \text{ AND}...\text{AND } t_k = u[i_k]\}$
Selection: $\sigma_F(R) = \{t \mid R(t) \text{ AND } F(t)\}$, where F is a condition on tuples that can be either TRUE or FALSE.

The Domain Calculus

The tuple calculus as given can yield infinite results. The relation defined by {t | NOT (TITLE(t))} describes an infinite set of tuples, all those not in the 5-tuple relation, TITLE. To restrict our definitions to finite relations, we appeal to the domain calculus, which applies to what are called *safe expressions*. We will not give the formal rules for safe expressions here, but refer the interested reader to [Ullman, 1982]. It can be shown that the domain calculus is equivalent to the relational algebra. That is, the set of functions or relations definable using safe expressions is the same set definable through the relational algebra.

There appears to be general agreement that, of the three models mentioned, the relational calculus is by far the easiest to understand and use. The problem with both the hierarchical and network models is that a fairly sophisticated knowledge of links and records is needed to negotiate a database. However, both hierarchies and networks are closer to the physical view of data and provide a basis for very efficient systems.

EXERCISES

1. Complete the JRNL branch in the publications hierarchy.
    a. Do you really need to repeat the AUTHOR, TITLE, and SUBJECT fields?
    b. How could you devise a JRNL record to avoid the redundancies mentioned in (a) above?
    c. Besides wasting space, why is it a bad idea to keep more than one copy of data? Try to think of two reasons.
2. What table results from the equijoin$_{\text{AKEY}}$ of AUTHOR-1 and TITLE? From the equijoin$_{\text{AKEY}}$ of AUTHOR-2 and TITLE?
3. What is set-difference (A – B) if A = TITLE and B = $\sigma_{[\text{NAME} = \text{'Cats'} \lor \text{NAME} = \text{'Cows'}]}$ (TITLE)?
4. What is PUBLISH X TITLE? TITLE X PUBLISH? TITLE X PUBLISH X AUTHOR-2?
5. What is the natural join$_{\text{AKEY}}$ of TITLE X AUTHOR-2?

SQL

SQL stands for structured query language and is pronounced "ess que ell" by some and "sequel" by others. It is sometimes written SEQUEL to enforce the second pronunciation. Its basis is intermediate between the relational algebra and calculus and was originally developed in the early seventies in San Jose, California, by IBM for the R Database System. It is not fully functional in the sense of being as powerful as a procedural language, but does provide operations sufficient for most database applications. We discuss it here instead of one of the many other possible database languages because there are more than one hundred commercial products based on it and it has recently been standardized by the American National Standards Institute and the International Standards Organization [ANSI-X3135, 1989] and [ANSI-X31351, 1989].

Publishing a standard has many advantages in that personnel trained at one location will be able to use their same skills if they change jobs; applications are portable from one machine to another and will be usable for a long time; systems can communicate from one to another; and customers can choose the big or the little version of the same language, depending on their needs. C.J. Date [Date, 1989], however, warns of numerous deficiencies in SQL as it presently exists. The most serious is that it was never really designed in accordance with either the relational algebra or calculus and is filled with numerous hard-to-remember restrictions, *ad hoc* constructs, and special rules. In other words, SQL is far from orthogonal. The standard also omits several widely used functions, such as those controlling cursor movement and anything like DROP TABLE, to remove a table from a database. These functions are usually added on in a nonstandard way to particular implementations. However, "vendors are scrambling to support it, and customers are demanding such support" [Date, 1989, p. 6].

We will continue to use the library database of Figure 8.4, including the PUBLISH and TITLE tables, but will use the Union of AUTHOR-1 and AUTHOR-2 and call it AUTHOR. We will also leave the third field null in Cohen's record, indicating that his book, *Sheep*, has no publisher as yet. Discussion below follows Date's *Guide to the SQL Standard* [Date, 1989]. In Lab XIX, you will find some differences, since the implementation is not strictly standard SQL.

AUTHOR

1001	Smith	MH
1002	Jones	MH
1003	Cohen	
1004	Brown	MH

SQL includes both a DDL and a DML. In order to have a database to work with, we must first define it. We will define our library database through a *schema*, as shown in Figure 8.5.

AUTHORIZATION means that MAVIS created this schema. Notice that the data definition includes formatted input. Each table has a field designated as a **PRIMARY KEY** that cannot be null. This designation must be unique to a row and is the primary way for looking up a record. AUTHOR and TITLE also have **FOREIGN KEYS** that facilitate referencing related tables. The fact that Cohen has no PNO causes no problem, since it does not appear in the PUBLISH table.

The SQL DML has four basic operations: **INSERT**, **UPDATE**, **DELETE**, and **SELECT**. Our next job would be to enter the data into the three tables defined in the schema. For example,

```
INSERT
INTO AUTHOR (ANO, ANAME)
VALUES      (1003, 'Cohen')
```

```
CREATE SCHEMA AUTHORIZATION MAVIS

CREATE TABLE PUBLISH ( PNO      CHAR(2)    NOT NULL,
                       PNAME  CHAR(8),
                       PRIMARY KEY ( PNO ) )

CREATE TABLE AUTHOR  ( ANO      CHAR(4)    NOT NULL,
                       ANAME  CHAR(10),
                       PNO    CHAR(2),
                       PRIMARY KEY ( ANO ),
                       FOREIGN KEY ( PNO ) REFERENCES PUBLISH )

CREATE TABLE TITLE   ( ISBN     CHAR(8)    NOT NULL,
                       TNAME  CHAR(8),
                       ANO    CHAR(4),
                       PRIMARY KEY ( ISBN ),

                       FOREIGN KEY ( ANO ) REFERENCES AUTHOR )
```

Figure 8.5   Schema definition

When Cohen's book is indeed accepted by Bantam, we can:

```
UPDATE AUTHOR
SET    PNO = 'BA'
WHERE  AUTHOR.ANAME = 'Cohen'
```

The **SELECT** statement is generally of the form **SELECT** X **FROM** Y **WHERE** <expression>. One use is to implement the equijoin we saw when describing the relational algebra. Here we will use our **FOREIGN KEY**s.

```
CREATE TABLE AP
       AS SELECT AUTHOR.ANAME, PUBLISH.PNAME
          FROM    AUTHOR      , PUBLISH
          WHERE   AUTHOR.PNO = PUBLISH.PNO
```

The following table will result.

AP

Smith	McG-Hill
Jones	McG-Hill
Cohen	Bantam
Brown	McG-Hill

Standard SQL is not particularly suited for selecting a number of rows and performing some operation on them, as it is primarily intended for embedding in procedural languages, particularly COBOL and PL/I, which are not specially oriented to manipulate tables. One can achieve this sort of iteration by declaring a cursor, which moves around a table like a mouse-controlled cursor moves around a screen.

Suppose Bantam gets sold to some mystery company, to be read from a secret file, and we want to update all rows in PUBLISH where 'Bantam' is the PNAME. While we're at it, we might update the key, BA to the first two letters of the new name. This code needs to be embedded in a host language to read in the mystery name and pick off the first two characters. The code below is an outline of a PL/I program to do the job. **EXEC SQL** signals the PL/I compiler to switch to SQL. X and Y are PL/I variables that are written :X and :Y in the embedded SQL code so there is no confusion with SQL variables.

```
EXEC SQL DECLARE C CURSOR FOR
        SELECT  PUBLISH.PNAME, PUBLISH.PNO
        FROM    PUBLISH
        WHERE   PNO = 'BA'

DECLARE X CHAR(8);        /* PL/I declarations */
DECLARE Y CHAR(2);
EXEC SQL OPEN C ;
DO /* for all rows accessible via cursor */ C ;
        EXEC SQL FETCH C INTO :X, :Y;
/* read the new name into X & put first 2 letters in Y */
        EXEC SQL UPDATE PUBLISH
                    SET PNAME = :X;
                    AND PNO   = :Y;
                    WHERE CURRENT OF C;
END ;
EXEC SQL CLOSE C;
```

In the code above, there are five operations with cursors: **OPEN**, **CURRENT**, **FETCH**, **SET**, and **CLOSE**. **OPEN** sets the cursor at the top of PUBLISH and starts the **SELECT** moving over all the rows accessible by the cursor C. **CURRENT** is the row currently pointed to by C. **SET** reads values pointed to by the CURRENT value of C, while **FETCH** reads and then moves the cursor to the next row defined for it. **CLOSE** undeclares the cursor.

There are two security measures in SQL, one using a **VIEW** and another called **GRANT**. A **VIEW** can be used to hide some data from users, while operations are **GRANT**ed to them. Most users will probably not be **GRANT**ed **UPDATE** privileges. We can create a **VIEW** of McGraw-Hill authors using:

```
CREATE VIEW MH-AUTHORS AS
       SELECT * FROM AUTHOR WHERE AUTHOR.PNO = 'MH'
```

Many database languages, including the System R version of SQL, include a function for creating an index, e.g.,

```
CREATE INDEX AUTHOR-INDEX
       ON (ANO [order, either ASCending or DESCending]) AUTHOR
```

CREATE INDEX functions directly on the physical database and provides addresses of data rows to speed lookups. This function has been eliminated in Standard SQL, since programs are to be portable from machine to machine. Indexes are created in Standard SQL using the **TABLE** function, i.e.,

```
CREATE TABLE AUTHOR-INDEX
       AS SELECT ANO FROM AUTHOR
```

Two integrity constraints have been considered desirable in relational DBMSs. The first is *entity integrity*, which insists that a KEY, either primary or foreign, cannot be null. Second is *referential integrity*, which insists that each relation have at least one foreign key to allow relating two or more relations. System R did not enforce either rule, while Standard SQL enforces entity integrity but not referential integrity.

SQL has provision for concurrency through *transactions*, which are guaranteed to be independent of each other. A transaction terminates normally by executing **COMMIT WORK**. **ROLLBACK WORK** handles an unsuccessful transaction and returns the database to its state before the transaction began to execute. A **ROLLBACK** must be called by a transaction and the Standard provides no guidance for transactions running at the time of a system crash or those that terminate without having executed **COMMIT WORK**. Thus these abnormal situations must be handled by the particular implementation.

EXERCISES

1. If we wish to add ACMPress to the PUBLISH database, would we use SQL **INSERT** or **UPDATE**? Why?
2. Use SQL statements to create the natural join of AUTHOR and PUBLISH.
3. Create an SQL **VIEW** of TITLE giving only those titles by authors Smith or Jones. You first will have to find out from AUTHOR just what those titles are.
4. Use an SQL statement to **DELETE** all authors whose books are published by Bantam. ∎

LAB XIX: SQL

OBJECTIVES

1. To become familiar with SQL coding for defining and establishing a database for the PUBLISH database.

2. To use the report-writing facilities of a popular SQL-based package to produce a short report from the database. ■

8.1 SEMANTIC DATA MODELS

A relational model is certainly easier to use than either a hierarchical or network model, but its tables are still closer to the machine than to many of the natural relationships found in business. Semantic models were first introduced as schema design tools. A schema would be designed and then translated into one of the other three models. Let's look at a semantic model for the library database in Figure 8.6.

Semantic models are mainly distinguished by three things. First is the direct representation of object types, called *entities*. Many models distinguish between *abstract* and *printable* or *representable* types. Abstract entities are represented in the diagram by triangles, and subentities by circles with double arrows pointing to the parent type.

The second fundamental mechanism found in semantic models is the notion of *attributes*, or functions between types. For example, lives-at maps AUTHOR into ADDRESS, while is-residence-of maps ADDRESS back to AUTHOR. These attributes are often thought of in the relational sense, AUTHOR lives-at ADDRESS and ADDRESS is-residence-of AUTHOR.

Third is the ability to represent *isa* relationships between supertypes and subtypes. Here we have ACADEMIC isa AUTHOR and EDITOR isa AUTHOR. As subtypes, both ACADEMIC and EDITOR inherit all the attributes of an AUTHOR, including ADDRESS, ANAME, and BOOK. One difference between a semantic model subtype and a subclass in the object-oriented sense is that attributes cannot be redefined. A subentity inherits *unchanged* all the attributes of the parent entity, the isa relationships of the library database model subsets of AUTHORs.

There are essentially two sorts of semantic models, entity relationship (ER) and functional data models (FDM). ER tends to emphasize abstract data types, while FDMs are more concerned with attributes related to entities through functions. Figure 8.6 represents a combination of both ER and FDM techniques, with ADDRESS and PUBLISHER being structured abstract types, and AUTHOR related to its attributes through functions.

Query languages for semantic databases can be much like SQL, such as:

```
for each X in AUTHOR
    such that Y = 'Tampa' and
             X lives-at ADDRESS.Y and
             X has-name Z
    print Z
```

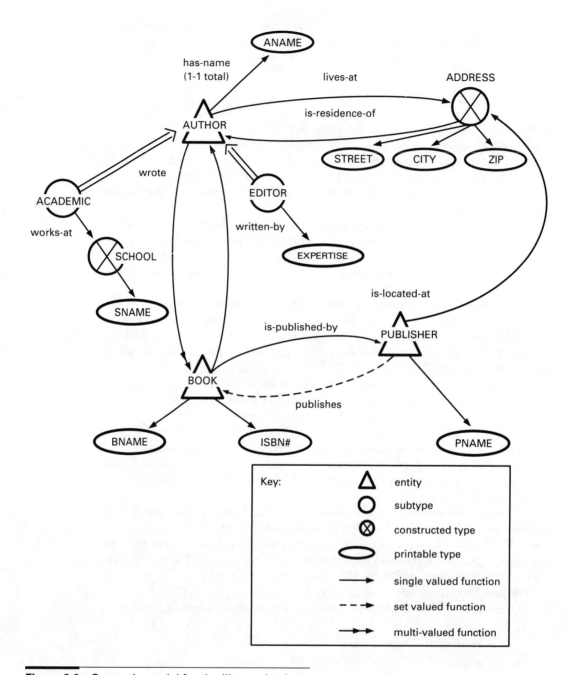

Figure 8.6 Semantic model for the library database

Subtypes can be created "on the fly" during program execution if wished.

```
create subtype SCIENCE-EDITOR of EDITOR
       where EXPERTISE includes SCIENCE
for each X in SCIENCE-EDITOR
       where X has-name Y
       print Y
```

If we add **record** SCIENCE-EDITOR, the subtype will be added to the database. This is known as a *derived subtype*, since it is derived from properties already existent in the database.

There are a number of implemented semantic data models, especially as front-ends to other database managers. Most run on VAX systems or workstations under either the UNIX or VMS operating system. Hull and King [Hull, 1987] list these models as:

Name	DBMS interface	Implementation lang.
DAPLEX	ADAPLEX extension	Ada
FQL	Functional Data Model	Pascal, CODASYL
TAXIS	Relational front-end	Pascal R
Semdal	SEMBASE	C
GEM™	INGRES front-end	Relational Interface Lang
ARIEL	Relational front-end	Pascal
Galileo™	GALILEO	VAX machine code

The languages listed above are geared to data-intensive applications within a standard procedural language. Other experimental languages provide graphical interfaces as well. There are also moves toward both object-oriented and logic-based database languages. As we have seen, objects are fairly close to database entities, while logic-based languages incorporate the relational calculus in their theoretical base.

EXERCISES

1. In the semantic model of Figure 8.6, which function(s) should probably be "1 – 1 total" besides "has-name"?

2. a. Why is there a double-headed arrow from AUTHOR to BOOK?
   b. What would it mean if the arrow from BOOK to AUTHOR was also double-headed?

3. What is the difference between a set-valued (- - ->) and a multivalued (———>->) function? When might you use each?

4. Why is ADDRESS represented as a constructed type, rather than an entity? (Think about this one. Your answer depends on what you think is the difference between an entity and an attribute.)

5. Write queries to the semantic library database to produce:

   a. All AUTHORs who works-at 'City U'

   b. A list of books published by McGraw-Hill

6. Redo number 5 a different way, i.e., if you didn't already do so, create a subtype for what you want. ∎

8.2 SUMMARY

The database paradigm is relational, and closely related to logic-based languages. It differs from logic-based languages in that database languages support persistence. By this we mean that the relationships between database entities are preserved offline. Relational databases and their languages are now the most prevalent systems, but those based on hierarchies (tree structured) or networks (graph structured) still exist.

A database management system (DBMS) usually includes two languages, a data definition language (DDL) and a data manipulation language (DML). The DML is often embedded in another high-level language, e.g., an SQL segment within a PL/I program.

SQL is the most-used database language, if not the best. It has provision for concurrency through independent transactions.

8.3 NOTES ON REFERENCES

Among his many books, James Martin has written a two-volume set on the 4GLs. The first volume [Martin, 1985] is *Fourth-Generation Languages: Principles*, and the second [Martin, 1986] is *Fourth-Generation Languages: Representative 4GLs*. Both books, directed toward the beginning DP professional, are quite thorough and easy to read. The second volume condenses some of the material from Volume I, and then presents 13 language "perspectives" followed by tutorials. Fifteen other 4GLs are discussed briefly without tutorials.

Three standard theoretical texts on database design and languages are [Wiederhold, 1983], [Ullman, 1982], and the two volumes by C.J. Date [Date, 1983 and 1985]. The second is most often used as an undergraduate text, perhaps because of its smaller size. Both Ullman and Date emphasize the relational models, with Ullman more theoretical and Date combining applications with theory. Wiederhold's text is divided into three sections, "File Structures and Design," "Database Structures and Design," and "Security and Operations."

The ACM *Computing Surveys* series provides several tutorials on database systems. One of these tutorials is an entire volume [Atkinson, 1987] dealing with types and persistence in database languages. Two others, [Hull, 1987] and [Peckham, 1988], are concerned with semantic data models. Hull is a particularly accessible tutorial on semantic notions, including implementations as well as areas of research interest.

V

LANGUAGES FOR SPECIAL PURPOSES

9

LANGUAGES FOR RAPID PROTOTYPING

Prototypes are often used to explore a problem before committing to a production-quality solution. They are regularly used by engineers and architects and may be called mockups, breadboards, or simulations. After proposing a solution to a given problem, a prototype can be used to answer three questions:

1. Is the proposal really a solution to the problem?
2. Is the proposed solution acceptable in performance, cost, and reliability?
3. Is it a solution to the right problem, i.e., was the initial problem framed correctly?

The Department of Defense (DOD) proposes the following definition for software prototyping [Gabriel, 1989]:

> *Prototyping* is the process of constructing software for the purpose of obtaining information about the adequacy and appropriateness of the designers' conception of a software product. Prototyping is usually done as a precursor to writing a *production* system, and a prototype is distinguished from a production system by typically being more quickly developed, more readily adapted, less efficient and/or complete, and more easily instrumented and monitored. Prototyping is useful to the extent that it enables information to be gained quickly and at low cost.

So far, no languages have been designed specifically for prototyping, and most prototypes have been programmed in the language in which the production system was to be written eventually. The Defense Department has drafted a report on requirements for a common prototyping system (CPS), including a common prototyping language (CPL) and a common prototyping environment (CPE).

We will look briefly at the draft requirements report for CPS, as it describes what a prototyping language should be, at least in the eyes of the U.S. Department of Defense. We will then consider a specific experimental language for prototyping, SETL, based on set theory.

9.0 CPS

The DOD envisions four difficulties in developing a language and accompanying environment suitable for prototyping.

1. It must be able to build prototypes across many applications, including parallel, distributed, real-time, and knowledge-based applications.

2. It must be able to import modules from and compile directly into many different programming languages. In particular, the DOD is interested in Ada, an imperative object-based language, and Common LISP, a declarative function-based language.

3. It should be implemented within four years, i.e., by 1994, although capabilities for parallelism may be only potential by then.

4. The technology for computer architectures and operating systems is not currently optimal for prototyping. Thus CPS must be based on an open architecture, capable of change.

Since prototyping is largely exploratory in nature, it must be quick and able to use existing modules where available, regardless of the language they are written in. To achieve this, both efficiency and completeness may be sacrificed. By efficiency, we mean speed of execution and economy of memory. Completeness refers to complete solutions to problems.

Prototypes are of two kinds, behavioral and structural. A behavioral prototype is a black-box procedure that models *what* the system is supposed to do. A structural prototype is a clear box, which shows *how* the system being explored will accomplish its task. Up until now, a task has been outlined manually through a program *specification*. Specification languages exist, but are largely formal, rather than operational. A prototype can serve as a specification, but will necessarily be less flexible, since it must be able to be interpreted or compiled and executed. Ideally, after a prototype has been approved by all involved, it could be transformed into a full production program, (semi-)automatically.

The DOD lists five objectives that any language must meet to be chosen as its CPL. It must:

1. Provide for the collection, analysis, and evaluation of information

2. Be fast and easily produce a prototype

3. Facilitate easily made changes

4. Combine behavioral and structural usage

5. Facilitate the incorporation of improved technology

In addition to these objectives, the system must be easily learned by experienced programmers, particularly those working in Ada and LISP.

The common prototyping environment (CPE) will provide such things as editors, debuggers, and browsers, as well as windows and multitasking facilities. *Browsing* involves the examination of data structures, variables, and procedures. For example, when parallel procedures share data, an easily understood display of these relationships, possibly in graphical form, can aid in understanding how a system operates. In particular, a prototyping environment must enable turning on and off information-gathering tools. In the next sections, we will look at one very high-level language designed with prototyping in mind. But first, we must look at its theoretical base.

9.1 SET THEORY AS A LANGUAGE BASIS

As we have seen, most programming languages have been modeled around an existing mathematical theory, e.g., algebra, mathematical logic, the lambda calculus, or relational calculus. Set theory is yet another system that includes most of scientific reasoning. By this statement, we mean that most scientific facts can be expressed in the language of set theory and shown to be either true or false using its methods.

Set theory is practical for prototyping because it forms the basis for a very high-level language. It is built on data structures that are powerful aggregates, and one can say much using very few statements. We will look at set theory and the Set Language (SETL) as an example of a language for rapid prototyping.

BRIEF THEORETICAL EXCURSION 10: Set Theory

As we saw in Chapter 6, valid reasoning can be assured if we follow the five axioms of the predicate calculus. These are the logical axioms of *Principia Mathematica* (PM), which can be extended to include various sets of proper axioms. For example, if we add the five Peano axioms to PM, we have the theory of natural numbers, which was considered to be the origin of all mathematical thought. In the words of Leopold Kronecker (1823–1891), "God made the integers, all the rest is the work of man."

The theory of sets encompasses all of existing mathematics, including the integers. The set of natural numbers, $N = \{0, 1, 2, ...\}$, can be defined by:

1. $\phi \in N$
2. If $n \in N$, then the successor of $n = n \cup \{n\} \in N$.

   ```
   N = {φ, {φ}, {φ,{φ}}, {φ,{φ},{φ,{φ}}}, ...}.
   ```

This definition of counting numbers is satisfying in that the set representing the nth number contains n elements. It is tedious to notate, however. Just try writing out 42 using this convention, which suggests that we rewrite N as

```
N = {0, 1, 2, ...}
```

The set N can be extended to include the integers, Z; Z^1 extended to the rationals, Q; Q extended to the reals, R; and R extended to the complex numbers, C.

HISTORICAL VIGNETTE 13: Georg Cantor

The life of the great mathematician, Georg Cantor, was like the lives of some other creative geniuses throughout history. He was an eccentric laughed at by many of his peers; supersensitive, suffering several nervous breakdowns; and he spent the end of his life in a mental institution. He was also brilliant in his field, and despite all the personal problems he faced, had faith in the validity of his own ideas in the face of objections that came from philosophers, theologians, and other mathematicians. To understand this complex man and his work, it is necessary to look at his personal history.

Cantor's father, who was born in Copenhagen, Denmark, and educated in an evangelical Lutheran mission, was a successful businessman. His mother, born in St. Petersburg, Russia, came from a musically gifted family, which included several violinists. The couple wed in St. Petersburg in 1842. The union was a combination of creative, artistic, pragmatic, and religious traditions that were to form the core of Cantor's life.

At an early age, Cantor took an interest in topics such as "the finespun arguments of medieval theologians concerning continuity and the infinite" [Dauben, 1979]. His parents encouraged him in these interests, as well as in music and art, and fostered his enduring faith in God.

During his early years in school, Cantor performed very well, much to his father's satisfaction, who wished him to study engineering. Cantor, however, preferred pure science. In his studies at Zurich, Göttingen and Berlin, he combined philosophy, physics, and mathematics. Luckily, Cantor's father supported his decision to devote his life to mathematics, which he considered a religious calling.

Cantor received a doctorate in pure mathematics in 1867 for a thesis on the theory of numbers, but his interests were focussing on the provocative word, *infinity*. For centuries theologians had been discussing its meaning and mathematicians were trying to

---

1 "Z" is the conventional notation for the integers, and represents the German word *zahlen*, meaning numbers. Q is used for quotients of integers, or rational numbers.

sort out its inherent paradoxes. However, such studies had yielded at best vague and confusing results. Into these deep and murky waters Cantor plunged.

In 1874, he married, and for a honeymoon, took his bride to Interlaken, where they met Dedekind, another mathematician deeply into study of the infinite. Both recognized that there were certain fundamental properties common to all infinite sets. Unlike Dedekind, Cantor did not believe that all infinite sets shared the same properties. He set out to build a hierarchy of sets based on their "power" or size, an entirely new field of mathematical research.

Many of the theories that Cantor developed were so paradoxical that Cantor himself was amazed by his own work. Friends were enlisted to check it, and publishers were reluctant to publish such unorthodox papers. Much of Cantor's energy was spent defending his work, which was often dismissed, since his contemporaries were reluctant to accept the notion of a "completed infinity." That the counting numbers, 1, 2, 3, ..., continued indefinitely, was accepted by all, but that one could complete the count, and then proceed on to more numerous aggregates was strongly resisted. One of the most outspoken critics was Kronecker, who demanded that arithmetic operations apply only to finite objects. These criticisms greatly wounded the supersensitive Cantor, who blamed Kronecker for preventing his appointment to a professorship at the University of Berlin. Cantor spent most of his career at Halle, a small school with a modest reputation.

In spite of the criticism, Cantor held to his ideas. He believed that set theory was divinely inspired and thus true. The stress took its toll, and in 1884, he suffered his first nervous breakdown. Believing that the friction with Kronecker was instrumental to his illness, Cantor successfully sought a reconciliation.

Cantor was hospitalized for depression twice in 1899. The sudden death of a son that same year weighed heavily on the fragile mathematician. He continued teaching at Halle for three more years, when a rapid decline forced him into permanent residency in a mental hospital, where he died in 1918.

Looking at his work, "later generations might forget the philosophy, smile at the abundant references to St. Thomas and the Church fathers, overlook his metaphysical pronouncements, and miss entirely the deep religious roots of Cantor's later faith in the veracity of his work. But all these contributed to Cantor's resolve not to abandon his transfinite numbers for less controversial and more acceptable interests. Instead his determination seems actually to have been strengthened in the face of opposition. His forbearance, as much as anything else he might have contributed, ensured that set theory would survive the early years of doubt and denunciation to flourish eventually as a vigorous, revolutionary force in scientific thought of the twentieth century" [Dauben, 1979, p. 299].

When using sets as a basis for computer languages, we need not concern ourselves with transfinite sets, as computers are, of course, finite, and cannot represent other than finite aggregates. Although Cantor's interests were inspired by glimpses of the infinite, his work on axioms was meticulous and provides a foundation for the theory of finite as well as infinite sets.

AXIOMS FOR SETS

A presentation of set theory requires a rigorous specification of the proper axioms and a proof that they are independent of each other, i.e., that we can't get by with fewer of them. Six of the axioms were published between 1904 and 1930 by Zermelo. We state them here informally, which should be adequate for our purposes.

In what follows, anything enclosed in curly braces, {...}, represents a set.

I. The Axiom of Extensionality   Two sets A and B are equal, iff they have the same elements.

II. The Union (Sum) Axiom   If A is a set, then there is another set, S = ∪A, and x ∈ S iff x ∈ B and B ∈ A.

An example will help here. If A = {{a,b},{a,{c}},Kilroy}, then ∪A = {a,b,{c}}. Notice that sets are elements of A as well as the individual, 'Kilroy'. Kilroy is not in ∪A, because there is no set, B in A, with Kilroy as an element.

III. The Power Set Axiom   If A is a set, then the power set of A, pow(A), is also a set. B ∈ⁿ pow(A) iff B is a subset of A.

Using our set A, from Axiom II,

```
pow(A) = { φ, {{a,b}}, {{a,{c}}}, {Kilroy},
{{a,b},{a,{c}}}, {{a,b},Kilroy}, {{a,{c}},Kilroy},
{{a,b},{a,{c}},Kilroy} }
```

We have listed the eight elements of pow(A) in order of size, i.e., the φ with zero elements, the three 1-element sets, the three 2-element sets, and finally the one 3-element set, A itself.

IV. The Axiom of Regularity   This axiom is hard to understand intuitively, but was added to Cantor's original axioms by Zermelo to eliminate circular reasoning.

If A is not φ, then there is an x ∈ A, and for all y, if y ∈ x, then ¬(y ∈ A)). As an example, this axiom eliminates the set A = {A}. We will have more to say about this elimination in the next section on paradoxes.

V. The Axiom for Infinity   This is the two rules combined for forming the set N of natural numbers of Figure 9.1. It is easy to see that this set is infinite.

VI. The Axiom Schema[2] of Replacement   If f is a function defined on a domain D, then there is a set, R, which is the range of f. That is, y ∈ R iff there is an x ∈ D, and y = f(x).

An ordered pair, [x,y], can be represented as the set {x,{x,y}}. A function is then just a set of ordered pairs with special properties. If the pairs are completely specified, i.e.,

---

2 Axiom VI is called a schema because it is really many axioms in one. For each function, f, and each domain set, D, there is a different instance of the axiom.

listed between set braces, Axiom VI is not needed, but if f is a rule, such as $f(x) = x^2 - 1$, and $D = Z$, the integers, the range set B can only be constructed using Axiom VI.

The seventh axiom deals with the size of sets, called their *cardinality*. It is not due to Zermelo but to Tarski, and states that:

VII. Axiom for Cardinals　　Two sets A and B have the same cardinality, $\#A = \#B$, iff there is a one-to-one correspondence, f, between their elements. That is, A is the domain of f and B is the range. Also, B is the domain of f^{-1} and A is its range, where f^{-1} is the inverse of f. As an example, if $A = \{1, 2, 3\}$, and $B = \{4, 5, 6\}$, then $\#A = \#B = 3$. One possible map is: $f = \{[1,4], [2,5], [3,6]\}$, and $f^{-1} = \{[4,1],[5,2],[6,3]\}$.

Relations among set elements need not be one-to-one functions. In fact, they need not be functions at all. The general term for a binary relation between two sets is called a **map**. A mapping may be a function, or not. A multivalued map may have several values for a given x-value, such as $g = \{[1,2], [1,3], [1,4]\}$. Here $g\{1\} = \{2,3,4\}$. A multiparametered map may or may not be a function. The map $h = \{[[1,2,3],1], [[1,2,3],2], [[1,2,3],3]\}$ is both multiparametered and multivalued.

You may have noticed that each of our axioms which declares the existence of a new set, Axioms II, III, V, and VI, depends on another set already being available. We have designated this preexisting set, A, in each of the axioms. To get started, we need to define just what a set is.

```
Def: y is a set iff there is an x, & x ∈ y, or y = φ.
```

We can then use the axiom of replacement to define ϕ as the range of the empty function.

EXERCISES

1. Assume with Kronecker that you already have the set Z of integers. How might you extend this to the rationals Q?

2. An important theorem of set theory is called the axiom of separation. It isn't really an axiom, since it can be derived from Axiom VI above. It allows us to construct a new set, B, from an already existing set, A, and some condition, C.

   Separation:　There is a set, B, such that $x \in B$ iff
   　　　　$x \in A$ and $C(x)$ is true.

   In other words, the predicate C separates the elements of B from the rest of A. This can be written, $B = \{e: x \in A \mid C\}$, where e is an expression involving x. For example: $B = \{2*x: x \in Z \mid 0 < x <= 50\}$ represents the set of even numbers, 2..100.

   a.   Write a definition for the odds between 1 and 300.

   b.   Write a definition for the set of primes less than 100. Assume the **mod** function already exists.

3.   What "special properties" do ordered pairs need to constitute a function?

4.   If f is a function represented by the set of ordered pairs, f = { {1,{1,2}}, {2,{2,5}}, {23,{23,–1}} },

   a.   What is the domain set D?

   b.   What is the range set R?

   c.   How could you construct R without using Axiom VI? (Hint: Apply Axiom II twice.)

5.   If N = {0,1,2,...}, and E = {0,2,4,...},

   a.   Is #N = #E?

   b.   Find the function f described in Axiom VII.

6.   A projection is a multiparametered map that picks out the ith coordinate from a vector. Suppose v = [1,5,7,9]. Write an ordered pair for the projection on the third coordinate, e.g., p(v,3) = 7, using the square bracket notation, [x,y]. Write it again using set notation, {x,{x,y}}.

7.   The axiom of regularity specifies the existence of a special element in any nonempty set. If N is defined as in Section 9.1, what is this special element?

8.   A common definition for the empty set is ϕ = the set y, such that for all x, $\neg(x \in y)$. Does 'Kilroy' fit this definition? any individual? What's wrong with the definition? ∎

PARADOXES AND THEIR RESOLUTION

Sets and the theory about them arose from intuitive notions. We all have some concept of a set as a collection of items. The hazards in constructing a consistent theory, however, are many. Even such an innocuous-seeming rule as Axiom I, which states when two sets are equal, can cause trouble. Recall that a natural number was defined to be the set containing its predecessors. Thus 3 = { ϕ, { ϕ}, {ϕ {ϕ}}} = {0, 1, 2} and 4 = {0, 1, 2, 3}. Good idea!

   How about describing an individual as the set of her predecessors [Halmos, 1960]? I will describe myself as, Doris = {EdleAmaliaSophia, Harry, Edle, Berndt, Annie, George, ..., Eve, Adam}. But my twin sister Donna would be described by the same set! An application of Axiom I would give us Doris = Donna, which surely is not true. Evidently such a set definition is not correct.

   In Cantor's original theory of sets, the abstraction principle included the axiom of separation (see exercise 2 above). Abstraction states that given any property P, there is a set A = {x | P(x)}. N = {x | x is an integer}, and CitizensOfUSA = {x | x is a citizen of the USA} are examples.

Bertrand Russell found the following paradox in 1903. Let $A = \{x \mid \neg(x \in x)\}$. Cantor proposed that P could be any property at all, so why not $P \equiv \neg(x \in x)$? The paradox arises when we ask the question, Is $A \in A$? If the answer is "Yes," then P(x) is true, and A is not an element of A. If the answer is "No," then $\neg(A \in A)$ is true.[3] But this puts A in A by the abstraction principle. In either case, we have the statement, $(A \in A)$, and its negation true, which is the mark of an inconsistent theory.[4]

Russell's was not the first paradox discovered. Cantor himself found one regarding cardinal numbers, which measure the size of sets, in 1899. Paradoxes fall into one of two categories. The first are logical or mathematical, of which Russell's is an example. The second are semantical, arising from the language itself. An example of the latter is the dilemma of the crocodile, which dates from antiquity [Suppes, 1960, p. 9]. "The crocodile has stolen a child and says to the father, 'I will return the child if you guess correctly whether or not I will return the child.' The father replies, 'You will not return the child.' What should the crocodile do?" This dilemma is easily expressed using abstraction, as A = {child | crocodile returns child after father guessed correctly}.

The problems appear to arise because of a confusion of language and talking about language, as in the crocodile paradox, or a confusion between sets and talking about sets, as in Russell's paradox. Axioms I through VII above appear to have eliminated the known paradoxes. The lesson is, however, that one had better be careful and follow the rules.

This lesson is particularly important in automated systems (e.g., computer programs). They process so many statements so fast that humans cannot follow the argument. It is absolutely vital that a programming language be based on a consistent theory, where we are assured that valid results follow from valid input and faithfully following the rules!

DEFINITIONS AND OPERATIONS ON SETS

Sets can be defined in two ways: by specification or by using set formers. MyPets = {Abelard, Heloise, Anna} is an example of specification. We could accomplish the same objective by writing

```
MyPets = {x | x ∈ Pets & x BelongsToDoris}.
```

Notice that this second method follows the dictates of the axiom of separation, since MyPets assumes the existence of the set Pets and the relation BelongsToDoris.

Odds = $\{2^*n + 1 \mid n \in N\}$ is also legal, since the set N = {0, 1, 2, ...} already exists. Obviously we will have to build up a store of defined sets before we can do much.

Three binary operations are defined for sets, all of which can be derived from the axioms, as shown in listing (9.1). The bold symbol in parentheses is the SETL symbol for

---

3 You proved in exercise 4 of Chapter 6, "The Propositional Calculus," that (P or ¬P) is a theorem of the propositional calculus. If we let P be $(A \in A)$, then $((A \in A) \text{ or } \neg(A \in A))$ is a theorem of set theory, which was thought to be one of many logically valid theories.

4 Consider as a practical example "I love you" and "I don't love you." Now there's your garden variety definition of inconsistency!

the operation, while the definition uses the common mathematical notation (see listing (9.1)). SETLS is a subset of SETL (Set Language), which we will look at in the next section.

```
Union:   A ∪ B = {x | x ∈ A, or x ∈ B }        (+)                    (9.1)
Intersection:  A ∩ B = {x | x ∈ A & x ∈ B }    (*)
Difference:   A - B = {x | x ∈ A & ¬(x ∈ B) }  (-)
```

There are also three unary operations:

```
Cardinality:   card(A) = # elements in A              (#)             (9.2)
PowerSet:   P(A) = {B | B is a subset of A}          (pow)
Choice:   c(A) ∈ A                                    (arb)
   (A choice function, c, chooses one element from set A.)
```

Finally, we have six predicates:

```
Membership: x ∈ A   (x is an element of A.)         (in)              (9.3)
Non Membership: ¬(x ∈ A)                            (notin)
Set Equality: A = B (A & B have the same elements.)  (=)
Inequality: A /= B                                   (/=)
Subset: B ⊆ A   (x ∈ B -> x ∈ A)                    (subset)
Includes: A ⊇ B   (B ⊆ A)                           (incs)
```

From here on, we will use the SETL symbols, rather than the mathematical ones, when there is a choice.

SEQUENCES, VECTORS, AND TUPLES

A sequence is a function from the natural numbers (usually starting with 1). If s = (1, 1, 2, 3, 5, 8), the first six Fibonacci numbers, then s(1) = 1, s(2) = 1, s(3) = 2, s(4) = 5, s(6) = 8. If a sequence is finite, we can write it as a vector, [1, 1, 2, 3, 5, 8]. Vectors are also called *tuples*, with the one above being a six-tuple. The tuple [1, 1, 2, 3, 5, 8] is an abbreviation for the function {[1,1], [2,1], [3,2], [4,3], [5,5], [6,8]}, with the two-tuple [x,y] more commonly called a *pair*, an abbreviation for the ordered pair {x, {x,y}}.

A tuple differs from a finite set in two ways. First, it can have duplicate elements, and second, it is ordered. Sets, {1, 2, 2, 3} = {1, 2, 3} = {3, 1, 2}, but the tuple [1, 2, 2, 3] has no other representation. Tuples can be formed just as sets can by specifying all the values, or using a tuple former, such as t1 := [2*x | x **in** {1, 2, 3}] or t2 := [2*x | x **in** [1, 2, 3]]. These two tuple formers may define different tuples. t1 may be [6, 2, 4] or [2, 6, 4], while t2 will always define the tuple [2, 4, 6]. Do you see why this might be so?

We can define a *map* as a set of pairs and a *function* as a map where the first coordinate of each pair occurs only once. The set of first coordinates of a map is called its *domain*, and the set of second coordinates, its *range*. We can also define the range of a function using a rule to compute an image for each domain element. This definition is similar to our two ways of defining sets or tuples, by specification or using a set former, with one important difference. A rule need not specify the domain of the function. Consider the SETL function

```
proc Fib(i);
  if i = 1 or i = 2 then return 1;
  else return Fib(i-1) + Fib(i-2);
  end;
end proc;
```

We can call Fib, where i is, say 6, with Fib(6). The single value 8 will be returned. Although we don't have the entire set of counting numbers at our disposal, we can define a tuple of Fibonacci numbers using

```
F := [Fib(i) : i in [1..SomeBigNumber]];
```

or the map,

```
M := {[[i,Fib(i)] : i in [1..SomeBigNumber]];
```

If SomeBigNumber is too large, the definition of F or M above will initiate a lengthy computation that will stop only when memory is exhausted.

We can, however, successfully define:

```
F2 := [Fib(i) | i in [1..SomeSmallerNumber]];
```

and the function,

```
M2 := [[i,Fib(i)] : i in [1..SomeSmallerNumber]];
```

In this case, **range**(M2) will return

```
{1,2,3,5,8,...,Fib(SomeSmallerNumber)},
```

implementing the axiom of replacement for Fib restricted to the domain, 1..SomeSmallerNumber. The built-in functions **domain**(f) and **range**(f) assume that the map f has been defined as a set of tuples. **Range**(Fib); will produce an error. Can you see why?

To return to MyPets, in SETL we can form by specification the set:

```
Pets := {'Heloise','Abelard','Anna','Jessie','Saunders'};
```

the map (sometimes called a *relation*):

```
BelongsTo := {['Doris','Heloise'],['Doris','Abelard'],
              ['Doris','Anna'],
              ['Karen','Jessie'],['Karen','Saunders']};
```

and, using a set former:

```
MyPets := BelongsTo {'Doris'};
```

which is equivalent to,

```
MyPets := {y : [x,y] in BelongsTo | x = 'Doris'};
```

(Read, "MyPets is the set of all values of the expression y, where the tuple [x,y] is in BelongsTo such that x satisfies the condition x = 'Doris.' ") MyPets would then be {'Heloise','Abelard','Anna'}.

EXERCISES

1. The oldest semantical paradox is Epimenedes' paradox of the Cretan who said, "I am lying." Why is this a paradox? How can this paradox relate to set theory?

2. Draw Venn (circle) diagrams to represent each of the set operations of listings (9.1) and (9.2) and predicates of listing (9.3).

3. Do you think `[x : x in {1, 2, 3}]` = `[x : x in {3, 2, 1}]`? Are you sure of your answer?

9.2 SETL

SETL, its subset, SETLS, and its interactive version, ISETL, are very high-level languages. They allow the direct manipulation of composite data structures, namely sets, tuples, and maps. An implicit assumption is that individuals wishing to devise preliminary versions of large, complicated systems know a fair amount about set theory and are comfortable expressing ideas in it. The price paid for this expressive power is a loss of efficiency. SETL was never intended as a production language, but as a vehicle for rapid experimentation. When and if such an experimental system looks promising in SETL, it can be translated into a more efficient language before being marketed.

SETL is completely type free. An identifier may have a value of any type at any time during the run of a program. For this and other reasons, SETL code is compiled into an intermediate language, which is interpreted at run time, accounting for some of the slowness. Compilation of a SETL program occurs in three phases:

1. A parse or grammatical analysis phase (PRS), checking for syntax errors.

2. A semantical analysis (SEM) phase, which checks for possible errors in meaning and identifies needed library files.

3. A code-generation phase (COD), which generates code that will actually be interpreted at run time.

Data Types

Although variables are untyped, SETL has four simple data types:

- Integers, e.g., (5, –22, 0, 1000000); SETL integers have infinite precision so, 1000000**3; returns 1000000000000000000.
- Floating-point numbers, e.g., (0.0, .362, –5.5, 38769.1E-4)

- Character strings ('Que sera, sera',",'Elmer"s Tune')
- Boolean values (**#T, #F**)

OM[5] is a special SETL constant that represents an undefined value. A SETL program never aborts because the programmer forgot to initialize a variable. SETL does, however, truncate trailing **OM**s. Thus `[1,2,OM,3,OM]` = `[1,2,OM,3]`.

We have already seen SETL's composite types—tuples, sets, and maps. SETL uses [ ] and { } for the empty tuple and empty set respectively.

To handle maps defined as sets of ordered pairs, **domain**(f) and **range**(f) define the domain and range sets of the mapping f. `f{x}` defines the range set of the element x. SETL maps may be many valued, as is the map BelongsTo above. If f is a function (i.e., single valued), `f(x)` provides the functional value of x. If `f{x}` contains more than one value, `f(x)` returns **OM**.

If f is a function, such as

```
f = {['cat','gato'],['dog','perro'],['rabbit','conejo']},
```

the following expressions to iterate over f are all equivalent.

```
(for p in f)        (for [x,y] in f)     (for y = f(x))
   x := p(1);          ...                  ...
   y := p(2);       end;                 end;
   ...
end;
```

SETL also has a built-in, 0-parameter function, **newat**, as shown in listing (9.4). **Newat** is similar to **gensym** in LISP, and generates a new atom. No operations are permitted on atoms, but they can be compared for equality or inequality. One use of atoms is to provide unique keys in a database, since **newat** produces a uniquely new atom at each invocation.

```
program IdList;                                          (9.4)

NameList := {};                 $Initialize NameList
(for i in [1..10])
   Id := newat;                 $Create a unique new atom
                                $and assign it to Id.
   print ('Enter name and address');[6]
   read (Name, Address);
   Info := [Id, Name, Address];
   NameList := NameList with Info;
       $Add Info to NameList
end;
```

---

5 In both SETL and ISETL syntax, **OM, Om, oM**, and **om** are all the same. ISETL differentiates upper- and lower-case in identifiers except in the case of OM. X and x are thus different ISETL identifiers, as are true and True.

6 The SETL **read** function reads SETL objects, i.e., sets, tuples, strings, etc. Thus values for Name and Address that contain spaces will have to be delineated by single quotes, e.g., 'Tom Jones', '105 Main'.

```
print (NameList);

end program;
```

This program will create a NameList of 10 records, each with a unique Id. Names and addresses may change, but Id will remain constant and unique.

Operators

The three binary set operators, three unary operators, and six set predicates were defined in "Definitions and operations on sets," along with their SETL symbols.

If S is a set, `S := S with x;` produces the set S, with x inserted. This statement can also be written with the operator on the left side, as in C. `S with:= x;` If T is a tuple, `T with:= x;` appends the element x to T, enabling the implementation of the "push" operator for a stack or "enque" for a queue. An element can be removed from the beginning or end of a tuple using **fromb** or **frome**. `x frome T;` removes the end item from T and assigns it to x, behaving like a "Pop" from a stack, and `x fromb T;` "deques" the first element from the tuple T, assigning it to x. If S is a set, `x from S;` removes an arbitrary element from S and assigns it to x, and is equivalent to the code:

```
x := arb S;        $Choose any element of S
S := S less x;     $Remove it from S
```

Besides the usual arithmetic operators, SETL includes the Boolean operators, **not, and, or,** and **impl** (implication). A statement such as

```
(not(raining_tomorrow) and car_working) impl go_swimming;
```

will return **#T** or **#F**, depending on the truth values of raining_tomorrow, car_working and go_swimming. SETL also provides the logical predicate symbols, **exists** and **forall**, which behave as defined in Chapter 2, for the predicate calculus.

exists x **in** S | C(x), where C(x) is a Boolean condition, is equivalent to [Baxter, 1989, p. 233]:

```
{x : x in S | C(x)} /= {};
```

and **forall** x **in** S | C(x) is equivalent to the loop:

```
G := {};
for x in S do
  if C(x) then G with:= x; end;
end;
G = S
```

SETL supports compound operators, as in APL. `+/[0,1,2,3]` yields 6, `*/{0,1,2,3}` gives 0, and `*/{x in [0,1,2,3] | x > 0}` yields 6. `+/[0,1,2,3]` also produces 6. `+/[]` gives **OM**, while `1 +/[]` returns the value 1. The 1 preceding the +/ provides a user-defined default value instead of the language defined **OM**. In ISETL, compound operators are written %op instead of op/, as in SETL.

Variables are never undefined, and the ? operator queries whether a variable is **OM** or not. X ? Y returns the value X, if X is defined. If X is **OM**, X ? Y returns Y. X := X ? 0 + 1 provides an abbreviation for

```
if X = OM then X := 0;   end;
X := X + 1;
```

? can also skip over **OM**s in a list. ?/[OM,OM,2,1] will return 2, the first non-OM value of the tuple.

SETL allows user-defined prefix or infix operators. The names of such operators must be preceded by ".". The operator .dot, defined as

```
op .dot(u,v);
    if #u /= #v then
        print ('mismatched length,'u,v);
        return OM;
    else  return +/[u(i)*v(i):i in [1..#v]];   end;
end op;
```

will return the dot product of two tuples. Thus, [1,3,5] .dot [2,4,20] = 1*2 + 3*4 + 5*20 = 114.

EXERCISES

1. SETL makes no provision for the complementation operator on sets, i.e., A' = {x | x **notin** A} is not defined. Why do you think this decision was made? Consider the set, MyPets of "Definitions and operations on sets." How would you define MyPets'?

2. The composite operator */[x **in** t | x /= 0] is the product of all nonzero components of t. If t = [0,5,0,5,0,5], this product is 125. If we write, */{x in t | x /= 0}, the product is 5. Why are the answers different? ■

Control Structures

Conditionals and loops

The SETL conditional is the usual

```
if...then...{elseif...}[else...]end;
```

The general SETL loop structure is

```
loop [init istatement]
     [doing dstatements][while wtest][step sstatements]
     [until utest][term tstatement]
do statement
end;
```

The simplest loop is

```
loop do                         ()
  statements        or        statements
end;                          end;
```

Iteration in SETL can be over the following:

strings   `(for c in 'zippedy-doo-dah') | c /= '-')...end;`

sets   `(for x in S)...end;`, or

tuples   `(for x in ['A','B','C','D'])...end;`.

The following loops all achieve the same objective [Schwartz, 1986, p. 137].

```
a: (for i in [1..10]) print (i); end ;
b: i := 1;
     (while i <= 10 step i +:= 1;) print (i); end;
c: (init i := 1; while i <= 10 step i +:= 1;)
     print (i); end;
d: loop init i := 1; until i >= 10 step i +:= 1; do
        print (i); end;
```

equivalently,

```
   (init i := 1; step i +:= 1; until i >= 10) print (i); end;
e: (init i := 0; doing i +:= 1; while i <= 10) print (i);
end;
```

Look at these loops carefully. Do you see the differences?

An iteration of a loop can be broken with a **continue** statement. When **continue;** is encountered, any remaining statements in the loop will be skipped and the next iteration started.

Procedures

SETL does not differentiate between procedures and functions. A procedure can **return** any data object, be it a simple data type, set, tuple, or string. OM is returned if the **return** statement is omitted. In ISETL, a **func** may include a **return** statement or not. ISETL 3.0 includes a **proc**, which generates an error if a **return** is included. Let's consider in listing (9.5) a simple program example for sorting and then printing a set of names. (Line numbers are for reference only and are not a part of SETL.)

```
1  program Sort_and_Print;                    (9.5)
2    proc sort, I_O;

3    S1 := {6,5,3,9};
4    I_O(S1);
5    T1 := sort(S1);
6    I_O(S1);
7    I_O(T1);
```

```
8  proc sort (s);
9    t := [];
10   while s /= {}
11     t with:= (x := min/ s);   $find minimal value of s
                                 $ & add it to end of t
12     s less:= x;               $remove it from s
     end;
13   return t;
   end proc;

14 proc I_O (x)
15   print (x);
   end proc;

end program;
```

The algorithm for sort is simplicity itself:

Until s is empty repeat
    find the least element of s
    append it to t;
    remove it from s;
end;

Notice in line 2 that we announce to the SETL compiler that two procedures are coming, and then write the main program statements. Since SETL variables are untyped, **print** accepts any variable, determines the type of its value, and prints it out (line 15).

SETL, like C, does not allow nested procedures, i.e., neither sort nor I_O may have any subprocedures. Sort could call I_O and I_O could call sort, however. In interactive ISETL, where procedures precede program statements, sort could not call I_O. Do you see why?

If you ask to have some of the local variables printed after a procedure is no longer active, you may get **OM**, a nonsense value, or the most recent value of the variable. This is very much implementation dependent, and there are no guarantees about what may or may not occur.

Scope In SETL the scope of each variable is the single procedure in which it is used. SETL has a very simple structure, with only the main program block and separate blocks, one after the other, for each of its procedures. A variable, x, can, however, be made global by placing **var** x; in the main block before any executable statements.

SETL offers other parameter-passing alternatives than pass-by-value. We can declare procedure parameters to be read-write (**rw**), write-only (**wr**), or read (**rd**).

In procedure sort above, if s were read-write (**procedure** sort (**rw** s)), the value of S1 would be copied into s (which must be a left-hand-side identifier, not an expression) when sort(S1) is called at line 5. If `s := t;` is substituted for **return** `t;` (line 13), the new value of s will be written back into S1 when the procedure, sort, terminates. As we have seen, this procedure is passing a parameter by *value-result*.

If a parameter is write-only (as in Ada's **out** parameters), the value of the actual parameter will not be read into the formal parameter, but its new value will be transmitted back to the caller at procedure termination. This is useful for initialization procedures, where actual parameters would have a value of **OM**. The read designation is for documentation purposes only, as variables are read by default.

Recursion SETL supports recursion. The simplest recursion is the factorial function, so we will use it in listing (9.6).

```
program main;                                          (9.6)
proc fact;
n := 4;
num := fact(n);
print(n,' factorial is: ',num);

proc fact(n);
  if n = 1 then return 1;
  else return n*fact(n-1);
  end if;
end proc;

end program;
```

A more complicated recursive procedure is quick-sort, so named because it is one of the most efficient in terms of execution time of all sorts based on comparison of keys. The algorithm is shown in listing (9.7).

Algorithm quick-sort   (9.7)

1. Remove the first element, x.

2. Separate the remaining elements into two piles,
   small-pile = {y | y < x}
   large-pile = {y | y >= x}.

3. Quick-sort small-pile and large-pile.

4. Assemble the sorted parts into:
   small-pile + [x] + large-pile.

The SETL procedure is even easier to write than the algorithm [Schwartz, 1986, p. 191].

```
proc quick_sort(t);              $t is a tuple              (9.8)
  return if #t < 2 then t
         else
            quick_sort([y : y = t(i) | y < t(1)]
            + [t(1)]
            + quick_sort([y:y = t(i) | i > 1 and y >= t(1)]
         end;
end proc;
```

EXERCISES

1. Rewrite the SETL fragment of listing (9.4) so that the NameList of records represents a SETL function.

2. SETL has a built-in nonzero step when iterating over numbers. Thus [1,3..9] represents the sequence 1,3,5,7,9, with a step of 2. List the sequences represented by the following tuples.
   a. [2,5..17]
   b. [2,5..15]
   c. [1,1..100] (Careful here! If you have SETL or ISETL, try it out.)
   d. [20,17..–8]
   e. [ ]

3. In "Conditionals and loops," four different loop constructs were given to print out in succession the numbers 1 to 10.
   a. What is the purpose of the parentheses?
   b. When does the **doing** get evaluated—before or after the loop body?
   c. What is the difference between the **for**, **while**, and **until** construct? Be precise!

4. Write a SETL procedure to implement minval, which returns the minimum value from the set s. If you have access to a SETL or ISETL implementation, try it out to see if it works properly. Do not use **%min** if you are using ISETL or **/min** in SETL.

5. Pascal, Modula-2, and some other languages allow nested procedures, which SETL does not (although SETL2 does). Discuss the advantages and disadvantages of this rule.

6. Consider the following SETL program [Schwartz, 1986, p. 199]
```
program esoteric;
proc manipulate;
var x,y;              $x and y are now global.
x := 'initial_val of x.';
y := 'initial_val of y.';
manipulate(x, x, y);
```

```
proc manipulate(u, v, rw w);
  print('u is ', u, '  v is ',v);
  u := 'changed.';
  print('u is ', u, '  v is ',v);
  w := 'mangled';
  print('w is ', w, '  y is ',y);
end proc;

print('x is ', x, '  y is ',y);

end program esoteric;
```

a. Reread the description of passing by value-result, in Chapter 1, "Parameterization", and then state what will be printed at each of the **print** statements in **proc** manipulate.

b. What do you think will be printed at the final **print** statement just before the call to manipulate?

7. a. Using the tuple, [3,1,5,3,7], follow through the quick_sort algorithm of listing (9.7) to be sure you understand how it works.

b. Draw contour diagrams for the SETL quick_sort procedure of listing (9.8). Let your diagram represent the situation after the fourth activation of quick_sort. ∎

LAB XX: SETL1

OBJECTIVES

1. To become acquainted with the built-in data structures of SETL, in particular, sets, tuples, and maps.

2. To experiment with the various methods of representing sets and tuples by specification, iteration, and using set or tuple formers.

3. To use the various ways of retrieving entities associated with maps, such as the domain and range, domain of an element, value of an element, etc.

∎

Syntax

Reserved words and op_defs

When translating source code into an intermediate lower-level language or machine code, a compiler or interpreter must recognize certain keywords of the language. For example, if the word **procedure**, or its abbreviation **proc**, is encountered, a compiler must recognize that what follows until the corresponding **end** is a separate block that may be called repeatedly. The system must know where this block is located to be able to transfer control when a procedure call is encountered.

Different languages handle this recognition differently, some using keywords and some employing reserved words. A keyword is generally recognized in the context of the rest of the statement. For example, an **if** must be followed by a **then** to be meaningful. FORTRAN has no reserved words, which makes it difficult to translate, and PL/I has both keywords and reserved words.

Reserved words are keywords that may not be used by the programmer as identifiers. If an **if** is encountered, it *always* represents the first word of an if_statement. SETL tends to overuse reserved words, as there are 150 of them! (ISETL has 47.) Two disadvantages arise with the reserved words. The first is the obvious burden they impose on the programmer to remember all of them or have a list handy. The second is more important, however: the reserved word makes the language difficult to extend. If at a later date, new reserved words are added, old programs using these now-forbidden words as identifiers will not run.

LAB XXI: SETL2

OBJECTIVES

1. To use sets, tuples, and maps in a practical application.
2. To see and modify an example of good programming style in SETL, demonstrating prototyping techniques. ■

Syntax diagrams

In the old days, if you got syntax errors that you couldn't resolve, you walked down the hall and asked somebody. Hopefully, somebody was available. Manuals tended to be extended lists of examples, poorly indexed, and hard to read. To define a language completely and unambiguously requires more regular methods. The Backus-Naur form (BNF) has become the standard method for this task, as was discussed in Chapter 5.

Although BNF provides the precision needed, it is hard to read, particularly for a novice programmer. The syntax of a language is just a description of what comprises legal terms, expressions, statements, etc. We need some way to check syntax quickly and easily when writing a program. Charts or diagrams (sometimes called railroad charts) have become popular methods of conveying this information. They often are concise and can be carried around in a pocket or purse, but may be somewhat simplified.

SETL syntax is defined in 12 pages of diagrams [Schwartz, 1986]. Figure 9.1, for example, shows how a statement is defined.

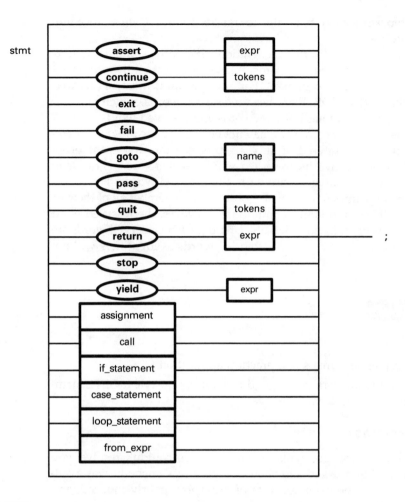

Figure 9.1

Any path entering the diagram from the left and exiting at the single exit on the right at the ";" forms a legal statement. Each of the forms listed above is defined subsequently in the chart, as shown in Figure 9.2.

To fully define the if_statement, we would have to find definitions for term, operator, and simple_iterator as well.

Some programmers find these brief charts useful, but they cannot take the place of the full BNF, which has additional advantages when constructing a parser in an interpreter or compiler, as we have seen.

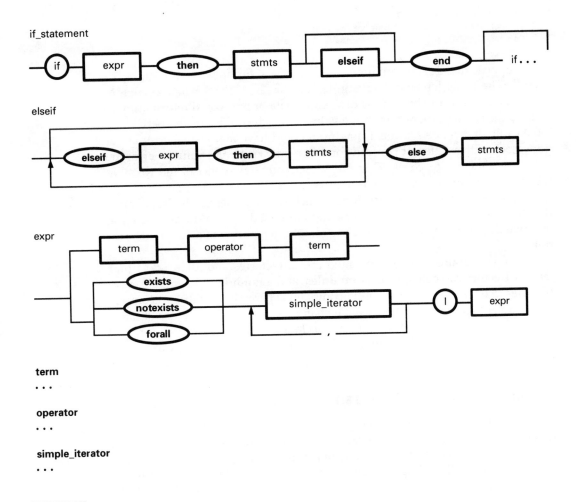

Figure 9.2

Advanced Features

SETL has several features that will only be mentioned here, as they have not been implemented so far in any of SETL2, SETLS, or ISETL. One of these features is provision for **macro**s. As you may recall, when the name of a macro appears in a program, its text is copied into the program by the compiler. For example, suppose in a program we want to check error conditions on a regular basis. We could write

```
macro check(condition, error_no);
   if not condition then return error_no; end
endm;
```

Suppose in a SETL procedure called say, Data_Input, we wrote, check(x < 5000,1). The compiler would substitute: **if not** (x < 5000) **then return** 1; **end**;. The effect would be that the procedure Data_Input would return immediately to the calling program with the value 1, which could transfer, perhaps, to a data_out_of_bounds routine. Data_Input could have many such error conditions, each with a different Boolean condition and a different value of error_no, using the same macro, check. Thus our source code stays concise, and we avoid the expense at run time of procedure calls.

SETL also supports backtracking, which we discussed in the last chapter. Backtracking utilizes the primitives **ok** and **fail**. **ok** divides a running program into two duplicate copies, and **fail** triggers the generation of an alternate solution.

Long programs can be segmented into **directories**, **modules**, and **libraries**. A **directory** can contain many **module**s, and a **module** can contain several **libraries**. Each of these units can be compiled separately, avoiding recompilation of an entire program when a small change is made and the re-use of libraries of utility procedures. Although type declarations are not required for SETL programs, they are available and used frequently when interfacing various program parts.

Efficiency: The Data Representation Sublanguage (DRSL)

SETL is inefficient in use of memory and execution time for two reasons. The first occurs in checking types. To evaluate the expression x **in** S, the type of both x and S must be determined. (As you remember, SETL has sets, tuples, maps, and strings, as well as simpler types such as integers or Booleans.) A tuple or string is stored as an array in most languages, with a header providing an index into the array.

A set or map is stored as a linked list, with an associated hash function to locate elements. A hash function, h(x), computes a memory address from the value of its argument x. A hash function, h, need not be one-to-one, so h(x) = h(y) may be true even if x /= y. That is, two different elements may hash to the same address. When elements are stored, this so-called collision must be resolved, and another storage location found for y. This storage and look-up method causes further inefficiencies.

The implementers of SETL developed a Data Representation Sublanguage (DRSL) to address these expenses. To speed up type checking, types may be declared in the DRSL. To address hashing problems, addresses of items placed in a set or map are remembered in a base set. Base sets are declared in the DRSL through basing declarations.

A program written in the pure SETL described briefly above is said to be a *supplemented program* when translated by the DRSL into a typed and based form. The output from the two programs should be the same, but a supplemented program may abort, where its pure version may run to completion, and the errors encountered in a pure program may be different from those in the supplemented version. The appearance of a supplemented program is a series of DRSL declarations surrounding the pure SETL code. The programmer is responsible for both the pure SETL and the DRSL supplement.

Applications

The Ada/Ed compiler

Ada, the language written on commission for the U.S. Department of Defense (DOD), is the largest and most complex language design project ever undertaken. Not only did it include separate compilation of packages and the facility for embedding programs in working military equipment, but parallel execution of program parts as well. The design was only part of the job. What was needed were "working sketches of the system in order to demonstrate its functionality to potential users" [Kruchten, 1984].

The NYUADA project at New York University was started as a small-scale optimization effort in 1978. As it proceeded, it became clear that the Ada definition at the time contained a number of ambiguities. SETL was used for two purposes, first as an interpreter of Ada code to a source code intermediate between Ada and machine code, and second as a rigorous definition of Ada. With an expenditure of only 100 person-months, Ada/Ed became the first validated Ada compiler in April 1983.

Being a large and complex language, Ada contained semantic problems— just what program code meant or just what it would do on execution. The semantics were of two kinds: static semantics, or name resolution, and dynamic semantics, or memory management. In Ada/Ed SETL maps are used to model variable names in various program environments. The environments, as realized dynamically in memory, are stacked on a tuple called ENV_STACK, and a composite map, CONTENTS(EMAP(E)), describes the value of each entity, E, in the environment currently executing. (For the time being, we can think of an environment as a procedure block, including the variables known within it.)

No attempt was made to devise an efficient Ada/Ed. The goal was to ignore all such distractions until all semantic questions about Ada had been fully resolved. The final version, Ada/Ed-C, was rewritten in C. Although still not very efficient, it was the first compiler to implement the complete Ada, demonstrating at least that it could be done.

Implementations

SETL2

SETL2 is being developed under the direction of W. Kirk Snyder at New York University as a successor to SETL [Snyder, 1990]. Its compiler is written in ANSI C. Compiling and executing a SETL2 program is accomplished in two steps, STLC <program name>, followed by STLX <program name>. The SETL2 compiler requires 600K bytes of memory, but the 80286 version can take advantage of any available extended memory.

Its main differences from SETL are:

1. It allows nested block structure of procedures, as in Pascal or Ada.

2. SETL2 procedures are first-class objects that may be passed to and returned from procedures.

3. An iterator, such as a **for** or **while** introduces a block, with its bound variables local to that block, as in Pascal, e.g., in **while** x **in** S **loop** ... **end**; the variable x will be renamed to a new atom and will have the value **OM** on exit from the loop.

4. SETL2 allows the separate compilation of modules, called packages, following the notions of Ada packages. SETL's typeless variables make this compilation much simpler than in Ada.

5. Several of SETL2's control structures are more Ada-like than before, e.g., a SETL while loop is written:

```
loop while <condition> do
  <statements>
end [optional tokens];
In SETL2, this is:
while <expression> loop
  <statements>
end;
```

6. SETL2 does not include SETL's macro or backtracking facilities.

In ISETL, funcs and procs are assigned names, e.g.,

```
Square := func(x)
        return x*x;
      end;
```

This notion was not implemented in SETL. SETL2 does so through lambda expressions, e.g.:

```
Square := lambda(x)
        return x*x;
      end;
```

As of January 1990, SETL2 was available from the project director for MS-DOS 3.0 or higher, Apple Macintosh, Sun-3™ running UNIX, Sun-4™ running

SunOS™, and DEC VAX running VMS or BSD UNIX. No efforts are being made to disseminate SETL2 widely, as it is still being developed. The finished version will probably be distributed as SETL3.

SETLS

SETLS is a subset of SETL, closer to the full SETL than SETL2 or ISETL and designed for microcomputers. It requires only 80K bytes of memory. It was developed originally by Nigel Chapman at the University of Leeds and is being maintained and developed at New York University by J. VandeKopple [Vande-Kopple, 1989].

The system consists of a translation and an execution phase. The first phase, based on SPITBOL, compiles SETLS code into an intermediate language, Indirect Threaded Code (ITC), which is interpreted on execution. This code runs substantially faster than ISETL.

The major omissions from the full SETL are (as of 12/90):

1. Real numbers

2. Modules and directories (not in ISETL)

3. Macros (not in ISETL or SETL2)

4. Backtracking (not in ISETL or SETL2)

5. User-defined operators (not in SETL2)

6. Arbitrary precision integers

7. Labels and goto (not in ISETL or SETL2)

8. Representation sublanguage and all REPR declarations (not in ISETL or SETL2)

SETLS is currently available for MS-DOS 2.1 or higher from NYU (see the Appendix). An 80386 version is also being developed for future release.

We will consider here a SETLS program to find an Euler path in a directed graph. A graph is a set of nodes and edges between nodes. If x and y are nodes, and [x,y] is an edge, then you can travel from x to y. If g is an undirected graph, an edge between node x and node y also indicates an edge between nodes y and x. A path from node a to node b means that you can go from a to b, following edges from various nodes, starting at a and ending at b. Thus a path might be [a,e,f,g,b], where [a,e], [e,f], [f,g], and [g,b] are all edges.

An Euler path in a graph is a path that traverses all edges without repetition. It is a well-known theorem that a graph has an Euler path if all the nodes (except possibly the start and finish nodes) have the same number of paths into the node as out. Finding the path, however, is more complicated than deciding whether there is one or not.

Consider the undirected graph shown in Figure 9.3.

The program below to find an Euler path was first presented in [Schwartz, 1986] and translated to SETLS by J. VandeKopple (see [VandeKopple, 1989]).

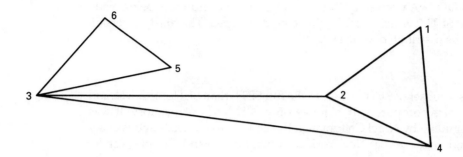

Figure 9.3

```
$Sample program
program euler;                  $ Eulerian path construction
proc euler_path,build_path;     $SETLS proc predeclarations
var g;                          $permit use of g in procs

g := {[1,2],[2,3],[3,4],[4,1],[4,2],[3,5],[3,6],[5,6]};
print('initial graph: ',g);
g +:= {[y,x]: [x,y] in g};      $form undirected graph
print('Euler path: ',euler_path);

proc euler_path;                $constructs eulerian path for g
  nodes := domain g;            $all nodes in the graph
    if #(odds := {x in nodes | odd(#g{x})}) > 2 then
      print('too many odd ordered nodes');
      return om;                $since more than two nodes
    end if;                     $are touched by an odd
                                $number of edges

      $odds is the set of all nodes of g that are touched by
      $an odd number of edges

    x:= (arb odds) ? arb nodes; $pick a node of odds if
                                $possible
                                $otherwise pick any node of g
    path := [x] + build_path(x);

    (while exists z = path(i) | g{z} /= {})
      new_p := build_path(z);   $insert new section into path
      path := path(1..i) + new_p + path(i+1 ..);
    end;

    return path;
end proc;
```

```
proc build_path(x);    $builds maximal path section starting
                       $at x, and deletes all edges traversed
  p := [];
  (while (y := arb g{x}) /= om) $while there exists an edge
                               $from the last point
      p with:= y;              $extend path to y
      g -:= {[x,y],[y,x]};     $delete edge just traversed
      x := y;                  $step to y
  end;
  return p;
end proc;

end program;
```

Rather than discuss here the generation of one such path, [2, 1, 4, 2, 3, 5, 6, 3, 4], the reader should trace the program from its input graph,

```
{[1,2],[2,3],[3,4],[3,5],[3,6],[4,1],[4,2],[5,6]}.
```

Notice that at each step an arbitrary path is chosen (lines 15 and 27). The key action occurs in the **while** of lines 19 through 22. While untraveled edges remain

```
(while exists z = path(i) | g{z} /= {}),
```

new path sections are built and inserted. Using this clever device, backtracking is automatic if a dead end is reached. Try it!

ISETL

ISETL [Levin, 1987] is an interpreted, interactive version of SETL and is being used at several colleges as a first programming language and in discrete mathematics courses. Since there is no need to declare variables to get started, it is as easy to use as BASIC, but supports numerous data structures automatically. Students can manipulate stacks and queues, sets, vectors, and lists without having to implement them themselves. This low level of needed programming expertise makes both SETL and ISETL attractive to beginners as well as researchers.

ISETL differs from SETL in some ways. Since it is interactive, a ";" is used as a request for output as well as a statement terminator. Thus 2 + 3; will return 5. **func**s as well as **proc**s are provided, with an error returned if a **proc** contains a **return** statement. Both procedures and functions are assigned to variables, e.g.:

```
Fib := func(n);...end;
```

Fib can then be passed or returned from other functions.

Like SETLS, ISETL is smaller than SETL. The omissions generally represent unimplemented features like modules and libraries. A few inconsistencies are annoying, such as the use of the double quote (") to delineate strings, rather than SETL's single quote ('), and the substitution of **image** for SETL's **range**. ISETL variable names are case sensitive, so that MyFile is different from MYFILE.

One of the big differences is in the handling of global variables. As was mentioned, variables in SETL are local to a procedure unless declared to be global through a **var** statement. In ISETL, this is not the case. Variables must be declared **local** in a procedure or they are considered global, even though they have not appeared in the calling program.

The **value** declaration causes the value of the global variable at the time the **func** or **proc** is created to be used. As an example, consider the definition of the function gs [Levin, 1988, p. 14].

```
gs := [func(x); value N; return x + 3 * N; end :
             N in [1..3]];
```

gs(2)(4) is 4 + 3 * 2. gs is not created until N is passed a value, in this case 2. In this way, tuples of functions, e.g., $[gs_N(x) : N$ **in** $[1..3]]$, can be created.

ISETL was developed at Clarkson University for use in freshman-level mathematics courses, but has recently moved to the West Publishing Co., where some of the unimplemented SETL features will be added. It is currently available for MS-DOS 3.0 or Macintosh systems, and possibly others.

9.3 SUMMARY

In this chapter, we have reviewed the axiomatic foundations of set theory, noting particularly the extreme care needed when forming sets to avoid inconsistencies. Sets are unordered collections of items, so iteration over them will occur in an arbitrary order. If one wishes an ordered collection, a tuple is used. A set of pairs, [x,y], is the basis for a map or single-valued map, called a function. A potentially infinite map may also be defined using

```
proc <function name>... return <value>...end;
```

Sets have proved useful in solving problems of various types, and are very high-level abstract data types. Sets can be implemented in rather limited ways in many imperative languages, but the first language to implement sets directly as an ADT including all the usual set operations is SETL. Three later versions are still being developed: SETL2, SETLS, and an interactive educational version, ISETL.

All versions include sets, tuples, and maps as built-in data types, and variables are completely untyped. Although SETL, SETL2, and SETLS are compiled, execution is through interpreting intermediate code into which source code was compiled. The compiled versions are particularly useful for rapid prototyping, while the interactive version can be used by naive programmers to explore sophisticated mathematical and logical notions.

9.4 NOTES ON REFERENCES

Two excellent books on set theory are [Halmos, 1960] and [Suppes, 1960]. The latter is a strictly axiomatic development, while the former provides a more casual approach. It is hard to say which is easier to read, although Halmos is certainly shorter.

A complete text with many examples, written for beginners wishing to program in SETL, is [Schwartz, 1986]. An interesting description of the prototyping of an early version of the NYU Ada compiler using SETL is described in [Kruchten, 1984].

The "Draft Report on Requirements for a Common Prototyping System" can be found in [Gabriel, 1989]. The future programmer or software engineer might find it interesting to see how requests for proposals (RFPs) are written up and the big jobs assigned.

ISETL systems come with a *very* brief user's guide [Levin, 1987] and [Levin, 1988]. A user's manual, written by Jeannie Dauterman should be available in late 1991. An ISETL user can determine most of what is needed using *Learning Discrete Mathematics with ISETL* [Baxter, 1989]. Guides for SETLS [VandeKopple, 1989] and SETL2 [Snyder, 1990] are available from the developers.

10

LANGUAGES FOR NOVICES, BUSINESS, AND SPECIFIC APPLICATIONS

Organizing programming languages into paradigms may give the (false) impression that a well-grounded theory preceded the development of each language. This has definitely not been the case, and will probably continue not to be the case. Real life is much more complicated than that. One way that languages arise is to meet special needs. These needs may be for particular groups of users or particular application areas. We will look at a few such "special-purpose" languages here. There is no particular reason for choosing the examples, and they are neither exhaustive nor do they represent one of each sort.

10.0 LANGUAGES FOR NOVICES

FORTRAN was developed in the fifties as the first high-level programming language and was directed toward the scientific community. Scientists can be expected to be mathematically sophisticated and comfortable with symbolic notation. They also understand vectors and arrays and have a general feel about equipment of various sorts. Many others who could benefit from using computers do not. We will call such people novices. They are naive about computers, the hard sciences, or both.

LOGO for Learning

As with most issues involved in raising children, the idea of toddlers in front of computer screens horrifies some while delighting others. Video games have become a big commercial success and occupy many hours of time for the young and not so young. Research in how to harness computer power to the benefit of children and others with learning styles different from the norm resulted in the computer language LOGO. Scholastic learning is heavily geared to those with well-developed language skills. Those who reason best in terms of pictures and objects in space, rather than words, are at a disadvantage. It was to tap concrete spatial skills and relate them to more abstract geometric concepts that LOGO was first devised.

HISTORICAL VIGNETTE 14: LOGO: Seymour Papert

When one thinks of LOGO, images of pretty pictures drawn with the LOGO "turtle" on elementary school computer screens might come to mind. The LOGO language is widely used to teach kids about computers, and some contend that it should replace BASIC as the most widely used educational language. LOGO's success in becoming an educational tool stems from its stable groundings in psychology.

LOGO was first devised in the late sixties by Seymour Papert, an educator and mathematician at the Massachusetts Institute of Technology (MIT). Papert had spent several years working with the famous Swiss developmental psychologist, Jean Piaget, who saw intellectual development as having four main stages: sensorimotor, pre-operational, concrete operational, and formal operational.

The sensorimotor stage covers the period when children move from a newborn's reflexes to a more highly organized sort of activity. In this stage, children learn such things as seeing themselves as different from objects around them, defining things by manipulating them, and regarding an object as constant despite a change in its location or the child's point of view: for example, learning that closing your eyes does not make everything disappear.

The preoperational stage covers roughly ages two to seven. During this time, children are busy using and learning language and developing general concepts about the physical world about them. They learn to classify and arrange objects according to their attributes, such as shape, size, or color. The world is quite concrete.

The concrete operational stage stretches from 7 to about 11 years of age. Children still deal with the world on a concrete level, but become capable of various logical operations on concrete objects. Geometric notions of area and volume are quite understood and manageable.

It is the formal operational stage, which lasts from about 11 to 14, in which children finally learn to think abstractly. Abstract thinking can be defined as the ability to deal with what could be possible in addition to what is here and now. At this stage, children can draw conclusions, offer interpretations, and develop hypotheses.

None of these age spans are written in stone. Generally, children have a difficult time understanding and using formal operations and need to be guided into ways of thinking abstractly. Papert realized that learning many mathematical principles is an abstract process, especially in geometry where so much needs to be visualized. Wasn't there a way to make an abstract subject like geometry more visually concrete to enable young students to understand it? If they could just *see* geometry in action, if they could actively manipulate figures just as a young child can manipulate a ball, math anxiety might be lessened as understanding grew.

LOGO became Papert's concrete model. The language was designed in the mid-sixties by Papert and a group of researchers at Bolt, Berenak and Newman (BBN) in Cambridge, Massachusetts. The BBN group had been involved in computer-aided instruction (CAI) research in mathematics education before Papert joined them. When he came along, a new direction was taken to design a language for kids, based on LISP. Papert made it more user-friendly by including English-like commands and a powerful tool called "turtle graphics" for producing geometric figures.

The version of LOGO I worked with has more than 200 primitives from such things as **show** 1 + 7, which prints 8, through **forward** 22, moving a "turtle" 22 units in the direction it is heading, to **savepic** <filename>, which saves a screenful of graphics as a binary file named <filename>. LOGO is procedural and extensible. Users can create new units (essentially procedures) and the unit names become indistinguishable from the original LOGO primitives. As many new units as memory permits can be defined.

In 1948, Grey Walter, a British neurophysiologist, developed a mechanical tortoise that rolled around. Its state was defined by its position on the floor, the direction in which it was headed, called its *orientation*, and the status of its pen, either up or down. LOGO's real claim to fame was its moving of this tortoise robot to the computer screen through a group of primitives making up "turtle graphics." This package makes geometry concrete through an attractive animal metaphor. Imagine that the cursor on the computer screen is actually an animate creature, say a turtle. Imagine further that the turtle can be made to move around the screen. You give it instructions about which way to move and how far and how fast to go. Finally, imagine that the turtle is like a snowplow that can ride along the street with its blade either raised or lowered. If you raise the turtle-plow, the turtle moves about the screen without leaving a trace. If you lower the plow, the turtle leaves a line in its wake. Recently, colors have been added to LOGO implementations and the ability to work with multiple turtles in different colors at the same time.

LOGO's extensibility and graphics capabilities are the two main features that have made it a popular educational tool. Extensibility encourages students to be creative, while graphics allow them to play with abstract mathematical concepts, helping to cross the bridge from the concrete to the formal operational stage.

The question remains about how well LOGO competes with BASIC as an educational tool. By the time LOGO hit the market, BASIC was already becoming the norm in elementary school classrooms. Some educators believe that BASIC is rigid and stifles creativity, while LOGO encourages it. Others advocate using BASIC in computer literacy courses, since it resembles standard imperative languages like FORTRAN and Pascal, and LOGO for teaching younger children to think.

LOGO, however, is not just for kids. Since Papert stressed its capabilities as an educational tool for children, it is often overlooked as an artificial intelligence programming tool. "As a direct subset of LISP, it is convenient for analyzing classes of information and the relationships between them because of its underlying list structure [Baron, 1986]." Unlike LISP, LOGO has small memory requirements (48K to 64K of RAM), which makes it ideal for home computer enthusiasts and classrooms where AI is the topic under discussion.

LOGO has also been used successfully with handicapped people. A dramatic example of how LOGO helped untrap the intelligence of Michael Murphy, a quadriplegic with cerebral palsy, is movingly described in *Cultivating Minds: A LOGO Casebook* [Weir, 1987]. Ten hours each week of work with LOGO over many years at the MIT Media Laboratory helped transform Murphy from a nonfunctioning individual into a successful college undergraduate. As Papert says in the introduction [p. x], "Cases like Michael Murphy exhibit one of these factors [among many] in a very pure and powerful form: empowerment of the most elemental kind. Put yourself, if you can, in the place of someone who has never made any physical thing, someone who has never made a mud pie or a drawing or an arrangement of flowers. Suppose also that your ability to speak is so restricted by severe dysarthria that you have never made a speech or even told a story. Then imagine what this machine can mean to you. You can draw on its screen. You can make texts out of words and keep them in your private space, no longer subjected to the favors and the scrutiny of a scribe. I don't think you can imagine these things. But you can grasp enough to know that an encounter with this machine could be the beginnings of profound change in your sense of who you are and of how you might shape your life."

With its user-friendliness, graphics capabilities, extensibility, and educational and AI programming capabilities, LOGO will probably be around for quite a while.

LOGO for "messing around"

LOGO is an interactive language, so a user must first enter the LOGO command environment by some such command as >**Logo**. One is then confronted by the LOGO turtle in the center of the screen. The turtle has two separate operations; it can turn any specified number of degrees and it can move either **forward** or **back**, with the "pen" either up (**pu**) or down (**pd**).[1] Moves can be accomplished by typing **forward** # (**fd** #) or **back** # (**bk** #), where '#' represents the number of steps to move.

---

1 LOGO commands can be spelled out in full, e.g., **penup** or abbreviated, **pu**. Most LOGO users move to abbreviated forms quickly.

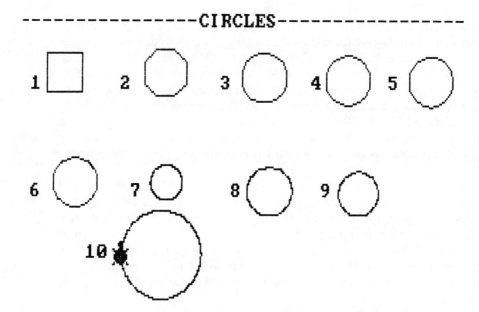

Figure 10.1

Each LOGO **page** has a flipside, accessed through <control> F, where any user-written procedures can be written and/or looked at. Listing (10.1) shows screen output from the procedure drawcircle.

```
to circle :angle :dist            to circle2 :x :y :angle :dist      (10.1)
circle2 xcor ycor :angle :dist    drawcircle
end                               end


to drawcircle
forward :dist    right :angle
if and (xcor = :x) (ycor = :y)
[stop]
drawcircle
end
```

We could have used only one procedure:

```
to circle :angle :dist
fd :dist rt :angle
end
```

and stopped the drawing with <control> BREAK, but using three procedures allows us to pass the starting *x* and *y* coordinates of the turtle (**xcor, ycor**) to circle2, without the user having to worry about it, and to pass no values to the recursive procedure drawcircle. "Messing around" with a procedure that stops when it arrives back at the starting point gives some very interesting results.

The exercise is a typical LOGO experiment in convergence. Students are told that a circle can be constructed by the turtle going a short distance and then turning right repeatedly. The first figure (Figure 10.1) is the result of the command, circle 90 25 representing a turn of 90°, and a distance of 25 units producing a square. Figures 2 through 6 resulted from reducing both the angle and the distance by half each time. But in figure 7, something interesting happened. The command, circle 1.95625 0.390625, was an error from the pattern of halving the previous parameters. This time, the turtle never stopped at all, but kept going round and round for a half-hour before the procedure was interrupted from the keyboard.

Correcting the inputs for figure 7 to circle 1.40625 0.390625 also produced an infinitely revolving turtle drawing, figure 8. In figure 9, circle 1 0.25, the turtle stopped after one revolution, but in figure 10, circle 1.5625 0.78125, it went around six times before stopping in the starting position. Why? Are there some magic numbers? Would the procedures drawing figures 7 and 8 have stopped if only they had run longer? Why six revolutions in figure 10? Is there something fairly interesting going on here, or is it just the limited precision of the computer being used?

It is these sorts of observations that give LOGO its reputation as a "language for learning." One does not, however, just turn students loose in a computer lab to mess around and expect them to learn anything important. As Sylvia Weir points out [Weir, 1987], using LOGO well requires a good computational environment and well-thought-out exercises that are usually the work of an interdisciplinary team involving computational, educational, psychological, and subject-matter specialists.

LOGO for the learning disabled

Just such a team has been working at a school for disabled children in Brookline, Massachusetts. The following story was created with teacher assistance by Chris, an eighth grader who had been working with LOGO for about a year [Weir, 1987, p. 104]. Figure 10.5 shows the procedures involved in the story.

The "gunfight" procedure pauses after "The bad guys showed up first!!!" before printing the left group of figures. The "good guys" appear similarly after a pause. That Chris has both a well-developed vocabulary and sense of humor is evidenced by the long pause between "Your mother" and "wears army boots!" (See Figure 10.2.)

Here, the "good guys" shoot the "bad guys" with "gunfire" that moves between the two groups, as shown in Figure 10.3. Chris had learned about procedures the previous year and used one called "shot," repeated four times, to accomplish the task.

On the final page, the "bad guys" fall down, and are finally erased from the scene, as shown in Figure 10.4.

Once upon a time there were four
bad guys who were stealing from
everybody!!! There were also four
good guys in this town so they
challenged the bad guys to a gun
fight at noon time!!! At the
dust street.
The bad guys showed up
first!!!
and then the good guys!!!!
They yelled insults back and forth
for almost 5 minutes!
Then a bad guy yelled "Your mother
wears army boots!"

Figure 10.2

That did it! The good guys opened
fire on the bad guys!!!!

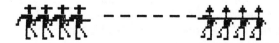

Figure 10.3

```
That ended it! The bad guys fell
to the ground and were never spoke
of again
```

Figure 10.4

Writing the story is awkward with LOGO, but better word processors are being added in newer versions. Each procedure begins with **to** <procedure name>, as shown in Figure 10.5.

Chris could see his story by entering the command, `gunfight` (line 1). The gang procedure (defined at line 14 and called at line 8), has a single integral parameter, `:num`, which will be 1, 2, or 3. **setpos** moves the turtle to the location where the gang is to be printed. The shape of each gang member is `:num + 5` (line 17), i.e., 6, 7, or 8, and was drawn and saved on a special "shapes" page previously. Shape 6 is a bad guy, shape 7 a good guy, and shape 8, a bad guy lying down. One brings a shape onto the screen by resetting a turtle's shape (**setshape**). To erase the bad guys at the end of the story, the command **penerase (pe)** is executed, followed by `gang 8` (line 13). **penerase** also occurs in the `shot` procedure (line 26), where the dashed line is first drawn (**pendown**) and then erased as the (invisible) turtle backs up (**back**) to the good guys. Line 24 together with line 26 creates animated shooting on the screen.

Weir reports that children given the opportunity to animate their stories can sometimes start writing when they have never done so before.

The most dramatic story in Weir's *Cultivating Minds: A LOGO Casebook* is that of Michael Murphy, a quadriplegic cerebral palsy patient. Michael's mind was literally trapped in a body that could neither write nor speak so that anyone could understand him. Given three years of work with LOGO, beginning at age 17, at the MIT Media Lab, Michael was able to communicate and gain admittance to a New England college as a computer science student. The computer allows him to be a participating member of the academic community, and eventually the world of work. Weir makes it plain, however, that years of tender loving care are needed in addition to the right computing environment.

```
1  to gunfight
2  print [Once upon a time ...]
   ...
3  print [The bad guys showed up]
4  print [first!!!]
5  wait 100
6  penup home²
7  sethead 90³  270 forward
8  gang 1 wait 50
...
9  print [That did it! The good guys opened]
10 print [fire on the bad guys!!!!]
11 wait 50
12 repeat 4 [shot]
   ...
13 penerase gang 8
14 end

15 to gang :num
16 penup
17 ifelse :num = 2 [setpos [55 -70]]
                   [setpos [-55 -70]]
18 setshape :num + 5
19 pendown
20 repeat 4 [pendown stamp penup  forward 10]
21 end

22 to shot
23 penup   setpos [55 -65]   sethead 270
24 repeat 7 [pendown forward 5 penup forward 5]
25 wait 4
26 repeat 7 [penup back 5 penerase back 5]
27 end
```

Figure 10.5

Advanced LOGO

Because of its ease of use and power, LOGO has been used and may have a future as a serious programming language. It has a built-in random-number generator and a facility for hiding procedures in "tools." Procedures can be imported from other LOGO pages (collections of procedures) and can pipe outputs into other procedures, as in C. LOGO's conditionals are:

```
if <predicate> [list of commands]
ifelse <predicate> [command list1] [command list2]
```

---

2 **home** is the center of the screen, with [**xcor, ycor**] = [0,0].
3 **sethead** <degrees> points the turtle's head in the direction represented by <degrees>, with 0° at twelve o'clock, 90° at three o'clock, etc.

As we saw above, LOGO supports an iterative **repeat** statement and recursion.

Interesting recursive applications such as the Towers of Hanoi (with animation) and MergeSort can be programmed easily through LOGO procedures, once the method is understood. In his book, *Advanced LOGO*, Michael Friendly [Friendly, 1988] describes learning about trees, natural language, and fractals, among other things, through recursive LOGO procedures.

In recent versions of LOGO, multiple different-colored turtles called "sprites" can be made active. Friendly describes various animated video games using different-shaped and -colored turtles.

LOGO has also been used for exploring the box world of robots, exploring language, and building a network model of memory called *ELINOR* [Norman, 1974]. A visual, easily programmable, extendable language like LOGO is particularly welcomed by researchers like social scientists, who do not want to spend a great deal of time developing programming skills. With only a few LOGO words, one can say some very interesting things.

EXERCISES

1. Another method for describing a circle as a limiting process is to consider both inscribed and circumscribed polygons with increasing numbers of sides and notice that the divergence between them becomes smaller and smaller. How would you write such a LOGO procedure?

2. The LOGO procedure, ARCR, to draw a right arc is defined as:

```
TO ARCR :DIST :DEG
REPEAT :DEG [FD :DIST  RT 1]
END
```

Write a LOGO procedure, ARCL, to draw a left arc, and a procedure, PETAL, to draw a flower petal.

3. Using your procedures from number 2, write a LOGO procedure to construct a daisy.

4. Write a LOGO procedure that calls other procedures to draw a house. Your procedures should include `DrawWindow`, `DrawDoor`, `DrawRoof`, etc. ∎

BASIC for Everybody

In the early sixties, it became apparent that in the future, almost all those in decision-making roles would need to know something about computing. It also became apparent that both FORTRAN and COBOL took too long to learn for anyone not intending to become a programmer. Thus a quickly learned, widely available language was urgently needed and Beginner's All-purpose Symbolic Instruction Code (BASIC) was born.

HISTORICAL VIGNETTE 15: BASIC: John Kemeny and Thomas Kurtz

In 1964, two Dartmouth professors, John Kemeny and Thomas Kurtz, developed BASIC, the most widely known computer language ever created. "Some 10 to 12 million school children have learned it. Professional programmers have exploited it to make millions of dollars in applications. More people have learned BASIC than Norwegian, Danish, and Swedish combined" [Slater, 1987, p. 244].

During the early 1960s, both Kemeny and Kurtz were professors of mathematics at Dartmouth University. Both were familiar with computers. Kemeny had been a consultant on computing to the Rand Corporation and Kurtz had worked with computers at MIT, General Electric, and the Institute for Numerical Analysis of UCLA. Both men wanted to get their students involved with computers, including those not majoring in the sciences. "Kemeny and Kurtz reasoned that nonscience students graduating from Dartmouth would be entering a world where they would need to make managerial decisions about computing" [Baron, 1986, p. 146]. How could decisions be made by people who knew little or nothing about these machines? An elementary course was clearly needed.

Two main problems had to be overcome. First, computers were not accessible. A program had to be punched on cards and then brought to a computer operator who would run it—a lengthy and troublesome process. Kemeny and Kurtz solved this problem by implementing a time-share system so that students could get hands-on computer experience. As Kurtz stated, "Lecturing about computing doesn't make any sense, anymore than lecturing on how to drive a car makes sense" [Wexelblat, 1981, p. 538]. The second problem led directly to the development of BASIC. A language for the mathematically unsophisticated was needed that was easier to learn than the complex languages available.

Kemeny and Kurtz originally tried to solve these problems through a language called DARSIMCO (DARtmouth SIMplified COde). It was still too mathematical, and FORTRAN soon made it obsolete. Simplified versions of both FORTRAN and ALGOL were also not successful among novice students.

In 1963, Kemeny began working on a rough draft of BASIC, always choosing simplicity over efficiency when there was a choice. Dartmouth students started using it in 1964. "Neither Kemeny nor Kurtz thought in grand terms then. They only hoped that BASIC would help students work with, and learn something about, computers. The two men put their invention into the public domain right away, and so they made no money from it" [Slater, 1987, p. 243].

BASIC was a success in the classroom and students did not need either a technical or mathematical background to learn it. Unlike other available programming languages, the syntax and vocabulary were simple. Users had to know only a few statements to write effective programs. This simplicity sparked the spread of BASIC in the schools. In 1976, Microsoft Corporation threw some gasoline on BASIC's wildfire spread when they got a version called Microsoft BASIC® working on a microcomputer. In the late seventies and early eighties, BASIC was the language microcomputer enthusiasts learned, as FORTRAN and COBOL were too large to fit in the memories available.

Because of its popularity, different versions of BASIC began to surface all over, much to the annoyance of Kemeny and Kurtz. Different versions made it difficult to transport a BASIC program from one machine to another and some violated the original design principles of Dartmouth BASIC.

BASIC also came under fire for its lack of structured programming support. Unlike Pascal, it is quite possible to write very unstructured programs in BASIC, due in part to the unrestricted GOTO statement. Edsgar Dijkstra [(1975). "How do we tell truths that might hurt?" from *Selected Writings on Computing*, quoted in Baron, 1986] says that "It is practically impossible to teach good programming to students that have had a prior exposure to BASIC: as potential programmers they are mentally mutilated beyond the hope of regeneration." Strong views like this prompted the College Board to use Pascal instead of BASIC for its advanced placement courses in computer science.

Kemeny and Kurtz, furious about the misuse and rapidly deteriorating good name of their language, took action. In 1985, a new version, True BASIC, became available. It is completely portable, since standard compilers are available for all machines on which it runs. It is highly structured and supports interactive graphics. True BASIC is copyrighted to avoid nonstandard versions being made available. Kemeny is chairman and Kurtz vice-chairman of True BASIC, Inc. Although you can't declare as many structured data types in it as in Pascal, the designers claim that the graphics and string-handling facilities are superior. They hope it will become a true competitor in teaching high-school and college programming courses.

The original BASIC

Since BASIC was intended for students who knew little about computers, it combined an interpreter, an editor, and parts of an operating system. BASIC monitors later included a compiler as well. When you turned on a computer, you were in the BASIC system, where you could write and run programs, execute single statements, edit programs, and so on. Students who later "graduated" to another language were quite surprised to find that they had to learn a whole list of operating system commands as well as the language itself to accomplish what had been done so easily in BASIC.

Any line that started with a line number, e.g.:

```
10 X = 35
```

was considered to be part of the current program, while those without, e.g.:

```
LIST
```

were BASIC commands. Line numbers facilitate the use of subroutines, as **GOSUB** <line #> transfers execution to <line #>, where a subroutine begins. A

RETURN statement at the end of the subroutine then transfers back to the line after the **GOSUB**.

BASIC had four control structures: **IF..THEN** statements, **FOR...NEXT** loops, **GOTO** <line #>, and **GOSUB** <line #>. That was it. Variable names were also restricted to single capital letters or a capital followed by another letter or digit (X, X1, etc.) or single letters followed by a "$" for character variables. Clever students could write quite workable programs that were unintelligible to anyone else. It was the **GOTO** that inspired the wrath of those advocating structured (i.e., planned-in-advance) programming. BASIC got a bad name for inspiring the young and impressionable to develop undisciplined programming habits.

Since BASIC was uncopyrighted, multiple incompatible versions sprang up. When it migrated to microcomputers, each vendor developed a different version. Part of the natural competition between hardware companies produced BASICs to take advantage of particular machine features. Thus BASIC became a machine-specific language, rather than a portable language in itself. Enter standardization.

True BASIC

The first standard for BASIC was published by the American National Standards Institute (ANSI) in 1978. It was for a very minimal BASIC so that implemented versions always included various enhancements. Programs using only standard BASIC would run on any system, but those using nonstandard features ran only on versions including the enhancement. Thus BASIC quickly became scores of different BASICs.

Kemeny and Kurtz's True BASIC contains all the ease of the original BASIC, but adds features that take advantage of modern microcomputers, including graphics, mathematics, and text processing.

Some of the first enhancements to Dartmouth BASIC were the **ELSE** and **ELSEIF** branches to the **IF...THEN...ELSEIF...ELSE** statement, and **DO WHILE** and **DO...UNTIL** loops. Thus Dartmouth instructors were able early on to forbid the use of **GOTO**s in student programs. True BASIC also includes various forms of **CASE** statements. String handling is also well developed. The following True BASIC code reverses a string:

```
def ReverseString$ (s$)
let Answer$ = ''''                    !The empty string
for I = len(s$) to 1 step -1
    let answer$ = answer$ & s$[I:1]   !concatenate Ith char.
next I
let ReverseString$ = Answer$
end def
```

A previously defined string, A$, can then be reversed and printed by:

```
print ReverseString(A$)
```

True BASIC includes graphics that will **PLOT POINT**s, **LINE**s, **TEXT**, or **AREA**s without having to refer to screen coordinates. A **DRAW** statement allows the user to draw various figures, **shift**ed, **rotate**d, **scale**d, or **shear**ed (tilted) by user input amounts.

True BASIC also takes advantage of windowing capabilities of microcomputers and will run on any machine.

LAB XXII: BASIC and Pascal

OBJECTIVES

1. To write the same program in an "advanced" version of BASIC and Pascal.

2. To include procedures, string handling, and graphics in the program.

3. To make judgments about the merits of each program regarding ease of implementation, error checking, and debugging. ■

SNOBOL for Naive Programmers

SNOBOL is included in this section on languages for novices, not because its potential users are young or uneducated but because they are naive as programmers. It is also interesting in its origins as a tool to fill special needs. The language began in the Programming Research Studies Department at Bell Labs, with a group of three working on methods for formula manipulation. One such activity is the factoring of multinomial expressions, such as $P(x,y,z) = (z+1)x^2 + (x + y)z^2 + xyz + zx + (x + z)y$. There are no sure-fire methods like the quadratic formula for finding the linear factors, $(x + y)(x + z)(z + 1)$. Another is symbolic integration:

$$(2x + y + z)dx = x^2 + (y + z)x + C.$$

These are nonnumerical applications, where both the expression of the problem and the results are symbolic. If the variables x, y, and z are given specific or limiting values, we could find factors or a particular value of the integral using entirely different numerical estimation methods. With nonnumerical applications, general results are desired.

In 1963, the Bell team found the languages available to them awkward as tools for their work and thought they could do better by developing a new language themselves, which they named SNOBOL.[4] They also wanted a language with research applications other than their own—including text processing and graph manipulation—a language that was simple for the naive programmer to

---

4 Ralph Griswold [Griswold, 1981] says that the name SNOBOL arose while "messing around" with the language, and his coworker Dave Farber liked it, since "it [the new language] doesn't have a snowball's chance in hell."

use. AT&T's Bell Labs is an interesting place, with young researchers sometimes allowed to go their own way for long periods of time, with no thought to developing products for AT&T. It was in this same setting that Kernhigan and Ritchie developed C. It is just coincidence that one of the first genuine applications of SNOBOL was to generate a FORTRAN program to perform analyses of telephone networks.

The designers of SNOBOL chose the string as their fundamental data type, since many systems can be represented as strings, including all existing programming languages. In the original SNOBOL everything was a string, and anything would compile without error. Of course, not everything would run. Functions were built into SNOBOL2, while other data types and the machinery for defining recursive procedures were first found in SNOBOL3.

SNOBOL4 is a different story. In 1968, new hardware was becoming available, and the developers wanted SNOBOL to run on whatever equipment they or their colleagues might have. Thus SNOBOL4 was designed to be *portable*. The most common implementation, which was distributed without cost from Bell Labs, is based on macros. A SNOBOL program is translated into code strings in Polish prefix notation, e.g., (* + 2 5 3) for ((2 + 5) * 3), which is then interpreted in software simulating a SNOBOL virtual machine. (We will not discuss virtual machines here, but refer the reader back to Chapter 6 to see one for PROLOG. Recall that a SNOBOL virtual machine is executed in software and makes the actual machine appear as if it were specially built to run only SNOBOL programs.)

In the SNOBOL virtual machine, central memory is divided into two parts: a symbol table, where all currently defined identifiers are stored and retrieved through a hash table, and a heap[5] where table values, arrays, patterns, and executable code are kept. Such storage simulation methods do not promote fast execution. However, several faster SNOBOL compilers operating quite differently have been developed. Three of these are SPITBOL (Illinois Institute of Technology), CISBOL (University of Arizona), and FASBOL (UC, Berkeley). Our examples below were coded and tested in MACRO SPITBOL VERSION 3.6(2.15) for IBM PC DOS.[6]

SNOBOL provides little incentive for structured programming or thinking ahead before starting to program. No variables need be declared, and identifiers can be assigned values of any type during execution. No facilities are provided for block structure, with its scope rules for variables and other structures. It does, however, provide two rather unique methods for programming computers, pattern matching and associative programming.

---

5 A hash table is referenced by addresses computed from the element itself. A hash function, h, is associated to the table such that h(element value) = address. A heap is unordered storage that is accessed through storage addresses. Thus if X = 'Ginny crack corn', 'Ginny crack corn' will be stored in the heap at address a and (X,a) will be in the hash table, with access via h(X).
6 Copyright © 1983, 1984, Realia, Inc.

Pattern matching

SNOBOL4 provides a data type called a *pattern*. This type defines a class of strings, with substrings matching the pattern. Two types of statements involve patterns. The first is: [label] <subject> <pattern> [:GOTO] where subject is a string in which pattern is to be found if possible. A label is optional, but the space between a label and the subject is not. Thus any unlabeled statement must start with one or more spaces. The GOTO is also optional and provides for execution transfer to different code depending on the success or failure of the match. If GOTO expressions are omitted, execution defaults to the next statement.

Matching occurs from left to right in subject and from top to bottom in a list of alternative patterns.

One of the innovative features of SNOBOL is delayed or lazy evaluation. In SNOBOL4 *E means to delay evaluation of the expression E, if possible. Let's look at the string a^2b^2, as a representative value of the class of strings, a^nb^n. If you remember from "Type 2: Context-free grammars (CFGs)" in Chapter 5, such strings can be recognized as valid in context-free grammars, and the production system for producing a^nb^n is:

S => ab | aSb

A SNOBOL4 pattern used to recognize such strings is:

```
WORD = 'ab' | 'a' *WORD 'b'
```

Here, "|" means *or* as usual. The blank between strings means concatenation, thus 'a' *WORD 'b' indicates that when WORD is evaluated, we are to concatenate an 'a' on the left, and a 'b' on the right to the string which is the current value for WORD.

Strings are surrounded by single quotes, and unquoted strings such as WORD are identifiers. A SPITBOL program to recognize strings of the form a^nb^n, follows.

```
line
nos.
*                 SPITBOL listing code, anbn.lst

1                 &anchor = 1
2                 terminal = 'Enter string of form a^n b^n :'
3                 X = terminal
4                 WORD = 'ab' | 'a' *WORD 'b'
5                 WPAT = WORD rpos(0)
6                 X WPAT                          :S(OK) F(NOTOK)
7        OK       terminal = X ' is OK.'          :(END)
8        NOTOK    terminal = X ' is not OK.'
9        END
```

Starting with line 1, **&anchor** is a toggle. When set to 1, the pattern must match, beginning with the first character of input. When **&anchor** is set to 0, the default value, a match can be found anywhere within the subject string. Anchored searching is more efficient than unanchored, since failures may be recognized without scanning the entire subject string.

In line 5, the pattern WPAT is set to WORD **rpos**(0). This setting indicates that when WORD is matched, there must be 0 characters to the right of the match remaining to be scanned. In line 6, the blank between X and WPAT indicates that SPITBOL is to try to match WPAT with some substring in X. This use of a blank is not to be confused with its use to indicate concatenation. The GOTO is **:S**(OK) F(NOTOK), where **S** stands for success and will transfer control to the statement labeled "OK" if X matches WPAT **rpos**(0). If the match fails (**F**), control will be transferred to "NOTOK."

Matching will proceed as:

String	Pattern
'aabb'	WPAT
'aabb'	WORD **rpos**(0)
'aabb'	'a' *WORD 'b' **rpos**(0)

Here the second alternative succeeds, so *WORD is evaluated using the first alternative, yielding:

```
'aabb'    'a' 'ab' 'b'  rpos(0)
```

The concatenated pattern matches an initial substring of the subject 'aabb', and there are no characters to the right of the cursor, i.e., `rpos(0)` is true. Thus the subject matches WORD and control is transferred to the statement labeled OK, where "aabb is OK." is printed.

The second pattern-matching statement is of the form:

```
[label] <subject> <pattern> = [PatternToBeSubstituted].
```

The Pattern to be substituted is optional. If there is no pattern on the right side, the null string is substituted for <pattern> if a match is found in <subject>. This pattern match corresponds to an erasing rule. If X = 'Ginny crack corn', then:

```
X 'corn' = 'nuts'
```

gives X, the value 'Ginny crack nuts'.

```
X 'corn' =
```

makes the value of X, 'Ginny crack'.

We will use this statement type in a SNOBOL procedure to recognize strings from a context-sensitive grammar. This use is possible, since there are no restrictions to the number of symbols appearing in <pattern>. Remember that a context-free rule requires a single nonterminal on the left of the assignment (=)

sign, but context-sensitive grammars allow any number of symbols on the left, as long as one is a nonterminal.

As you may recall from "Type 2: Context-free grammars" in Chapter 5, "$a^n b^n c^n$" is an example of a word pattern that is context sensitive but not context free. The rules to generate strings, such as 'aaaabbbbcccc', are:

1. S → aBC
2. S → aSBC
3. CB → BC
4. aB → ab
5. bB → bb
6. bC → bc
7. cC → cc

Since we are attempting to recognize an already-formed string, we will reverse the steps used to generate it. For example, the last production rule to generate strings of the form $a^n b^n c^n$, is cC → cc, so reversing it yields cc → cC. There is, however, one problem. All our production rules scanned from left to right, so to reverse the procedure, we need to scan from right to left. SNOBOL also scans strings from left to right, so we will reverse X before proceeding, to simulate a right-left scan.

Lines 2 through 4 of the SPITBOL code below reverse string X. The local variable Y is first assigned the null string (line 2). Line 3 repeatedly removes the first character from X, assigning it to C. C is then concatenated onto Y (line 4). We are then ready to analyze the reversed string from left to right.

The first match and replace statement can be found on line 5:

```
Y 'cc' = 'Cc'
```

This means when traversing the string Y from left to right, if the pattern, 'cc' is encountered, it is to be replaced with 'Cc'. When the match fails, execution will continue at line 6, where 'cb' will be replaced with 'Cb'.

```
1              DEFINE('MATCH3N(X)','START')            :(MAIN)
   * First reverse the input string, X, to simulate
   * right to left scan
2    START   Y = ''
3    REVERSE X len(1) . C =                        :F(LOOP1)
4      Y = C Y                                     :(REVERSE)
   *
5    LOOP1   Y 'cc'   = 'Cc'                   :S(LOOP1)
6            Y 'cb'   = 'Cb'
7    LOOP2   Y 'bb'   = 'Bb'                   :S(LOOP2)
8            Y 'ba'   = 'Ba'
9    LOOP3   Y 'CCB'  = 'CBC'                  :S(LOOP3)
```

```
10   LOOP4    Y 'CBa'  =                    :S(LOOP4)
11            IDENT(Y '')                   :S(RETURN)F(FRETURN)
12
13   MAIN     terminal =
14            terminal = 'enter string of form anbncn:'
15            A = terminal
16            MATCH3N(A)                     :S(OK)  F(NOTOK)
17   OK       terminal = A ' is OK.'        : (MAIN)
18   NOTOK    terminal = A ' is not OK.'    : (MAIN)
19   END
```

The production statements of Chapter 5—7, 6, 5, 4, 3, and 2—correspond in the SPITBOL program above to lines 5, 6, 7, 8, 9, and 10 respectively. The action of lines 5 through 9 changes reversed input such as Y = 'cccbbbaaa' to CBCBCBaaa. LOOP4 repeatedly erases the pattern 'CBa' (X 'CBa' =), corresponding to production rule 2. The final erasure corresponds to rule 1. If the input string X is of the correct form, the value of Y (line 11) should then be the null string ('').

This program uses a procedure, MATCH3N, which is defined at line 1. When MATCH3N(A) is called at line 16, control is transferred to the label START (line 2). Return is from line 11 to line 16. If the match at line 11 fails, return to line 16 is through **FRETURN**, where MATCH3N(A) also fails, transferring control to the line labeled NOTOK. If the match succeeds, line 11 and line 16 both succeed, and control will be transferred to the line labeled OK.

Three sample runs gave:

```
Enter string of form anbncn: aabbcc
 aabbcc is OK.

Enter string of form anbncn: aabc
aabc is not OK.

Enter string of form anbncn: is OK.
```

This last result represents input of empty string, which is $a^0b^0c^0$.

Associative features

Associative programming involves the *"association* of objects with other objects in a completely arbitrary way" [Maurer, 1976, p. 52]. The simplest sort of association is a variable, where a value is associated with a name. Another sort is an array, where A[I] is associated with its value. Index values are usually restricted to a finite set of scalars. As we have seen, variable-length arrays have not been very common, with the usual implementation being the use of only part of a fixed-length array. Arrays cannot usually be described as "completely arbitrary."

SNOBOL has two unusual features that make associations arbitrary. The first is the unary *indirect reference operator* $. If we write a SNOBOL4 program:

```
        X = 'Y'
        Y = 'Z'
        OUTPUT = $X
END
```

the output will be Z. Here the $X means to look up the identifier X in the internal SNOBOL hash table, find its string value 'Y', and output the *value* Z of Y. Identifiers can be indirectly referenced to any level. If we added z = 2, to the program above, **OUTPUT $$**X would yield 2.

In the original SNOBOL, an array could be built only indirectly, through such statements as:

```
        I = 2
        $('A' I) = 'Bobby Jones'
```

Then the value of 'A2' is 'Bobby Jones'. The array A is referenced as usual through the hash table, where 'A2' is stored as a string that has a value. 'Bobby Jones' is, of course in the heap, unless we assign, **$(**'Bobby Jones') = 'golfer', when Bobby Jones will be entered in the hash table, with 'golfer' in the heap.

SNOBOL3 added an array type, for speed, which can be declared, A = **ARRAY**('1:100'), A = **ARRAY**('100'), or A = **ARRAY**(100). In SPITBOL 3.6, only the last declaration is valid. We have, of course, lost the arbitrary associations of the string method above. Arrays can also be created dynamically so that A = **ARRAY**(N ',' N) is a perfectly valid declaration, where the value of N is computed at run time. An element of the array A is denoted by A<i>, where i is an index variable or value.

An array constructed through methods such as **$(**'A' I) is called a *simulated array*. It can save one level of unrelated association. For example, if we have an array of 100 employee names constructed as Employee = **ARRAY**(100), we can add addresses through the following device:

```
        ADDR = 'ADDR'
        I = 2
        $('EMPLOYEE' I 'ADDR') = '22 Main St.'
```

Now suppose **$(**'EMPLOYEE' 2) = 'B. Jones'. Then '22 Main St.' will be output by any of:

```
        OUTPUT = $('EMPLOYEE' 2 ADDR)
        OUTPUT = $('EMPLOYEE' I 'ADDR')
        OUTPUT = $'EMPLOYEE2ADDR'
```

$ can also be used in GOTO statements so that program statements can be *associated* with computed values as well.

Arrays are usually thought of as having ordered indices, but this is not necessary in SNOBOL since lookup is through the hash table, where entries can be any string (or number for that matter).

The second novel feature of SNOBOL is an array with completely unrestricted indices called a *table*. Unlike an array, indices need not be ordered. In SNOBOL4, a table can be declared and assigned, e.g.:

```
T = TABLE()
Y = 2
T<Y>    = 'hello'
T<'Y'> = 'goodbye'
terminal = T<Y> ' ' T<2> ' ' T<'Y'>
```
END

The terminal output will then be, "hello hello goodbye".

The table declaration may have two arguments, e.g.:

```
A = TABLE(20,15)
```

The initial table will have 20 elements, but if more are needed, its size will be increased to 35, 50, etc. Declaring arrays and tables may improve efficiency over using indirect definitions.

The ability to build unrestricted tables removes the programmer further from the machine than do indexed arrays. Thus SNOBOL is *higher level* than most imperative languages. A SNOBOL compiler may translate source code into a more conventional intermediate language, but the user doesn't see it.

EXERCISES

1. Trace through the SPITBOL programs above for input of:

   a. 'aaabbb', 'aab', and 'aabbcde' in Program anbn.

   b. 'aaabbbccc' and 'aabbbccc' in Program anbncn.

2. What will be output by the following SNOBOL programs?

   a.
```
         N = 10
         X = 0
         C = 1
LOOP     X = X + C
         C = C + 1
         GT(C,N)      :F(LOOP)
         OUTPUT = 'The sum of the first ' N 'nos. is ' X
END
```

   (*Note*: GT means "greater than.")

   b.
```
         Y = 'MISSISSIPPI'
         X = Y
         C = 0
NEXTS    X 'S' =              :F(DONE)
         C = C + 1            :S(NEXTS)
DONE     terminal = 'Y is ' X ' after removing S ' C 'times.'
END
```

```
c.          X = 'Y'
            Y = 'X'
            terminal 'X ' X ' ' $X ' ' $$X)
END

d.          X  = 'Y'
            $X = 'Z'
            terminal = X $X Y
END
e.          I = 1
            A = 'A'
MORE        $(A I) = I
            I = I + 1
            GT(I,100)        :F(MORE)
            terminal = $(A 23)
END
```

3. Why wasn't the reverse of production rule 3, Y 'CB' = 'BC', used in line 9 of the procedure MATCH3N instead of Y 'CCB' = 'CBC'? ∎

10.1 LANGUAGES FOR BUSINESS

Without a doubt, the biggest computer user is the business community. They store and access data, analyze it, and write reports with computers. In the late fifties, this was not the case. The original high-level languages such as FORTRAN and ALGOL were developed to perform complicated computations quickly and manipulate algebraic forms. Many business calculations use little beyond arithmetic, but the amount of data that needs to be stored, retrieved, and organized is massive.

Business professionals are usually not trained in the methods and notations of science and need languages that are easy for them to read and understand and that include textual as well as numeric input and output. Business languages were developed independently, but parallel to scientific languages. In many ways this was unfortunate, as the two communities might have contributed more to each other than is the case.

COBOL

The first and still most widely used business language is COmmon Business Oriented Language (COBOL), which has many detractors in the computer science community. Ben Shneiderman [Shneiderman, 1985] cites five historic reasons why COBOL is held in such low esteem. First is that the developers came from the world of commerce and government instead of academia and thus were not "part of the club." Second, they did not conduct or report their work in a scholarly fashion, including reference to previous efforts and the development of a body of increasingly worthwhile work. Third, although Backus-Naur form was available, COBOL was not described using it. Fourth, well-written user manuals and textbooks were very slow to appear, and fifth, computer scientists were not interested in business applications anyway.

Complaints centered around the lack of procedures with parameters and local variables, poor string-handling facilities, some error-producing syntax rules, such as the need for a period to delimit an IF-THEN-ELSE statement, rather than a keyword such as ENDIF, and general wordiness. Some of these earlier faults have been remedied in later versions, particularly by the new standard, COBOL-85.

Shneiderman cites six contributions that the original COBOL made to the development of programming languages. We will look at these plus special data management facilities one at a time.

The environment division

A COBOL program has four divisions: an *identification, environment, data*, and *procedure* division. In COBOL-85, all but the identification division are optional. A program ends with an *end-program-header* statement, e.g.:

```
END PROGRAM myprog.
```

These two organizational revisions to COBOL-74 allow the nesting of programs and the inclusion of variables local to a particular *contained* program. Thus we might have a program like Figure 10.6.

In the figure below, prog1 can be separately compiled, while the two programs contained in it cannot. Programs can be nested to any level.

```
IDENTIFICATION DIVISION.
PROGRAM-ID. prog1.
ENVIRONMENT DIVISION.
...
DATA DIVISION.
...
PROCEDURE DIVISION.
...
IDENTIFICATION DIVISION.
PROGRAM-ID. prog2.
END PROGRAM prog2.
IDENTIFICATION DIVISION.
PROGRAM-ID. prog3.
END PROGRAM prog3.
END PROGRAM prog1.
```

Figure 10.6 Containing program with two contained program stubs

The identification division includes a program name, or ID, and may include information about the author of the program and its security. New to COBOL-85 is the optional specification of a program as **COMMON** or **INITIAL**. A **COMMON** program can be called from any unit of a containing program. For example, if prog2 above were identified as **COMMON**, it could be called from either prog1 or prog3. An **INITIAL** declaration restores all program variables to their initial state (usually undefined) each time it is entered. Ordinarily, COBOL variables behave like **own** variables in ALGOL 60 and contain values from the most recent previous invocation.

The environment division is unique to COBOL. It describes the operating and compilation environment of a program and has two sections. The *configuration section* describes the computer being used to compile the program and the computer, which may be different, on which the program will run. The *input-output section* describes files, which can be random access, sequential, or indexed, and record structures. It also can be used to specify run-time storage allocation, such as which files can share memory locations.

Describing data is an important activity in business programs, thus the COBOL data division provides many options. COBOL data and program statements conform to card images, with entries required to start in particular columns. Columns 1 through 6 are reserved for line identifiers, column 7 for indicating a continuation, debugging, or comment line, columns 8 through 11 for area A, and columns 12 to the end of the line, being area B. Some implementers have eliminated the need for line identifiers, while others extend area B to column 72, and still others, to column 80. Unfortunately, this holdover from the days of card input is still preserved in COBOL-85. It does have the advantage, however, that old programs still run, and old data is still readable. We will discuss the data division more when we look at file and record structures below.

The procedure division contains program statements, preceded by optional *declaratives*. These declaratives are for error control and allow the user to specify what should happen when particular error conditions occur.

Record and file structures

COBOL has a rich collection of record and file structures, and its designers pioneered the implementation of data structures composed of items of different types. But first, we should look at just what simple types are available.

COBOL provides for two literal types, numeric and string. Examples of numeric literals are –117, and 120.3. String literals are enclosed in quotes, e.g., '117 Main St.' The declaration of an elementary data item in the data division is preceded by 77 in data area A. The most common way of declaring 77-level variables is through the PICture statement, for example:

```
77 X PICTURE 9999V99.
```

declares X to be a decimal number with one to four places before and two places
after the virtual decimal point (V).[7]

```
77 NAME PIC X(10).
```

or

```
77 NAME PIC XXXXXXXXXX.
```

declares NAME to be a string of 10 alphanumeric characters.

Arrays are declared using levels in place of the 77s:

```
01 TABLE-X.
    02  X PIC S9V99 OCCURS 100.

01 TABLE-Y.
    02 ROW-Z OCCURS 10.
        03 Z PIC XXXX OCCURS 5.
```

This example describes a one-dimensional array of 100 decimal elements and a
10 X 5 array of four-letter strings.

COBOL also includes record variables defined by level.

```
01 STUDENT.
    02 NAME PIC X(30).
    02 GRADES.
        03 TEST1     PIC 999.
        03 TEST2     PIC 999.
        03 TEST3     PIC 999.
    02 ABSENCES      PIC 99.
```

Now suppose we keep these student records in a file called STDNTS, with
each line being 80 characters long and each student's record contained on a single line. The record is declared in the data division as:

```
FD STUDENT-INPUT-FILE
    RECORD CONTAINS 80 CHARACTERS
    LABEL RECORDS ARE OMITTED
    DATA RECORD IS STUDENT-INPUT-RECORD.
01 STUDENT-INPUT-RECORD.
    02 NAME    PIC X(30).
    02 GRADES.
        03 TEST1 PIC 999.
        03 TEST2 PIC 999.
        03 TEST3 PIC 999.
    02 ABSENCES  PIC 99.
    02 FILLER    PIC X(39).
*fills the line with anything
```

The file is associated with these records in the input-output section of the
environment division:

```
SELECT STUDENT-INPUT-RECORD ASSIGN TO 'STDNT.DAT'.
```

---

7 A virtual decimal point does not appear in data. Thus 125643 is a 9999V99 numeral, representing
1256.43.

Control structures

Arithmetic (and other) statements allow for user-defined error recovery. For example:

```
ADD INC TO N ROUNDED
    ON SIZE ERROR <statement1>
    NOT ON SIZE ERROR <statement2>
END-ADD
```

The **END**-verb is an optional addition to COBOL-85 and may be replaced with a period.

COBOL also includes **SUBTRACT**, **MULTIPLY**, and **DIVIDE** statements. If the result of an arithmetic expression such as `P*(1 + I)**N` is desired, one uses **COMPUTE** <expression>, which can also include error handling.

As conditionals, COBOL includes an **EVALUATE** and an **IF** statement. **EVALUATE** is new to COBOL-85 and is similar to the case statements of other languages. Suppose SELECT is an integer-valued variable used as a case selector. Then a simple use of **EVALUATE** is:

```
EVALUATE SELECT
    WHEN 1
        PERFORM <procedure name>
    WHEN 2
        ADD 1 TO N
    WHEN 3
        CONTINUE
    WHEN OTHER
        DISPLAY "Some sort of error here!"
END-EVALUATE
```

The **IF** statement has been modernized to avoid having to match up **ELSE**s with every **IF**. In COBOL-74, we would use:

```
IF <condition-1>
    IF <condition-2>
        <statement for inner IF goes here>
    ELSE
        NEXT SENTENCE
ELSE
    <statement for outer ELSE goes here>.
```

However, in COBOL-85, we would have:

```
IF <condition-1>
    IF <condition-2>
      <statement for inner IF goes here>
    END-IF
ELSE
    <statement for outer ELSE goes here>
END-IF
```

Notice two improvements here: first, the ability to end an if-else anywhere, and second, the substitution of the **END-IF** for the period, which apparently caused many programming errors.

COBOL also includes the much-maligned **GO TO** statement and a **CALL** statement to call other programs.

Loops are implemented with **PERFORM** statements. In COBOL-85 there are four **PERFORM** formats. The first calls a procedure or executes an imperative statement before executing **END-PERFORM**. The second performs a procedure N **TIMES**. The third performs a procedure **UNTIL** some condition occurs, and the fourth performs a procedure **VARYING** id-1 **FROM** id-2 **BY** id-3 **UNTIL** <some condition>. This last format provides a for loop with several variations.

One thing to notice is that the **PERFORM** statement always calls a procedure, enforcing block structure in most COBOL programs. To repeatedly loop through a sequence of statements, control must be transferred to a separate block.

Compiler directives

Compiler directives are available, including **COPY**, **REPLACE**, and **USE** statements. **COPY** copies text from a library into a source program, optionally replacing some identifiers. It is particularly useful for copying complicated data descriptions that are common to more than one program unit. **REPLACE** is new to COBOL-85 and is simply a macro used to replace text with other text. Only one **REPLACE** can operate at a time and executes after all **COPY** statements. Thus copied library text can be modified as well.

The **USE** statement is similar to the **ON** statement used above in connection with errors occurring during the computation of arithmetic statements. A **USE** statement is placed immediately following a section name in a procedure division and will be invoked whenever the specified condition occurs. **USE FOR DEBUGGING** <procedure> transfers control to <procedure> only in debugging mode, while **USE BEFORE REPORTING** is activated only when using the Report Writer facility.

Facilities for data management

Although at present COBOL does not include database facilities, it does provide powerful built-in functions for data management. The **ACCEPT** and **DISPLAY** for interactive execution, **READ** and **WRITE** for file input and output, and **MOVE** statements transfer data from one location to another. **STRING** concatenates strings in various ways, and **UNSTRING** breaks existing strings apart.

COBOL also has ordering statements to rearrange data. **MERGE** merges two already-ordered files, while **SORT** sorts a file on keys in either ascending or descending order. Various options allow one to delete duplicates and perform other housekeeping tasks.

Portability and standardization

One of the primary design goals for COBOL was to provide a language that would be common to all business applications. The Conference on Data Systems Languages (CODASYL) was formed in the late fifties. The committee included representatives of both business and the government. A standard was approved in 1960. Revisions led to COBOL-61 Extended, COBOL-68, COBOL-74, and finally, COBOL-85. Standardization of the language itself plus the provisions of the environment division make COBOL programs executable on almost any machine, including personal computers.

COBOL-85 includes 116 changes to COBOL-74. Many of these are minor syntax changes, but some are more far-reaching. Increasing the number of dimensions of a table from three to seven takes advantage of the larger memories of most modern machines, while provision for the nesting of programs makes a top-down programming style more practical. Parameters in procedure calls are less restricted and a **TEST AFTER** phrase in a **PERFORM** statement allows testing to occur either at the beginning or end of a loop. Variable-length records, often a problem, have been defined more precisely. Some of the more archaic features, such as capital letters only have been eased.

Nelson [Nelson, 1988] lists 70 other changes anticipated for inclusion in the mid-nineties. The most far-reaching of these is the inclusion of a database description language. Unfortunately, the work of the DataBase Language Task Group (DBLTG) has been focussed on the network database model, which has received little acceptance since the emergence of relational models. A screen management system is also anticipated.

Another interesting revision of COBOL would be the inclusion of object-oriented features [Sherer, 1989]. This suggestion comes from Hewlett-Packard, which wishes to include object-oriented programming (OOP) in its new COBOL compiler. Their proposal has been submitted to the ANSI X3J4 (COBOL) Committee and will be considered by them.

A COBOL program

We will end this section with a simple COBOL program for the reader who has never seen one. (See Figure 10.7.) It performs the sort of task one uses COBOL for, the computation of salaries from a file containing employee names, hourly rates, and number of hours worked. It was executed using the WATBOL compiler from the University of Waterloo, running on a DEC PDP-11-84 computer.

The first line of SALARY.DAT is:

```
Jean Barnes              800        20
```

with output to SALARY.OUT:

```
Jean Barnes                    $160.00
```

```
     $JOB WATBOL DOE
1          IDENTIFICATION DIVISION.
2          PROGRAM-ID.      SALARY.
3          AUTHOR.          JOHN DOE.
3          INSTALLATION.    WIDGET COMPANY.
4          DATE-WRITTEN.    07/01/90
           *
           * READS EMPLOYEEE NAME, HOURS, AND HOURLY RATE,
           * THEN COMPUTES SALARY.
           *
5          ENVIRONMENT DIVISION.
7          CONFIGURATION SECTION.
8          SOURCE-COMPUTER.        PDP-11-84.
9          OBJECT-COMPUTER.        PDP-11-84.
           *
10         INFPUT-OUTPUT SECTION.
11         FILE-CONTROL.
12             SELECT EMPLOYEE-CARD-FILE ASSIGN TO 'SALARY.DAT'.
14             SELECT EMPLOYEE-REPORT-FILE ASSIGN TO 'SALARY.OUT'.
           *
16         DATA DIVISION.
17         FILE SECTION.
           *
18     FD  EMPLOYEE-CARD FILE
19         RECORD CONTAINS 80 CHARACTERS
20         LABEL RECORDS ARE OMITTED
21         DATA RECORD IS EMPLOYEE-INPUT-RECORD.
22     01  EMPLOYEE-NAME-INPUT
23         05  EMPLOYEE-NAME-INPUT              PIC X(20).
25         05  FILLER                          PIC X(6).
27         05  EMPLOYEE-SALARY-RATE-INPUT      PIC 99V99.
29         05  FILLER                          PIC X(8).
31         05  EMPLOYEE-HOURS-INPUT            PIC 99.
33         05  FILLER                          PIC X(40).
           *
35     FD  EMPLOYEE-REPORT-FILE
36         RECORD CONTAINS 133 CHRACTERS
37         LABEL RECORDS ARE OMITTED
38         DATA RECORD IS EMPLOYEE-REPORT-RECORD.
39     01  EMPLOYEE-REPORT-RECORD.
40         05  CARRIAGE CONTROL               PIC X.
42         05  EMPLOYEE-NAME-REPORT           PIC X(20).
44         05  FILLER                         PIC X(11).
46         05  EMPLOYEE-SALARY-REPORT         PIC $$, $$99.99.
48         05  FILLER                         PIC X(92).
           *
50         WORKING-STORAGE SECTION.
51         77  END-FILE       PIC X(3)        VALUE 'YES'.
           *
```

Figure 10.7 (continued next page)

```
54        PROCEDURE DIVISION.
55        CREATE-SALARY-REPORT.
        * MAIN PROGRAM READS INPUT RECORDS AND PROCESSES THEM
        * UNTIL END-OF-FILE
        *
56            OPEN INPUT  EMPLOYEE-CARD-FILE
56                 OUTPUT EMPLOYEE-REPORT-FILE.
57            READ EMPLOYEE-CARD-FILE
57                 AT END MOVE 'NO ' TO END-FILE.
59            PERFORM FORMAT-OUTPUT-RECORD
59                 UNTIL END-FILE = 'NO '.
60            CLOSE EMPLOYEE-CARD-FILE
60                  EMPLOYEE-REPORT-FILE.
61            STOP RUN.
        *
62         FORMAT-OUTPUT-RECORD.
        * PROCEDURE FORMATS SALARY RECORDS IN THE OUTPUT REPORT
        *
63            MOVE SPACES TO EMPLOYEE-REPORT-RECORD.
64            MOVE EMPLOYEE-NAME-INPUT TO EMPLOYEE-NAME-REPORT.
65            MULTIPLY EMPLOYEE-SALARY-RATE-INPUT BY EMPLOYEE-HOURS-INPUT
65                 GIVING EMPLOYEE-SALARY-REPORT.
66            WRITE EMPLOYEE-REPORT-RECORD
66                 BEFORE ADVACING 1 LINES.
67            READ EMPLOYEE-CARD-FILE
67                 AT END MOVE 'NO ' TO END-FILE.
    $END

STATEMENTS EXECUTED:     31; PAGES PRINTED:       1; VER=V2L2C
OBJECT CODE (BYTES):  710 WORK AREA (BYTES):  17520
MESSAGES: EXTENSIONS=    0 WARNINGS=    0 ERRORS=       0
```

Figure 10.7   (continued from previous page)

Notice in line 46 the declaration:

```
EMPLOYEE-SALARY-REPORT              PIC $$,$$9.99.
```

This is for output format control and will display the value of EMPLOYEE-SALARY-REPORT with a dollar sign preceding up to four figures before a decimal point and two after. Such variables cannot be reassigned, except to an output medium.

The WATBOL compiler was developed for teaching purposes and provides good error detection and reporting. An error will cause a program to abort, while a warning will not, but calls attention to some irregular program feature. The line numbers were added by the compiler at run time and provide easy reference to any error messages. Only a few comments are necessary here.

Lines 12 through 14 SALARY.DAT and SALARY.OUT are user-prepared input and output files. EMPLOYEE-CARD-FILE and EMPLOYEE-REPORT-FILE are variables containing pointers to these files and provide access to them during program execution. Just how these variables work depends on the particular COBOL implementation.

Line 40 CARRIAGE-CONTROL contains a single (nonprinting) character. In this program, the ASCII carriage control code will be inserted automatically each time line 66 executes because of the **BEFORE ADVANCING** 1 **LINES**.

Line 51 END-FILE is a level-77 (simple) variable used with both EMPLOYEE-CARD-FILE and EMPLOYEE-REPORT-FILE as an end-of-file marker.

Line 54 The **PROCEDURE DIVISION** contains a main program, CREATE-SALARY-REPORT, terminated by **STOP RUN** at line 61, followed by a single procedure, FORMAT-OUTPUT-RECORD, beginning at Line 62. This procedure is called by the **PERFORM** statement at Line 59.

FORTRAN + COBOL + ALGOL = PL/I

Programming Language/I (PL/I) appeared at IBM in 1965. It was developed as a conscious effort to combine the best features of the myriad languages then in existence. It included the nested block structure and recursion of ALGOL 60, the file and record structures and error handlers of COBOL, and the formatted I/O of FORTRAN. It also included pointer variables and dynamic storage allocation as found in LISP, but there was no facility for garbage collection, and the programmer was responsible for avoiding dangling pointers.

PL/I never became very popular, and was considered to be a dinosaur from the beginning. It is huge and includes many complex, hard-to-learn features. However, its facilities for defining generic subroutines, bit strings, and concurrently running tasks have influenced other languages. Tasks are coordinated by methods similar to semaphores, with the two operations **WAIT** and **COMPLETION** (signal).

We will end this brief section with a PL/I procedure to test equality of two generalized lists. A generalized list includes a collection of atoms, which contain data items, and a linked structure of pointers. A PL/I declaration for both types of nodes is the following:

```
DECLARE PTR POINTER;
DCL    /*Abbreviation for DECLARE*/
    1 LIST_NODE, BASED(PTR),
        2 NOTATOM        BIT(1),
        2 DATA_PTR       POINTER,
        2 NEXT           POINTER;
```

```
DCL 1 ATOM              BASED(PTR),
      2 ISTATOM         BIT(1),
      2 DATA_ITEM       CHAR(1);
```

LIST_NODES or ATOMS can be created dynamically using **ALLOCATE** LIST_NODE or **ALLOCATE** ATOM. For a LIST_NODE we would assign PTR->NOT-ATOM = '0'B; for an ATOM, we would assign PTR->ISTATOM = '1'B. Here PTR->ISTATOM is an abbreviation for PTR->ATOM.ISTATOM. PL/I allows such assignments without any "with" clauses. PL/I does not have a Boolean type, but uses bit strings of length 1 for true ('1'B) and false ('0'B). As with Pascal's variant record, we can create two types of nodes based on the same pointer. However, PL/I is more efficient than Pascal. When we **ALLOCATE** LIST_NODE, storage for three fields is allocated. When we **ALLOCATE** ATOM, storage for only two fields is allocated.

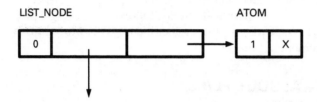

A list could terminate one of two ways. The NEXT field of the final LIST_NODE can contain NULL, where NULL is the PL/I null pointer:

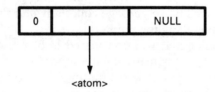

or a special ATOM:

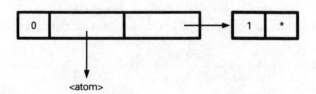

could be set up, to which the final NEXT points. We leave as an exercise the advantages of each implementation.

A function, EQUALS, can then be defined as:

```
1  EQUALS: PROC(X, Y) RECURSIVE RETURNS (BIT(1));
2     DCL (X, Y) POINTER;
3     IF X = Y THEN
4        RETURN ('1'B);      /*True*/
5     ELSE
6        IF (X->ISATOM | Y->ISATOM) THEN
7           RETURN ('0'B);
8        ELSE IF EQUALS (X->DATA_PTR, Y->DATA_PTR) THEN
9           IF EQUALS(X->NEXT, Y->NEXT) THEN
10             RETURN ('1'B);
11          ELSE
12             RETURN ('0'B);
13       ELSE
14          RETURN ('0'B);
15 END;
```

(Line numbers are not part of PL/I code, but added to facilitate discussion.)

Line 1 Notice two things: first, that a recursive procedure must be declared so, and second, that functions are just procedures which return a value, as in ALGOL, Modula-2, and SETL.

Line 2 X and Y are declared to be **POINTER**, but with no particular type pointed to. A PL/I pointer is just a variable that contains an address.

Line 6 The -> operator discriminates fields of a record. Bit strings have associated logical operations. Here, we are looking at one-element bit strings representing true and false.

EXERCISES

1. How does COBOL's ability to declare programs as **INITIAL** coincide with object-oriented programming? What do you think a COBOL object would be?

2. The **PERFORM** statement allows iteration of a procedure. One form is:
```
PERFORM <SomeProcedure> N TIMES
   <imperative statement>
END PERFORM.
```

Other variations are similar to for or while loops. A change in COBOL-85 allows the omission of <SomeProcedure>. This is called an inline perform, since the code to be executed is in the same line as the **PERFORM**.

   a. If <imperative statement> is **MULTIPLY** X **BY** N **GIVING** X, what is achieved by the inline perform?

   b. Why is this a desirable change?

3. Draw figures representing the generalized lists L1 = (A B C) and L2 = (A (B C)). Trace the execution of the PL/I procedure, EQUALS(L1, L2), where L1 and L2 are pointer types, and A, B, and C represent the same atoms in both L1 and L2.

4. Consider the two methods mentioned for representing the end of a generalized list. Does either work with the EQUALS function? Can you see any advantages to either method? ■

10.2 LITTLE LANGUAGES

When one thinks of programming languages, big production systems come to mind, like FORTRAN, Ada, C, etc. But there are many "little languages" around as well. Jon Bentley [Bentley, 1986a] qualified his definition of a programming language for little languages. After much difficulty, he settled on a language "specialized to a particular problem domain" and one that "took only a few days to implement."

When there is a "particular problem domain," a little language will usually be an interface to an existing larger language. This is nothing new. All high-level programming languages are interfaces to other languages, be they assembly, machine, or another high-level language. We have also seen some languages that are first translated into intermediate code, e.g., LISP into the lambda calculus, and SETL into ITC. Most languages have special languages for input and output whose implementations are machine dependent. For example, FORTRAN includes format statements such as F5.3, while COBOL would use PIC 99.999 for the same purpose. A compiler must seek out this code for special treatment on different machines. The little languages we will consider here compile into existing languages.

An individual confronted with a special computer application has three options:

1. An interactive program in an already known language
2. A library of subroutines in a particular language
3. The development of a little language.

The first option involves questions and answers, such as:

```
OUTPUT "What is the name of your file?"
INPUT F$
```

or mouse or key signals. A Pascal example of an interactive program that behaves like a little language is Turtle Graphics, implementing the LOGO turtle, which was provided in Turbo Pascal Version 3. One accesses it by running the Pascal program, Turtle. After verifying that the user does indeed have a color graphics adapter, a split screen is presented with a "turtle" in the center of the top portion. At the bottom one sees the list of possible key commands:

```
SPEED: 0-9  TOGGLES: Pen, Wrap, Turtle, Color
TURN: F1,F2  HOME: +     RES: Hi, Med
```

The "turtle" moves forward if SPEED is set to anything other than 0. Although Turbo didn't do it, one could easily write a 10- to 15-page user manual describing the little language. In fact, one of my students did so and tried it out with second graders, to their great pleasure.

The second option calls for a program in a host language, with a library of subroutines imported. A good example of this approach are the I/O packages in Ada. They are not part of the Ada standard, but are part of the standard Ada environment, and include various packages, such as IO_EXCEPTIONS, SEQUENTIAL_IO, DIRECT_IO, and TEXT_IO. SEQUENTIAL_IO provides procedures for I/O to and from files of objects of the same type, reading or writing from beginning to end. DIRECT_IO provides random access to and from indexed files of objects of the same type. TEXT_IO provides access to files in human-readable form. Each of these packages uses the little language IO_EXCEPTIONS, which provides procedures for recovery from such errors as trying to read an item of the wrong type, trying to read from or write to an unopened file, trying to read past the end of a file, etc. All these little languages are system dependent.

Are the two examples above applications or little languages? Although opinions may differ, that the user is confined entirely to the little language and need know nothing of the host language justifies calling each a little language.

The third option is more justifiably called a little language and provides the interface between the user, the existing language, and the operating system. It can be built in any existing language. All that is necessary is that it provide a facility for arbitrary user input (not in response to direct questions, as in an interactive system) and that the user can access the language without knowing the niceties of the host language.

One such language is the UNIX shell or command interpreter, which manages C and other programs. UNIX is written in C, so the distinction between a program and an operating system command is not as big as in other languages. When the shell runs a program, it opens three files, designated 0, 1, and 2. The first is standard input, the second, standard output, and the third, error output. Normally, all three files are connected to the terminal, but files 0 and 1 can be redirected through "<" and ">". <infile, means that "infile" provides input, while > indicates a file providing output. The C statement:

```
prog <infile >outfile
```

redirects file 0 to whichever file is named by infile, and file 1 to outfile. Many UNIX shell programs (also written in C) begin with:

```
main (argc, argv)
```

where argc is the argument count and argv is the argument vector.

For example, the UNIX utility, **cp**, to copy one file to another would set argc = 3. Argv[0] is a pointer to the cp.c file; argv[1], a pointer to a source file; and argv[2], a pointer to the destination file. The shell has functions to open, create, close, and unlink (remove a file from the system) files. It also provides for sequential and random access to files and the creation and deletion of temporary buffers. A user can also allocate and deallocate storage as needed. Thus the UNIX shell is truly a little language, providing user interface with the operating system. It did not, however, take only a few days to implement.

PIC, CHEM, GRAP, and DOTCHART

PIC is a large language for drawing pictures in the UNIX environment. PIC code is first analyzed by a preprocessor, which translates it into TROFF (UNIX typesetting) code so that its pictures can be "drawn" right in the middle of a surrounding program. Ordinarily, a compiler translates source code into object code in six steps, as shown in Figure 10.8.

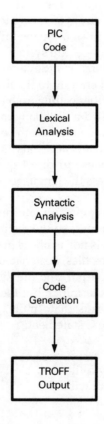

Figure 10.8   A typical compiler

When compiling the little language PIC, four of these steps are followed, leaving out optimizations and semantic analysis, as shown in Figure 10.9. High speed is usually not needed for executing a little language, and semantic analysis will be performed on the language TROFF, into which PIC is compiled.

Execution of an infile using the schema above is easy to do in UNIX, with:

```
>infile | pic | troff >outfile
```

where "|" indicates a UNIX pipe. Output from a program preceding a pipe is input to the program after it. PIC is a fairly low-level graphics language with several primitives, such as BOX, LINE, ELLIPSE, etc. When a primitive is called, followed by a list of attributes, such as:

```
BOX height, width, label
```

the appropriate figure will be drawn.

Jon Bentley [Bentley, 1986a] describes other little languages that feed into PIC. One of these is CHEM, which is specialized to chemical drawings. Here the UNIX pipeline would be:

```
<Infile | chem | pic |troff> outfile
```

CHEM incorporates commands that are meaningful to its chemist users. Thus a CHEM command is:

```
backbond up from R1.V1 ; H
```

which draws the ladderlike backward-bonding symbol up from vertex 1 of box R1 and labels it "H".

The little language GRAP [Bentley, 1986b], is larger than something like CHEM and was written to be translated into PIC, which in turn is translated to TROFF. GRAP describes graphs to be included in documents printed with TROFF typesetting commands. GRAP code is inserted in a program between the delimiters .G1 and .G2. It also provides primitives for drawing graphs from supplied data and is host to a variety of other specialized little languages, such as DOTCHART for drawing scatter diagrams, where we would have:

```
<infile | dotchart | grap | pic | troff> outfile
```

If the desired graph is part of a C program, the sequence would be:

```
<infile | dotchart | grap | pic | troff | Ccompiler> outfile
```

GRAP took about four days to write in AWK, which is a string-processing language oriented to data fields. GRAP lets the user produce graphs embedded

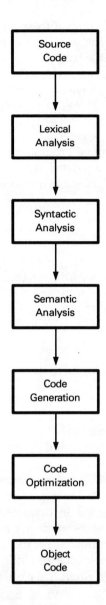

Figure 10.9   Processing PIC code

in text. They are not fancy, like those printed with commercial business software, but serve the purposes of the Bell Labs personnel who use them.

When devising a little language, Bentley recommends that the following design principles be kept in mind [Bentley, 1986a, p. 720]:

1. Orthogonality: keep unrelated features unrelated.
2. Generality: use an operation for many purposes.
3. Parsimony: delete unneeded operations.
4. Completeness: can the language describe all objects of interest?
5. Similarity: make the language as suggestive as possible.
6. Extensibility: make sure the language can grow.
7. Openness: let the user "escape" to use related tools.

LAB XXIII: Writing a "Little Language" for a Particular Task

OBJECTIVES

1. Paying heed to Bentley's seven principles above, to devise a little language to perform a well-defined task.

2. To implement the "language" as a subroutine library or interactive program in a language with which you are comfortable.

3. To write a user manual so that others can learn and use the language quickly. ■

10.3 SUMMARY

We have not begun to survey the variety of languages that exist for special purposes. One large group is those for statistical analysis. Many are English-like command languages accessible to both programmers and nonprogrammers. Some packages, like BMDP (Bio-Medical Data Package), are libraries of (in this case FORTRAN) subroutines, including data manipulation facilities. Others, like MiniTab or SyStat, provide both interactive and batch modes. Statistical Analysis System (SAS) offers more programming facilities than the others, while Statistical Package for the Social Sciences (SPSS) is well documented at beginning, intermediate, and advanced levels. Most newer implementations offer enriched graphics. The following SAS procedure definition provides a little of the style of these "languages":

```
proc print label;
   where sex = 'M' and age >= 65;
   label idnum = 'Policy Number' damage = 'Estimated Auto Damage';
run;
```

Several of these little procedures, either built in or user written, can be combined to manage, analyze, report, and display data. Interfaces are provided to many popular fourth-generation packages for managing databases or spreadsheets.

The tension between all-purpose languages and languages tailored to special needs will continue, but the ability to incorporate special languages into fully functional programming languages, e.g., a database or statistical language into C, could limit language proliferation to a few programming languages plus many compatible special-purpose languages or subroutine[8] libraries.

10.4 NOTES ON REFERENCES

Sylvia Weir's book, *Cultivating Minds: A LOGO Casebook,* is a fascinating account of how children with abnormal learning styles can benefit from well-designed learning experiences using LOGO. To autistic children, who hardly communicate with the rest of the world at all, it can be their only friend. The mix of graphics and text has successfully bridged language and cultural gaps among some. To capture LOGO fever, one couldn't do better than to read Papert's book, *Mindstorms* [Papert, 1980]. The group working at the MIT Media Laboratory are humanists first, using technology to foster human interconnections.

A very elementary but readable and reliable book surveying 22 languages, from Ada through QBE (Query By Example) to SNOBOL, is Naomi Baron's *Computer Languages: A Guide for the Perplexed* [Baron, 1986]. She provides information on available implementations, as well as a brief description and history of each language.

Introductory texts on COBOL abound. One of my favorites is Dan Mc-Cracken and Don Golden's *A Simplified Guide to Structured COBOL Programming* [McCracken, 1988]. For an early history of COBOL, see Wexelblat's *History of Programming Languages* [Sammet, 1981]. This same book includes a personal history of the development of PL/I [Radin, 1981].

---

8 The term *subroutine* originated in FORTRAN, where a program was composed of one main routine and any number of subroutines or procedures. One of FORTRAN's strengths is its well-developed libraries that can be incorporated into programs.

APPENDIX

This appendix contains information about software for PCs running in the DOS environment. Since the programming languages course requires a number of different compilers and interpreters, I have chosen inexpensive implementations where possible. Lab assignments and code within the main text have been tested on the software listed below.

No attempt was made to survey all implementations available or make a judgment on the merits of different products.

CHAPTER 1: ABSTRACTION

Modula-2

Modula-2 is available from:

LOGITECH, INC.
6505 Kaiser Drive
Fremont, CA 94555
(800) 231-7717; or in California, (800) 552-8885.

Pascal

Because of its popularity on college campuses, we used Turbo Pascal Version 5.0 from:

Borland International
4585 Scotts Valley Drive
Scotts Valley, CA 95066
(408) 438-5300

Ada

Code in both the text and the Ada MiniManual has been tested on PCs using the Meridian Student Ada Compiler and Janus/Ada. Meridian has, however, discontinued the Student compiler, in favor of a new implementation called AdaZ.

Meridian Software Systems, Inc.
10 Pasteur Street
Irvine, CA 92718
(714) 380-9800 or (800) 221-2522

Janus/Ada

R.R. Software Inc.
2317 International Lane #212
Madison, WI 53704
(608) 244-6436, (800) PC-ADA, or (800) 722-3248

We also used VAda on an AT&T 3B2/400 under UNIX.

Verdix Corporation
Sullyfield Business Park
14130-A Sullyfield Circle
Chantilly, VA 22021
(703) 378-7600

CHAPTER 2: BLOCK STRUCTURE

C

We used Turbo C from Borland International.

CHAPTER 3: OBJECT-BASED LANGUAGES

Object Pascal

Turbo Pascal 5.5 (or 6.0) is an object-oriented extension to Turbo Pascal. It is available from Borland International at the address listed above.

C++

Turbo C++ is an object-oriented extension to Turbo C. It is available from Borland International.

CHAPTER 4: DISTRIBUTED PROGRAMMING

Ada

Addresses for providers of Ada implementations are listed above.

CHAPTER 6: LOGIC PROGRAMMING

PROLOG

micro-PROLOG is available from:

> Logic Programming Associates, Ltd.
> 10 Burntwood Close
> London SW18 3JU England
> 01-874-0350 (24-hour phone)

> In the United States, LPA PROLOG is distributed by:

Programming Logic Systems, Inc.
31 Crescent Drive
Milford, CT 06460
(203) 877-7988

> A compiled version of Edinburgh PROLOG is available in an educational
version from:

> Arity Corporation
> 30 Domino Drive
> Concord, MA 01742
> (508) 371-1243 or (800) 722-7489

CHAPTER 7: FUNCTIONAL (APPLICATIVE) PROGRAMMING

LISP

There are many versions of LISP available for microcomputers. We chose PC
SCHEME Version 3.03, because of its ease of use, closeness to the lambda calculus, and minimal cost. It is available from:

> Texas Instruments Incorporated
> Data Systems Group
> P.O. Box 2909
> M.S. 2151
> Austin, TX 78769

CHAPTER 8: LANGUAGES FOR DATABASES

SQL

Lab XIX is written for use with dBASE III PLUS. The implementation is a limited functionality version, available for training and demonstration purposes.
    dBASE student editions are available from:

Ashton-Tate Corporation
1-800-2ASHTON

CHAPTER 9: LANGUAGES FOR RAPID PROTOTYPING

SETL

SETL2 is an experimental version of SETL. It is available without technical support, but at minimal cost from:

W. Kirk Snyder
Courant Institute of Mathematical Sciences
New York University
New York, NY 10012

In the text, I used SETLS, Version 2.1, a subset of SETL for PCs. It is available at minimal cost from:

J. VandeKopple
Courant Institute of Mathematical Sciences
New York University
New York, NY 10012

ISETL is an interactive version of SETL, and is available in Version 3.0, from:

Ron Pullins
Hamilton Gateway Building
5 Market Square
Amesbury, MA 01913
(508) 388-6688

CHAPTER 10: LANGUAGES FOR SPECIAL PURPOSES

LOGO

LOGO is available from:

LCSI
3300 Cote Vertu, Suite 201
Montréal, Québec, Canada H4R 2B7
(514) 331-7090

It is distributed in the United States by:

LCSI
330 West 58th Street, Suite 5D
New York, NY 10019
(212) 765-4780 or (800) 321-LOGO

BASIC

The BASIC that was used for Lab XXII is Turbo BASIC from Borland International.

SPITBOL

SPITBOL is a compiler for SNOBOL. MACRO SPITBOL Version 3.6 (2.15) for the IBM/PC family is available at minimal cost from:

Robert B. K. Dewar
SPITBOL ORDERS
73 5th Avenue
New York, NY 10003

BIBLIOGRAPHY

Abelson, 1985 Abelson, H., Sussman G.J., and Sussman, J. (1985). *Structure and Interpretation of Computer Programs*. Cambridge, MA: MIT Press.

Agha, 1987 Agha, G. and Hewitt, C. (1988). Actors: A conceptual foundation for concurrent object-oriented programming. In *Research Directions in Object Oriented Programming* edited by B. Shriver and P. Wegner, pp. 49–74. Cambridge, MA: MIT Press.

Aho, 1979 Aho, A.V. and Ullman, J.D. (1979). *Principles of Compiler Design*. Reading, MA: Addison-Wesley.

Aït-Kaci, 1983 Aït-Kaci, H., Lincoln, P., and Nasr, R. (1983). Le Fun: Logic, equations, and functions. In *Proceedings of the 1987 Symposium on Logic Programming*, pp. 17–23. Washington, DC: Computer Society Press.

Andrews, 1983 Andrews, G.R. and Schneider, F.B. (1983). Concepts and notations for concurrent programming. *ACM Computing Surveys* 15(1):3–43.

Anscombe, 1981 Anscombe, F. (1981). *Computing in Statistical Science Through APL*. New York: Springer-Verlag.

ANSI/IEEE, 1983 *American National Standard Pascal Computer Programming Language*. New York: IEEE, Inc.

ANSI-1815A, 1983 *Military Standard: Ada® Programming Language*. Washington, DC: American National Standards Institute, Inc.

ANSI-X3J11, 1986 *Draft Proposed American National Standard for Information Systems—Programming Language C*. Washington, DC: American National Standards Institute, Inc.

ANSI-X3135, 1986 *Database Language SQL*. Washington, DC: American National Standards Institute, Inc.

ANSI-X31351, 1989 *Database Language SQL Addendum*. Washington, DC: American National Standards Institute, Inc.

Appleby, 1988 Appleby, K., Carlsson, M., Haridi, S., and Sahlin, D. (1988).Garbage collection for Prolog based on WAM. *CACM* 31(6):719–741.

Atkinson, 1987 Atkinson, M.P. and Buneman, O.P. (1987). Types and persistence in database programming. *ACM Computing Surveys* 19(2):105–190.

Auer, 1989 Auer, K. (1989). *Which Object-oriented Language Should We Choose? Hotline on Object-oriented Technology.* New York: SIGS Publications, Inc.

Backus, 1978 Backus, J. (1978). Can programming be liberated from the von Neumann style? *CACM* 21(8):613–641.

Bal, 1988 Bal, H.E. and Tannenbaum, A.S. (1988). Distributed programming with shared data. *Proceedings of the 1988 International Conference on Computer Languages.* Washington, DC: Computer Society Press.

Bal, 1989 Bal, H.E., Steiner, J.G., and Tanenbaum, A.S. (1989). Programming languages for distributed systems. *ACM Computing Surveys* 21(3):261–322.

Ball, 1989 Ball, M.S. (1989). Implementing multiple inheritance. *The C++ Report* 1(9):1–6.

Barnes, 1982 Barnes, J.G.P. (1982). *Programming in Ada.* London: Addison-Wesley.

Baron, 1986 Baron, N. (1986). *Computer Languages.* Garden City, NY: Anchor Press/Doubleday.

Baxter, 1989 Baxter, N., Dubinsky, E., and Levin, G. (1989). *Learning Discrete Mathematics with ISETL.* New York: Springer-Verlag.

Beidler, 1986 Beidler, J. and Jackowitz, P. (1986). *Modula-2.* Boston: PWS.

Bentley, 1986a Bentley, J. (1986). Programming pearls: Little languages. *CACM* 29(8):711–721.

Bentley, 1986b Bentley, J. and Kernighan, B.W. (1986). GRAP—A language for typesetting graphs. *CACM* 29(8):782–792.

Bergin, 1989 Bergin, J. and Greenfield, S. (1989). What does Modula-2 need to fully support object-oriented programming? *Journal of Object-oriented Programming* 1(6):31–38.

Blair, 1989 Blair, G.S., Gallagher, J.J., and Malik, J. (1989). Genericity vs delegation vs conformance vs... . *Journal of Object-oriented Programming* 2(3):11–17.

Bobrow, 1983 Bobrow, D.G. and Stefik, M.J. (1983). *The LOOPS Manual.* Palo Alto, CA: Xerox.

Booch, 1986 Booch, G. (1986). *Software Engineering with Ada* (2nd ed.). Menlo Park, CA: Benjamin/Cummings.

Branquart, 1971 Branquart, P., Lewi, J., Sintzoff, M., and Wodon, P. L. (1971). The composition of semantics in Algol 68. *CACM* 14(11):697–707.

Brender, 1981 Brender, R.F. and Nassi, I.R. (1981). What is Ada? *Ada: Programming in the 80's.* Reprinted from *Computer* 14(6):17–24.

Brinch Hansen, 1975 Brinch Hansen, P. (1975). The programming language Concurrent Pascal. *IEEE Transactions on Software Engineering* 1(6):199–207.

Brinch Hansen, 1978 Brinch Hansen, P. (1978). Distributed processes: A concurrent programming concept. *CACM* 21:934–941.

Budd, 1987 Budd, T. (1987). *A Little Smalltalk*. Reading, MA: Addison-Wesley.

Buzzard, 1985 Buzzard, G.D. and Mudge, T.N. (1985). Object-based computing and the Ada programming language. *Computer* 18(3):11–19. Also in *Tutorial: Object-oriented Computing*. Vol 1: *Concepts*, edited by G.E. Peterson (1987), pp. 115–123. Washington, D.C.: Computer Society Press.

Calingaert, 1988 Calingaert, P. (1988). *Program Translation Fundamentals: Methods and Issues*. Rockville, MD: Computer Science Press.

Caromel, 1989 Caromel, D. (1989). Service, asynchrony, and wait-by-necessity. *Journal of Object-oriented Programming* 2(4):12–22.

Carriero, 1989 Carriero, N. and Gelernter, D. (1989). Linda in context. *CACM* 32(4):444–458.

Chomsky, 1965 Chomsky, N. (1965). *Aspects of the Theory of Syntax*. Cambridge, MA: MIT Press.

Chomsky, 1966 Chomsky, N. (1966). *Cartesian Linguistics*. New York: Harper and Row.

Chomsky, 1988 Chomsky, N. (1988). *The Culture of Terrorism*. Boston: South End Press.

Church, 1941 Church, A. (1941). *The Calculi of Lambda Conversion*. Princeton, NJ: Princeton University Press.

Clark, 1984 Clark, K.L. and McCabe, F.G. (1984). *micro-Prolog: Programming in logic*. Englewood Cliffs, NJ: Prentice Hall.

Clark, 1973 Clark, R.L. (1973). A linguistic contribution to goto-less programming. *Datamation* 19(12):62–63.

Clocksin, 1984 Clocksin, W.F. and Mellish, C.S. (1984). *Programming in Prolog* (2nd ed.). Berlin: Springer-Verlag.

Cohen, 1986 Cohen, D.A. (1986). *Introduction to Computer Theory*. New York: Wiley.

Cohen, 1985 Cohen, J. (1985). Describing Prolog by its interpretation and compilation. *CACM* 28(12):1311–1324.

Cohen, 1988 Cohen, J. (1988). A view of the origins and development of Prolog. *CACM* 31(1):26–37.

Colmerauer, 1985 Colmerauer, A. (1985). Prolog in 10 figures. *CACM* 28(12): 1296–1310.

Cooling, 1988 Cooling, J.E. (1988). *Modula-2 for Microcomputer Systems*. London: Van Nostrand Reinhold (International).

Cooper, 1982   Cooper, D. and Clancy, P. (1982). *OH! PASCAL*. New York: W.W. Norton and Co.

Cooper, 1983   Cooper, D. (1983). *Standard Pascal User Reference Manual*. New York: W.W. Norton.

Cox, 1984   Cox, B.J. (1984). Message/object programming: An evolutionary change in programming technology. *IEEE Software*, January 1984:50–61. Also in *Tutorial: Object-oriented Computing*. Vol 1: *Concepts*, edited by G.E. Peterson (1987), pp. 150–161. Washington, D.C.: Computer Society Press.

Dahl, 1966   Dahl, O. and Nygaard, J. (1966). SIMULA—An Algol based simulation language. *CACM* 9(9):671–681.

Date, 1983   Date, C.J. (1983). *An Introduction to Database Systems* (Vol. 2, 1st ed.). Reading, MA: Addison-Wesley.

Date, 1985   Date, C.J. (1985). *An Introduction to Database Systems* (Vol. 1, 4th ed.). Reading, MA: Addison-Wesley.

Date, 1989   Date, C.J. (1989). *A Guide to the SQL Standard* (2nd ed.) Reading, MA: Addison-Wesley.

Dauben, 1979   Dauben, W. (1979). *Georg Cantor*. Cambridge, MA: Harvard University Press.

DeGroot, 1984   DeGroot, D. (1984). *Prolog and Knowledge Information Processing: A Tutorial*. Unpublished manuscript, IBM, T.J. Watson Research Center, Yorktown Heights, NY.

Denning, 1989   Denning, P.J., Comer, D.E., Gries, D. Mulder, M. C., Tucker, A., Turner, A.J., and Young, P.R. (1988). Report of the ACM task force on the core of computer science (Order #201880). Baltimore: ACM Order Dept. Also condensed in *CACM* 32(1):9–23.

Digitalk, 1986   *Smalltalk/V: Tutorial and Programming Handbook*. Los Angeles: Digitalk, Inc.

Dijkstra, 1968a   Dijkstra, E.W. (1968). *Cooperating Sequential Processes*. In *Programming Languages*, edited by F. Genuys. New York: Academic Press. (Reprinted from the Technological University, Eindhoven (1965).)

Dijkstra, 1968b   Dijkstra, E.W. (1968). Go to statement considered harmful. *CACM* 11(3):147–148.

Duncan, 1990   Duncan, R. (1990). A survey of parallel computer architectures. *Computer* 23(2):5–16.

Dybvig, 1987   Dybvig, K.R. (1987). *The SCHEME programming language*. Englewood Cliffs, NJ: Prentice Hall.

Emery, 1986   Emery, G. (1986). *BCPL and C*. Oxford, UK: Blackwell Scientific Publications.

Falkoff, 1976 Falkoff, A. (1976). Some implications of shared variables. In *Formal Languages and Programming*, edited by R. Aguilar. Amsterdam: North Holland.

Feigenbaum, 1983 Feigenbaum, E.A. and McCorduck, P. (1983). *The Fifth Generation: Artificial Intelligence and Japan's Computer Challenge to the World.* Reading, MA: Addison-Wesley.

Feuer, 1982 Feuer, A.R. (1982). *The C Puzzle Book.* Englewood Cliffs, NJ: Prentice Hall.

Feuer, 1982b Feuer, A.R., and Gehani, N.H. (1982). A comparison of the programming languages C and PASCAL. *ACM Computing Surveys* 14(1):73–92.

Friedman, 1987 Friedman, D.P. (1987). *The Little Lisper.* Cambridge, MA: MIT Press.

Friendly, 1988 Friendly, M. (1988). *Advanced Logo.* Hillsdale, NJ: Lawrence Erlbaum.

Gabriel, 1989 Gabriel, R.P. (ed.) (1989). Draft report on requirements for a common prototyping system. *ACM SIGPLAN Notices* 24(3):93–165.

Gage, 1984 Gage, N.L. and Berliner, D.C. (1984). *Educational Psychology* (3rd ed.). Boston: Houghton-Mifflin.

Gallaire, 1984 Gallaire, H. and Minker, J. (1984). Logic and databases: A deductive approach. *ACM Computing Surveys* 16(2):153–185.

Gehani, 1983 Gehani, N.H. (1983). *Ada: An Advanced Introduction.* Englewood Cliffs, NJ: Prentice Hall.

Gehani, 1986 Gehani, N.H. and Roome, W.D. (1986). Concurrent C. *Software Practice and Experience* 16(9):821–844.

Genesereth, 1985 Genesereth, M.R. and Ginsberg, M.L. (1985). Logic programming. *CACM* 28(9):933–941.

Ghezzi, 1987 Ghezzi, C. and Jazayeri, M. (1987). *Programming Language Concepts* (2nd ed.). New York: John Wiley.

Goguen, 1984 Goguen, J.A. and Meseguer, J. (1984). Equality, types, modules and (why not?) generics for logic programming. *Journal of Logic Programming* 1(2):179–210.

Goldstein, 1989 Goldstein, T. (1989). Tutorial: Part I: Derivation. *The C++ Report* 1(1):4–6.

Gordon, 1979 Gordon, R. (1979). *The Denotational Description of Programming Languages.* New York: Springer-Verlag.

Graham, 1980 Graham, S.L., Harrison, M.A., and Ruzzo, W.L. (1980). An improved context-free recognizer. *ACM Transactions on Programming Languages and Systems* 2(3):415–462.

Gries, 1971 Gries, D. (1971). *Compiler Construction for Digital Computers*. New York: Wiley.

Gries, 1981 Gries, D. (1981). *The Science of Programming*. New York: Springer-Verlag.

Griffiths, 1965 Griffiths, T.V. and Petrick, S.R. (1965). On the relative efficiencies of context-free grammar recognizers. *CACM* 8(5):289–300.

Griswold, 1971 Griswold, R.E., Poage, J.F., and Polonsky, I.P. (1971). *The SNOBOL4 Programming Language* (2nd ed.). Englewood Cliffs, NJ: Prentice Hall.

Griswold, 1973 Griswold, R.E. and Griswold, M. (1973). *A SNOBOL4 Primer*. Englewood Cliffs, NJ: Prentice Hall.

Griswold, 1975 Griswold, R.E. (1975). *String and List Processing in SNOBOL4: Techniques and Applications*. Englewood Cliffs, NJ: Prentice Hall.

Griswold, 1981 Griswold, R.E. (1981). *A History of the Snobol Programming Language*. In *History of Programming Languages*, edited by R.L. Wexelblat, pp. 601–660. New York: Academic Press.

Grune, 1977 Grune, D. (1977). A view of coroutines. *ACM SIGPLAN Notices* 12(7): 75–81.

Guttag, 1977 Guttag, J.V. (1977). Abstract data types and the development of data structures. *CACM* 20(6):396–404.

Halmos, 1960 Halmos, P.R. (1960). *Naive Set Theory*. New York: Van Nostrand Reinhold.

Hansen, 1988 Hansen, G.W. (1988). *Database Processing with Fourth Generation Languages*. Cincinnati, OH: South-Western.

Harmon, 1985 Harmon, P. and King, D. (1985). *Expert Systems: AI in Business*. New York: John Wiley.

Hayes-Roth, 1985 Hayes-Roth, F. (1985). Rule-based systems. *CACM* 28(9): 921–932.

Helmbold, 1965 Helmbold, D. and Luckham, D. (1985). Debugging Ada tasking programs. *IEEE Software* 2(3):47–57.

Hoare, 1969 Hoare, C.A.R. (1969). An axiomatic basis for computer programming. *CACM* 12(10):576–583. Also in *Tutorial: Programming Language Design*, edited by A.I. Wasserman (1980), pp. 500–505. Los Alamitos, CA: Computer Society Press.

Hoare, 1972 Hoare, C.A.R. (1972). Proof of correctness of data representations. *Acta Informatica* 1:271–281.

Hoare, 1985 Hoare, C.A.R. and Shepherdson, J.C. (1985). *Mathematical Logic and Programming Languages*. Englewood Cliffs, NJ: Prentice Hall International.

Hodges, 1983 Hodges, A. (1983). *Alan Turing: The Enigma*. New York: Simon and Schuster.

Hofstadter, 1985a Hofstadter, D.R. (1985). Lisp: Atoms and lists, lists and recursion, and recursion and generality. In *Metamagical Themas*, pp. 396–424. New York: Basic Books.

Hofstadter, 1985b Hofstadter, D.R. (1985). Review of *Alan Turing: The enigma*. In *Metamagical Themas*, pp. 483–491. New York: Basic Books.

Hopcroft, 1979 Hopcroft, J.E. and Ullman, J.D. (1979). *Introduction to Automata Theory, Languages and Computation*. Reading, MA: Addison-Wesley.

Horowitz, 1984 Horowitz, E. (1984). *Fundamentals of Programming Languages* (2nd ed.). Rockville, MD: Computer Science Press.

Horowitz, 1987 Horowitz, E. (Ed). (1987). *Programming Languages: A Grand Tour* (3rd ed.). New York: W.H. Freeman.

Hudak, 1989 Hudak, P. (1989). Conception, evolution, and application of functional programming languages. *ACM Computing Surveys* 21(3):359–411.

Hughes, 1968 Hughes, G.E. and Cresswell, M.J. (1968). *An Introduction to Modal Logic*, pp. 1–21. London: Methuen.

Hull, 1987 Hull, R. and King, R. (1987), Semantic database modeling: Survey, applications, and research issues. *ACM Computing Surveys* 19(3):201–260.

ISO, 1980 *Second DP7185—Specifications for the Computer Programming Language Pascal*. (1980). British Standards Institute (BSI).

Iverson, 1962 Iverson, K. (1962). *A Programming Language*. New York: Wiley.

Jackson, 1986 Jackson, P. (1986). *Introduction to Expert Systems*. Reading, MA: Addison-Wesley.

Jacobson, 1982 Jacobson, P. and Pullum, G.K. (eds.). (1982). *The Nature of Syntactic Representation*. Boston: D. Reidel.

Jensen, 1974 Jensen, K. and Wirth, N. (1974). *Pascal User Manual and Report* (2nd ed.). New York: Springer-Verlag.

Johnson, 1988 Johnson, R.E. and Foote, B. (1988). Designing reusable classes. *Journal of Object-oriented Programming* 1(2):22–35.

Jonsson, 1989 Jonsson, D. (1989). Next: The elimination of goto-patches? *ACM SIGPLAN Notices* 24(3):85–92.

Kaeler, 1986 Kaeler, T. and Patterson, D. (1986). *A Taste of Smalltalk*. New York: W.W. Norton.

Kernighan, 1978 Kernighan, B.W. and Ritchie, D.M. (1978). *The C Programming Language*. Englewood Cliffs, NJ: Prentice Hall.

Knuth, 1967 Knuth, D.E. (1967). The remaining troublespots in ALGOL 60. *CACM* 10(10):611–617. Also in *Programming Languages: A Grand Tour* (3rd ed.), edited by E. Horowitz (1987), pp. 61–68. New York: W.H. Freeman.

Kowalski, 1985 Kowalski, R.A. (1985). The relation between logic programming and logic specification. In *Mathematical Logic and Programming Languages*, edited by C.A.R. Hoare and J.C. Shepherdson, pp. 11–27. London: Prentice Hall International.

Kowalski, 1988 Kowalski, R.A. (1988). The early years of logic programming. *CACM* 31(1):38–43.

Krasner, 1983 Krasner, G. (1983). *SMALLTALK-80: Bits of History, Words of Advice*. Reading, MA: Addison-Wesley.

Kristensen, 1987 Kristensen, B.B., Madsen, O.L., Moller-Pedersen, B., and Nygaard, K. (1987). The BETA programming language. In *Research Directions in Object-oriented Programming*, edited by B. Shriver and P. Wegner, pp. 8–48. Cambridge, MA: MIT Press.

Kruchten, 1984 Kruchten, P. and Schonberg, E. (1984). The Ada/ED system: a large-scale experiment in software prototyping using SETL. *Technology and Science of Informatics* 3(3):175–181.

Kuhn, 1962 Kuhn, T.S. (1962). *The Structure of Scientific Revolutions*. Chicago: University of Chicago Press.

Kuhn, 1970 Kuhn, T.S. (1970). *The Structure of Scientific Revolutions* (2nd ed., enlarged). Chicago: University of Chicago Press.

Lesk, 1975 Lesk, M.E. (1975). LEX-a lexical analyzer generator. CSTR 39. Murray Hill, NJ: Bell Labs.

Leler, 1990 Leler, W. (1990). Linda meets Unix. *Computer* 23(2):43–54.

Levin, 1987 Levin, G.M. (1987). *An Introduction to ISETL*. Unpublished manuscript. Clarkson University, Potsdam, NY.

Levin, 1988 Levin, G.M. (1988). *A Gentle Guide to Using ISETL: A Supplement to the Intro*. Unpublished manuscript. Clarkson University, Dept. of CS and Math., Potsdam, NY.

Lewis, 1981 Lewis, H.R. and Papadimitriou, C.H. (1981). *Elements of the Theory of Computation*. Englewood Cliffs, NJ: Prentice Hall.

Liskov, 1975 Liskov, B.H. and Zilles, S.N. (1975). Specification techniques for data abstractions. *IEEE Transactions on Software Engineering* 1(1):7–19.

Liskov, 1977 Liskov, B, Snyder, A., Atkinson, R., and Schaffert, C. (1977) Abstraction mechanisms in CLU. *CACM* 20(8):564–576. Also in *Programming Languages: A Grand Tour* (3rd ed.), edited by E. Horowitz (1987), pp. 254–266. New York: W.H. Freeman.

Liskov, 1986 Liskov, B. and Guttag, J. (1986). *Abstraction and Specification in Program Development*. Cambridge, MA: MIT Press.

McCracken, 1988 McCracken, D.D. and Golden, D.G. (1988). *A Simplified Guide to Structured Cobol Programming*. New York: Wiley.

MacLane, 1968 MacLane, S. and Birkhoff, G. (1968). *Algebra*. New York: Macmillan.

MacLennan, 1987 MacLennan, B.J. (1987). *Programming Languages: Design, Evaluation and Implementation* (2nd ed.). New York: Holt, Rinehart, and Winston.

Madsen, 1987 Madsen, O.L. (1987). Block structure and object-oriented languages. In *Research Directions in Object-oriented Programming*, edited by B. Shriver and P. Wegner, pp. 113–128. Cambridge, MA: MIT Press.

Malpas, 1987 Malpas, J. (1987). *PROLOG: A relational language and its applications*. Englewood Cliffs, NJ: Prentice Hall.

Mandrioli, 1986 Mandrioli, D. and Ghezzi, C. (1986). *Theoretical Computer Science*. New York: Wiley.

Marcotty, 1976 Marcotty, M., Ledgard, H.V., and Bochmann, G.V. (1976). A sampler of formal definitions. *ACM Computing Surveys* 8(2):191–276.

March, 1989 March, S.T. (ed.) (1989). *ACM Computing Surveys* 21(3). Special Issue on "Programming Language Paradigms."

Markov, 1954 Markov, A.A. (1954). *The Theory of Algorithms*. (Trudy mathematicheskogo instituta imeni V.A. steklova 42 375 pp. (in Russian).) English translation, Jerusalem: Israel Program for Scientific Translations, 1961.

Martin, 1985 Martin, J. (1985). *Fourth Generation Languages*. Vol. 1: *Principles*. Englewood Cliffs, NJ: Prentice Hall.

Martin, 1986 Martin, J. (1986). *Fourth Generation Languages*. Vol. 2: *Representative 4GLs*. Englewood Cliffs, NJ: Prentice Hall.

Maurer, 1976 Maurer, W.D. (1976). *The Programmer's Introduction to SNOBOL*. New York: North Holland.

McCarthy, 1960 McCarthy, J. (1960). Recursive functions of symbolic expressions. *CACM* 4(3):184–195. Also in *Programming Languages: A Grand Tour* (3rd ed.), edited by E. Horowitz (1987), pp. 203–214. New York: W.H. Freeman.

McCarthy, 1965 McCarthy, J. and Levin, J. (1965). *LISP 1.5 Programmers Manual*. Cambridge, MA: MIT Press. Also in *Programming Languages: A Grand Tour* (3rd ed.), edited by E. Horowitz (1987), pp. 215–239. New York: W.H. Freeman.

Mendelson, 1979 Mendelson, E. (1979). *Introduction to Mathematical Logic*. Princeton, NJ: D. Van Nostrand.

Meyer, 1988 Meyer, B. (1988). Eiffel: Harnessing multiple inheritance. *Journal of Object-oriented Programming* 1(4):48–51.

Michaelson, 1989 Michaelson, G. (1989). *An Introduction to Functional Programming Through Lambda Calculus*. Wokingham, UK: Addison-Wesley.

Moon, 1986 Moon, D. (1986). Object-oriented programming with Flavors. *ACM SIGPLAN Notices* 21(11):1–16.

Moskowitz, 1989 Moskowitz, R. (1989). Object oriented programming: The future is now. *PC Times*, October 2, p. 3.

Mueller, 1990 Mueller, R.A. and Page, R.L. (1990). *Symbolic Computing with Lisp and Prolog*. New York: Wiley.

Naur, 1963 Naur, P. (ed.). (1963). Report on the algorithmic language ALGOL 60. *CACM* 6(1):1–17. Also in *Programming Languages: A Grand Tour* (3rd ed.), edited by E. Horowitz (1987), pp. 44–60. New York: W.H. Freeman.

Nelson, 1988 Nelson, D. (1988). *COBOL 85 for Programmers*. New York: North Holland.

Norman, 1974 Norman, D.A. and Rumelhart, D.E. (eds.). (1974). *Explorations in Cognition*. San Francisco: W.H. Freeman.

Nygaard, 1981 Nygaard, K. and Dahl, O-J. (1981). The development of the Simula languages, and transcript of presentation. In *History of Programming Languages*, edited by R. Wexelblat (1981), pp. 439–491. New York: Academic Press.

Papert, 1980 Papert, S. (1980). *Mindstorms: Children, Computers and Powerful Ideas*. New York: Basic Books.

Parnas, 1971 Parnas, D.L. (1971). Information distribution aspects of design methodology. *Proc. 1971 IFIP Congress*, pp. 26–30.

Parnas, 1972 Parnas, D.L. (1972). On the criteria to be used in decomposing systems into modules. *CACM* 15(12):1053–1058.

Pascoe, 1986 Pascoe, G.A. (1986). Elements of object-oriented programming. *Byte*, August, 1986. Also in *Tutorial: Object Oriented Computing*. Vol 1: *Concepts*, edited by G.E. Peterson (1987), pp. 15–20. Washington, D.C.: Computer Society Press.

Peckham, 1988 Peckham, J. and Maryanski, F. (1988). Semantic data models. *Acm Computing Surveys* 20(3):153–190.

Peterson, 1987 Peterson, G.E. (ed.), (1987). *Tutorial: Object Oriented Computing*. Vol 1: *Concepts*. Washington, D.C.: Computer Society Press.

Peyton Jones, 1987 Peyton Jones, S.L. (1987). *The Implementation of Functional Programming Languages*. Hemel Hempstead, Hertfordshire (UK): Prentice Hall International Ltd.

Plauger, 1990 Plauger, P.J. and Brodie, J. (1990). *Standard C*. Redmond, WA.: Microsoft Press.

Plum, 1987 Plum, T. (1987). *Notes on the Draft C Standard*. Cardiff, NJ: Plum Hall, Inc.

Poe, 1984 Poe, M.D., Nasr, R., and Slinn, J.A. (1984). Kwic bibliography on Prolog and logic programming. *Journal of Logic Programming* 1:81–142.

Post, 1943 Post, E.L. (1943). Formal reductions of the general combinatorial decision problem. *American Journal of Mathematics* 65:197–215.

Pratt, 1975 Pratt, T. (1975). *Programming Languages: Design and Implementation.* Englewood Cliffs, NJ: PrenticeHall.

Proc. SPL, 1986 *Proceedings of the 1986 Symposium on Logic Programming.* (1986). Washington, DC: IEEE Computer Society Press.

Radin, 1981 Radin, G. (1981). The early history and characteristics of PL/I. In *History of Programming Languages,* edited by R. Wexelblat (1981), pp. 551–574. New York: Academic Press.

Randall, 1960 Randall, J.H., Jr. (1960). *Aristotle.* New York: Columbia University Press.

Rees, 1987 Rees, J. and Clinger, W. (eds.). (1987). Revised report on the algorithmic language Scheme. MIT Artificial Intelligence Laboratory, AI Memo 848a. Cambridge, MA: MIT AI Lab.

Rentsch, 1982 Rentsch, T. (1982). Object-oriented programming. *ACM SIGPLAN Notices* 17(9):51–57. Also in *Tutorial: Object-oriented Computing.* Vol 1: *Concepts,* edited by G.E. Peterson (1987), pp. 21–27. Washington, D.C.: Computer Society Press.

Rich, 1983 Rich, E. (1983). *Artificial Intelligence.* New York: McGraw-Hill.

Richards, 1979 Richards, M. and Whitby-Stevens, C. (1979). *BCPL—The Language and its Compiler.* Cambridge, UK: Cambridge University Press.

Ringwood, 1988 Ringwood, G.A. (1988). Parlog, 1986 and the dining logicians. *CACM* 31(1):10–25.

Robinson, 1965 Robinson, J.A. (1965). A machine-oriented logic based on the resolution principle. *JACM* 12(1):23–41. Also in *Automation of Reasoning.* Vol. 1.: *Classical Papers on Computational Logic, 1957–1966,* edited by J. Siekmann and W. Graham (1983), pp. 397–415. Berlin: Springer-Verlag.

Robinson, 1983 Robinson, J.A. (1983). Logic programming—past, present and future. *New Generation Computing* 1:107–124.

Rogers, 1967 Rogers, H., Jr. (1967). *The Theory of Recursive Functions and Effective Computability.* New York: McGraw-Hill.

Ross, 1923 Ross, D. (1923). *Aristotle.* London: Methuen.

Royce, 1987 Royce, W. (1987). Managing the development of large software systems: Concepts and techniques. Reprinted in *Proceedings of the Ninth International Conference on Software Engineering,* Monterey, CA, March 30–April 2, pp. 328–338. Washington, DC: IEEE Press.

Rubin, 1987 Rubin, F. (1987). "GOTO considered harmful" considered harmful. *CACM* 30(3):195–196.

Sammet, 1969 Sammet, J. (1969). *Programming Languages: History and Fundamentals.* Englewood Cliffs, NJ: Prentice Hall.

Sammet, 1981 Sammet, J. (1981). The early history of COBOL. In *History of Programming Languages*, edited by R. Wexelblat (1981), pp. 199–242. New York: Academic Press.

Saunders, 1989 Saunders, J.H. (1989). A survey of object-oriented programming languages. *Journal of Object-oriented Programming* 1(6):5–13.

Scholz, 1961 Scholz, H. (1961). *Concise History of Logic* (K.F. Leidecker, Trans.). New York: Philosophical Library.

Schwartz, 1986 Schwartz, J., Dewar, R.B.K., Dubinsky, E., and Schonberg, E. (1986). *Programming with Sets: An Introduction to SETL*. New York: Springer-Verlag.

Sergot, 1986 Sergot, M.J., Sadri, R.A., Kowalski, F., Kriwaczek, P.H., and Cory, H.T. (1986). The British nationality act as a logic program. *CACM* 29(5): 370–386.

Sethi, 1988 Sethi, R. (1988). *Programming Languages: Concepts and Constructs*. Reading, MA: Addison-Wesley.

Shapiro, 1989 Shapiro, E. (1989). The family of concurrent logic programming languages. In "Programming language paradigms" [Special issue, P. Wegner (Guest editor)]. *ACM Computing Surveys* 21(3):412–510.

Shatz, 1989 Shatz, S.M. and Wang, J-P. (1989). *Tutorial: Distributed Software Engineering*. Washington: IEEE Computer Society.

Sherer, 1989 Sherer, P.M. (1989). COBOL vendors take up issue of OOP standards. *PC Week* 6(31):67, 69.

Shneiderman, 1985 Shneiderman, B. (1985). The relationship between COBOL and computer science. *Annals of the History of Computing* 7(4):348–353. Also in *Programming Languages: A Grand Tour* (3rd ed.), edited by E. Horowitz (1987), pp. 417–421. New York: W.H. Freeman.

Shopiro, 1989 Shopiro, J.E. (1989). An example of multiple inheritance in C++: A model of the iostream library. *ACM SIGPLAN Notices* 24(12):32–36.

Shriver, 1987 Shriver, B. and Wegner, P. (1987). *Research Directions in Object-oriented Programming*. Cambridge, MA: MIT Press.

Shumate, 1988 Shumate, K. and Kjell, N. (1988). A taxonomy of Ada packages. *Ada Letters* 8(2):55–76.

Silvester, 1984 Silvester, P. (1984). *The Unix System Guidebook: An Introductory Guide for Serious Users*. New York: Springer-Verlag.

Simonian, 1988 Simonian, R. and Crone, M. (1988). InnovAda: True object-oriented programming in Ada. *Journal of Object-oriented Programming* 1(4): 14–23.

Slater, 1987 Slater, R. (1987). *Portraits in Silicon*. Cambridge, MA: MIT Press.

Smedema, 1983 Smedema, C.H., Medema, P., and Boasson, M. (1983). *The Programming Languages Pascal Modula Chill Ada.* Englewood Cliffs, NJ: Prentice Hall.

Snyder, 1990 Snyder, W.K. (1990). The SETL2 programming language (Tech. Rep. No. 490. Robotics Rep. No. 221). New York: New York University, Dept. of Computer Science, Courant Institute of Mathematical Sciences.

Sosnowski, 1987 Sosnowski, R.A. (1987). Prolog dialects: A déjà vu of BASIC-s. *ACM SIGPLAN Notices* 22(6):39–48.

Steele, 1978 Steele, G.L., Jr. and Sussman, G.J. (1978). The revised report on Scheme, a dialect of Lisp. (Artificial Intelligence Memo 452). Cambridge, MA: MIT, Artificial Intelligence Lab.

Steele, 1984 Steele, G.L., Jr. (1984). *Common LISP: The Language.* Burlington, MA: Digital Press.

Stefik, 1986. Stefik, M. and Bobrow, D.G. (1986). Object-oriented programming: Themes and variations. *AI Magazine*, Winter, pp. 40–62. Also in *Tutorial: Object-oriented Computing.* Vol 1: *Concepts,* edited by G.E. Peterson (1987), pp. 182–204. Washington, D.C.: Computer Society Press.

Stroustrup, 1986 Stroustrup, B. (1986). *The C++ Programming Language.* Reading, MA: Addison-Wesley.

Suppes, 1960 Suppes, P. (1960). *Axiomatic Set Theory.* New York: Van Nostrand Reinhold.

Sussman, 1975 Sussman, G.J. and Steele, G.L., Jr., (1975). Scheme: An interpreter for extended lambda calculus. MIT Artificial Intelligence Memo 349.

Tanenbaum, 1976 Tanenbaum, A.S. (1976). A tutorial on ALGOL 68. *ACM Computing Surveys* 8(2):155–190.

Tennent, 1976 Tennent, R.D. (1976). The denotational semantics of programming languages. *CACM* 19(8):437–453.

Tesler, 1985 Tesler, L. (1985). Object Pascal report. *Structured Language World* 9(3):10–14.

TI, 1987 *Revised SCHEME User's Guide, Tutorial, and Reference Manual.* Austin, TX: Texas Instruments.

Tu, 1986 Tu, H-C. and Perlis, A.J. (1986). FAC: A functional APL language. *IEEE Software* 3(1):36–45.

Tukey, 1977 Tukey, J.W. (1977). *Exploratory Data Analysis.* Reading, MA: Addison-Wesley.

Turbo 5.0, 1988 *Turbo Pascal Reference Guide.* Scotts Valley, CA: Borland International, Inc.

Turbo 5.5, 1988 *Turbo Pascal 5.5 OOP Guide.* Scotts Valley, CA: Borland International, Inc.

Ullman, 1982 Ullman, J.D. (1982). *Principles of Database Systems* (2nd ed.). Rockville, MD: Computer Science Press.

VandeKopple, 1989 VandeKopple, J. (1989). *SETLS Users Guide: A Short Introduction to the SETLS Compiler.* New York: New York University. Dept. of Computer Science, Courant Institute of Mathematical Sciences.

Warren, 1977 Warren, D.H.D., Pereira, L.M. and Pereira, F. (1977). PROLOG—The language and its implementation compared with LISP. *ACM SIGPLAN Notices* 12(8):109–115.

Warren, 1988 Warren, D.S. (1988). The Warren abstract machine. *SIGPLAN '88: Advanced Implementations Tutorial Notes,* pp. 1–18. Baltimore: ACM Press.

Watson, 1987 Watson, S.E. (1987). Ada modules. *Ada Letters* 7(4):79–84.

Wegner, 1976 Wegner, P. (1987). Programming languages—the first 25 years. *IEEE Transactions on Computers,* C-25(12):1207–1225. Also in *Programming Languages: A Grand Tour* (3rd ed.), edited by E. Horowitz (1987), pp. 4–22. New York: W.H. Freeman.

Wegner, 1980 Wegner, P. (1980). *Programming with Ada: An Introduction by Means of Graduated Examples.* Englewood Cliffs, NJ: Prentice Hall.

Wegner, 1983 Wegner, P. and Smolka, S.A. (1983). Processes, tasks, and monitors: A comparative study of concurrent programming primitives. *IEEE Transactions on Software Engineering* SE-9(4):446–462 Also in *Programming Languages: A Grand Tour* (3rd ed.), edited by E. Horowitz (1987), pp. 360–376. New York: W.H. Freeman.

Wegner, 1987 Wegner, P. (1987). The object-oriented classification paradigm. In *Research Directions in Object-oriented Programming,* edited by B. Shriver and P. Wegner, pp. 479–560. Cambridge, MA: MIT Press.

Wegner, 1988 Wegner, P. (1988). Object-oriented concept hierarchies (draft). *Tutorial Notes: Object-oriented Software Engineering.* International Conference on Computer Languages '88. (IEEE).

Wegner, 1989 Wegner, P. (Guest editor). (1989). Introduction to programming language paradigms [Special issue]. *ACM Computing Surveys* 21(3):253–258.

Wegner, 1990 Wegner, P. (1990). Concepts and paradigms of object-oriented programming. *OOPS Messenger* 1(1):8–84.

Weiner, 1988 Weiner, J.L. and Ramakrishnan, S. (1988). A piggy-back compiler for Prolog. *Proceedings of the SIGPLAN '88 Conference on Programming Language Design and Implementation,* pp. 288–296. Baltimore: ACM Press.

Weir, 1987 Weir, S. (1987). *Cultivating Minds: A Logo Casebook.* New York: Harper and Row.

Wexelblat, 1981 Wexelblat, R. (ed.). (1981). *History of Programming Languages.* New York: Academic Press.

Whitehead, 1910   Whitehead, A.N. and Russell, B.A.W. (1910–1913, 1st ed.; 1923–1927, 2nd ed.). *Principia Mathematica* (Vols. 1–3). Cambridge, UK: Cambridge University Press.

Wiederhold, 1983   Wiederhold, G. (1983). *Database Design* (2nd ed.). New York: McGraw-Hill.

Wiener, 1989   Wiener, R.S. and Pinson, L.J. (1989). Smalltalk-80 on the Macintosh. *Journal of Object-oriented Programming* 2(1):67–68.

Wirth, 1971   Wirth, N. (1971). The programming language Pascal. *Acta Informatica* 1:35–63.

Wolfe, 1981   Wolfe, M.I., Babich, W., Simpson, R., Tholl, R., and Weissman, L. (1981). The Ada language system. *Computer* 14(6):37–45.

Zilles, 1986   Zilles, B. and Guttag, J. (1986). *Abstraction and Specification in Program Development*. New York: McGraw-Hill.

INDEX